Fakesong

DAVE HARKER

FAKESONG

The manufacture
of British 'folksong'
1700 to the present day

Open University Press

Milton Keynes · Philadelphia

Open University Press
12 Cofferidge Close
Stony Stratford
Milton Keynes MK11 1BY. England
and
242 Cherry Street
Philadelphia, PA 19106, USA

First Published 1985

British Library Cataloguing in Publication Data

Harker, David, 1946-
    Fakesong : the manufacture of British folksong
    1700 to the present day.—(British popular
    music in the nineteenth and twentieth centuries)
    1. Folk music—Great Britain—History and
    criticism
    I. Title   II. Series
    781.741   ML3650

    ISBN 0-335-15066-7

Library of Congress Cataloging in Publication Data

Harker, David.
    Fakesong : "folksong" and working people.

    Bibliography: p.
    Includes index.
    1. Ballads, English—Great Britain—Texts—History and
criticism.   2. Folk-songs, English—Great Britain—
Texts—History and criticism.   3. Laboring class
writings, English—History and criticism.   4. Labor
and laboring classes in literature.   5. Great Britain—
Popular culture.   6. Oral tradition—Great Britain.
7.   Labor and laboring classes—Great Britain. I. Title.
PR976.H37   1985   821'.044'09   85-5670
ISBN 0-335-15066-7 (U.S.)

Typeset by Mathematical Composition Setters Ltd, Salisbury, UK.
Printed in Great Britain by M. & A. Thomson Litho Limited,
East Kilbride, Scotland.

For Maureen

Ex-secretary,
Cutty Wren
Folk Club,
Redcar,
Yorkshire

Contents

THE SOLUTION

After the uprising of the 17th June
The Secretary of the Writers' Union
Had leaflets distributed in the Stalinallee
Stating that the people
Had forfeited the confidence of the government
And could win it back only
By redoubled efforts. Would it not be easier
In that case for the government
To dissolve the people
And elect another?

Bertolt Brecht

Editorial Preface

What *is* British popular music? Does such a thing exist? What makes certain music and songs popular? And who made the musical cultures of these islands? What did Scots, Welsh, Irish and North American people have to do with the process? What part did people in the English regions play — the Geordies, Cockneys, midlanders and all the rest? Where did the Empire fit in? How did European 'high' culture affect what most people played and sang? And how did all these factors vary in significance over time? In the end, just how much do we know about the history of musical culture on these tiny patches of land? The truth is that we know very little, and this realisation led to this series.

The history of British people and culture has been dominated by capitalism for centuries; and capitalism helped to polarise people into classes not only economically, but culturally too. Music was never *simply* music: songs were never *simply* songs. Both were produced and used by particular people in particular historical periods for particular reasons, and we have recognised this in the way in which we have put this series together.

Every book in this series aims to exemplify and to foster interdisciplinary research. Each volume studies not only 'texts' and performances, but institutions and technology as well, and the culture practices and sets of social relationships through which music and songs were produced, disseminated and consumed. Ideas, values, attitudes and what is generally referred to as ideology are taken into account, as are factors such as gender, age, geography and traditions. Nor is our series above the struggle. We do not pretend to have helped produce an objective record. We are, unrepentently, on the side of the majority, and our main perspective is from 'below', even though the whole musical field needs to be in view. We hope that by clarifying the history of popular musical culture we can help clear the ground for a genuinely democratic musical culture of the future.

Dave Harker and Richard Middleton

Introduction

What is a 'folksong'? What is a 'ballad'? Aren't they those songs which are sung in folk clubs, or get taught to children at school — simple, unaccompanied tunes, with words about country life, seafaring, love and perhaps the odd one dealing with mills, mines and masters? Well, yes, that's what 'folksongs' are to most people today, but these commonsense ideas have a very long and a *very* strange history. For almost three centuries, arguments have been raging amongst collectors, editors and singers about where these songs come from, who made them, what they really meant and what relevance they are today. Now and again that argument surfaces, as part of the general debate about working people's history and culture, and more and more people believe that it is important to find out as much as we can about how our ancestors experienced life — what they felt, thought and believed. The problem is that when historians examine the tens of thousands of songs which appeared in print and were collected by generations of antiquarians, scholars and folklorists, they find that it is very hard to be sure about what, precisely, this evidence represents. So songs get used to embellish chapter-headings in the history books, or are inserted apologetically as an 'illustration' of what the vast majority of the population may, have felt or thought. Then the narrative goes back to the *real* history, perhaps not so much to kings and queens, now, but to politicians and trade union leaders.

Most *people* still get left out. All they left behind as an official record of their lives tended to be an entry in a church register, a birth, marriage and death certificate, and perhaps a few lines in a court record, or a newspaper. But, as historians have lately begun to find out, most people can talk, and have interesting memories which can be recorded. They even *sang*; and for the period which oral history cannot reach, we have these thousands of songs, waiting for a way of using them as historical evidence to turn up. So, what *Fakesong* wants to do is to develop ways of understanding *precisely* what 'folksongs' and 'ballads' *really* are. And to do that, we have to examine how they have come down to us, to establish how they have been affected by their passage through time, and through the heads and hands of collectors, antiquarians and folklorists. By doing this, we will not only help to clear the ground for those of us who want to write history from the 'bottom' up, but we will also learn some interesting facts about those people who have got between the makers and singers of these songs and us — their descendants.

At this point, professional historians and political activists may heave a sigh and ask, why bother? What have these 'folksongs' got to do with really important issues today? The answer is: More than you might think. Noel Halifax[1]* has shown that apparently marginal aspects of culture like 'folk' traditions, rituals, forms of dress, music and song have been, and are, of some importance in official culture on both sides of the Iron Curtain. Eastern European states maintain 'peasant' and 'folk' museums, encourage the collection of 'folk' songs, music and stories, and the reintroduction or invention of 'folk' or 'national' costume for special occasions. So-called 'Third World' states, such as Zimbabwe, have reconstructed (or invented) 'tribal' and 'folk' customs; and even a racist state such as South Africa follows a similar policy in the 'black homelands', where certain 'tribal' traditions and rituals are systematically fostered. In Britain, both Labour and Conservative councils finance 'folk' and 'country life' museums, and royalty lends its support to the English Folk Dance and Song Society. In the United States, after a massive programme of 'folk' research sponsored during the economic depression of the 1930s, the academic study of 'folksong', 'ballad', 'folk' dance, music, traditions and tales has become a significant component in university and college education in the humanities and social sciences, with enormous undergraduate teaching programmes and postgraduate research departments, and a myriad of academic 'folk' journals.

What do such states with their apparently conflicting official ideologies get out of this patronage? The self-styled 'socialist' countries of Europe evidently need to foster 'national' unity, in order to maintain the outward appearance of being a workers' states. Such things help to paper over, or distract workers' attention from, the struggles which threaten to tear apart a country like Poland. Additionally, this emphasis on the 'national' in the various Warsaw Pact states helps the drive to encourage competition between them, as part of the process of increasing production and exploitation so as to compete with NATO militarily. An analogous process is taking place in a state like Zimbabwe, where the official sponsorship of 'folk' culture helps to promote the notion of 'national unity' in the face of political competition from within, (which threatens to run over into armed struggle) and of military aggression from without, with South Africa. South Africa's own policy, on the other hand, aims to prevent the emergence of a politically-potent sense of black nationalism, precisely by splitting up the majority population both geographically and culturally into 'tribal' enclaves, lest independent and *genuinely* national institutions emerge to challenge white power. In Britain, where working-class trade union and political organization has a long history, the state has no need to take 'folk' issues seriously at a

---

* Superscript numerals refer to numbered notes at the end of this book.

national level, except where such things contribute marginally to tourism, and so such patronage as is offered comes at a lower level of civil government. In the USA, the official ideology is based on individualism, on the famous 'American Dream'. But at the same time, there is a very evident cultural heterogeneity in what is, after all, a comparatively new state. There, the celebration of 'ethnic' and regional cultures has to operate within the framework of a raw 'national' culture, with new institutions. Cultural identity is, therefore, *both* important to the pluralist self-image, *and* a threat to the development of a 'national' bourgeois culture.

What these states have in common is that they are *all class societies*. In Britain, as I write, the Conservative government has succeeded in reminding many people that the class system is far from dead. Thousands of striking miners have felt the full force of police violence operating in the interests of capital and the ruling class, and against the interests of those who need to have a job in order to live. In Zimbabwe, the creation of a one-party state and the crushing of all political opposition goes hand in hand with the advertising of luxury houses (complete with resident servants) in the one and only newspaper, and state power is used against workers who dare to strike against the construction of 'socialism'. In the USA, trade unions are systematically attacked in the name of 'freedom', and when they get too powerful for the state's liking — as they did in the Air Traffic Controllers' dispute not so long ago — then the freedom to organize collectively is proscribed, (This idea was promptly taken up by the British Cabinet and applied to GCHQ.) In the Soviet Union, trade unions have been absorbed into the state, and a sizeable body of bureaucrats performs much the same role in relation to workers as did the employers before 1917, quite contrary to Lenin and Trotsky's arguments about the need for independent workers' organizations. Should autonomous workers' organizations dare to appear, as they did in Poland, then 'socialist' tanks are sent in to crush resistance in a state which never saw a successful socialist revolution. In South Africa, of course, blacks are as free to join trade unions and to organize politically as they are to be shot or pushed out of tower-block windows whilst undergoing 'questioning'. Now, this is obviously a *mess*, but haven't we come some way from 'folksong'?

The truth is that what these apparently different kinds of state have in common is their *need to deny the primacy of class*, and *anything* which can help do that, however modestly and marginally, is of use. Their support for 'folk' culture is a small but significant part of their attempts to reinforce *nationalism*, and so help fend off danger of the only power which can challenge them — international working-class solidarity. So, while superficially competing states use state ideologies, however unsuccessfully, to contain class-struggle within the boundaries of their various patches of land, most of us recognize that we live in a world of besieged national cultures, which face the threat of Soviet or American imperialism, or both. And yet the world has never been so closely integrated, economically: capitalism, as Nigel Harris[2] has demonstrated conclusively, in its 'free-market' or state forms, is international. So nationalism, with its 'folk' components, has to be understood as part of the world's ruling classes' ideological armoury against the material forces which drive the working classes of each state closer together. It is impossible (without self-deception) to consider 'national', 'peasant', 'tribal' or 'folk' culture merely as subjects of academic interest, and if we can show that these general considerations apply specifically to the concepts used by even the most progressive 'folk' scholars, then those who associate themselves with bourgeois ideology will have a clearer idea of the *real* function of their work, and those who see themselves as socialists will be encouraged to rethink their theory and adjust their practice accordingly.

Even in a sane world, after the revolution, it will not be possible to take concepts such as 'folksong' and 'ballad' out to be shot. However, they stand a fair chance of being put on trial, and then being locked up, or subjected to a lengthy period of political re-education! The aim of this book, then, is to put the case for the prosecution, as a small contribution to that ideological struggle which goes on all the time, but which so often gets masked. I recognize that such concepts and the people who use them, innocently or otherwise, cannot be denounced or incriminated simply for having bourgeois origins.[3] But I hope to show that these concepts *do* have class origins, and that their continued use will help to mystify workers' culture in the interests of bourgeois ideology and therefore of capitalism, east and west. If we are serious about finding out as much as we can about how working women and men *really* lived, felt, thought and acted, then all those 'commonsense'ideas about 'folksong' have to be understood historically. For some people, this may be a painful process. They may feel that my approach is merely destructive, though I believe it to be both descriptive and analytical. They will no doubt accuse me of negativity. But what I hope to have done is to show that concepts like 'folksong' and 'ballad' are intellectual rubble which needs to be shifted so that building can begin again. They may even challenge me to produce my own ideas about 'folksong' and 'ballad', yet I feel that the whole purpose of *Fakesong* is to demonstrate that there is no point in attempting, as Bert Lloyd and others did, to rehabilitate such concepts. They are conceptual lumber, and they have to go. The aim of this book, then, is not to provide a fully worked-out set of alternative concepts and methods. That task has only begun, and it is far too important to be left to the historians.[4]

* * * * *

Fakesong is not a social history, in the broad sense, but it assumes a certain perspective on the general history of Britain, and of England and Scotland in particular. Similarly, it has no pretensions to being a general history of British culture, but I have tried to locate what I am going to call the *mediation* of songs within a wider framework. The analysis is not and cannot be ideologically innocent, so I have tried to *situate* myself, materially and intellectually,[5] and I have resolutely struggled to keep this book as free of jargon as possible. The ideas of marxism are far too important to be allowed to become the property of professional intellectuals, who so often fail to observe Marx's injunction on the need to *combine* theory and practice, especially in an uncomfortable period for socialists such as the present. A reader who is familiar with Edward Thompson's *The Making of the English Working Class*,[6] Raymond Williams' *Culture and Society*[7] and *The Country and the City*,[8] and Tony Cliff's *Lenin*,[9] will have little difficulty in following the historical, cultural and political assumptions and ideas which underpin this book.

The scope and content of *Fakesong* were partly determined by the need to present a substantial historical account of the *mediation*[10] of songs. By *mediation* I understand not simply the fact that particular people passed on songs they had taken from other sources, in the form of manuscript or of print, but that in the very process of so doing their own assumptions, attitudes, likes and dislikes may well have significantly determined what they looked for, accepted and rejected. Not only that, but these people's access to sources of songs, the fact that they had the time, opportunity, motive and facilities for collecting, and a whole range of other material factors will have come into play. Ideological and material factors in this process did not occur separately, of course. So, while we cannot 'read off' what a person did with songs from, say, their class position, it is still the case that their social origins, education, occupation (or lack of it) and so on were obviously connected with how they felt, thought and acted, in relation to songs as to everything else. These things happened, not in a mechanical or an inevitable way, but they were *linked* all the same. *Fakesong* aims to show why these people mediated songs, who they did it for, and how their practices and the results of their mediations related to more general cultural and historical tendencies and developments. But in order to do this with any degree of thoroughness, we have to know who the people were, and that in itself sets limits on the historical period and the range of materials we can examine.

Before the early eighteenth century, printed songs appeared in substantial numbers as broadsides, chapbooks and small songbooks or 'Garlands', but they almost always did so anonymously. Even the printers did not inevitably print their name or address, especially if the songs were likely to incur official displeasure. The state of knowledge on seventeenth century song-printers is somewhat rudimentary, and in need of considerable research.[11] Our knowledge of eighteenth and nineteeth century broadside printers is hardly more advanced;[12] and this fact alone has meant that the task of attempting to understand their mediations has had to be deferred. In order to *situate* the analysis of song-mediation effectively, in a particular history and culture, a further constraint had to be taken into account. Irish, Welsh and Gaelic Scots history and culture has been markedly different from that of England and English-speaking Scotland, and all three deserve separate study. Then again, since my interest in mediation includes not only the collecting but also the publishing of songs, it seemed inconsistent to try to deal with those people who collected but did not publish, or who published mainly in out-of-the-way journals aimed at a specialist audience. Unfortunately, this has meant that the work of three women, Kate Lee,[13] Anne Gilchrist[14] and Janet Blunt,[15] has not been examined. Fortunately other researchers have begun to take up this task and to produce good work. Similarly, it has meant that the collection of John Clare[16] could not be analysed here, even though he was one of the few song-mediators of his period from a labouring background. Lastly, given the book's key concern with workers' song-culture, I have obviously chosen to concentrate on those mediators who published songs deriving wholly or in part from that culture. Of course, this in itself is a highly problematical selection, and no doubt I have been influenced by the way in which people interested in 'folksongs' and 'ballads' have chosen their own ancestors.[17] In order to try to cope with this problem I have decided to concentrate on these mediators who set out their ideas in substantial essays, notes or similar material, from which a clearer idea of their aims and practices can be legitimately deduced. If this has meant a disproportionately large Scots component in the book, this is simply because the Scots have provided fuller materials than the English.

In spite of this set of constraints, I have been unable to examine all the mediators, or even all the publications of those I have studied. However, I have tried to give a historical analysis of a substantial cross-section — if so it is — of the publications of English and English-speaking Scots song-mediators, from around 1700 until the middle of the present century, which contain songs derived, wholly or in part, from workers' culture, and especially from adult, secular song-culture. (Children's rhymes, and hymns and carols need books of their own.) I have felt it important to include examples of all the mediators' works which people with a serious interest in 'folksong' and 'ballad' have customarily referred to as important to the development of those concepts, but I do not suppose that I have included all of the lesser figures, and I recognize that I have not been able to examine all the publications of the major ones. Sometimes, this has been because of the material constraints of book-length imposed by my publishers. At other times, it is because I simply could not get hold of the works, or did so too late.[18] I believe that my analysis will be *generally* applicable even to those mediators and publications not specifically examined here, though fellow-researchers may bring out interesting differences in specifics. This section of the book had to be doggedly chronicled, but readers may decide to take my word for it and read quickly through, so as to get to the more interesting material and analysis in Part 2!

Given that one aim of *Fakesong* was to show how concepts like 'folksong' and 'ballad' were produced, historically, it has not been possible to present a straightforward chronology, or even to remain neatly within the boundaries of a particular culture or nation state. Francis James Child was a North American scholar, yet his work was crucial to the development of the concept of the 'ballad'. Similarly, Cecil James Sharp did not invent 'folksong', but his collecting and publishing was of profound significance. Simply to pick out some of these key figures, and to treat them as either quite typical or totally exceptional, as so often happens, would radically distort history. So, while this book acknowledges these men's work in its structure, it also tries to *situate* them as part of a complex historical process, to show how and why their interventions were crucial. A related structural problem has been that of presenting each mediator's work in such a way as to show how that work related to the wider cultural, historical and political issues and tendencies in any given period. Partly, this problem derives from the theoretical difficulties inherent in attempting to relate what marxists call 'base' and 'superstructure'.[19] There is an enormous and mostly pretentious literature developing on this crucial issue, but the reader who chances not to know the debate does not need to break off at this point and dive into it. Suffice it to say that the structure of this book is intended to give no comfort to those who believe that history is based on a conspiracy theory, or to those who claim that socialism is 'inevitable' so let's sit back and wait for it to happen, or to those who seek to write off marxism on the grounds that generations of Stalinists and the example of the Soviet Union have demonstrated where it leads.

The consequences for the structure of the chapters of this book are that after a short introductory sketch of the key economic, political and cultural changes which were taking place in England and Scotland in the first decades of the eighteenth century, we move on to look at how early song-mediators in both countries were located in relation to those changes. I hope to have shown that what they *were* was closely connected with what they *did*; so the structure of later chapters is different. The next three chapters examine three historical periods of song-mediation, roughly 1760–1800, 1800–1830 and 1830–70. Of course, neither individual lives nor dates of publication fit neatly into such periodizations; but I hope to have shown that the 1790s and the years around 1830 were not only political watersheds but were also, allowing for the complex relationships between economic, political and cultural change, decisive 'breaks' in the mediation of workers' songs. There were lags and there were precocious innovators, as in any other process of combined and uneven development, but ideas and practices in general clearly changed. In order to try to explain why, each of these three chapters is divided into four sections. Mediators' class positions, material interests and general ideology are discussed in relation to key processes of material and intellectual development, and, secondly, in relation to their specific aims and intentions in mediating songs. Thirdly, we examine where they got songs, from whom, how and why; and finally we analyse how those songs were further mediated in the processes of editing and publishing. A reader who so wished could easily read 'across' the boundaries of chapters and historical periods on each of these themes; and the whole book could be read, as it were, backwards, which was of course how it was conceived and written!

The end of the period examined in Part 1 marks the entry of Child into 'ballad' scholarship, so Part 2 tries to show not only how his ideas developed between 1859 and the publication of *The English and Scottish Popular Ballads*,[20] but also where those ideas came from, notably in relation to previous workers in the field, and above all the Danish scholar, Grundtvig. The chapter on Child has a similar structure to those on his predecessors, and while I hope to have shown that his class position, education, occupation and ideology do have clear connections with his aims, methods and theories, I have tried to avoid the pitfalls of doing so in a mechanical or in a crudely determinist fashion. What is much more important than the work of this US scholar is the way in which his ideas and practices related to bourgeois attitudes towards workers' culture on both sides of the Atlantic, and to bourgeois strategies — notably, a form of cultural imperialism — in relation to workers' culture. This leads to the brief analysis, in Chapter 6, of the apparent paradox that while many of Child's ideas have been successfully attacked since his death, the kernel of what I term the 'ballad' consensus survives, not only in customary usage, but even amongst scholars. At the same time, the fact that debate around 'ballads' has taken-off into academe, above all in the USA, partly explains why the concept of 'folksong' had a stronger hold in Britain, where 'ballad' study has been successfully marginalized in academic circles and in some cases banished altogether. In separating 'ballad' from 'folksong' in this way, it is not intended to suggest that these concepts were somehow separate from each other; but it *is* meant to show that their development after the 1860s was to some extent different.

Part 3 follows a similar pattern to Part 2, in that the work of Sharp is first of all shown to have roots in that of the earlier 'county' collectors, and especially in the ideas of the German émigré, Carl Engel. The use of the term 'folk' in English has a long history, but its application to aspects of workers' culture dated from the 1840s, and to workers' songs apparently only after the 1870s. Chapter 7 deals with these issues, and shows the developing tradition in which Sharp intervened after 1900. Chapter 8 goes on to examine Sharp's work in some detail, analysing how what began as a somewhat radical cultural intervention was transformed, in the 1900s and 1910s, into one which was not only culturally exploitative but reactionary too. By way of partial contrast, Chapter 10 looks at the work of one of the very few song-mediators from a working-class background, Alfred Williams, whose conservative attitudes and ideas resulted, contradictorily, in some of the most progressive and suggestive work on the culture of an English region. There then follows a 'silence' which seems to have occured in the history of 'folksong' mediation during the later 1920s, the 1930s and the early 1940s, before the work of Albert Lancaster Lloyd began to appear. Chapter 11 scrutinizes Lloyd's intervention, and demonstrates, I believe, that in spite of his socialism and his internationalism, Lloyd's contribution was hobbled by his debts to the work of Sharp, and by his reliance on that deformation of marxism which, even today, rattles on in the brains of older members of the Communist Party of Great Britain. In a sense, this whole book is an attempt to have an argument with the ideas of Lloyd, and with comrades in the CPGB and the left of the Labour Party, over whom he exercised considerable influence, and still does after his death. The pity of it is, from a personal point of view, that 'Bert' can't answer back.[21]

The Conclusion sets out some ideas for further research, which were suggested by problems discovered in writing this book, or which have been brought home to me even more now that it is written. Hopefully, many of the ideas mentioned will be taken up by future contributors to this series. There then follows a rather peculiar Appendix, the writing of which caused me more problems than the rest of the book. Basically, I felt obliged to attempt to situate myself to some extent, if only because I have had the hardihood to do it to so many other people. Anyway, it's there if readers want it; and, of course, it's *totally unbiassed*.

* * * * *

Making this book has left me in many people's debt. Without the consistent help of the people in the Inter-Library Loan Unit and the Reprographics Unit at the All Saints building of Manchester Polytechnic, dozens of books couldn't have been consulted and copies of earlier drafts couldn't have been sent out for comments. Douglas Bond of Newcastle Central Library and Malcolm Taylor of the Vaughan Williams Library at Cecil Sharp House have helped dig out valuable information. Mike Yates kindly helped to check quotations from Cecil Sharp's diaries. Peter Wright of the Open University Press has been continuously supportive, in spite of the frequent breaking of deadlines; and Richard Middleton, my fellow series editor, has shown heartbreaking forbearance. Richard Middleton, Mike Pickering, Georgina Boyes and Matthew Kelly have spared considerable time from their own work to help make mine better, and Dave Arthur has sent me useful information about Bert Lloyd's life. I hope they feel that their effort was worthwhile; but, in any case, I want to express my gratitude to them, because writing this book has not been part of my 'academic' job and I have needed all the feedback I could get.

Most of the work has been done in the evenings and at week-ends, and during what are nominally holidays, with the unstinting support of a woman who, in spite of fair warning, chose to share a house with me and in line with one of the 'folk' traditions of provincial England to endure a peculiar ceremony known as 'marriage'. That woman has *suffered*, not so much by my continued absence in an upstairs room (which has certain advantages), but by putting up with days of combing dusty second-hand bookshops, with the cost of buying second-hand books at inflated 'antiquarian' prices, and with their distinct odour of decay, which hits you half way up the stairs. Then again, apart from the Chinese torture of faintly-perceptible two-fingered typing, and putting up with the sight of a man hardly drying out from an overdose of facts, quotations and other people's insane ideas, she has often done more than half of the socially-necessary labour involved in feeding three of us, keeping the house free of fatal disease, and ensuring that Michael develops no more delinquent traits than is customary in the North Midlands English culture of this period. Just to rub all this further in, she has also corrected the proofs. In a very material sense, then, this book is just as much Maureen's work as mine, but none of it is her fault.

Dave Harker, Whaley Bridge, 15th September 1984.

PART I

Two Centuries B(efore) C(hild)

And as in private life one distinguishes
between what a man thinks and says of
himself and what he really is and does,
still more in historical struggles must
one distinguish the phrases and fancies
of the parties from their real organism
and their real interests, their
conception of themselves from their
reality.

Karl Marx, *The Eighteenth Brumaire of Louis Bonaparte*, 1852

No song-mediator produced a book without an intellectual reason, even if their primary aim was material gain, and none of them was free of an ideological tendency. So, no song-book could fail to be, however marginally, a kind of ideological intervention whether its producer admitted it or not. Some mediators set out their aims on title pages or in Prefaces and Introductions. Others allowed their ideas and assumptions to 'leak out' in footnotes, asides, or statements on particular issues. Sometimes, the real ideological thrust of a song-book might remain partly hidden, even from its maker. Similarly, no song-book was made for wholly altruistic reasons. Each mediator occupied a specific position in society, had a personal and intellectual history, made a living, had opinions on economic and political issues and acted upon them. Each person can, to some extent, be located in relation not only to ideological developments, but also material ones, such as urbanization, the transformation of agriculture, the factory system, industrialization, the rise of the bourgeoisie to economic (and finally political) power over the landed aristocracy, and the making of the working class. In the period 1700–1870, it would be astonishing if people who made song-books did not have clear ideas about political crises such as the Jacobite Rebellions of 1715 and 1745, the American War of 1775–83, The French Revolution of 1789, the War with Revolutionary and then Bonaparte's France between 1793 and 1815, the post-war economic and political crisis leading up to Peterloo in 1819, the Reform agitation of the late 1820's and early 1830's and the Chartist years of the late 1830s and 1840s.

Of course, this is neither a social nor political history book, but the first chapter will make clear, I hope, that in order to understand song-books we have to understand their makers and their purchasers in the specific ideological and material history of England and Scotland. Once it becomes clear why we need to be interested in mediators' social origins, education, geographical and social mobility, occupations, relations to both rising and declining classes and so on, it will be easier to understand their attitudes to workers' and then *working-class* culture, and their mediating practices in relation to that culture. Such relationships cannot be 'read off' from mediators' material positions and interests, of course, and there is always the danger of falling into the trap of presenting a conspiracy theory of history. On the other hand, there is an even greater danger of being so wary of the over-reductiveness of stalinized marxism, where the economic 'base' determines the political and cultural 'superstructure', that we remain trapped in the idealist limbo where everything is hopelessly complex and 'problematical', and only *very* clever people can keep it all in their heads. I hope to show that there *was* a general relationship between mediators' class position, their ideology and their practices, and that that relationship can be fully understood only in terms of a historical materialist and dialectical analysis of British history.

* * * * *

1   *The Early Mediators*

(i) England[1]

Song-books did not suddenly appear in England and Scotland in the early eighteenth century, but the period *c.* 1700–1725 marks a qualitative change, in that a district market seems to have separated itself out from the centuries-old trade in broadsides and chapbooks. The roots of this process can be traced back to the end of political suppression of song-publishing in the later sixteenth century; but when the court of Charles I patronized Italian music, part of a nationalistic reaction came in the form of a spate of *Drolleries* and *Garlands* of English songs aimed at the polite end of the market. This development, far from being suppressed during the Civil War and its aftermath, merged with a tendency in polite culture for a populist attitude towards workers' culture. John Playford produced the first of what turned out to be many editions of *The English Dancing Master* in 1651, for example, to cash in on the fashionable vogue for 'country' dancing. On the other hand, the production of new songs by professional composers and singers was made more difficult at this period, because what was mainly aristocratic patronage kept 'wits' such as Martin Parker in business. Those who did not emigrate to the courts of foreign princes and nobles worked the country houses of English Cavalier gentry, sometimes venturing to perform in town taverns until Cromwell passed an Act to stop them. (Very few song-writers sided with Parliament.)[2]

At the Restoration, in 1661, these conservative writers' work appeared in Playford's *Antidote against Melancholy*, along with mildly erotic anonymous material, some of which may have derived from workers' culture. Their monarchical and generally reactionary songs were also in demand at new institutions such as the 'Musick-House' at the Mitre, near St Paul's Cathedral in London, and at another such resort near the Temple, where, for the substantial sum of a shilling, the well-to-do male audience could hear original compositions, or pieces learned from sheets published at Playford's nearby shop. That shop stocked musical instruments as well as printed music, and acted as a rendezvous for the many musical lawyers and other leisured gentry of the period. Henry Playford, John's son, later promoted formal concerts and music clubs at Oxford, whither scions of the nobility and the aspiring bourgeoisie came to eat their dinners in London's schools of law. By the 1680s 'all the quality and *beau monde* repaired'[3] to a purpose-built music room in London's Villiers Street, to avoid the ale, tobacco and less refined company of the City taverns. After the Glorious Revolution of 1688 there seems to have been a further polarization, as the adherents of the exiled King James divided the '*beau monde*' and formed the basis of the Jacobite song-culture of the next half century. The courts of William and then Anne provided a countervailing source of patronage and a ready-made market for suitable cultural products. This was important because at a period when it was not yet possible to earn a consistent living as a song-writer in the provinces, as the freemason-poet Thomas Whittell discovered in the north-east.[4] This, then, was the state of the song-market in London when Thomas D'Urfey entered the Inns of Court in the 1670s.

D'Urfey had impeccable political credentials for a Restoration literary figure.[5] His grandfather had been a French protestant who escaped from La Rochelle and settled in Exeter in the 1620s. D'Urfey's father was prosperous enough to marry the daughter of a Huntingdon-shire gentry family and to send his son to London to learn to be a lawyer. Having a certain literary facility, D'Urfey soon abandoned the law and became effectively a freelance writer and entertainer to the gentry and nobility, using connections with the Playfords to get his songs into print. For 40 years he wrote plays, composed and performed songs, and established a reputation as being the 'indispensable entertainer' of not only the rising bourgeoisie and landed aristocracy, but even of royalty. He boasted that he had performed for every monarch from Charles II to George I; but though such notables might subscribe to his publications and patronize his plays, it was the lawyers, merchants and lesser gentry who formed the backbone of his market. These were the people who pro-fited more than most from the eclipse of the Stuarts, and from the aggressive foreign policy of the government which helped expand overseas trade and the domestic economy. Even when income from play-writing dropped off, in the 1700s and 1710s, D'Urfey's political reliability continued to pay. Queen Anne paid him 50 guineas for one song, and his various revisions of the Playfords' old song-books commanded substantial support from subscribers. Thus, the six-volume 1719–20 edition of *Wit and Mirth, or, Pills to Purge Melancholy* was dedicated to 'Right Honourable the Lords and Ladies', the people who had 'merry and vacant hours', and who stood in need of songs to help unbend their thoughts 'from the Times, Troubles and Fatigues'. Though the rigidly righteous had denounced D'Urfey for publishing 'Profaneness and Debauchery', and while sophisticated poets like Alexander Pope ridiculed him from their Augustan exclusiveness, D'Urfey well understood that his lack of intellec-tual pretensions was a key part of his appeal. 'The town may da-da-damn me for a Poet, but they si-si-sing my Songs for all that',[6] he claimed; and this same 'Town', by which he meant fashionable and leisured

London-oriented gentlefolk, gave him the confidence to produce 1500 copies of the first volume of an early edition of the *Pills*, in 1698. The widow of Henry Purcell, probably the country's foremost 'classical' composer, had risked a print-run of only 500 copies of volume one of *Orpheus Britannicus* that same year.

D'Urfey used the *Pills* to promote his own compositions, but he took care that his pieces had metres compatible with common tunes and could therefore be sung in the streets. This policy was directly counter to that adopted by would-be superior composers, and opened up his work not only to bourgeois singers but also to the wider market of people who still bought broadsides and chapbooks. He was evidently quite sure that his 'double Genius for *Poetry*, and *Musick*' had a potentially wide appeal; and he extended that appeal even further by including what he termed 'Scotch' songs. Songs dealing with 'rustic or humble life' had invariably been termed 'Northern' or 'Scotch' by genteel people since at least the 1650s;[7] and though D'Urfey's English 'Scotch' songs might not have penetrated workers' song-culture on either side of the Border, some of them do seem to have been taken up by polite society in 'North Britain', particularly after the political and military defeat of Jacobitism. In England, too, D'Urfey's published tunes were an important quarry for Gay's *Beggar's Opera*: 37 tunes, some of them probably deriving from workers' culture, fitted perfectly into a production specifically designed to ridicule the continuing fashion amongst the reactionary rich for Italian opera. The *Pills* cheerfully pillaged the printed songs and tunes of the preceding half century. Broadsides, engraved single songs, items from printed plays, drolleries, garlands, courtesy books, music books, song-books and books of poems are all laid under contribution; but D'Urfey also seems to have picked up some songs from street-singing, tavern song-culture and the oral culture of working people. He had few theoretical pretensions, however. His 'Alphabetical TABLE' differentiates simply between 'Poems' and 'Verses, Prologues and Epilogues' which were intended to be spoken, and 'Songs', which had texts and tunes designed for singing by a wide 'public'. *Chevy Chase* counted as a 'Song', for at this period a 'ballad' was customarily defined as a 'Common Song sung up and down the Streets.' Sophisticated theoretical distinctions probably seemed unnecessary. Many items in the *Pills* happen to have been composed by well-known authors, yet D'Urfey's penchant for self-promotion prevented him from acknowledging most of them, while he took care that the 350 out of 1144 which *he* wrote or rewrote were suitably attributed!

The market identified by D'Urfey was developed in a literary-antiquarian direction by a *Collection of Old Ballads*, which appeared between 1723 and 1725 and has been attributed to Ambrose Phillips. Phillips' father had been both a knight and a sergeant-at-arms, and had moved from Shropshire to Leicestershire. Ambrose went to school at Shrewsbury, and then to Cambridge in the 1690s. By 1700, he had both

an MA and a fellowship, and his political reliability led to his being
entrusted with various secret missions to Scotland, Utrecht and Denmark
during the politically crucial early 1700s, when the Protestant succession
was in jeopardy. He acted as secretary to the Hanover Club — formed
during Queen Anne's reign to ensure that the Stuarts remained in exile —
and was part of the literary component of court culture which centred on
the critic and essayist Addison, the champion of *Chevy Chace* and *The Babes
in the Wood* in his famous *Spectator* articles of 1711.[8] Phillips was rewarded
by George I with a JP's post in Westminster and a lucrative commis-
sionership in the state lottery; and he eventually moved to Armagh, first
to be the Bishop's Secretary and then the local MP, before ending as a
judge in the prerogative court. Thus, while song-editing was hardly a
major source of income, the connections Phillips established in both
literary and political circles no doubt helped ensure the market success of
his books of songs. Indeed, he mentions the support of a 'Gentleman'
noted for his parliamentary eloquence and his 'noble Behaviour in the
State', whose patronage, along with that of 'some Persons of the nicest
Taste' and the 'Generality of the Town', led to the exhaustion of volume
one in two months, even before a second print-run could be completed.
Phillips had a care for the marketing of his book, tried not to alienate
Catholics and Jacobites, and cited Addison's critical authority. But while
he was responsive to the 'thinking Man', who could be assumed to
understand French and Latin quotations, and might support the re-estab-
lishment of the London Society of Antiquaries, he also noted in his second
volume how he had been 'very much importun'd' by 'the ladie ' to
include a particular piece. He had no qualms in using a song wi.ich
sought to caricature a Welshman, an Irishman and a Scot, all of whom
were evidently suitable for 'low Humour', and the vogue for 'Scotch'
material of a genteel kind is to some extent catered for, though only one
item appears to be of Scots origin. So, when he notes that an item is
'very popular', it is important to realize that most British people outside
London and its polite society are excluded from that definition.

   Phillip's *Collection* proclaims its editorial intentions on the title page.
The reader is promised 'Old Ballads', 'Corrected from the best and most
Ancient Copies Extant', with 'Introductions Historical and Critical'
Some items had been sent to the editor by a 'Gentleman', and had been
written by the 'greatest and most polite Wits of their Age'. Such writers
had received a classical education, and could have aspired to be poets, but
had chosen instead to give 'the World a small Specimen of their Talents'
in the form of occasional songs. Phillips drew the line at using the work
of Suckling or Cowley, because he was reluctant to infringe on their
literary property, but he had no qualms in taking material from 'common
Tradition' when he had 'no better Authority'. He affected to apologize
to 'the many who perhaps will think it ridiculous to enter seriously into
a Dissertation upon Ballads' and tried to ensure that his second volume
was more 'careful' than the first, checking to see that it contained 'no vile

Conceit, no Low Pun, or double Entendre.' Only songs which were characterized by 'Majestick Simplicity', or were the sort of innocuous 'merry Songs' most missed by earlier purchasers, are included. His 'Introductions' to the songs had some literary and even scholary pretensions, though most are merely descriptive, and many are left incomplete, even after 'the strictest Search' for information, because of the 'difficulties we are forc'd to go through, when we undertake to reconcile the Inconsistencies and Contradictions of Authors'. Texts (for there are no tunes printed, though some are named) are arranged rather loosely. Items with historical content are mostly grouped together. 'Ballads written on Foreign Subjects', pseudo-'Scotch' songs and a few texts on 'Scripture Subjects' are arranged separately; yet there is no formal division in the 'Table of Ballads'. Phillips' intention of using 'nothing but old Songs' is contradicted by the inclusion of one 'modern' piece; but he has no theoretical distinction to make between 'Ballads' and 'Songs'. His was essentially a work designed as much for reading as for singing from, for passive and individual consumption as well as for private or public performance.

* * * * *

(ii) Scotland[9]

Scotland had only one broadside-song printer in the later seventeenth-century when England had 40, so not only did English prints reach as far as Aberdeenshire, but English editors and publishers could call almost anything 'Scotch' and get away with the imposition south of the Border. Printing in Scotland was politically controlled through a system of licensing. After the political defeat of the English Parliament and their Scots allies, Charles II granted a monopoly of publishing books to Andrew Anderson. For 40 years after 1671 this monopoly was strictly enforced, and opportunities for getting into print were further decreased by the political censorship imposed after 1688, first by the English state, and then by the Scots Presbyterian theocracy. So when, in 1700, James Watson printed a pamphlet attacking England's attempts to stifle Scots overseas trade, he was promptly imprisoned in Edinburgh's Tolbooth, though he was soon set free by those citizens who agreed with his views. Watson's father had been an Aberdeen merchant who had lent cash to Charles II when the king was in exile; and when two Dutch printers failed to prosper from another Watson loan, the merchant decided to turn printer, encouraged by the king's gift of a monopoly for printing almanacks throughout Scotland, and the perquisite of being printer to the royal household. Watson senior died just before 1688; and in the mid-1690s his son James set up as a printer in the Scots capital. During the early 1700s James published two newspapers; and in 1706 he issued the first of what were to be three volumes of songs and verse. *A Choice Collection of Comic and Serious Scottish Poems both Ancient and Modern* appeared in the period which spanned the heated political debate over the Union. Volume one was published five years before Anderson's licence expired, and at a period when propaganda in the form of song was believed to be especially potent. The Scots politician Andrew Fletcher claimed to know a 'very wise man' who 'believed if a man were permitted to make all the ballads, he need not care who should make the laws of a nation'.[10] Volume two was published when Watson set up as a bookseller, in 1709, and the third volume was printed in 1711, when his acceptability to the court party in London and North Britain was confirmed by his being awarded a share in the renewed Royal Patent to print books. When one of his partners supported the Jacobites in 1715, Watson benefited substantially, and he was able to leave his widow a 'very considerable estate'.

The *Choice Collection* contained songs which were 'Comic' because they were unexpurgated. Some were bawdy, some obscene, and many were written in a phonetic version of the vernacular, contrasting with the 'quite English' work which also appeared. With the benefit of hindsight, literary critics may perceive a 'marked split between the popular and cultivated elements' in this 'scrappy miscellany'.[11] But an earlier song-book, the Aberdeen *Cantus* of 1662, contained hardly any indigenous Scots material. The market which welcomed Watson's volumes was probably to some extent different to that which had bought the work of the older Scots poets — the Semphills, Montgomerie, Aytoun, Drummond and the two James's — in chapbook form. This old vernacular poetry and song was not only common in cheap printed versions found in Scots workers' cottages, but even had some life in oral song-culture. This fact, and the fact that the Union issue raised the question of the independence not only of Scots economic and political but also of its cultural life, point to a 'new' market for Watson's song-book. Scots upper-class culture was becoming progressively Anglified in this period, and the Kirk continued to tyrannize social life; so the songs in Watson's *Collection* would appeal both to a sense of Scots nationalism in culture, and to a vicarious enjoyment in 'low' life and character, as enjoyed by English polite society since the Restoration. Watson made little attempt to discriminate between the sources available to him, calling both poetry and songs 'Poems'. He takes texts from broadsides, and he also claims to have copied others 'from the most Correct Manuscripts', the 'Repositories of some Curious and Ingenious Gentlemen', in preference to chapbooks, where they had 'been formerly Printed most Uncorrectly, in all respects'. This was no scholarly edition, however. Occasionally he cites an author's name, a place and date of performance, but he names no tunes to those pieces which were made to be sung, and he is coy about his sources, so we cannot check his transcriptions. The *Collection* achieves its ambition of giving some of the songs and verse a more permanent home, but it does so primarily for a genteel market of readers.

Allan Ramsay built on Watson's foundations, after Culloden. Ramsay was the grandson of an Edinburgh lawyer, but his father worked as Lord Hopetoun's mine superintendent in Lanarkshire, and his mother hailed from Derbyshire. Though the family lived in what has been called 'poverty',[12] Allan was able to stay on at school until he was 15, and when his father died he was apprenticed to a wig-maker in Edinburgh, setting up shop in his own right after he had served his time. He was a founder member of the Jacobite Easy Club in 1712, became its acknowledged 'laureate', and immersed himself in the 'old racy vernacular ditties' which were enjoyed by the capital's 'middle and lower classes' in private, as part of a gesture of defiance against 'the repressive tendencies of the Kirk', and against the strange tradition of Latin versifying which dominated seventeenth century Scots polite culture.[13] After the first military defeat of Jacobitism, Ramsay turned to bookselling. He wrote occasional poems which sold as single or half-sheet publications, and gave him the reputation of being the 'poet of the jovial burgher'. His 'genial and epicurean'[14] talents, and his politics, endeared him to influential people in the city who managed to protect him from attack by the English state or the Scots Presbytry. (On one occasion, his shop was raided by the self-appointed cultural censors of the Kirk, looking for 'villanous profane and obscene books and playes printed at London', but Ramsay was tipped off, and had hidden 'a great many the worst'.[15]) In 1719, he published a volume of his own *Scots Songs*, which soon reached a second edition; but even more successful was his version of *Chryst's-Kirke on the Green*, which he published from an old manuscript with additional verses of his own. By 1723, this work had reached a fifth edition, and no doubt this success encouraged him to produce two song-books. In January 1724, he issued *The Tea-Table Miscellany*, a 'Collection of Choice Songs Scots & English'; and in November there appeared *The Ever Green*, a 'Collection of Scots Poems Wrote by the Ingenious before 1600'. Both went into several reprints, and the *Miscellany* had reached its twelfth edition by 1763, in a considerably enlarged form. Ramsay's material success was assured. One work netted him 400 guineas, and he eventually set up a shop in the Luckenbooths, which became the centre for the polite literary and musical culture not only of Edinburgh residents, but also 'country' gentry and professional people. By 1755, he retired to a substantial town house, independent of trade. Just as Hanoverian and Protestant victory in England had assured state patronage for D'Urfey and Phillips, so, contradictorily, political, military and religious defeat for Jacobitism ensured noble and bourgeois patronage for Ramsay, even after the extinction of Stuart ambitions in 1746.

Ramsay sought to appeal to the wider market for Scots cultural nationalism, and particularly to those who supported the wrong side in 1707 and at Preston. But he was realistic enough to dedicate the *Miscellany* to 'ilka lovely BRITISH lass' and *The Ever Green* to His Grace James Duke of Hamilton, and the rest of the gentry and respectable bourgeoisie who composed the 'Honourable MEMBERS' of the Royal Company of

Archers. He also recognized that he could not treat predominantly female and male markets in the same way. Thus, the *Miscellany* ostentatiously claimed to keep out 'all smut and ribaldry', so that the 'modest voice and ear of the fair singer might meet with no affront', given the editor's 'chief bent' was to gain the 'good graces' of each 'free-born chearful Briton' round the fashionable tea table. But since only one woman in 50 in that market could 'tolerably entertain with vocal or instrumental music', while the remaining 49 content themselves with 'the pleasure of hearing and singing without the trouble of being taught', such women needed Ramsay's song-book the better to integrate then into polite British society, and to make them fit to be members of a future ruling class. In *The Ever Green* he goes hard for the comparable male market, not scrupling to titillate them with the occasional 'wanton story', to appeal to their patriotism or to their sense of masculinity. Ramsay aimed at 'any SCOTS Man, who despises the Fopery of admiring nothing but what is either new or foreign, and is a lover of his Country'. He also puffed those 'serious and comick Performances of our old Poets', which are imbued with the 'Spirit of Freedom' and the 'Love of Liberty', and are characterized by a natural Strength of Thought' and an engaging 'Simplicity of Stile':

> When these good old Bards wrote, we had not yet made Use of imported Trimming upon our Cloaths, nor of foreign Embroidery in our Writings. Their Poetry is the Product of their own Country, not pilfered and spoiled in the Transportation from abroad.

Crucial both to that poetry and to Ramsay's song-books was the *vernacular*, the talisman of Scots not ashamed of their culture and their heritage, and not inclined to reject 'the most elegant Thoughts in a Scots Dress'. Even so, while labelling such pretentious and unpatriotic individuals as an 'affected Class of Fops' who 'would fain distinguish themselves' from the 'Vulgar', Ramsay is by no means implying that such a distinction is not necessary. The issue to him and conservatives like him was how to hang on to the best of the past 'national' Scots culture, and to make it a live component in what would inevitably become a 'national' British culture — that is, the culture of the amalgamating ruling class, penetrated by that of the rising bourgeoisie. In this strategy, however, it was precisely the culture of the 'Vulgar' which was used as a stick with which to chastise Anglicized Scots people.

The 'manners of his countrymen, and the peculiarities of the lower orders', are used by Ramsay both to underwrite his ideal of 'Doric simplicity' and to give a sense of Scottishness, of 'local colour', by the adoption of workers' sayings and a version of their spoken tongue. This construct could then be used as a moral critique both of workers' culture and that of the culturally treacherous in the nobility and gentry, with the added bonus that 'low life' vitality, sensuality and outspokenness can be enjoyed vicariously, and without risk to reputation or to health. The success of the *Miscellany* and the *The Ever Green* — and especially that of his play, *The Gentle Shepherd*, which appeared in 1725 and contained several songs — indicates that there was a sizeable section of actual and would-be polite Scots society which was keen to differentiate itself from both town and country workers' culture, while wanting to appropriate what they could salvage from that culture so as to retain at least a partial 'national' identity within the economic and political reality of Britain. These people could afford song-books, drank tea, were highly literate and yet not only understood but probably spoke vernacular Scots. For the men at any rate, institutions like the successors to the Easy Club represented one strategy for resisting cultural assimilation or the rapid decline to a merely provincial status. Similar stresses were, of course, being felt by the English bourgeoisie, the people who listened to Ramsay's songs being 'warbled, to rapturous applause, by the favourite vocalists' at London and provincial pleasure gardens and other 'places of popular resort'.[16] By 'popular', of course, is meant not only the bourgeoisie, but the strata who were to form the petty-bourgeoisie later in the century, and one or two cultural slummers from higher up the social scale, amongst whom the appeal of Ramsay's arcadian songs was 'abundantly testified by the song-books and sheet music' which sold so steadily throughout England.[17] It seems appropriate that the same people who expropriated workers' labour power in their economic activities, should also exploit elements of workers' culture in analogous ways, both sides of the border.

The *Miscellany* uses 'old verses' from manuscript and print, but Ramsay concedes that around 90 items were 'new verses to known tunes', his own work or that of 'some ingenious young gentlemen' who lent him their assistance. *The Ever Green* is equally careless of ascribing authorship, in spite of its title page advertisement, and Ramsay postpones an 'Account of the Authors' to a promised second volume, which never appeared. However, he claims that he got 'most' of his texts from a 'large Manuscript-book in Folio, collected and wrote by Mr. George Bannantyne in Anno 1568', which was made available to him by the Honourable Mr William Carmichael, Advocate, brother to the Earl of Hyndford. Bannantyne[18] was an Edinburgh merchant who compiled his manuscript in Forfarshire during an outbreak of plague in the capital, using 'copies awld, markit and vitillat', plus one or two of his own compositions. Where the other 'copies' came from is uncertain, but their anonymity fitted in well with Ramsay's strategy of absorbing such material into a largely impersonal and undifferentiated Scots 'national' culture. Where information was available, he chose to play it down. Thus many of the tunes had strong Jacobite associations and were set to pseudo-arcadian poetry, while what had been unashamedly erotic material is renovated ruthlessly so as to leave only 'merry images of low character', acceptable to Scots and 'British' gentility alike. His song-books had few scholarly

pretensions. *Chryst's-Kirke* now had *two* extra cantos of his own composing: the pseudo-antique *Hardyknute* appeared without comment, and
various 'faults of omission and commission' were committed with the
Bannantyne MS.[19] What Ramsay termed the 'dross of blundering
transcribers and printers' was a fragile and disingenuous cover for his
own tinkering; and, in any case, 'old songs with additions' and 'new
words by different hands' far outnumber the 'old songs', or those with
'authors unknown', whose authenticity is often highly suspect, even if
some did originate or remain current in workers' culture. The truth was
that Ramsay did not rate real vernacular poetry and song highly enough,
according to bourgeois literary standards, to treat them with respect, and
he was ready to doctor even the most famous and those by named authors
so as to make them singable over tea cups or at the convivial club.

The pull of London-oriented culture was enormous. By the 1720s the
English market for 'Scots' songs was such that rather than simply import
the songs, the capital imported the people who made and sang them.
William Thomson[20] was born in Edinburgh about 1683, the son of one
of the King's Scottish state trumpeters. In his youth William became
'distinguished for the sweetness of his voice, and the agreeable manner
in which he *sung* a Scots song'.[21] Early in the eighteenth century he
moved to London, and his singing of Scots songs brought him favour at
Court. In 1722 he merited a benefit concert, and in 1725 he produced *Orpheus Caledonius*, a 'Collection of the best Scotch Songs' set to music by
the editor and dedicated to the Princess of Wales. The work was re-issued
in 1733, with a licence from the King granting sole publishing rights to
the book to Thomson for 14 years, and against the importation of pirated
copies or the use of any of its contents in other works. Its subscription list
represented huge swathes of gentry, nobility and even royalty in both
England and Scotland. The first edition sold 300 copies before it was
published, while the 1733 edition had almost 700 advance orders,
including those from 20 Dukes or Duchesses, a further 150 or so other
aristocrats, and over 300 lesser gentry and professionals, all no doubt impressed by Thomson's bold acknowledgement of the Queen's encouragement of him as a 'teacher and singer of *Scots* songs'. Before the copyright
ran out some material was pirated for another song-book, and the rights
were still worth 50 guineas to Dodsley the publisher in 1753. Songs and
now song-books were by this time very much like any other literary
property, and were treated as commodities in the market composed of
people who would need and appreciate Thomson's bass accompaniments,
or the melodies arranged for the flute. Later, particularly complex or
difficult material was cut or amended to make the songs more accessible
to less-gifted performers.

Thomson's very title was a deliberate echo of Purcell's posthumous
work. Like Ramsay, he used Jacobite tunes and even song-titles but with
notably apolitical texts, many of which were stolen without acknowledgement from Ramsay's song-books of 1724. Ramsay was a subscriber, but

he held his peace until the 1733 edition appeared, still with no reference to himself, and then published a restrained note in the 1734 edition of the *Miscellany* to set the record straight.[22] (Just possibly, the appearance of his and Stuart's *Musick for Allan Ramsay's Collection of Scots Songs*, which was published in 1725–6, was his way of getting some profit out of the enlarged and highly respectable market opened up by Thomson; but having his own compositions protected by copyright on behalf of someone who had no legal or moral right to such material must have been a little galling.) Thomson's second edition penetrated so far as the Edinburgh Musick-Society and Auchindinny, as well as to Bristol and even Paris. Presumably, to the British élite, Scots people and culture, even as mediated by Thomson, were sufficiently 'foreign' to excite curiosity, as well as fitting in neatly with the myth of rural arcadia. Being closer to 'Nature', Thomson's sanitized 'Lass' who scorned 'Brocade', and his idealized (and fashionably kilted[23]) 'Scottish Lads' could be enjoyed by the city 'BEAUS and BELLES' without problems like the odour of sheep-dung or the danger of physical work. At a period when social stratification added to political crisis made almost all workers' culture a matter for genteel curiosity, it will no doubt have been of comfort to both Scots and English people of fashion to believe that country life really was 'sweet' and 'unaffected' as portrayed in Mr Thomson's pretty little songs. In a way, Thomson developed the role of cultural importer and wholesale merchant, as well as that of song-tailor; and in his own modest fashion he helped the cultural assimilation which was to be a significant factor in the amalgamation of the future British ruling class. Such people did not wish to be troubled with elaborate introductions, notes, or dissertations on theoretical issues — only one piece is loosely characterized as a 'ballad'. They wished only to be amused, and they were prepared to pay Mr Thomson to do it.

* * * * *

These early song-books were made by people who came from modest social origins, but who were also upwardly-mobile. Because they were all men, they received more than average formal education and were able to move from the English or Scots provinces to the capital cities, where connections not only with one faction or another within the ruling-class but also with the legal profession and the print-trade seem to have been particularly significant. Song-writing and the making of song books was not yet a secure way of making a living, and patronage of one kind or another remained crucial for those not of independent means. Their tendency to support reactionary political positions evidently helped to make these mediators fit to be recipients of patronage. It also predisposed them to patronize or even to expropriate the products of workers' culture, and to treat those products cavalierly as property and as commodities,[24] as part of the cultural as well as economic and political struggle to construct a

'British' state and culture out of two 'national' states and cultures. In this process, song-mediators performed what seems to have been a minor but interesting role, though they clearly had no significant intellectual or theoretical contribution to make, and scholarly questions hardly impinged on their consciousness, let alone their editorial practice. In so far as workers' song-culture is present in their books it functions as the raw material for mediators' own compositions, or as a source of genteel amusement or titillation. Already, social stratification was resulting in a clear distinction between what was 'national' and what was 'popular' in culture. Just as most people were a source of economic gain to those whose culture dominated the 'nation', so majority culture began to take on significance as a source of cultural exploitaton, with members of the rising bourgeois class performing the crucial mediating role. From now on, therefore, we will examine mediators' class position and general ideology thematically, rather than at the level of the individual, to see how they related to economic, political and cultural change.

2 From Thomas Percy to Joseph Ritson

In the 40 years between the first edition of Ramsay's song-books and the appearance of Percy's *Reliques* Jacobitism had been militarily annihilated, agriculture had been rapidly transformed, what we now know as the Industrial Revolution had begun and British towns and cities had begun to attract workers from the countryside in significant numbers. After Culloden, the landed aristocracy and big bourgeoisie not only began to close ranks against the rest of the population politically, but they saw to it that their collective economic interests were supported by a series of overseas wars for control of international trade. The consequent expansion of the economy not only helped the formation of a new ruling-class with a sizeable bourgeois component, but it also necessitated the development of what we now refer to as the petty-bourgeoisie. Upward social mobility became possible for more people — that is, if they were men — than at any previous period of history, and especially in the professions, if they could get access to at least some formal education. Thus, while the next 'generation' of song-mediators tended to have humble provincial origins, they also tended to be both geographically and socially mobile, to receive more formal education than most of the population, and to have ambitions to achieve and then consolidate their position higher up the economic and social scale. However, the American War of Independence, the French Revolution of 1789 and the political crises in Britian during the Wilksite struggles of the 1770s and the republican struggles of the 1790s, also helped to concentrate bourgeois minds on the 'people' as a newly-politicized power in society.

* * * * *

(i) The people

Thomas Percy[1] was born in Shropshire in 1729, the son of a Bridgenorth grocer. He went to the local Grammar School, and then to Christ Church College, Oxford before entering the established church. David Herd[2] was born into a Kincardineshire farming family in 1732, had some education at a local school, and was probably apprenticed to a country lawyer before moving to Edinburgh and working as an accountant's clerk. Thomas Evans,[3] born in London in 1742, served an apprenticeship to a bookseller before setting himself up as a bookseller and publisher in his own right. Joseph Ritson's[4] parents had origins in the Westmoreland yeomanry. He was born in Stockton-on-Tees in 1752 in very humble circumstances, but he managed to get some education under the tuition of a local church minister, served his time with a local solicitor and conveyancer, and finally shifted to London to become managing clerk in a conveyancing firm. In a few years he set up in business for himself, became High Bailiff of the Liberty of the Savoy, and was called to the Bar. John Pinkerton[5] also came from a family with yeoman ancestors, but his father moved from Scotland to Somerset, rose to become a merchant, and returned to Edinburgh, where he married a widow who had been a merchant's daughter. John was born in Edinburgh in 1758, went to a small school in the Edinburgh suburbs and then to Lanark Grammar School. He was prevented from going to Edinburgh University by his father's objections. Instead, he spent five years apprenticed to an Edinburgh lawyer. After his father's death in 1780, he went to London, lived as a man of independent means, and pursued a literary career. Robert Burns,[6] like Herd, was the son of a Kincardineshire farming family. His father suffered 'domestic embarrassments' and moved to Alloway, where he failed to compete with better-capitalized farmers who rose from 'the head of the commonality to the tail of the gentry' during the so-called 'agricultural revolution'. William Burns sank to the level of a 'mere ploughing and harrowing machine', before giving up his independence and going to work for wages as a gentleman's gardener.[7] Robert was born in Alloway in 1759 and spent four years at a local 'adventure school', before working with his father on the land. Poverty and the lack of patronage made apprenticeship or training impossible. His future collaborator, James Johnson,[8] was born, probably at around the same period, at Ettrick on the Border. We know nothing of his parents, education or training, but when we first hear of him it is as an engraver and music-seller in Edinburgh, so he will have been apprenticed to his trade. So far, with the exception of Evans and Burns, these men were quite typical of that stratum of professional people we have identified; and, conversely, they were quite atypical of the majority of British people, who still lived in the country, worked with their hands, received little or no formal education and lived and died in poverty. But if their origins and early lives were unusual, their careers and material success were even more so.

* * *

Percy benefited from patronage from his Oxford college, an Earl, a Duke, and finally the King, as he moved to a Northamptonshire vicarage, through the Deanery of Carlisle, to the Bishoprick of Dromore in Ireland. He also had connections in London's literary world, and at Oxford and

Cambridge, including professed antiquarians like Birch, Farmer and Steevens, and literary critics and practitioners such as Johnson, Goldsmith, Garrick, Warton, Gray and Shenstone. His less than onerous church duties allowed him to produce literary work during the 1760s and 1770s, and to pursue his antiquarian-literary interests in conjunction with London booksellers and publishers as a profitable sideline. Macpherson's studies in Gaelic and Erse poetry and the scholarly concern with the Norse *Edda* — a debate to which Percy contributed — represented a fashionable and fresh injection of spirit into what had become a rather turgid and formalistic lyric poetry. In the later 1760s and after, Herd had leisure and money enough to pursue antiquarian hobbies, and to get involved with booksellers and publishers. He also took an active part, being a lifelong bachelor, in Edinburgh's all-male convivial clubs, which cut across what were increasingly class divisions. The Cape Club,[8] of which Herd was an active member, included literary and musical amateurs and professionals, but also tradesmen, artisans, lesser professionals and only the occasional representative of the gentry. Yet its 'democratic' reputation contrasted with the fact that it took the poet Robert Fergusson three years before he was allowed to join. The Cape had its provincial siblings, not only in Glasgow, but also in Manchester and London; and we know that one of its members, Stephen Kemble,[9] later moved to Newcastle and joined a similar club. Across Britain, such clubs helped migrants and rising tradesmen, professionals and performers maintain (or even construct) a sense of comradeship and of a common culture in the increasingly stratified city society in which they found themselves. In Scotland the sense of cultural displacement was of course exacerbated by a progressively Anglified upper bourgeoisie and ruling class on the one hand, and a rapidly proletarianized majority of land-workers on the other. Financial gain — and even fame — were of minor importance to a man like Herd: both his song-books appeared anonymously, and readers were referred to the publishers rather than to the editor.

During the 1770s, and up to his death in 1784, Evans not only sold books aimed at 'every man of taste', ranging from polite literature to works on 'antiquities', from Samuel Johnson to Montesquieu, but he also edited and published one or two himself. He acted as a link between his patrons and literary acquaintances and his fellow booksellers, who had their own convivial club at the Grecian Tavern; and his companionable qualities attracted the friendship of leading figures like Garrick, Reynolds and Sheridan, not to mention Goldsmith, whose writings were first published in London by Evans himself. Evidently, the combination of a significant expansion in the market for printed books and in the opportunities for talented young men from the provinces combined to provide the material basis both for Evans' success and for that of his literary friends from equally humble and obscure families. Ritson came to London in the late 1770s after the Wilksite struggles. His increasing material wealth enabled him to explore the literary treasures and antiquities in the British Museum, and to indulge himself in publishing several collections of songs without fear of offending patrons or incurring any serious financial loss, though he often published anonymously, and probably none of his productions made a profit. He was strongly anti-aristocratic, hated George III, and was fully in sympathy with the French *sansculottes*. After 1789, he adopted throughgoing republican views. He visited revolutionary France with a fellow north-easterner, William Shield[10] the composer, in 1791, and returned to declare England 'ripe for the long-delayed parliamentary reform.'[11] He read Paine's works, befriended outright republicans (including Eaton), corresponded with the radical William Godwin and, during the politically repressive years of the middle and late 1790s, had to 'walk warily for fear of being reported to the authorities as a radical'.[12] Though he seems not to have written openly on political issues, the appearance of his work on *Robin Hood* in the politically turbulent year of 1795, with its barely coded references to contemporary struggles, seems to locate Ritson's ideology clearly enough. At a period when working people in the north-east were taking over markets and selling food at the old prices, Ritson described Hood as:

> a man who, in a barbarous age, and under a complicated tyranny, display'd a spirit of freedom and independence which has endeared him to the common people, whose cause he maintained, (for all opposition to Tyranny is the cause of the people); and in spite of the malicious endeavours of pitiful monks, by whom history was consecrated to the crimes and follies of titled ruffians and sainted idiots, to suppress all record of his patriotic exertions and virtuous acts, will render his name immortal.[13]

Such a statement must have had considerable political resonance, and the attack on churchmen links to Ritson's campaign against the practices of the man who had now become Bishop Percy.[14] After *Robin Hood*, however, Ritson seems to have kept his head down. He produced no more song-books until the year 1802, when an uncharacteristic gamble in the state funds went badly wrong during the financial crisis following the Peace of Amiens, and swept away over a thousand pounds of his small fortune, forcing him to part with much of his very valuable library. Ritson died, in a 'deplorable state of mental derangement', four months after war had again been declared on France. Though he had helped many literary figures, including Walter Scott,[15] he was left largely unsupported and was belittled after his death. His friend, Shield, conforming to the dominant culture, went on to become Master of the Musicians-in-Ordinary to the King in 1817.

Pinkerton went to London to 'obtain access to books of reference' in 1781, after his father's death made him materially secure, and permitted him to devote himself to literary, historical and antiquarian interests. He made the acquaintance of booksellers and publishers, and of literary figures like Horace Walpole, Gibbon, Bishop Percy, Douce and

Southgate of the British Museum. Publishing followed. He had some curious ideas for an émigré Scot, notably a firm belief in the 'inveterate inferiority of the Celtic race', whose 'features, history, actions, and manners indicate a fatal moral and intellectual weakness, rendering them incapable of susceptibility to the higher influences of civilisation'. He died in Paris in 1826, separated from his wife (who was the Bishop of Salisbury's sister), and left behind a reputation for 'peculiar prejudices and eccentricities', for being 'a somewhat spiteful enemy', and for having 'infirmities of temper'. By contrast, James Johnson had an 'honest Scotch enthusiasm', a little capital, some skill in engraving music and a desire to be 'a Patriot for the Music' of his country.[16] Once he had met Burns, probably at one of Edinburgh's convivial clubs, Johnson abandoned control over his publishing project to the up-and-coming poet, but he seems to have made little if any profit from the venture. Certainly, he died poor, and his widow ended her days in the Charity Workhouse.

Burns' youth and early manhood in Alloway were strongly influenced by the economic and ideological upheavals which disturbed Scotland during the early phases of the Industrial Revolution. He was inspired both by the robust country culture in which he grew up and by the vernacular literature he was exposed to at school. As a young man, he began to 'regard with a sort of sullen aversion and disdain, all that was sordid in the pursuits of his peers',[17] and joined not only the convivial Tarbolton Bachelors Club, but also the local Freemasons, where he had access to a sprinkling of lesser gentry and to other Freemasons across Scotland and into England. In 'absolute defiance'[18] of his strictly Calvinist father's wishes, he attended the Tarbolton dancing class. In their different ways, all these institutions were, of course, a focus of opposition to the Kirk's oppressive ideology and practices; and this 'alternative' and largely male culture provided Burns not only with an audience for his own creative work as poet and song-writer, but also, in the later 1780s, with a *market*. Some 'gentlemen' evidently proposed a subscription on Burns' behalf, to enable him to emigrate to the West Indies; but when the first edition of his poetry and songs was published at Kilmarnock, the combination of anti-kirk sentiments and elements of (especially the bawdy) old vernacular culture, ensured the sale of all 612 copies. Burns' work appealed not only to all the farmers in the parish, but also to 'plough-boys and maid-servants'[19] of his own age, who saved up three shillings for a copy. This small-scale market success gave Burns a springboard to get to Edinburgh, where a second edition of his book attracted 1500 subscribers from a book-buying public which had got wind of the ploughman's reputation. In fact, the publisher risked a print-run of 2800 copies, and paid Burns 100 guineas for the copyright two days after publication.

Burns's success was possible in Edinburgh literary circles precisely because of the growing crisis in 'national' culture. He was catapulted into fashionable New Town society, lionized during the 1786–7 'season' , and welcomed by the male 'leaders of intellect and society'[20] at their prestigious Crochallan Fencibles Club, as much for his skills as a conversationalist as for those as a poet and song-writer. The Freemason's Grand Lodge of Scotland hailed him as 'Caledonia's Bard', and the upper-crust Caledonian Hunt supported the re-publication of his book. Because of this rapid fame, ideas about emigration faded; yet once his curiosity-value as a 'Heaven-born ploughman' or 'untutored clodhopper' had been exhausted in the city's West End salons, Burns still had to make a living. His investment of £700 of his proceeds from publishing (in a farm-tenancy at Ellisland) failed, but the invitations to the tables of nobility and gentry continued, and genteel patronage enabled him to get a commission worth £50–70 a year in the Excise service. In spite of the apologists, there was clearly no way he wanted to remain a ploughman, or return to those he once called his 'Compeers, the rustic inmates of the Hamlet'[21] as their equals in material wealth. Nor did he court success amongst 'the Million', the newly-urban workers who by the 1780s and 1790s had become the Scots proletariat. Even in his early days, Burns proclaimed that he 'would abhor every Prentice mouthing my poor performances in the streets'[22]. And while he may have had an intellectual sympathy with both American and French revolutionaries, he also affected a sentimental attachment to Jacobitism, and was drawn to a strongly reactionary conception of what constituted Scots history and culture — that same 'Scottish prejudice'[23] he imbibed as a child when he read a chapbook on Wallace. Rather than seek to expand the considerable market he had established for his early poetry amongst urban workers and artisans, Burns largely abandoned original poetry to join with the engraver, James Johnson, in the production of *The Scots Musical Museum*. By this time, Burns was effectively distanced from the embryo working class, and his donation of talent and labour power, unpaid, was to the liberal elements within bourgeois culture. Even when he wrote *Scots Wha Hae* and laid himself open to state prosecution, it was his friends in court and not radicals or workers who protected him. His pen was usually at the service of a 'popular' candidate at parliamentary elections, but he also wrote against a bad landlord who chanced to be a Whig rather than a Tory, and he was one of the first to join the Dumfries Volunteers during an anti-French scare, though he could not afford to buy his uniform — a debt which dogged him until his death in poverty in 1796. Yet before he died, broadside songs with his name on them were being hawked through Dumfries, and many of his earlier songs and poems were being marketed in chapbook form from most major printing centres in England and Scotland. While he busied himself with the demands of polite culture, which certainly cost him rather than earned him money, the work he created out of the experience of country workers' culture was carried along in the pockets and the memories of the proletarianized workers into the culture of what was to be the urban working class.

* * * * *

(ii) Their aims

Percy's *Reliques of Ancient English Poetry*, 'consisting of Old Heroic Ballads, Songs, and other pieces of our earlier poets; together with some few of modern date', was published in London in 1765. His market was both 'the judicious antiquary and the reader of taste', yet he and his literary advisors doubted whether the hitherto unpublished material he had chanced upon might be 'deemed worthy of the attention of the public' in the 'present state of improved literature'. They understood that the style and content of the poetry and songs cut across the grain of formal Augustan literature; and, true to form, eminent critics and scholarly anti-quarians poured scorn on the venture. But the young men who turned out to be the next generation of fashionable poets devoured the *Reliques* — including Wordsworth, Southey, Coleridge, Scott and Burns — and a wider public bought up the first edition in two years. By 1794 the publication was in its fourth edition. The 'Simplicity of style and senti-ment' combined with the nationalistic appeal of 'the Genius of antient English poetry' led to its commercial success amongst 'readers of taste' in the rising bourgeoisie. They liked the idea of Percy's allegedly homogeneous 'national' culture at some date prior to 1600, partly because the split into what he termed 'art' could be neatly traced as the origins of their own class culture, but also because the presumably non-'art' elements could be shunted off as the heritage of 'vulgar' culture of their own day. This underlying assumption of the perfectibility of bourgeois culture rested on certain strange ideas about the role of the medieval 'minstrel' and about 'gradations in the development of the language'. According to Percy, the 'minstrel' produced songs for a 'martial and unlettered people, the majority of whom remained passive consumers of his professional products. In other words, he foisted onto cultural history the same hierarchical and élitist view of artistic produc-tion — with its patronage-system, social exclusiveness, and so on — that prevailed in his own day. Not only does he systematically downgrade workers' creativity, but he lambastes the 'low and insubordinate correct-ness, sometimes bordering on the insipid', in the products of the seven-teenth century broadside song-writers who wrote for a comparatively broad market. In this way, Percy fostered apparently contradictory ideas of a past 'national' culture and individualism in 'art'-production, of a supposed contemporary cultural unity at the level of the élite and of a distinctive 'English' identity, which chanced not to include the culture of the overwhelming majority of the population. Individuals, of course, could 'escape' from that majority culture — become Bishops, even — and carry along with them a little cultural baggage to add to the stock of the class which was readying itself to amalgamate with the old landed aristocracy, and take on 'national' responsibilities.

David Herd's 1769 Edinburgh publication, *The Ancient and Modern Scots Songs, heroic ballads, &c.*, 'Now Collected into one Body, From the various Miscellanies wherein they formerly lay dispersed', and 'Containing likewise, A great Number of Original Songs, from Manuscripts, never before published', was the first new important song-book of Scots material for almost half a century. Like Ramsay, Herd had a ready-made market for this anonymous publication in the Edinburgh Cape Club and its analogues, which — rather like his book — represented part of the same culturally-defensive strategy against creeping Anglization amongst actual or would-be gentility, but were also an enclave in an urban culture which was being rapidly proletarianized. Herd and his kind came from provincial Scotland, retained social and occupational links there, and yet formed a significant part in the developing city culture. What they had to offer that culture — and what also helped them keep some sense of cultural identity, given their relatively rapid geographical and social mobility — were things like their spoken language, and those elements of their culture of origin which fitted the Edinburgh of the early phase of the Industrial Revolution. There was also a link with polite Scots culture. Herd's friends, James Balfour and Stephen Clarke, who helped promote the interest in 'Scots' music and song every time they performed in front of genteel audiences, needed 'new' material, which was also welcome in the clubs, where singing was evidently of considerable importance. Thomson's *Orpheus* had 'become very scarce', and the old political conflicts had become somewhat muted, so it seemed possible to produce a 'national' song-book, containing all old pieces 'of any repute', and some 'Originals, purely Scottish'. And while some purchasers might, like Herd and his acquaintance, be 'learned in antiquities', the inclusion of a glossary underlines the editor's fear that the political and economic fact of Britain had begun to undermine and dilute precisely that sense of Scottishness which he and they felt needed to be reasserted.

This first edition sold out in only five years; and when a second edition was mooted, Herd's publishers had no qualms in accepting an offer of help from Percy, which fortunately never came.[24] By 1776, Herd had so much 'new' material that the second edition had to grow to two volumes, crammed with songs to the exclusion of almost all scholarly apparatus. *Ancient and Modern Scottish Songs, Heroic Ballads, etc.*, 'collected from memory, tradition and ancient authors' no longer had the definite article in its title, but it was still aimed at both literary and antiquarian markets, at the 'Gay and Chearful' and the 'Speculative and Refined', who were *defined* by Herd as *a*typical of the 'people' from whom some of the 'common popular songs' had come. He recognized the dichotomy between a genuinely 'national music' and the 'natural and striking traits of character, genius, tastes and pursuits' which he saw as typical of the 'people' at large. In a sense, Herd saw the dichotomy as the problem. His song-culture of origin had become separated from his culture of destination. So, while he could claim a 'national' music for Scotland (and Ireland, though, notably, not for England), and while he knew it to be approved by the 'unbiassed suffrage of foreigners of the best taste', what he wanted to do was somehow re-insert elements of the old song-culture into that of his own day and class. It wasn't that Herd didn't perceive the forces which were polarizing Scots culture and society. After all, the second edition was prepared during the period of sharpest struggle between provincial oligarchies and lesser burghers and townspeople, it appeared after the beginning of what turned out to be the American War of Independence, and his Preface recognized the political impact of some songs on the 'machine of government'. But since he started from the idea that 'Every nation, at least every ancient and unmixed nation, hath its peculiar style of musical expression, its peculiar mode of melody', which was supposedly 'modulated by the joint influence of climate and government, character and situation, as well as by the formation of the organs [sic]', then the political and economic crises which had characterized eighteenth century Scotland necessarily meant that anything like a genuinely national Scottish culture was problematical indeed. Herd's book signalled this contradiction by acknowledging the expropriation of elements of the song-culture of a 'great part of its inhabitants' (whimsically described as leading a presumably arcadian 'pastoral life', title page vignette and all), for the benefit of the 'classical reader', and others seeking 'amusement' from a work of such 'slight importance'. His foregrounding of songs from workers' culture, and his unwillingness to acknowledge an English 'national' music (as opposed to 'Poetry'), also represents a mildly combative form of cultural nationalism.

After the publication of Percy's third edition and Herd's second, other song-book makers in both countries cashed in on the markets that had been developed. Evans' *Old Ballads, Historical and Narrative, with some of modern date,* was totally reliant on Percy and Addison for ideas; and though he claimed his work contained nothing published in the *Reliques,* but only material 'Now first collected, and reprinted from rare Copies, with notes', Evans' was largely an up-date of Phillips' edition of the 1720s. John Pinkerton was another literary-antiquarian retailer. His *Select Scottish Ballads,* containing 'Ballads in the Tragic Style' and 'Ballads of the Comic Kind', was highly derivative. Its London publication no doubt helped him to exploit the émigré market for his 'Scottish' song-books during the 1780s, and particularly that for the 'really great poets' of the Middle Scots period, who he felt had been neglected. Given that much of this material was still circulating in workers' culture, in chapbook form, it is strange to note Pinkerton's stated aim of keeping this part of the literary heritage out of the hands of the 'vulgar'. But he was simply following the tradition of Thomson and Percy, by associating the cultural products of a whole 'nation' with that of its current ruling class, including not only the Duke of Buccleuch, to whom *Select Scottish Ballads* was dedicated, but now even those descendants of the losing side in 1746, who had recently got back their material property, as part of the process of ruling-class consolidation. Pinkerton pushes the logic of Percy's assumptions even further, equating the advance of 'Literature' with the supposed disappearance of 'Oral Tradition', and associating the art of the ancient bards with the products of children, from which the editor had to select 'only the very best'. Contemporary workers' culture was, to Pinkerton's élitest and literary way of seeing, like that of 'an ignorant person', devoid of 'common sense'; and so his acquaintance with Bishop Percy of Dromore is given prominence, while the supposed errors of a more humble (and safely dead) person such as Allan Ramsay can be patronized at length.

Though Ritson took on members of the literary establishment such as Johnson, Warton and Steevens, and song-mediators like Percy and Pinkerton, he did so not so much because he disagreed with their élitism, their literary values and assumptions, but because of their dubious scholarship. Buyers and readers were not getting what they paid for; and to a man whose job depended on the careful scrutiny of titles, deeds and suchlike artefacts, the sloppy or dishonest use of sources was tantamount to fraud. Ritson's motivation during the 1780's, then, was both scholarly and antiquarian in the best sense, and his three-volume *A Select Collection of English Songs* of 1783 aimed to satisfy the expectations raised, but not met, by Percy. He wished to 'exhibit all the most admired and intrinsically excellent specimens of lyric poetry in the English language', and thereby promote 'real instructive entertainment', 'satisfy the critical taste of the judicious', 'indulge the nobler feelings of the pensive' and 'afford innocent mirth to the gay', but only with *authentic* material. He believed the propaganda about cultural perfectibility fostered by the Enlightenment, and he accepted that 'National Song' stemmed from earlier courtly culture, while the song-culture of the 'common people' was simply the residue of what had been produced by minstrels and was sometimes passed on by the 'illiterate vulgar', though with little accuracy or success. According to Ritson, at this date, 'not more than two' such items were 'known to exist'. He firmly associated himself with the culture of the bourgeois book-buying 'public', the people who had 'stamped' the songs in his collection with their 'approbation' and claimed them, whatever their origins, as their own. But like Herd and many other upwardly-mobile migrants, Ritson also felt a sentimental attachment to his own culture of origin. He decided to collect songs from the north-east and to publish them in 'garlands', like *The Bishopric Garland; or Durham Minstrel*, which he published at Stockton in 1784. This 'Choice Collection of Excellent Songs, relating to the above county', was not only 'Full of agreeable Variety, and pleasant Mirth', but represented potential raw material for Shield's ballad operas, once the lyrics and their associated tunes had been removed from bibliophile-antiquarian aspic. Handel, Haydn, Arne and Dibdin dominated fashionable taste, yet Ritson and Shield wished to assert 'simple national melody' over the 'florid Italian fashion' of decades before. This cultural chauvinism, and the bourgeois prejudices which informed it, formed a significant part of the motivation to find and then to appropriate and assimilate the musical culture of

English regions, 'North Britain'and Ireland. And once the French Revolution and then the War boosted British, and especially English nationalism, Shield was well-placed to benefit from the ruling-class 'discovery' of 'ancient' and 'English' texts and tunes, free from alien influence and unambiguously patriotic.

By the time of Ritson's 1790 *Ancient Songs, from the time of King Henry the Third, to the Revolution*, the issue of 'national' culture had already become closely bound up with that of political loyalty to the state. Historical questions were, therefore, of more than antiquarian importance in settling that was 'English' about English culture. So Ritson's choice of 1688 as the closing date of this book's time-span, his attack on Percy's ideas about cultural development in general and about Minstrels in particular, and his stress on the authenticity of this 'small but genuine collection' have to be seen in a political as well as a cultural framework. Ritson saw himself as Percy's rival as mediator to the 'public' of 'the history, the poetry, the language, the manners, or the amusements of their ancestors'. His work on north-eastern song-culture, and his experience of the political polarization of the later 1780s and early 1790s, caused Ritson to question the cultural homogeneity of English society. He knew there were both amateur and professional musicians, song-writers and singers amongst the labouring population 'in some of the least polished or less frequented parts of the kingdom', such as Derbyshire and the outskirts of London. He had no difficulty in conceiving of a historic division of labour on class-based lines, as between the rise of the 'artist' and the decline of the 'minstrel', when literacy, print and 'Calvinistical bigotry' had seen off the products of an older culture, except for the *eight* 'minstrel' items he had now discovered! He also acknowledged that such 'scanty gleanings' of 'our Ancient Songs and vulgar music' as existed, made anything like a proper 'History' impossible. But his comparatively progressive political ideas did not overcome his scholarly prejudices sufficiently to stop him lining up with 'the more critical reader' in his bourgeois market when it came to questions of cultural quality, or distancing himself from those 'common people' who represented the only chance for the permanent overthrow of the aristocrats he so much hated.

When he edited a two-volume edition of *Scotish Songs*, in 1794, Ritson was ready to pronounce 'tradition' in workers' culture as a 'species of alchemy which converts gold to lead'. Yet his repeated visits to Scotland to garner materials and his correspondence with Scots collectors made him recognize that what they had found in Scotland (and he had to some extent discovered in north-east England) *was* different to the material available in manuscript and in print. Ritson rationalized this difference along lines set out by Herd. He liked 'Scots' songs because of their 'pastoral simplicity', compared to the 'more of art than of nature' he found in 'English' texts. He used the analogy of the attraction of a 'beautiful peasant, in her homespun russet', as opposed to the 'fine town lady, patched, powdered, and dressed out, for the ball or opera, in all the frippery of fashion'. But Ritson's position had moved: he now lamented that a 'considerable' number of 'ancient printed songs and ballads' had 'perished' because they had fallen 'chiefly into the hands of the vulgar, who had no better method of perserving their favourite compositions, than by pasting them upon the wall'. Clearly, his attitude towards songs on broadsides had changed since his dismissiveness of 1790, and though his division of Scots and English song-culture along black and white lines is arbitrary — arcadia versus modernity, nature against art — it necessarily led him to consider the possibility of there being a valuable song-culture amongst working people, and to concentrate his endeavours on the pursuit and preservation of whatever he could find. By the early 1800s, Ritson's attention had shifted decisively away from those of 'readers of taste and genius', and towards those of scholarly anti-quarianism and the serious 'student of traditional song'.

Strangely enough, Burns' interest in songs was partly the result of his fondness for Ritson's *English Songs*, his 'vade mecum' for many years; but his Scots patriotism was a far more important factor in the dedication of many years of his life and much of his creative talent after 1787 to Johnson's project, *The Scots Musical Museum*. The original idea had been for a collection of 'sentimental' songs, including Irish and English as well as Scots material, but the support of two 'gentlemen interested in the anthology of Scotland',[25] and above all Burns' involvement, was decisive. Burns became 'absolutely crazed'[26] about the project, spurned the idea of payment, and set about exploiting his new-found acquaintance in the interests of making the *Museum* as musically complete as he could. He wished to publish 'every Scotch air worth singing'.[27] By 1803, the six volumes contained 'Six Hundred Scots Songs with proper Basses for the Piano Forte &c.'. The work was dedicated to the Society of Antiquaries of Scotland, though at first it had been dedicated to the fashionable Edinburgh Catch Club. Originally, the publication was aimed at especially the female owners of harpsichords or pianos; but the price of seven shillings a volume (and two guineas a set) did not prevent later volumes from being advertised as available in Glasgow, Dumfries and Dundee, and even in Manchester and Newcastle. The *Museum* appealed not only to expatriate Scots, but, like Burns' poetry, to members of the liberal bourgeoisie and petty-bourgeoisie in England. And even before Ritson, Burns placed importance on the vitality of workers' culture — 'Nature's Judges',[28] he called them — though, as the *Museum's* title shows, he had little confidence in the continued vitality of that culture. This pessimistic attitude partly explains his willingness to act as a cultural archivist, for the tunes at any rate, on behalf of the 'people' and the 'public'.

Burns always understood that his books would be mused over and perhaps used by a bourgeois market, not by the country singers and musicians whose work formed its raw material; so there was a constant pressure to make the publication fully acceptable to bourgeois taste. Pieces which seemed to him to be historical and romantic 'Ballads' were sent off to his friends Tytler and Riddell, because they would not suit; and when he became involved with George Thomson's *Select Collection of Original Scotish Airs* (which began to appear in London in 1793), Burns almost invariably bowed to Thomson's businessmen's instincts to 'accommodate our tastes to our readers'.[29] This half-guinea a volume work had to have texts fit to be sung in polite society, which would please 'the Ladies', and Burns' role was the literary equivalent of Haydn, Bishop and even Beethoven, who accepted commissions to compose 'introductory and concluding symphonies and accompanyments for the violin and pianoforte'. In this company, Burns felt constrained to apologize for his own affection for 'inelegant and vulgar' strathspeys, even though they had been in vogue during the 1770s Edinburgh craze for 'Scots' country dancing amongst people of 'undisputed and cultivated taste'.[30] Burns' face was turned squarely towards the bourgeois market for printed song, and he successfully policed his own tastes and instincts in the interests of popularizing elements of workers' culture in that quarter. Like every other song-mediator whose work appeared in this period, the production of Burns' *Museum* would not have been possible without the bourgeois book-buying public, with its interest in its own cultural history and its growing power in commercially-oriented cultural production and consumption. On the other hand, the rise of a petty-bourgeois element within the larger market, and the ideological struggles of the period of the reaction to the French Revolution, directed politically progressive mediators' attention towards workers'culture in a more sympathetic way.

* * * * *

(iii) Their sources

The Percy MS. has been characterized by its editors as the 'foundation document of English balladry'.[31] It was bought by Percy's friend, Humphrey Pitt of Shifnal in Shropshire, at a library sale. Percy discovered it 'lying dirty on the floor under a Bureau in ye Parlour', where it was being used 'by the maids to light the fire'.[32] He begged it, had it suitably bound to show his literary friends — though the binder pared off the tops and bottoms of certain pages in the process of beautification — and then used it to prepare the *Reliques*. After 1765, the manuscript went through the hands of several of Percy's 'learned and ingenious' acquaintance, and spent a whole year at Mr Nichol's house. It was described in the 1790s as having 'half of every leaf' of the first 54 pages 'torn away', and several others at the end 'injured':

Before he learned to reverence it, as he says, he scribbled notes over its margins and put brackets for suggested omissions in its texts. After he learned to reverence it, he tore out of it two leaves containing its best ballad.[33]

According to Percy, the MS had been transcribed for and belonged to Thomas Blount, a London lawyer and author who hailed from Worcestershire. But the Victorian editors, Hales and Furnivall, identified a Lancashire idiom in the form of spelling and were satisfied that the texts had been written down, 'from dictation, and hurriedly', about 1650.[34] Percy's nephew believed the scribe 'grew so weary of his labour as to write without the least attention to sense or meaning', perhaps from 'defective copies' or from 'the imperfect recitation of illiterate singers'.[35] Possibly, the copyist was Blount's clerk, who reluctantly recorded the 'Curious Old Ballads' his master 'occasionally ... met with'; but we have no hard information as to Blount's sources.

Though he claimed that the 'greater part' of his texts came from this MS', Percy used perhaps only 30 items from this source in something like their entirety, while another 15 were used in part. The first 50 were '*crossed through* by the Bishop's own hand' because they were 'objectionable on the score of indelicacy', and he would 'admit nothing immoral or indecent'.[36] The remaining 131 items were culled from libraries to which Percy had access because of his rank and connections, or were sent to him by a network (as it became) of genteel correspondents and literary friends. He aimed to 'ransack the whole British Empire' for material, yet most of the extra items came from the Bodleian and Ashmolean Libraries at Oxford, the collection of broadsides made by the later seventeenth century state official, Samuel Pepys, in Magdalene College Cambridge, the Library of the London Society of Antiquaries and the British Museum. But while he was careful to acknowledge the help of Lord Hailes, to whom he was 'indebted for most of the most beautiful Scottish poems', Percy makes no mention of his own silent borrowings from the conveniently accessible works of Ramsay. Of an important acquaintance of a 'much lower stamp', the broadside-publisher Dicey of Bow Church-Yard, London, the *Reliques* contains not a trace; yet the 'greatest printer of ballads in the kingdom' promised 'copies of all his old Stock Ballads, and engaged to rommage into his Warehouse for everything curious that it contains'. He delivered over 80 items by 1761, some of which Percy had never seen before.[37] Given Dicey's commercial interest in producing material for a wider audience than metropolitan-oriented litterateurs, the chances are that some of these texts derived ultimately or even directly from workers' culture, through the mediation of what Percy termed 'the imperfect recitation of itinerant ballad-singers'. However quiet he kept about it, Percy recognized that workers' song-culture existed in England, and that it had close contact with commercial song-publishing of a less fashionable kind than his own.

Herd's 1769 edition contained texts taken openly from Thomson, Ramsay and Percy and 'all the various miscellanies hitherto printed', as well as many items hitherto unpublished. He already had 'some prospect of materials' for a second volume, and the publishers solicited readers for 'more perfect copies' of 'imperfect copies and detached pieces of a great many more' which remained in their possession, or for 'any Scots songs of merit' they might have, or which 'can by any means be obtained'. This hint that songs might be found outside the culture of the book-buying 'public', and beyond the existing printed books or manuscripts of 'modern songs, by celebrated authors', must have been based on what had already been collected in the Herd manuscript. This manuscript eventually contained 188 items, and its relatively large size cautioned Herd about the impossibility of getting an exhaustive collection. (He used only 93 of these pieces in the 1776 edition, and found 277 more texts elsewhere.[38]) The Herd MS. contains material sent from Tweedside, and a text, sent by J. Grossett from Breadishome near Glasgow, found in a 'large Collection in the hands of Mr Alex[ander] Morice', a Lisbon merchant, which was 'now suppos'd to be lost'.[39] Andrew Plummer — Scott's predecessor as Sheriff-depute of Selkirkshire — sent Herd another song, as 'received by a carrier from a lady, and lost'.[40] Yet another was taken by Herd from William Bell, about 1770,

who had picked it up in Annandale; it was all in detached scraps of paper, wrote down by himself at different times, as he met with those who remembered any thing of it — part of these he had lost, and some of the remainder were illegible, being chaff'd in his pocket.[41]

Two songs are noted as from an 'Irish Harper',[42] and another from 'the mouth of a Milk Maid in 1771 by W.L.'.[43] Therefore, while there is no direct evidence of Herd himself collecting texts from working people directly, his MS. does contain such items, and he sometimes mentions in his notes that he had 'heard this sung to a very good tune not in any Collection',[44] or that another text 'is sung to a very fine old Scots Tune',[45] indicating that he was alive to the song-culture he and his correspondents had begun to penetrate or had recently left. Other texts he knew to be mere fragments, and he mentions 'a great many other verses which I could not recover'[46] though he must have heard them sung. Through his own and George Paton's library, Herd also had access to scarce works like Forbes' *Aberdeen Cantus*, 'Nicoll's Poems' and *The Charmer* (a song-book of 1759), and copied texts from some of them into his collection. A few pieces by known authors also get copied, though usually without acknowledgment. Evidently, Herd saw little point in attaching people's names — and especially those of milk-maids or harpers — to texts which were Scottish 'national' property.

Evans' *Old Ballads* may well have contained texts 'Now first collected, and reprinted from rare Copies', but his largely commercial motives precluded any urge to discover songs from oral sources. On the other hand, he did have access to a manuscript collection owned by Mr

Barrett, a Bristol surgeon, to black-letter garlands (notably, *The Garland of Delights*), and to a fairly wide range of other printed sources. He used song-books, magazines, plays and poems, the work of one John Price, a 'land-waiter' at Poole, a 'Lady of Quality' and one item 'supposed to be written' by an ancient bard, which chanced to be a forgery.[47] Pinkerton was equally unfortunate, when he claimed Lady Wardlaw's poem, *Hardyknute*, was taken from the 'memory of a lady in Lanarkshire', and that snatches of it were known to the 'common people' of that county. He later had to admit that he had lied about the source of the poem, after having denounced the author of *Ossian* as a forger![48] Pinkerton had a contradictory attitude to the 'nurses and old women' who allegedly provided a text (thus proving its authenticity) but who then 'corrupted' its title. Yet he uses an item sent by his friend Percy because it agreed with 'the stall copies, and the common recitals'. He takes several items from Ramsay while lambasting him for his editorial practices, and lifts texts from Aytoun and D'Urfey without comment. The 'late Dr Austin of Edinburgh' supplied Pinkerton with some items, and he seems to have had a 'quarto Manuscript' of material in his own possession, but he was later found to have tried to 'palm off as old certain productions of his own'.[49] Little wonder that a scholar such as Ritson should have taken on the pseudonym of 'Anti Scot' to denounce such cavalier treatment of every kind of source.[50]

At first Ritson relied on printed sources for his earlier compilations, but not on the broadside holdings of the British Museum, which he found not 'of sufficient merit'. Perhaps inspired by Herd's success, he collected materials for his *Bishopric Garland* from the Stockton shoemakers James McLean and George Knight, and he noted he had heard other pieces 'sung in the market-place' or by a 'north-country blacksmith' in his youth. Moreover, he seems to have taken the trouble of going to Boltsburn, to record *Rookhope Ryde* 'from the chanting of George Collingwood the elder',[51] who had died by 1785; and we know he encouraged his musician-friend William Shield to 'collect several of the airs that are still traditionally sung in the counties of Northumberland, Durham, and Cumberland, which in his infancy he had been taught to sing and play'.[52] Ritson mentions that he had 'frequently heard of traditional songs, but has had very little success in his endeavours to hear the songs themselves'. He thought that it was 'barely possible' that songs 'may still be preserved in the country' with any accuracy by 'tradition'[53], though he does not define what he means by the term. He relied instead on the 'multitude of MS. and printed collections' preserved in the British Museum, in the Harleian MS., Bodleian Library MS., Fairfax MS. and suchlike, but also in a private MS. collection owned by one John Baynes, and the Tytler and Bannantyne MSS. which he got from Scotland. He used books, broadsides and other printed materials, and by the 1790s he could claim to have all but exhausted those which were available to him. Except for the Percy MS. and certain private collections, 'there is scarce a public library which has not been explored'.[54] This and his changing political position, encouraged him to try again to find songs preserved 'by tradition among the country people',[55] which he knew to be qualitatively different to those found in manuscript and print. So, while the *Northumberland Garland* contained items by known poets like the playwright John Cunningham,[56] the earlier Newcastle-based bon viveur and wit Thomas Whittell, and the playful Rev. Robert Lambe[57] (whose fabricated *Laidley Worm* was allowed to appear without comment), it also had material produced by 'the late ancient and famous Northern poet, Mr. Bernard Rumney, a musician or country fiddler, who lived and died at Rothbury'. Even more significantly, this *Garland* contained three anonymous items which appear to have been collected orally, and perhaps from working people — *The Collier's Rant*, *Bonny Keel Laddie* and *Weel May the Keel Row* — all concerned with the manual workers in the burgeoning Tyne and Wear coal trade. This tendency continued, as 40 of Herd's texts appeared in Ritson's *Scotish Songs*; and though he got hold of the Herd MS. only afterwards, Ritson was so impressed with the new kinds of songs in it that he sent off a list of titles he had heard of, in the hope that Herd or one of his friends knew of them.[58] The turn to oral sources was now decisive, and it was being done by people who were far closer to workers' culture than to that of fashionable society.

Burns went 'collecting old stanzas, and every information regarding their origins, authors, etc, etc.'[59] for the *Museum's* second volume, and in under ten months he had 'begged, borrowed and stolen' enough material.[60] Some songs he had learned from his mother and an old woman, as a boy: others he collected from Jean Armour, his wife, and songs which were 'well known, but never in notes before' he collected from people like Kirsty Flint.[61] His Cape Club friend, Stephen Clarke,[62] transcribed the tunes, while Drs Beattie and Blacklock and Mr Tytler of Woodhouselee sometimes assisted in collecting the 'poetry'.[63] Very few notes were printed, but an annotated copy of the *Museum* sometimes indicates a piece was 'a very popular Ayrshire song', or from 'our Peasantry in the West', 'west country folks', 'oral tradition in Ayrshire', or had been 'pickt up' from 'a country girl in Nithsdale' and 'never met with ... elsewhere in Scotland'.[64] Burns roamed far and wide, made a Highland 'pilgrimage', and collected tunes and texts from 'my compeers, the common people'. But in his notes these people's names are absent, and songs are said to be from the singing of 'a girl', 'country lasses', 'an old man', 'an old woman in Dunblane', 'my old Hostess in the principal inn' in Dunblane, and 'a Lady in Inverness', or there is the throwaway, 'Every country girl sings it'.[65] Sources of higher social status do get named, including William Marshall (the Duke of Gordon's butler), Thomas Fraser (oboeist at Edinburgh concerts), Alan Masterton (an Edinburgh schoolmaster), Miss Jenny Graham of Dumfries, and the Rev. Mr. Clunyie.[66] Texts written or remade by Burns, Fergusson's songs, and tunes composed by well-known figures such as Oswald and Riddell, are usually credited. Genteel sources are left unnamed only when they might feel embarassment, such as the 'Revd Doctor of the Church of Scotland'[67] who gave Burns an erotic song, or perhaps when deference was called for from the poet, as with an 'Irish gentleman' and a 'countess'.[68] Burns has no qualms in characterizing a working woman he knew, Jean Glover, as 'not only a w[hore] but also a thief', who had 'visited most of the correction houses in the west' of Scotland.[69] Like most of his Crochallan Club acquaintances and his West-country convivial cronies, Burns had access enough to erotic songs from 'respectable' people, including Herd's network and (probably) his manuscripts. He had known broadside and chapbook material from his boyhood,[70] and had access to most if not all of the many 'old collections' of printed music, from which he could 'pick out songs' and tunes.[71] He was, therefore, uniquely placed to attempt this welding together of elements of country workers' song-culture and that of the fashionable minority in Scots towns and cities.

* * * * *

(iv) Their editing

Percy's *Reliques* was designed to be read rather than sung from, so he gave a tedious Preface and Essay and lengthy notes, to conform to his scholarly pretentions. His conscious imitation of Dodsley's *Collection of Old Plays* in terms of his format, and the attempt at a chronological arrangement of texts — though he chose to use the period of the Civil War as a cut-off point — were all intended to 'shew the gradation of our language, exhibit the progress of popular opinions, display the peculiar manners and customs of former ages, or throw light on our earlier classical poets'. In spite of his poet friend, Shenstone, who had ideas about making a clear distinction between 'song' and 'ballad' — the latter becoming such 'with the common people' as it 'grows in years'[72] — Percy steered clear of theorizing. Indeed, only after decades of accusations of 'forgery' by Ritson did the reluctant Bishop make his MS. available for proper public inspection, and thus have to come clean about his treatment of the texts. In 1794, through his nephew, Percy claimed that

> a scrupulous adherence to their wretched readings would only have exhibited unintelligible nonsense, or such poor meagre stuff, as neither came from the Bard, nor was worthy the press; when, by a few slight corrections or additions, a most beautiful or interesting sense hath started forth, and this so naturally and easily, that the editor could seldom prevail upon himself to indulge the vanity of making a formal claim to the improvement; but must plead guilty to the charge of concealing his own share in the amendments under some such general title, as a 'Modern Copy', or the like.[73]

In fact, when Hales and Furnivall eventually managed to edit the MS., 50 years after Percy's death, all his 'tawdry touches' were revealed.[74] The 'best ballad' he 'had evidently touched up largely himself'.[75] He 'puffed out the 39 lines of the *Child of Ell*; he pomatumed the *Heir of Lin* till it shone again; he stuffed bits of wool into *Sir Cawline*, *Sir Aldingar*: he powdered everything'.[77] Perhaps only 30 texts were genuinely 'extracted' from the MS., and even they were seen 'as a young woman from the country with unkempt locks, whom he had to fit for fashionable society' by giving her 'the correct appearance'.[78] This 'young woman' was, effectively, maimed beyond recognition in order to conform to the taste of 'Polite Society' in its bourgeois manifestation.[79] She would have been quite unrecognizable in the culture from which she came, and her new appearance speaks volumes about the perception of literary value and standards of taste of those who bought and read the *Reliques*. Ritson was vindicated, and he also discovered that Percy couldn't use even broadside texts with any degree of accuracy![80]

Herd was neither poet nor theorist, and was therefore less likely to abuse his sources.[81] Besides, in his 1769 edition he confessed 'the warmest attachment, not only to the music, but to the poetry' of the songs he published, and apologized for including 'modern words' to fit 'ancient tunes', though done by '*Poets* natives of North Britain', for want of the originals. Considerations of volume size provided an opportunity for Herd to defer 'notes to the more ancient and historical poems'. Problems with 'modernized' texts excused him from any attempt at a chronological arrangement; and his only attempt at a theoretically-based categorization is in placing what he terms 'songs' in one section, and new items together with 'larger ballads or poems' in another. His textual editing, seemingly, was restricted to an attempt at 'collating different copies'[82] of the older song-texts from 'all the miscellanies hitherto printed', according to the standards and tastes of his assumed readership. His 1776 edition contained many pieces freshly collected and not previously in print, and while he did make minor alterations in some texts, notably by enhancing their interest to the antiquarians by changing spellings 'into the northern Doric',[83] a careful scrutiny of his editing shows Herd to have been 'one of the most trustworthy of the old collectors'.[84] This might not have been the case had Percy had his way. After he had seen the MS. collection, and before some of it was published, he wrote:

> most of them are fragments too mutilated and imperfect to afford much pleasure to a reader in their present state; and ... most of them contain charming hints, which might give occasion to very beautiful songs, if supplied and filled up, in the manner that old broken fragments of antique statues have been repaired and completed by modern masters. I think I could fill up the breaches of some of them myself.[85]

Fortunately, Percy failed to deliver; but his observations reinforce the fact that he saw the culture from which Herd was still collecting songs as though it were dead, stiff and with parts missing, which could be 'filled up' by a person deeply embued in another culture, according to that culture's notions of beauty. That such restoration might be tantamount to forgery, and that preservation was not far short of expropriation, were issues not worth raising let alone debating. Herd took some of Percy's advice and waited for what he found to be 'more perfect versions of some songs', 'expunging some of the most imperfect fragments'[86] and checking the remainder for erotic material which might be collected by enthusiasts, and recorded in manuscript form (as Herd did conscientiously),[87] but could not yet be published with impunity. His transcriptions were almost certainly faithful;[88] so we can reasonably credit Herd with being the first song-book mediator to print *texts* which came, some of them at least, straight from the mouths of working people. Tunes, unfortunately, he seems not to have noted at all.

Evans' publication marked a small gain for scholarship, in that, in imitation of Phillips, but more fully, he notes doubts about authorship, cites new texts, makes careful references to other song collections and works of history, supplies historical, topographical and suchlike material where appropriate, and makes some effort to track down variants and the geographical locations of stories. His attempt at a chronological arrangement, with most modern pieces being placed at the end, underlines his generally historical approach. His scrupulousness with texts corresponds to Herd's practice rather than to that of Percy. Yet his principles of selection were geared to market considerations, just as his appeal to authority — combined with a total failure to indicate what a 'Ballad', old or modern might be — represents an intellectual timidity quite in keeping with his aims. Unlike Pinkerton, for all his display of scholarly training, Evans was at least honest. In fact, Pinkerton's scholarship was soon doubted by Herd,[89] who would also have noted his habitual Anglicization of vernacular Scots texts.[90] Yet Pinkerton was confident enough to produce two elaborate 'Dissertations' in the 1783 work on 'The Tragic Ballad' and 'The Comic Ballad', in which he attempted to theorize the editorial decision to chop up the texts into two separate volumes, but which rely heavily on the authority of Percy's Essay in the *Reliques*. Pinkerton proceeds to justify his selection of texts by pretending to abstract certain characteristics of 'Oral poems'. Yet 'commonplaces', 'land-marks' such as 'The Burden' or chorus, the use of alliteration and 'rime', and the centrality of music, were hardly unique to the 'Ballad' he claims to characterize, with its allegedly typical 'ballad stanza'. His barefaced offering of the factitious *Hardyknute* in its 'original perfection', and his publishing of many items supposedly 'given much more correct' than elsewhere, were soon exposed by Ritson, who roundly denounced him for 'forgery'.[91] Pinkerton's claims to be 'correct', his pretentious use of 'emendatory criticism' in relation to the 'absurdity' of an 'ignorant person' who he claims to have been 'at a loss for the original expression', and his open contempt for the 'dross' added by a mediator such as Ramsay, came back at him all the more violently once his own forgeries and lies were exposed.

By contrast, Ritson brought talents of 'accuracy and integrity'[92] to song-mediation from his conveyancing work; but he too felt constrained by questions of taste and had to make some concessions to marketability in his exclusion of

> every composition, however celebrated, or however excellent, of which the slightest expression, or the most distant allusion could have tinged the cheek of Delicacy, or offended the purity of the chasest ear.[93]

Thus, while not faking a text, Ritson was still in danger of faking a *culture*. In his *English Songs* he took up Shenstone's ideas and attempted a definition of 'songs', which were characterized by 'sentiment, expression or even description', and 'ballads', which were 'mere narrative compositions'. The book's form derived from this distinction. 'Ancient Ballads' are separated from 'Songs', which are also divided into crude sections by content or function — 'Love', 'Drinking', 'Miscellaneous'. Ritson devotes one of his three volumes entirely to the music to many texts; and indicates that this separation was intended to make his work easier to use by singers. Known authors are cited scrupulously; composers and setters of tunes are credited, and yet the 'Ancient Ballads' texts are set aside as anonymous in order to fit in with Ritson's ideas about their origins. He collated differing texts of these 'old popular tragic legends, and historical or heroic ballads', but took as few 'liberties' with his sources as he could, simply modernizing spellings and correcting any 'manifest blunder of the press'. Occasionally, he removed a 'supplemental stanza' of 'inferior merit' from a text, on the grounds that it had been 'added, as it should seem, according to an ordinary practice of ballad printers, to fill up the sheet', thereby underlining his contempt for commercially-written and -published texts, and, by implication, for the market for which they were produced. He continued to have difficulty in rationalizing his affection for those 'many ballads, or legendary and romantic songs, composed in a singular style' with his prejudice against 'vulgar poetry', especially in its broadside forms, right up to his death; and this contradiction relates to his love–hate attitude towards workers' culture in general, and to embryo working-class politics in particular. By 1802, he saw the role of the song-editor as being to 'correct obvious errors of an illiterate transcribeër, to supply irremediable defects, and to make sense of nonsense'; but his sense of scholarship remained linked to his belief in 'improvement' *and* 'entertainment' for his chosen market of both 'readers of taste and genius' as well as the 'austereëst antiquary'.[94] So his scholarship effectively acted, albeit in marginal and vastly superior ways to Percy, in the cultural interests of that class-based culture.

Burns understood that workers' culture contained more than one 'droll Scots song more famous for its humour than its delicacy',[95] and that this alone would 'mar the progress' of such pieces 'to celebrity'.[96]

Therefore, while many such items were passed around in manuscript form amongst like-minded men, and reached the Crochallan Fencibles (who published many of them after Burns' death), for the *Museum* and Thomson's book Burns rewrote or re-cast texts, and 'completed' or 'brushed up' fragments, so as to get a tune into print. Sometimes he is known to have put texts 'wholly in Scottish orthography', or used a text simply as a 'model', though on occasion he found 'stuff' that would not 'bear mending'.[97] *Duncan Gray* appears in the *Museum* 'very much in the spirit of the old song', in Thomson's work 'with nothing left in it to offend the morals of the Edinburgh West-end salons', and in the posthumous *Merry Muses* in what may have been its form when Burns found it.[98] It is clear that Burns was prepared to produce 'many silly compositions',[99] to put together a 'parcel of rhymes', a 'few lines *smooth and pretty*' or any old '*random clink*' for polite book-buyers.[100] Not that he admitted this publicly, but to his friends he stressed that the tunes always took precedence: 'I often gave Johnson verses, trifling enough perhaps, but they served as a vehicle to the music'. In a 'good many of them, little more than the chorus is ancient, though there is no need for telling everybody this piece of intelligence'.[101] This habit carried over from the erotic pieces, and became a normal practice. He rarely baulked at Englishing a text, and resisted Thomson only over *Scots Wha Hae*.[102] Therefore, while he could claim a closer relationship to the culture from which many of the songs came, his editing was directed conscientiously at getting tunes taken up by the culture to which he partly aspired, by the strategy of patching up original texts to fit the aesthetic ideals of their culture of destination. Apart from one or two pieces copied into letters or his Commonplace Book, none of the original texts remain, so only the suppressed erotic material (which appeared in 1800) remains in bulk to indicate what the workers' song-culture he edited was really like. The fact that Burns had to die before even this material, edited by another hand, could get into print, speaks eloquently about the power of cultural and sexual repression in polite society. Not being a professional musician, he seems to have touched the tunes only to cut out the florid embellishments from the basic melody. Unlike lyrics, music could not so easily give offence on account of rudeness or vulgarity.

* * * * *

The increasingly stratified society in which the mediators came to live was in stark contrast with that from which most of them had come, and songs took on what seems to have been a disproportionate cultural significance. Two tendencies can be discerned in what the mediators did. Most of them felt the attraction of polite culture, where their interest in songs helped establish their cultural credentials and so, hopefully, ensure their material security. On the other hand, the upheavals of the petty-bourgeoisie against the ruling cliques in town corporations during the

1770s, the political wedge struck into bourgeois and petty-bourgeois consciousness by the American War and then the French Revolution, and the
intense political struggles of the 1790s all helped to focus interest among
the more liberal of the mediators on the issue of the 'people'. The pull
of these forces can be seen quite clearly in Ritson's changing attitudes
towards workers' song-culture, and in Burns' whole life; and while
neither man resolved this problem, what they and Herd actually achieved
was to open up workers' song-culture to a predominantly bourgeois and
petty-bourgeois market. What is important to remember is that they did
so on that market's terms: songs were transformed into property, and
song-books into commodities, as part of the servicing of a growing
bourgeois reading 'public'. From our point of view, of course, and in
spite of what most of them did to the songs, their contribution was crucial.
Without their collecting, and irrespective of their mediations and their
motives, we would not have had hundreds of songs recorded and
published for posterity. In fact, without their example, the modest boom
in song-book publishing which followed might not have happened at all.
In the work of Ritson, too, we see the beginnings of a genuinely scholarly
approach to mediation, which remained as a standard and a source of
editorial guilt for generations.

3 *From Walter Scott to Robert Chambers*

The first three decades of the nineteenth century marked the end of a recognizably separate Scottish political life, and it was the Parliamentary Reform of 1832 which put paid to it formally. Economically, of course, Lowland Scotland and England had been closely integrated well before that; and so when the French Revolution encouraged sympathetic responses in Britain and the maturing Industrial Revolution concentrated workers in towns and cities, the result was the making of the English and Lowland Scots working class. Given all this, perhaps it is less surprising that most of the song-mediators in the period 1800–1830 were Scots. They centred on the person of Walter Scott, an important 'national' literary figure in Britain and a writer of novels about Scots history.[1] But what we need to examine, here, is precisely how Scott and his circle mediated songs during this turbulent period of history, and especially how they responded to the culture of a class of labouring 'people' which was becoming unmistakably distinct as British society was stratified by the development of industrial capitalism.

(i) The people

Walter Scott was born in Edinburgh in 1771. His mother was a professor's daughter, and his father was a well-known lawyer, the first of his family to move from the country into the capital's Old Town, and then to the more fashionable New Town, purpose-built for the genteel across the Nor' Loch, away from the insanitary centre of the city. Walter was sent to a dame school, then to a school at Kelso, and had a spell with a private tutor because Edinburgh was bad for his health; but he came back to attend the High School, and to be apprenticed to his father to learn the lawyer's trade. His protégé, James Hogg,[2] was a year older, and was brought up in Ettrick on the Border in the family of a failed farmer. He managed only a few months at a local school and then had to work as a shepherd for a living, so he quickly forgot the little learning he had acquired. Robert Jamieson[3] was born in Morayshire around 1780 and left the Lowlands when he was 15. He acquired an M.A. from one university or another, and so was qualified to take up an appointment as an assistant classical teacher, though he had to move to Macclesfield in Cheshire to find suitable work. His close contemporary, Charles Kirkpatrick Sharpe,[4] was much more privileged. He was born into a gentry family in Dumfriesshire, at Hoddom Castle, had an uncle who was a knight, and was related distantly to a countess. He was sent to Christ Church College, Oxford, and was intended for the church, but he was wealthy enough not to have to work at all and returned to Edinburgh to indulge his hobbies. Alan Cunningham[5] was also born in Dumfriesshire, at Keir in 1784, in more humble circumstances. His mother was the daughter of a Berwickshire farmer-turned-merchant, and his father worked as a gentleman's factor, or steward, after five years learning his trade in County Durham. Cunningham had some schooling, but he was apprenticed to his brother to learn to be a stonemason, and worked for a while at the trade as a young man.

This mixture of backgrounds, education and occupations is also present amongst those Scots song-mediators born in the 1790s and early 1800s. Peter Buchan's[6] father was a pilot at Peterhead, and the boy, born in 1790, had enough schooling to bring him to the attention of a local noble patron, who hinted at putting him through university. Peter was eventually let down, but this was after he had taken part of an apprenticeship with a mill-wright, then with a turner and carver in Aberdeen, before setting up on his own account as a jobber. James Maidment, born around 1795, was the son of a Northumberland solicitor who had moved to London. After some formal education, James was called to the Scottish Bar, and joined other lawyers with an interest in song in that city. George Richie Kinloch was born in Stonehaven, probably in 1796, and he also became a lawyer, working as clerk to three successive Advocates-Depute at Stirling, before becoming secretary to Scott's friend, George Cranstoun, Lord Corehouse. William Motherwell's[7] father was an ironmonger who hailed from Stirlingshire, and his mother the daughter of a respectable farmer in Perthshire, who left her a fortune of £2000. William was born in Glasgow in 1797, attended a private school in Edinburgh, went on to the High School, and finally spent a year at Glasgow University. He served his time in the office of the Paisley Sheriff-Clerk, before becoming Sheriff-Depute of Renfrew in his own right, apparently on his own merits. Robert Chambers[8] was born at Peebles in 1802, the son of a draper-merchant who went bankrupt, and who had to work for wages as manager of a salt-pan business near Edinburgh. All the same, Robert completed his education at the burgh and grammar schools at Peebles, and followed his family to Edinburgh where he attended the High School. Only the fact that relatives let him down and failed to provide the cash they had promised prevented him from going on to university. He set up in business as a bookseller when he was only 16, and made his own way in life.

Robert Hartley Cromek was born in Hull in 1770, and seems to have had some connection with the law as a young man, but he worked as an engraver and publisher in London for most of his adult life. John Bell's[9] mother came from a well-to-do County Durham family, and his father was a Northumberland farmer's son, who was apprenticed to a Newcastle land-surveyor and combined that trade with bookselling. John probably had some formal training at a local school, apart from the educative influences of the print trade, and he certainly learned both his father's trades. In 1803, Bell was set up by his father as a bookseller in his own right on Newcastle's Quayside. Why were there only two English people involved in making song-books comparable to all those being put together in Scotland? Why were so many of them involved with the law or the print-trade? Why was there such a wide range of social status, not only in their origins but also in their occupations? Why were they *still* all men? And how did such an apparently diffuse bunch get involved with mediating songs? To answer these questions we need to look more closely at their lives and their ideas.

* * *

Scott was a snobbish, romantic Tory from his early manhood,[10] with professional, political and social connections which secured him the patronage of Robert Dundas and the Duke of Buccleuch in getting the Sheriff-Depute's job in Selkirkshire. He was clubbable and loyal, acting as Quartermaster to the Royal Edinburgh Light Dragoons in the war, and breaking the heads of three Irish supporters of the French Revolution. His literary interests, including a penchant for German literature and language, brought him into contact with the 'first literary characters of the age' — people like 'Monk Lewis', Richard Heber, George Ellis, John Leyden and Joseph Ritson — as well as helping him make friends with the Edinburgh booksellers. His literary interests extended to the songs and stories told at convivial meetings at places such as Dowie's Tavern, where Burns had once been a regular,[12] and where David Herd and George Paton might still be found.[13] By 1804 he was clearing over £1000 a year, including some earnings from the various editions of the *Minstrelsy*; and in 1808 Constable offered him 1000 guineas for a poem, unseen. In 1812, he slipped gracefully into a job worth £1300 a year, and paid out £4000 for his Tweedside estate at Abbotsford. By the late 1810s he cleared £2000 a year, had turned down the poet-laureateship, and virtually retired to his estates to write novels for his bourgeois and petty-bourgeois readership, who, like him, needed to take spiritual solace in pre-working class mythified history. He netted £10 000 a year by the end of the decade, and became obsessed with the purchase of land. At Abbotsford, he became the centre of a large network of like-minded Tories and literary people, many of them interested in songs and 'ballads', to whom he dished out patronage and hard cash. His loyalty to patrons in power got him a baronetcy from George IV, who shared his fear of the emergent working class.[14] In 1819, Scott helped form a force of volunteers to resist any assault on property by Northumberland colliers and Glasgow weavers — logically enough, given that one of those 50 000 'blackguards' he feared were 'ready to rise between Tyne and Wear'[15] would have had to work seven years underground to earn what Scott received for the *Minstrelsy*. Eventually, his partisan generosity and massive expenditure of over £76 000 on Abbotsford put his finances at risk. The economic crash of 1825–6 left him having to give a bond for £10 000 on his estates to creditors and with a debt of some £40 000, which he worked to pay off over a period of several years. (His wine-cellar seems to have remained intact to comfort him, however.) This experience did not alter his reactionary political views. He agitated in print and in speeches against parliamentary reform, against the interests of workers like those at Selkirk, and those at Hawick — who offered to 'Burke Sir Walter' — before accepting the loan of a frigate from the First Lord of the Admiralty to ferry him off to a milder climate for the benefit of his health! When he died in 1832, the year of Reform, his fictionalized version of Scots history, based on unassimilated antiquarian interests and sentimentality for lost causes[16] was already part of the cultural support for the violent reaction he and his class (and their hangers-on in other classes) felt for the burgeoning democratic forces represented by urban and industrial workers, that 'Jacquerie'[17] which threatened the corrupt system of patronage and power with which Scott was closely associated and from which he had benefited substantially.

Scott's collaborator and protégé, Hogg, began work as a shepherd in 1777, when he was only a child, and spent the 1790s working for a Mr Laidlaw of Blackhouse, Yarrow. Though he had lapsed into virtual illiteracy in his teens,[18] the stimulus of printed vernacular songs and stories from Ramsay's time and before, and especially the poetry and the fame of Burns, encouraged him to become a poet. 'Jamie the poeter'[19] became known to Laidlaw's son, who introduced him to his friend, Scott. Scott consulted Hogg when he was putting together the *Minstrelsy*. Hogg's first printed poem was a 'spirited patriotic'[20] piece about Napoleon's threatened invasion, and he used a trip to Edinburgh to sell stock from his parents' small farm in order to publish a book of his poetry. He badly wanted to become Burns' successor, but he had to earn a living, and tried settling on a large sheep farm in Harris in 1803. He lost money, and had to go back to being a shepherd, this time in Nithsdale, where he met another aspiring poet, Allan Cunningham. An 1807 book of poems netted Hogg £300 under Scott's guidance, but it was lost in another unsuccessful farming venture in Dumfriesshire. He tried Scott's patronage further, asking for an ensign's post in the militia, and then for that of an Excise officer; but he returned to Ettrick a discredited bankrupt. A further attempt to establish himself financially with the proceeds of *The Queen's Wake* failed, because his publisher went bankrupt, though Scott saw to it that the Countess of Dalkeith (later the Duchess of Buccleuch) handed over 100 guineas. Scott knew Hogg had talent enough to spoil him for his own trade, but insufficient to earn a living writing for the predominantly bourgeois literary market. Yet Hogg's aspirations were kept up by his membership of Edinburgh clubs, his acquaintance with established poets like Wordsworth, Southey and Byron (who lent him money, and recommended his work to a London publisher), and by the continued receipt of patronage, like the 1817 subscription from Edinburgh literati and the Duchess of Buccleugh's bequest of a farm at nominal rent at Altrive Lake. Scott kept bailing Hogg out, even during his own financial crisis, and tried to get him on the Royal Literary Society's 'pecuniary list', though the poet went on to produce only a strange novel and a notably unsuccessful edition of Burns' works with the arch-reactionary, Motherwell.[21] Twice-yearly public dinners in Candlemaker's Row, Edinburgh, a public dinner at Peebles, his lengthy association with descendents of Jacobites, and the pull of patronage meant that Hogg, like Burns, was ever more distanced from the former friends and neighbours he thought of as 'the poor illiterate people' of Ettrick. Hogg evidently believed that he had 'got on' and 'got out' of what was virtually the rural proletariat, and the ideological gap between those he left behind on the Border widened as he struggled to become a 'rustic Sir Walter Scott'.[22]

Another Scott protégé, Jamieson, was qualified by his M.A. to become assistant classical teacher at a school in Macclesfield, Cheshire, and then to take up a post in Riga as a tutor. His song-related work was the hobby of a self-styled 'obscure individual', but through it he made the acquaintance of Scott, who got him a post as assistant to the depute-clerk-register in Edinburgh's General Register House, where he had time to work on Scottish historical records.[23] He already knew (or corresponded with) many 'persons of the greatest respectability', including fellow members of the London Society of Antiquaries, Oxford and Cambridge dons, London booksellers and even Bishop Percy. But his membership of Scott's circle was crucial, as it was (in a literary if not material sense) to Sharpe. After a childhood being 'nourished on Jacobite story and tradition', Scott's *Minstrelsy* rekindled Sharpe's interest, and he contacted the editor, who asked him for 'good hacking reviews' for a conservative periodical venture.[24] Sharpe turned out to be far 'too aristocratic' to use his art to assist his purse,[25] but he gladly joined Scott's Bannantyne Club, and no doubt his remarkable knowledge of 'scandalous' Scots genealogy and of indigenous and French erotic and pornographic literature endeared him to that all-male society. Maidment had similar interests, and was equally acceptable. He combined a flourishing career at the Scottish Bar with genealogical expertise, which proved very useful in disputed peerage cases. Like Sharpe, Maidment was able to pay for the publication of his own song-books, and he acted as editor for publications produced for various literary societies, such as the Bannantyne, Maitland, Abbotsford and Hunterian Clubs, and the Spottiswoode Society. These two men formed the cadre of the Scott circle, even after its founder's death in 1832, along with figures such as the antiquary, David Laing, Jamieson and Hogg.

There were other men who had contact with Scott and his circle, but who remained rather more marginal to it. Cromek won a reputation for being a 'shifty speculator' by allegedly thieving a Ben Jonson letter from Scott, exploiting the trust of artists like William Blake and Stothard, making money out of the vogue for Burns not long after his death, and luring the poet Allan Cunningham to London to work on a song-book.[26] Scott's reaction was to wish 'to God that we had that valuable and original young man fairly out of Cromek's hands again';[27] but Cunningham went willingly to London in 1810, to get out of being a stonemason all his life — his apprenticeship had begun when he was eleven — and to further his literary ambitions. In Scotland, he did not meet Burns, but went to walk in his funeral procession. He travelled to meet Hogg, and walked 70 miles to Edinburgh to see the celebrated author of *Marmion* and the *Lay of the Last Minstrel* on which he had spent 24 shillings, over a week's pay, but this last trip proved abortive. Cromek made his acquaintance through the good offices of an Edinburgh literary hostess, and though Cunningham contributed substantially to the production of the *Remains*, his reward was one single bound copy and a worthless promise of some cash on any second edition which might be called for. None was, and the two men fell out, probably over cash; but Cromek gave Cunningham an introduction to the rising sculptor, Francis Chantrey, another migrant of humble origins, for whom the poet went to work as secretary, where his 25 and then 32 shillings a week were supplemented by a guinea a week from a London periodical editor for poems or parliamentary reports. Cunningham spent 12 hours a day in the studio and then went back home to write creatively, eventually getting pieces into *Blackwood's* and the *London* magazines, and thereby helping keep six children. He eventually met Scott in 1820, when the writer sat for his bust in Chantrey's studio, and because they shared Toryism and literary interests these meetings were repeated on Scott's later visits to London. Cunningham gained in confidence and produced plays, tales and songs, some of which proved remunerative — he got £200 for his *Songs of Scotland*. He was well-placed to exploit Scott's patronage for his sons, who consequently got places in the armed forces, the audit office and the Indian service. Cunningham also drew on the goodwill of Scott's Edinburgh circle, and London-based antiquarians and established poets, to produce an 'annual' miscellany for a couple of years; and though public recognition (in the form of the freedom of Dumfries and a special dinner attended by Carlyle) was no doubt acceptable, the £100 annuity left by Chantrey to his secretary in 1841 was rather more in keeping with his real needs, even though he enjoyed it for only one year before he died.

Scott's influence reached into provincial England, too. John Bell took an active part in the intellectual and convivial societies of Newcastle, was one-time Secretary of the Stationers' Company, an enthusiastic Freemason, and became a member of the local Burns Club.[28] Above all he was a fanatical collector of things old and curious, and when he was only 30 he projected and established the Newcastle Antiquarian Society, with the patronage of the Duke of Northumberland and the consequent (if belated) support of some local gentry and professional men. He had a mania for publishing songs and verse which contributed to his bankruptcy in 1817, but he also had liberal political views which forced him out onto the fringes of the town's fashionable literary and anti-quarian society, and he had to turn to his second trade of land-surveying to make a living. The Abbotsford library benefited from Bell's enforced sales, and thus so did Scott's circle. Publication of songs stopped, as did a correspondence with Walter Scott, who saw him as an 'odd fish'.[29] But though he had snobbish tendencies, Bell also had the courage to associate himself with the struggles of the Tyne keelmen over mechanization of their trade, and joined in the campaign to liberate an important 'public' library from the church's bureaucratic neglect. Every attempt to publish works on local history and culture gained his support, and drew on the pasted-up collections of newspaper cuttings and printed ephemera which he was able to afford to make. At a period when Newcastle's culture had stratified politically, Bell tended to be drawn towards the radicals, to the tradesmen and lesser professionals who founded the Mechanics' Institu-tion (in opposition to the 'Dons' of the Lit & Phil). Such people formed the cadre of the 1819 Radical agitation, and that for Parliamentary Reform in 1832 (to which Bell contributed propaganda). Up to his death in 1864, at the age of 81, Bell remained a key source of local historical, biographical and cultural information, not only for nationally-known bibliophiles like Dibden, but even for the *Gentleman's Magazine*.

Kinloch was more marginal to Scott's circle, but he did join the Maitland Club and had powerful enough connections to get him the place of Assistant-Keeper of the Register of Deeds in Edinburgh Register House in 1842, two years before Jamieson died. He rose to become head of his department in 1851, retiring in 1869. Kinloch's attitude towards working people was less reactionary than many of his song-mediating predecessors. (He acted as treasurer of a relief fund for the 'deserving poor' for many years.) And though he helped Dr Jamieson with his Scottish Dictionary, and Scott with his revised edition of the *Minstrelsy*, Kinloch did little after Scott's death. Neither did Peter Buchan, whose poetry-writing first brought him to the attention of the Earl of Buchan, and then encouraged him to turn to printing. He learned the trade at Stirling and by inveigling himself into the workshops of leading members of Edinburgh's printing fraternity, posing as an itinerant bookseller; and he eventually set himself up as the first printer in Peterhead. The Earl and Charles Forbes M.P. gave some patronage, but Buchan spent much time cultivating Edinburgh literati, with the result that his business faltered and he lost the Earl's support. After a brief spell working for wages in

London, Buchan was forced by ill-health to return to Scotland to rejuvenate his business; and from the mid-1820s he interested himself in publishing songs, using Edinburgh contacts for getting access to privately-published collections. He eventually made the acquaintance of Scott, and through him Buchan's proposal to publish his own manuscript ballad collection went the rounds of Sharpe, Laing, Jamieson and the bookseller, John Stevenson, who used Scott's circle as tasters for the market. Buchan's proposal was accepted, conditionally on Sharpe and Laing controlling the publication and getting part of the proceeds. William Motherwell, the 'clerk of Paisley', offered £50 for the original manuscript — such things had by this date also become commodities. In the end, Buchan abandoned any idea of making even a supplement to his income by literary work, though he kept going into the 1830s, when he got John Bell's sympathy and support. He sold some of his manuscript collections for hard cash, moved to Aberdeen, and then to Glasgow in 1838, where his children were prospering as he was not. Later song-mediators contacted him for material — Chambers, S. C. Hall and Wright — and his manuscripts were used by Dixon and the Percy Society in the mid-1840s;[30] but a brief spell of financial security ended in law-suits and virtual ruin towards the end of that decade. Buchan was saved by two grants secured by Chambers from the Royal Literary Fund, and he migrated to Ireland and then London, where he died in 1854. Though the form of patronage had changed from individual and aristocratic to that of the state, Buchan proved that people without private means could not hope to survive by making only partly-commercial song-collections or song-books, even in mid-century.

Motherwell did not make direct contact with Scott's circle until the later 1820s, after he had virtually completed the preparation for his major song-book, but his work and his views were remarkably similar. While he began adult life as an '*extremely* liberal'[31] person, his official position as an officer of the law soon brought him into close contact with working-class activists, first during the 'Radical War' of 1818, and then during the political crisis of 1819. 'In obediance to the orders of his superiors' Motherwell had to perform 'many duties which rendered him un-popular', including wielding a truncheon on behalf of the state in Paisley's streets. On one occasion his efforts were met by a crowd of Radicals who raised him bodily on the top of a bridge parapet, before he was rescued. The experience changed his whole life[32]: from that point, his politics hardened into a 'determinate Toryism'[33]. He joined the Paisley Rifle Corps as a sergeant, and then the Renfrewshire Yeoman Cavalry as a trooper, and even took lessons in boxing and sword-play from professionals. During the early stages of the Reform agitation, Motherwell helped to found the *Paisley Monthly Magazine*, contributed towards and edited the *Paisley Advertiser*, and then resigned his secure legal job for the editorship of the *Glasgow Courier*, which he edited after 1830, on the principles of 'high church-and-king Toryism'.[34]

Motherwell's denunciations of the Reformers have been characterized as 'violent', and his paper became a 'fierce and uncompromising
champion'[35] of political reaction. But though his apologists claim that his
ideology was more the product of a 'political and indiscriminate admiration of everything connected with chivalrous antiquity'[36] — including
the Norse sagas which he imitated in his poetry — than of a consistent
and theoretically-based philosophy, this view does not square with
Motherwell's becoming one of the district secretaries of the Orangemen
in south-west Scotland. Certainly, even the partly-reformed House of
Commons had misgivings, and summoned him before one of their com-
mittees in 1835. Literature interested him all his life. He had edited a
book of Renfrewshire poets' work so early as 1819, and by 1825 he had
opened a correspondence with Scott, as he readied himself to produce his
Minstrelsy Ancient and Modern. In 1832, he published his own poems in a
collected form, and had the satisfaction of an encouraging review in
Blackwood's. But much of his leisure-time was spent in the company of
other minor poets and literati who were based in a bookshop and a
Trongate howf. This 'Whistle-Binkie' circle was a petty-bourgeois version of the Edinburgh clubs of 50 years before, and its members took an
interest in the literary work of their own class. They fostered an unsuccessful edition of Burns' works (done by Motherwell and Hogg), and
encouraged Motherwell's biography of the workingman poet, Tannahill.
Motherwell died of apopleptic fever in 1835 at the age of 37. Clearly, his
'essentially and ardently Scottish' tastes and feelings melded with 'in-
stinctively' Tory ideas and 'monarchical principles'.[37] In his adult life he
saw one after another of his most cherished prejudices first derided and
then destroyed',[38] and it would be remarkable indeed if his ideology did
not both inform and help structure his song-mediating work. What
Motherwell's career shows, however, is the way in which reactionary
political and cultural practices had penetrated down the social scale to
petty-bourgeois culture by the 1820s.

Robert Chambers' early life is usually presented as a heroic struggle;
yet both he and his brother William saw themselves as 'Scottish people
of the middle class', even while they exercised a 'vigorous frugality' in
their teens, and went to literary activities and print-trade sales in Edinburgh in order to escape their cold lodgings. Given this downward social
mobility, their father's 'harangues about independence' no doubt bit
deep into their minds. Robert's business prospered slowly; but when his
handwritten extracts from Scott's works reached the publisher Constable,
his fortunes improved dramatically. Constable got him to write out songs
from Scott's *Lady of the Lake*, showed the results to the author, who in turn
remembered the young man's efforts when his own patron, King George
IV, visited Edinburgh in 1822, and got him commissions to draw up
'loyal addresses'. Robert's material success was assured; but what finally
assured the brothers a niche in the Scott circle was their acquisition of a
hand-press (and better premises, using their £400 capital), and the pro-

duction during their considerable free time of a part-work titled *Traditions of Edinburgh*. Their material was culled from gentry and well-to-do contacts in the city, including Sharpe, who supplied 'the scandal of the time of Charles II', and then, through Scott, from Hogg, Wilson and Henry Mackenzie. This connection was what made the *Traditions* copyright worth over £300, but the Chambers brothers narrowly missed being ruined by the 'general storm of bankruptcy' which partly engulfed Scott, the Ballantynes and Constable, when they withdrew stock from their London publisher in the nick of time.

From this date, 1825, the Chambers' story is one of almost uninterrupted prosperity. Robert produced volume after volume of relatively inexpensive collections of Scots songs, tales, rhymes and 'ballads', which found a market amongst those Scottish people who recognized that the end of even slightly independent Scots political institutions was in sight — it came, in fact, in 1832, when the separate Scottish representative system was abolished, and that rupture was confirmed, 11 years later, with the Disruption of the Church of Scotland. The major factor in their material success, however, was that improved printing machines and paper-making machines made 'cheap literature' really possible, as it had not been when the brothers were young. They understood that the developing network of Mechanics' Institutions and of the Society for the Diffusion of Useful Knowledge, which had grown out of the reaction to cheap printed political propaganda pumped out by the radicals in the 1810s, had helped foster a rapidly-growing market for cheap books amongst workers.[39] The radical press of 1815–20 had produced works which, to their way of seeing, were 'low-priced and scurrilous prints, ministering to the fancies of the seditious and the depraved'. It was, then, their public duty — in line with what we know of Robert's orthodox Scots Episcopal faith and his attachment to the 'old Conservative interest' — to cater for that market with what became *Chamber's Journal*. This was a miscellany of factual matter and literary efforts, which, according to Allan Cunningham, appealed to those with '*poetic, ballad-scrap, auldworld, new-world, Scottish*' tastes, to the self-educating shepherds of Galloway (who are said to have left their copies under a stone on certain hill-tops, in place of the chapbook or broadside they once passed on amongst themselves in this fashion),[40] and to those working people who could be incorporated into what became Robert's philosophy of 'social progress within sound constitutional limits' through self-culture and some degree of social and economic advancement. The *Journal* deliberately set out to appeal to 'respectable' workers, to those who might feel the pull of Chartism and of the trade unions. It succeeded commercially beyond the Chambers's most sanguine hopes, so that Robert seems to have taken over some of Scott's patronage power by manipulating the Royal Literary Fund, making charitable donations, supporting Scots literary and antiquarian societies, and getting official acknowledgement in the form of membership of London's exclusive Athenaum Club and an honorary doctorate from the University of St Andrews. All this, then, was achieved on the material basis of his commercial literary wholesaling and retailing — including the production of books of songs — in the interests of his own financial prosperity and an essentially reactionary ideology.

* * * * *

(ii) Their aims

Scott's *Minstrelsy of the Scottish Border*, 'consisting of Historical and Romantic Ballads collected in the Southern Counties of Scotland, with a few of modern date, founded upon local tradition', was the first book-length work dealing with the song-culture of an English or Scots region, though Ritson had shown the way with his garlands.[41] Volumes one and two were published at Kelso in 1802, and volume three in Edinburgh in 1803, and the work sold massively in the relatively small literary market. The first two volumes had a print-run of 1000, but the third called for 1500. An edition of 1806 ran to 1250 copies of each volume, as did that of 1810. The 1812 edition was of 1500, and that of 1820 was of 500. In total, this publication netted Scott £600.[42] He later benefited financially from the customary egregious dedication to his patron, the Duke of Buccleuch, but his success depended more on the bourgeois market for 'popular superstition, and legendary history', who felt that the supposedly 'peculiar features' of Scottish 'manners and character' were 'daily melting and dissolving into those of her sister and ally' to the south. Of course, what is presented as 'national' was effectively class-based history and culture. Scott concentrates almost entirely on chiefs, kings, queens and princes in a 'barbarous nation' constantly at war, while ordinary women and men are mentioned collectively only as troops, victims of violence, or the entourage of the great and powerful. His 'hasty sketch' of 'border history', 'manners' and the 'character of the marchmen' is a lengthy, erudite and male-oriented account of the 'domestic economy' of the chieftain, of his attitudes to kings, wars, 'patriotism' and moveable property, and virtually excludes women, kinsmen and vassals. Moreover, that history is heavily ideological. Scott's own preference for lost reactionary causes, like that of Queen Mary and the Jacobites, and his antipathy towards any dangerously 'democratic' tendencies, such as aspects of the religious wars of the seventeenth century, fitted in with contemporary conservative bourgeois attitudes, and helped reconstruct history from that perspective.

Scott pays more attention to 'The Fairies of Scotland' than he does to the 'common people', 'peasants' or 'vulgar' whom he dismisses or patronizes for their 'superstitious' beliefs while exploiting them as sources. This is why Scott chose not to theorize about the 'ballad', and why he presented 'Tradition' as an almost impersonal force. Only when he felt sure that a particular ruling class song had been 'degraded' into a 'ballad', 'by the lapse of time, and the corruption of reciters', did he

make such pronouncements, safe in the knowledge that this would appeal
to the adherents of the theory of a perfectible bourgeois culture. Like
them, Scott did not know workers' culture. He was an agent of the state,
and relied on a man, Hogg, who aped many of his own ideas and
attitudes, referring to his former neighbours as 'the poor illiterate people
in these glens.'[43] According to Scott's fellow law-agent, Shortreed, 'baith
the country and its peculiar manners sat for their pictures' in their 1790s
'raids',[44] and provided the taste of apparent 'authenticity' which Scott
wished to convey in his song-book and his later novels, where tales,
superstitions, snatches of song and suchlike raw materials could be worked up for the benefit of an increasingly insecure bourgeoisie, including
'stereotypes of Scottish character' and elements of workers' culture as
'colouring and relief' — relief from a burgeoning working class presence,
in a romanticized and mythified past.[45]

Scott's *Minstrelsy* consolidated the bourgeois market for song-books,
both sides of the Border, so Jamieson's *Popular Ballads and Songs, From
Tradition, Manuscripts, and Scarce Editions*, 'with Translations of Similar
Pieces from the Ancient Danish Language, and a Few Originals by the
Editor', was able to be published both in London and Edinburgh in 1806.
His use of *Popular* in his title was original, and was probably designed to
widen the potential market, as were the somewhat heterogeneous contents
advertised on the title page. Jamieson stressed he had the idea for such
a work before his 'more happily situated fellow-labourer', Scott, but he
copies him in the style of his dedication (to the Duchess of Gordon, 'eminent among our Scottish matrons' for her 'taste' and 'patriotism') in the
appeal to both scholar and antiquary, and in the targetting on the 'most
refined reader' interested in 'the real state of traditional peotry, as it is
still preserved' in Scotland. Such people, and above all his 'expatriated
countrymen', might be expected to understand Ossian's Gaelic and Pin-
dar's Greek, but they were also aware that the 'extension of commerce
and manufactures among a people like the Scots' had led to a situation
where more mobile expatriates had begun to 'disregard and discontinue
the habits, usages, and amusements of their less enlightened and refined,
but not less virtuous and praiseworthy predecessors'. To such a bourgeois
market, the 'history and nature of traditional poetry' was an important
part of their shaken sense of Scots identity; and yet they, like Jamieson,
could be presumed to be contemptuous of the bearers of that 'tradition',
of the 'uncouth rhapsody' of 'illiterate minstrels', 'old nurses and grandmothers' and other 'ignorant' reciters. What the song-editor had to do,
then, was to 'discover what garb' a given piece appeared in 'some two
hundred years ago', when Scotland could be said to have its own national
identity, and before the royal link with England had been forged. The
gentlemanly (and partly-coded) struggle[46] between Jamieson and Scott
which is an undercurrent of *Popular Ballads* suggests that there was a
debate as to the precise nature of the 'Reliques' of that culture, and the
real nature of its history. It evidently mattered to them that their

bourgeois culture got the legitimizing support of having connections with the declining aristocratic culture.

Cromek's *Remains of Nithsdale and Galloway Song* of 1810 not only extended the geographical range of regional song-books, but also introduced the novelty of giving 'Historical and Traditional Notices, relative to the Manners and Customs of the Peasantry'. The book's aim, apart from making money from the London market for Scots nostalgia, was primarily antiquarian. Cromek sought to 'redeem some of those fine old ballads and songs' (which he did not differentiate theoretically), which were 'floating in the breath of popular tradition'. What made Scotland different, apparently, was that the 'influence of commerce' in England had 'gradually altered the character of the people' and 'weakened that strong attachment to the soil' which was yet to be found in the remoter Scots countryside. This residual culture bore the 'evident stamp of *Rusticity,*' and differentiated itself not only from the culture of the 'elegant and learned' who were meant to buy the book, but also from that of the emerging proletariat. According to Cromek, this uneven cultural development was a product of the defeated rebellion of 1745–6, after which 'Scottish rural character arose from the wrecks of feudal jurisdiction', while still managing to preserve that 'perfect individuality of character which had been forming itself ever since the Reformation'. In this way, what had previously been a 'national' culture had become, by 1810, a 'peasant' one, in districts somehow free from the 'bustle and contamination of foreign commerce' and foreign culture. The 'peasantry', in other words, were the legitimate heirs of the 'people':

> Taught by their fathers to regard every foreign fashion as a dangerous innovation, they preserved themselves unpolluted with the streams of refinement which was sapping the ancient manners and character of their nobility and chieftans.[47]

'Peasant' culture, therefore, acted as a moral standard against which to measure ruling class and bourgeois decadence, and as a talisman of cultural chauvinism, albeit that the *Remains* was proudced by a migrant Englishman and an émigré Scot at the heart of British capitalism!

The remarkable violence done to history and culture was only possible because of Cromek's promulgation of bourgeois myths about the supposedly idyllic country life, and because Cromek and Cunningham, his collaborator, believed that even the 'peasant' culture of Nithsdale and Galloway was changing under the influence of the industrialization of agriculture. In a 'few years', they claimed, the songs they printed would be 'irrecoverably forgotten'. The 'peasants' could not be trusted with their own culture, as they became absorbed into the rural or urban proletariat; and so their products had to be preserved through the agency of a 'guide' who had 'personal intercourse with the peasantry', who knew 'how the peasantry think and feel', and who could act as a kind of precocious anthropologist probing a culture miraculously immune from the 'more polished and artificial manners of their neighbours'. Cromek and Cunningham's wish to 'impress us with a noble idea of peasant abilities' and with a 'sacred reverence for their memory', has about it that 'noble savage' ideology which helped inform Romantic poetry, and acted as a critique of industrialism, commercialism, urbanization and utilitarianism *within* bourgeois ideology, where it provided an intellectual 'alternative' to the real processes of economic and social change.[48] In their ahistorcial landscape, songs and stories are like 'wild-flower seeds scattered by the winds of heaven'; though Cunningham, if not Cromek knew at first hand that the imbecilities of 'fabled Arcadians' in some genteel literature were the product of people who 'never smear sheep or blister their gloved hands with shepherds' crooks'. What they wanted to do was to inject the 'strongly marked rudiments of critical judgment' and 'genuine prompting of uneducated nature', which they perceived in the 'peasantry', into the bourgeois literary culture of their own day, so as to serve both as an antidote to the 'elaborate and polished effusions of what may be called the classic school of poetry', and as an alternative to the Romantics' 'abortive' attempts to 'revive this primitive style of poetry'. Yet even a conservative radical like Cobbett understood that 'peasant' was simply a '*new*' name given to the *country labourers* by the indolent boroughmongering and loanmongering tribes'[49] who benefited from the capitalization of agriculture which had penetrated almost all of the British Isles before 1800. So Cromek and Cunningham's use of the term marks the hardening of the sentimentalizing tendency (amongst those who thought they had 'escaped' from capitalist relations of production in the countryside or provinces) towards a country culture which they believed was dying out. Just as farmers and landlords exploited the working men and women in the British countryside economically, so Cromek and Cunningham did so culturally under the guise of preservation. Paradoxically, by treating cultural products as property in this way, Cromek and Cunningham demonstrated both the distinctiveness of country workers' culture and its vitality, some of which comes through in the 'real history of the Scottish Peasantry' Cunningham believed he had written in his Introduction and Notes.

John Bell's *Rhymes of Northern Bards*, published in Newcastle in 1812, appealed to English regional patriotism, and was advertised straightforwardly as a 'curious Collection of old and new Songs and Poems Peculiar to the Counties of Newcastle upon Tyne, Northumberland and Durham'. The *Rhymes* grew out of Ritson's initiative and represents an English response to the upsurge in Scots song-books.[50] The book sold at six shillings, and, taking booksellers' discounts off the top, Bell stood to make only a few pounds' profit, so this was hardly a major motive. He used the chapbook- and broadside-publishing firm of Margaret Angus, perhaps for the sake of cheapness, but also because he saw his work as part of the developing tradition of publishing of what the commercial song-publisher

John Marshall termed '*provincial songs*'.[51] The edition sold out quickly — the last copies going at 25 shillings from a bookseller who bought most of the 500 copies wholesale — largely because of its overtly regionally-patriotic aim, to rescue 'from the yawning jaws of oblivion the productions of the Bards of the Tyne; and by so doing, hand them down to future ages as Reliques of Provincial Poetry'. Bell, like Cromek, believed that flimsy broadsides and chapbooks, (let alone people's memories) could not preserve 'many of these simple, yet popular effusions', a 'day beyond the time they were written', whereas a book aimed at not only a bourgeois but also a petty-bourgeois market could. He felt no urge to theorize, and his genuinely antiquarian attitudes encouraged him to publish everything which came his way, irrespective of origin, form or literary pretentions. Bell did most of his collecting at a period when even British provincial culture seemed, to people of his own class, to be in danger of disappearing into London-oriented 'national' culture. He also demonstrates — as did his purely commercial fellow-publishers in and around Newcastle — that the very cultural vitality and distinctiveness that they and their class felt in danger of losing was, in spite of their claims, still present in the culture of working men and women.

Hogg's *The Jacobite Relics of Scotland* of 1819–21 was published in Edinburgh, but was made, virtually to order, for the Highland Society of London. It contains 'Songs, Airs and Legends of the adherents to the House of Stuart,' which might 'furnish us with a key to the annals of many ancient and noble families', and form a 'delightful though rude epitome of the history of our country during a period highly eventful, when every internal movement was decisive toward the establishment of the rights and privileges we have since enjoyed'.[52] As with Scott, that enjoyment and 'history' were the property of 'noble families', the kind of ruling class individuals who belonged to the Highland Society, and who, like the two royal Dukes who were members, could safely associate themselves with the families and the culture of their relatives who happened to be on the wrong side in 1745–6. All of them could afford song-books, have bare tunes harmonized for them by a 'composer' or 'professional player at the piano', and might well be members of those Scots Tory clubs who sang such songs at 'festive meetings during the late war, in detestation of those who deprecated the principles of Pitt'.[53] Hogg understood his market and, with ideological as well as material support from Scott, tended to use quotations from Jacobite sources rather than those from Whigs, whose songs were relegated to an appendix. At a period when the descendants of the foot soldiers on both sides were being hewn down in Manchester by yeomen cavalry, and harassed by the forces of the state up and down the country,[54] the unblushing use of original and politically reactionary song-texts signals the extent to which the *British* ruling class had patched up old wounds in the face of a threat to the security of all its constituent elements — whether Scots or English,

Catholic or Protestant, Tory or Whig — from working-class economic and political organizations.

Three small publications of the mid-1820s — Sharpe's *A Ballad Book* of 1823, Maidment's *A North Countrie Garland* of 1824 and Kinloch's *The Ballad Book*[55] of 1827 — were all privately published in Edinburgh, and were circulated largely to members of the Scott circle. Each 'little fairy volume',[56] published in tiny editions of 30 or so, was deemed to be worth 'a little time thrown away on its perusal, which most Antiquaries can spare'.[57] Apart from the antiquarian and bibliomaniac attraction of such collections, private publication (amongst what appears to be an all-male coterie) also allowed the editors to print material which could not yet appear in British books aimed at a commercial market. Sharpe aimed to 'preserve a few Songs that afforded me such delight in my early youth, and are not found at all, or complete, or in the same shape in other Collections', but he acknowledged that some items were 'not over delicate'. Maidment could indulge his penchant for faked antiquity with black-lettering and a deliberately crude woodcut, and justify his whim by claiming 'rarity' value of the texts. But he could also use material which he knew might 'shock the fastidious', just as Kinloch used at least one 'coarse production'. It is interesting to speculate, then, just how far anti-quarianism and an interest in the culture of 'the vulgar' legitimized the singing and now the printing of erotic songs for members of the all-male clubs of cultural slummers in Edinburgh and both Scots and English pro-vincial towns, at a period when the erotic aspects of bourgeois culture were coming to be repressed by Dr. Bowdler and other self-appointed censors. Sharpe, Maidment and Kinloch had to go to workers' culture for their bawdy songs, demonstrating the vitality of that culture and the poverty of their own, which encouraged them to seek to 'capture' texts for their own kind and treat such trophies as property amongst like-minded friends.

By the time of Cunningham's *The Songs of Scotland, Ancient and Modern*, which was published in London in 1825, Scott had taken over as a suitable dedicatee for such productions. Cunningham added 'an Introduction and Notes, Historical and Critical and Characters of the Lyric Poets', but his chief aim was a comprehensive edition of 'the pro-ductions of the lyricists of our native land'. He recognized that only 'national vanity' could elevate a 'few rude lines and a few questionable fragments' into a distinct set of older 'national melodies'. He also abandoned the attempt to find 'era and author to our ancient lyrics' amongst herdsmen, warriors and other 'Lyric Poets' of 'humble origin', and made no effort to distinguish between 'English' and 'Scottish' songs, which he termed a 'fruitless effort of patriotism'. Cunningham used the same historical perspective as in the *Remains*, claiming for himself the role of middleman, and adding 'what history has preserved' to his conception of what 'veritable tradition handed down', though he lamented 'the ravages of time and the imperfections of oral remembrance'. While he continued to have the perspective of a print-oriented literary poet, looking now from outside at a culture which seemed increasingly alien and distant, he still recognized that songs *did* 'descend from generation to generation' and were 'changed or amended according to the taste or caprice of the multitude, at whose mercy all oral things live', and were often 'softened in their progress'. That 'multitude', moreover, was the same 'half of mankind' which had been crushed by commerce and industry so as to now be 'slaves to the other half'; and though he found it incongruous that 'rustic' songs were 'warbled amid a multitude of people rustling in the richest dresses, and sparking in gold and jewels', this very situation was partly the result of his own efforts. In addition, he championed the idea that 'torn and bleeding members of old song' are legitimate raw material for literary poets, from Ramsay and Percy to his own day, since he believed that there were no property rights in workers' culture; and his inclusion of almost 100 pieces by 'Living Lyric Poets' — about two-fifths were his own productions — evidently did not contradict his aims of combining 'the more dainty and polished productions of the present time' with 'excellent old morsels of the lively Muse'.

Cunningham *defined* the work of the old 'oral poets' as 'national culture', and sought to elevate Scots 'rustic' culture above that of the 'English peasants' who he thought had no such 'literature of their own'. He also wanted to insert into contemporary 'national' song-culture the work of what he felt were the legitimate heirs (and some heiresses) of post-Reformation 'patriarchal' and 'peasant' culture. However, he also recognized that country workers' culture was far from dead, even in the 1820s. A 'vigilant and skilful collector' who could 'enter into the peculiar feelings of a shrewd and a suspicious people' might yet 'find his reward in many curious and instructive things which still linger among our hills and vales', including 'songs which are composed by the peasantry' — people defined as being 'unpractised in the arts of poetical composition' as known to his bourgeois readership.[58] Such an idea derived from Cunningham's first-hand knowledge of the 'parochial poets' who earned half a crown a week pocket-money from audiences of shepherds and ploughmen at country weddings, and who scattered throughout southwest Scotland 'a regular succession of lyrics, more or less impressed with the character of the people' for whom they were performed. He knew also of the 'travelling sellers of songs, ballads and histories' in chapbook-form, and of their importance in linking the developing print-oriented song-culture with that of 'the peasantry'. He placed greatest weight for having 'laid the foundation of the rustic or national poetry of Scotland' not on the 'royal race of bards', but on Allan Ramsay, a man who, like Cunningham, was a 'daily labourer for his bread' and had no time to go out collecting songs, yet who still 'strove to redeem from oblivion, or rescue from the changeful memory of tradition, the ancient lyrics of the nation'. That 'oblivion' of course was precisely the oral culture of working people;

and the 'rescue', as with Cunningham's own book, was a subtle form of expropriation. What he was trying to do was to place himself at the conjuncture of two related traditions, one being that of the mediators of Scots song, from Ramsay's 'first great sanctuary' onwards, and the other that of artisan and worker poets, stretching back to the anonymous 'minstrels' of the sixteenth century, and coming through Ramsay, Fergusson, Burns and Tannahill to Hogg. With such dubiously genuine credentials, Cunningham hoped to gain access to the bourgeois literary pantheon.

Motherwell's *Minstrelsy Ancient and Modern* concentrates on the 'Ancient Romantick and Historick Ballad of Scotland', and he uses 'narrative' as the chief theoretical criterion for a 'ballad', with other (and usually negative)[59] criteria derived from the materials he selects. The Introduction was written last, and reluctantly,[60] in 1827; but what was new about this Glasgow book was Motherwell's stress on the accurate transmission of texts by the 'unlettered and the rude', and on the need for collecting from 'the lips of "The spinsters and knitters in the sun" '. To Motherwell, 'tradition' was on a par with 'more efficient and less mutable channels of communicating the things of past ages to posterity', 'fragile and capricious as the tenure' might seem there. Variations of songs were still to be found, but differences between oral and manuscript texts were 'neither very numerous nor very important', and so the former was 'in all matters relative to popular poetry, a safe and almost unerring guide'. In fact, 'the lower and uneducated classes of society' were not those amongst whom 'oral song suffers vital and irremediable wrong': 'What they have received from their forefathers, they transmit in the same shape to their children:'[61]

Following Ritson, Motherwell believed that the 'conscientious antiquary' had most to fear from the 'pernicious and disingenuous practices' of other mediators — those who 'slightingly and slovenly executed' song-collection without 'scrupulous and unshrinking fidelity'. What was needed was careful and accurate transcription of the 'wreck' of what he termed 'Ancient National Minstrelsy' in Scotland, which was 'yet floating around us'. This position relates to his idealist belief that songs 'purely national and characteristick' had been somehow 'inwoven' with the 'feelings and passions of the people', and were thus 'an actual embodiment of their Universal mind, and of its intellectual and moral tendencies'. 'Tradition' was essential to this process, yet

> Though tradition may faithfully transmit to us the narrative uninjured and unshorn of any part of its circumstance, nay even give the sentiments of the poet unaltered, and preserve the character of the piece precisely as at first pourtrayed, yet it alters the language so completely, that not a word may be preserved which originally was there.[62]

By collecting 'every old traditionary ballad known', the editor was able to attempt to read this 'Universal mind', as it were, historically.

Motherwell's own naive and mystical notion of cultural history comes out clearly when he makes a distinction as between the 'patriotick children of an ancient race', and the contemporary urban working-class 'rabble', who might be 'gulled' by phoney song-editors as well as by political and trade union leaders. This longing for a golden age of Scots culture is then combined with a belief in a racial and cultural homogeneity of the 'Scandinavian provinces of Europe'. Yet while this internationalism is in some ways progressive in that it denies the imposition of political borders on cultural exchange, it is also reactionary, because of the implicit view that such internationalism in culture is only a survival of what had once been a 'curious and interesting species of national literature'.

Motherwell saw his editorial role as being to use his 'intuitive and auxiliary sense' for discerning the genuinely 'ancient' on behalf of the 'general reader' and the 'more industrious and accurate cultivator'. Since 'opportunities of recovering traditional song' were disappearing because of 'changes which, within this half century' had been effected in the 'manners and habits of our peasantry and labouring classes, with whom this song has been cherished', the time was approaching 'that take the sickle who likes in hand, it will be vain to expect it can reap anything but stubble and profitless weeds'. Workers had

> departed from the stern simplicity of their fathers, and have learned with the paltry philosophers, political quacks, and illuminated dreamers on Economick and Moral science, to laugh at the prejudices, beliefs, and superstitions of elder times.[63]

Like Cunningham, Motherwell could not conceive of any cultural continuity as between country workers and urban 'labouring classes' as they were transformed during the Industrial Revolution. There had been, as it were, a cultural *break*, and the song-editor's job was to tune into the wavelength of what remained of the 'Universal mind'. To change the metaphor, an editor had to glean the cultural stubble left behind in the economic and political development of the British working class for the benefit of the would-be intellectual (and economic) élite of late Georgian Britain, the automatic beneficiaries of the cultural heritage of a conveniently abstract 'people'.

Peter Buchan's *Ancient Ballads and Songs of the North of Scotland* was published in Edinburgh in 1828 and aimed explicitly at the bourgeois market — people who could 'cultivate a taste for polite literature amid the more weighty concerns of business', whose faculties were 'not contracted within the narrow sphere of sordid gain', and who cherished the 'national feelings' of 'all true and patriotic Scotsmen'. The book mentions Buchan's corresponding membership of the Scottish Society of Antiquaries, and is dedicated to the ubiquitous Duke of Buccleuch. Workers are notably absent: the editor scorns the 'vulgar mind' in favour of those concerned with 'the history of Scottish literature', such as the 'literary antiquary' and the 'man of letters', who indulged an interest in the 'decayed memories of their forefathers', who 'cherish a national spirit, and who are anxious to support the time-worn structure, and falling towers of Ancient Scottish National Song'. In other words, Buchan hoped to touch every chord which might widen the market for Tory pessimism at a period when the Scots Parliament's future was coming into question, along with the entire corrupt system of patronage. As with Motherwell, we can understand the ideological undertow of this publication as an attempt to shore up a peculiar description of a 'national' history and culture, coming under challenge by petty-bourgeois and even working-class organization at both economic and political levels. Once again, however, the contradiction Buchan faced was that he had to collect his 'hitherto unpublished' texts — without which he had no market-appeal — from 'the sons and daughters of the North', the descendants of the 'rural minstrels' and of 'European, and Scottish Bards', still be to found 'among the aged and venerated people' in the 'straw-covered cot'. These old people were evidently not a creative part of the 'regular process of civilisation', and simply preserved 'mutilated fragments', 'graphic relics' and a 'remnant of those wild flowers' which it was the mediator's task to save from the 'fast decaying hand of time' with 'the greatest industry and care'. To adapt Motherwell's notion, Buchan seems to imply that the 'Universal mind' had gone ga-ga, and cultural lobotomy and pickling was the only possible strategy for those who identified ideologically with the culture from which these songs derived, rather than with that in which they now survived. What is new is that Buchan, like John Bell, was from the urban petty-bourgeoisie, and sought to distance himself sharply from the culture of the 'vulgar' and the 'rabble' by producing, rather like a squirrel, a 'Ballad-store' which he could retail to a genteel market which he could not hope to reach in any other way.

The 1829 Edinburgh publication of Chambers' *The Scottish Ballads* represents an important stage in this transition towards cultural wholesaling. Its market success signalled the opening-up of a wider book-buying public than the older bourgeois trade, yet songs which deal with people who 'belong to a very humble class of society' have to be apologized for to 'the most fastidious reader'. Chambers cheerfully expropriates the cultural expropriators, both by pinching material and some ideas from the likes of Motherwell, and by proclaiming the rights of a much more broadly defined 'public' over those of the 'antiquary'. Such a public was assumed to want only the 'best of the whole mass of published ballads', could afford a 'very moderate price', and would need a gloss for Latin quotations. The concept of the 'general reader', in other words, had expanded, and Chambers' initiative marked the earlier stages of the exploitation of that market for cheap publications by entrepreneurs who had no incentive to grovel in public to noble patrons, or rely on the restricted literary-antiquarian market.

* * * * *

(iii) Their sources

During the 1790s, Scott's legal duties took him into Selkirkshire, and there he made some contact with farmers and professional people, though not as equals. He was 'Mr Scott, *the Advocate*' after all, and often as not rode in a low-wheeled phaeton.[64] But he came to make the acquaintance of the town-pipers of Jedburgh, and of Jonathan Graham, an itinerant clock-cleaner, who had a reputation at inns for being a singer and teller of tales. Graham was 'sent for' by Scott and his friend Dr. Elliott, in order to get his tune for the *Fray o' Suport*, was treated with drink, and sent away with a gratuity and a hangover.[65] Scott later romanticized about these Liddesdale 'raids', when, as Shortreed put it, they '*roved away among the fouk*'[66] for a few days *memorizing* songs 'chiefly' from 'shepherds' and 'aged persons' who lived in the 'recesses of the border mountains'. In fact, only one piece is known to have been taken by Scott 'from recitation'.[67] He relied on his memory and notches in sticks, and Shortreed 'never saw a pen'.[68] Only four texts written in Scott's hand survive.[69] After a break, Scott made another 'raid' in 1801, and his friend William Laidlaw put him in touch with Hogg. They met in 1802, by which time Scott took Hogg's transcriptions on trust.

Most of Scott's sources were allowed to remain in obscurity. Apart from Hogg's mother, he refers simply to a 'blind old man', 'old persons residing at the head of Ettrick Forest', or labels texts as an 'an Ettrick Forest copy', or even from 'tradition' itself. He was extremely trusting with genteel correspondents, like his 'early and dear friend', Robert Surtees[70] of Durham, another ex-Christ Church College lawyer with antiquarian interests. Surtees sent material he *said* he had collected from old people; but one item was certainly his own composition. Probably, they all were.[71] Sharpe sent texts, one said to be 'written down, from tradition, by a lady', another baldly termed a 'copy', and a third 'from an old magazine'.[72] Scott was well placed to examine the archives of Border gentry and the libraries of Edinburgh antiquarians, but other members of polite society chipped in, including the 'eccentric' Mr Bartram of Biggar. Robert Hamilton, another lawyer, recited 'several verses' to his friend; Mungo Park the explorer[73] contributed a couple of verses; Mr Plummer, Sheriff-depute of Selkirkshire, did the same; while Dr Elliott sent 'many valuable communications', from a 'large MS collection of his own', made 'for his own amusement',[74] which included songs from at least one 'reciter'. Mr Livingston of Airds got material from 'an old woman residing on his estate'. Miss Joanna Baillie[75] sent others and was coyly referred to as a 'lady of the highest literary eminence'. An Edinburgh music-seller, who also wrote 'Scottish' songs, recorded a piece which had been his mother's favourite; and a dozen more people of similar status followed suit. Scott seems to have cared little for specifying the people who did the singing (as opposed to those who recorded songs). He refers vaguely to 'an old woman, residing near Kirkhill in West

Lothian', to a piece 'still sung by the children', and to another from 'a lady of high rank'. He was often imposed on, as with a piece 'taken down from tradition', which he later found to have been 'composed by the late Mr Graham of Gartmore'.

Scott took over 90 unpublished items from Herd's collection.[76] Others came from the Glenriddell MS., owned by Robert Riddell, Burns' friend, and bought by Dr Leyden from a Carlisle bookseller in 1800. The Old Lady's MS. (written by an unnamed woman), one of Thomas Wilkie's MSS., the Bannantyne MS., and his own collection provided more. Mrs Brown's manuscripts of 'Romantic Ballads' came to Scott from his 'learned and respected friend', Alexander Fraser Tytler Esq. (later Lord Woodhouselee), who inherited them from his father, William Tytler, who in turn got them from Thomas Gordon, professor of philosophy at King's College, Aberdeen. Gordon's youngest daughter, the Mrs Brown in question, had learned almost all her songs from her aunt, Mrs Farquhar, the wife of the owner of a small estate in Braemar, and she had got them 'from the nurses and countrywomen in that sequestered part of the country'. Mrs Brown's songs were first taken down by Gordon's grandson, Mr (later Professor) Scott, and sent to William Tytler.[77]

Scott saw this Tytler MS. in 1795, and again in 1800. In 1800 he persuaded Fraser Tytler to approach Mrs Brown to collect any more songs she might have, thereby producing the Tytler-Brown MS. Mrs Brown was no peasant and no worker; and while David Buchan believed that she 'found it natural and satisfying to know her ballads' as Anna Gordon, as Mrs Brown of Falkland, the lady of the manse, she 'could not admit publicly to a knowledge of these rude though curious Scottish songs'. In fact, she was 'vexed' with Scott when he used her name in print. Her concern for 'propriety, gentility and station', and for the English bourgeois standards of decorum which had been adopted by her class in the wake of 1745–6, overlapped with the decay of the 'oral mode' of composition and transmission which was still important around 1759, when she learned her songs from her aunt, her mother and a Forbes family servant.[78] The relationship between her manuscript texts and the singing of those three women remains, however, highly problematical. Even Scott's suspicions were roused, because of her familiarity with the *Ossian* forgeries, the echoes of *Hardyknute* and the fact that she wrote poetry herself. Scott primed Dr Anderson to test her, and called a meeting of fellow collectors to debate the issue in the autumn of 1800, but they exonerated her simply on their estimate of her 'character'.[79] When Robert Jamieson was returning south through Edinburgh after collecting more texts from Mrs Brown for his own publication, Scott asked him to dinner, gave him some texts which did not fit his specification for the *Minstrelsy*, tried to settle the problem of 'poaching', and to 'bring the collectors to a good understanding' on the issue of who would publish what and from where.[80] Scott's access to song-books, broadsides and printed sources appears to have been substantial, though he shared Ritson's contempt for 'penny pamphlets' and 'printed sheets', because of their 'great corruption', and for literary forgery by previous editors. Texts he believed to be from 'tradition' he places at the top of his hierarchy of sources, be they Hogg's, Mrs Brown's or the dozens he extracted from Herd's publications; and this naïve assumption that the collector was the agent of 'tradition' is underlined when we learn that Hogg took at least one text down from 'a crazy old man, and a woman deranged in her mind', in 'plain prose', which the Ettrick Shepherd promptly worked up into verse. *Kinmont Willie* and *Jamie Telfer* remain under suspicion;[81] but questions of absolute authenticity were, for Scott and so many of his predecessors and contemporaries, secondary.

The network begun in Edinburgh by Herd and developed by Scott also helped Jamieson, but on its terms and not his, and especially after he went direct to a key source, Mrs Brown, over their heads. The price he paid for getting access to Herd's MS., which had been 'handed about' amongst Edinburgh antiquaries for years, was what he thought was a deal in relation to Mrs Brown's texts. In the event, however, Scott decided that since 'the greater part of the materials collected' from her was the same, there was no reason why he should not use the advantage of his material well-being and contacts to get into print first with the 'Romantic' items he had promised not to publish.[82] Jamieson preferred orally-collected songs, such as the one taken down by Leyden from 'a young lady (Miss Robson) of Edinburgh, who learned it in Teviotdale', and the 'number of pieces' he got from Mrs Arrot of Aberbrothick'. Jamieson's own childhood experience included hearing songs 'sung by the rustic maiden at her spinning-wheel', and he secured a few more items on a trip to his native Morayshire. He understood the importance of texts 'purchased of a pedling pamphlet-seller for a penny', but by 1806 saw fit to signal contempt for 'the very lowest description of vulgar modern English broadsides, which are sung about the streets in country towns, and sold, four or five for a half-penny, to maid-servants and children'.[83] Such 'paltry stuff' had to be apologized for to his genteel readers, whereas texts taken from a Danish 1695 edition of the *Kaempe Viser* did not. (They were less 'foreign' to song-book buyers than the culture of people who bought 'traditionary ballads and songs, and penny pamphlets' in the Scotland of his day.) Jamieson's understanding of 'tradition', like Scott's, had veered away from contemporary workers' culture, and towards isolated and exceptional sources of the 'genuine text', notably the very bourgeois Mrs Brown who conveniently sent him songs through the post, though some of her texts failed to appear in *Popular Ballads and Songs*.

Allan Cunningham was the chief source for Cromek's *Remains*. As a boy, he had 'committed to memory many of our ancient as well as our modern songs' and tunes, learning them from chapbooks, broadsides, magazines and song-books. Unlike Jamieson, he held those 'little cheap copies of our favourite works' in some respect.[84] Other songs he learned orally from his father, 'an honest cultivated farmer'[85] who had been a friend of Burns, and from various singers at country festivities — Beltane, New Year, Hallow-eve, sheep-shearing, harvest-homes, wool-combing, spinning, and both song and dance 'trystes'. These last had a 'great effect upon the youth of the district, and preserved an image of ancient manners'. They were 'a kind of initiation into the mysteries and beliefs and feelings of their ancestors'.[86] In his young manhood, Cunningham learned songs from a 'servant girl belonging to his father', from the singing of 'wandering mendicants', and from printed texts in the 'balladsinger's basket', not to mention at weddings, barn-dances, summer fair nights at inns, prentice bindings, and other occasions of 'fixed and casual conviviality'.[87] So, when he wrote of a piece being a 'great favourite' amongst people he *later* came to see as 'peasantry' he speaks with an authority beyond what Cromek could challenge.[88]

Yet in the *Remains* Cunningham felt under no more obligation to name his 'peasant' sources than did Scott or Burns: one-third of the songs remain totally unlocated, while others are described almost anthropomorphically as the product of 'Nithsdale' or 'Galloway' or 'the Lowlands'. A handful are ascribed to the singing of a 'young girl', a 'worthy old man', 'young lads' at haymaking, 'old people' or a 'peasant woman of Galloway, upwards of ninety years of age', probably Margaret Corson, aged 97; but only one woman who might have been a worker is named, Martha Crosbie, because she also gave a song to Burns. Jean Walker, another named source, may have been a country worker, but this young girl from Kirk-bean in Galloway wrote a highly literate letter, addressed Cromek as 'Mr', and supplied Cunningham with half a dozen pieces which are promptly labelled as 'From Tradition'. Genteel sources are, however, named. Mrs Copland of Dalbeattie, to whom the *Remains* was dedicated, sent ten items and 'notices and remarks' from what may have been a manuscript collection. Her niece, Catherine Macartney of Hacket Leaths, Galloway, recited two further texts, and 'recovered ' another fragment. Both women are congratulated for their 'exquisite taste', and for their association with the 'magic hand' of the 'Rural Muse of Galloway'. More, they are thanked for having 'rescued from oblivion many fine remains of Song', when that 'oblivion' happened to be the live song-culture which Cunningham had only recently left to go to London. Cromek's contribution appears to have been a few verses taken from an 'elderly gentleman', who learned them as a boy, in Yorkshire! Yet while both men had access to old broadsides, to some of Burns' manuscripts and to the *Museum*, and both rejected 'spurious works' from books such as Pinkerton's, they acknowledged that 'Historical notices' concerning songs were 'the most difficult things to be procured imaginable', since they were 'below the dignity of the historian.' Similarly, they claimed to respect the 'peasantry' for their ability to 'retain those noble touches of nature which are scattered among their songs and ballads, while the indifferent verses which encompass them, like dross from the pure ore, are rejected and forgotten'. They also felt confident in deciding when 'tradition' had so 'fabled' a given text that 'we dare scarcely trust her report'. Cunningham, in his own eyes, was now the very bearer of authentic 'tradition' and its self-appointed trustee.

Given his antiquarian motives, John Bell's range of sources was appropriately wide. He took whatever he could get from 'old MSS', a Haltwhistle tombstone, a sheet 'Pasted upon the Walls, and scattered about the Town of Rothbury, several Years ago', newspapers, street-singers, and 'Pitmen about Long Benton'. Ritson's garlands he uses almost exhaustively: Whittell[89] and John Cunningham's[90] poems and songs are cheerfully accepted; and the work of Henry Robson[91] (a Newcastle print-worker, originally from a pit village, who was Bell's friend and protégé) and Blind Willie Purvis[92] (a Newcastle pub-singer and musician) he used unproblematically. Two-thirds of Bell's texts appear as anonymously-made, yet many can be traced to local broadsides and chap-books containing locally-made songs, sometimes with known authors. Perhaps half his texts were from manuscript or oral sources, and he exploited his location at the heart of Newcastle's Lower Town social life to collect texts from urban workers and visiting 'country' labourers on Pay Saturdays and at holiday or market times. He used friends, acquaintances and contacts with fellow enthusiasts to secure new texts and tunes, and in this way he was able to reach out into *both* the polite *and* the workers' culture of the north-east. Though both he and they used primitive communications of horse-travel, carters and the rudimentary postal service to their limit, what they did was very much in line with the 'vacuum-cleaner' approach of more recent times,[93] and for this reason he did indeed produce a 'matchless collection'.

Hogg's *Jacobite Relics* was made to measure for the same kind of people who supplied him with material. Apart from items derived from Cromek, Ritson, Scott, and the occasional 'street ballad' and magazine, Hogg had to rely on manuscript and some oral sources. By 1819, he had amassed 'upwards of twenty collections of MS songs', 'Exclusive of casual correspondences' from people who had feared to sing such songs 'open and avowedly in mixed parties'. Songs which had been 'confined to the select social meeting of confirmed Jacobites' were still 'hoarded up in the cabinets of old Catholic families, where to this day they have been preserved as their most precious lore'. These manuscripts were handed over as 'beloved relics' and with the 'greatest liberality' by nobility, gentry and professional people, including John Stuart Esq. of Dalguise, who had no fewer than three volumes, the Honourable Miss Rollo, and other correspondents in Scots cities and country houses, and as far afield as England. The key to this generosity was Hogg's link with Scott, who 'must have picked out of every cabinet and portfolio in the kingdom' for his own 'Jacobite Collection', perhaps including Herd's MS., which is not acknowledged.[94] Fellow antiquarians like Surtees and David Laing helped Hogg collect from Scots literati, print-trade proprietors, academics and leisured gentry. Laing 'never let any old thing of that nature pass that came in his way', right up until 1821,[95] when Hogg professed he 'actually grew terrified when I heard of a MS volume of Jacobite songs'.

To Hogg the fact that he got up to 20 copies of a given text, 'the greater part of them quite different from one another', could only be explained by postulating a 'great original collection of Jacobite songs, from which others copied what suited or pleased them', making conscious or unwitting changes in the process. His manuscript-oriented conception of transmission underwrites his uniform ignorance of song-texts amongst the descendants of foot-soldiers on both sides. (He also privileged texts thought to be written 'by ladies, and those generally the best', even though those with named authors tended to be by men!) However, he was obliged to make more than one 'general application' to 'rural musicians', for all his claim to be 'perhaps better acquainted with the Lowland melodies of Scotland, as sung by the peasantry, than any person now living'. The truth was that his knowledge was less marketable than the results of his access to that culture. He did not understand, for example, why 'the people of every county in the eastern parts of Scotland' sang a given text 'to their own favourite tunes', and he was enough of a snob to apologize to his patrons and readers for his use of humble sources. One song he describes as a 'garbled copy taken from some singer, as almost every ballad is that is copied from a singer', and he prefers instead to use a manuscript text from Mr Gordon of Ford. Orally-collected songs are given as from a 'country singer', 'old woman' or 'girl', unless they chance to be socially significant, like Mr John Scott, his own uncle, or his 'late indulgent and lamented friend' the Duke of Buccleuch. When working people are named, Hogg refers to them with contemptuous familiarity as 'old Lizzy Lamb' a cottager at Ladhope on Yarrow, or exploits them for 'local colour', as with William Dodds, the 'half-daft man' who amused Hogg and his friends when they were children. Tunes are a different matter. Country fiddlers' and singers' better quality material is preferred to printed versions; and though note might be taken of local tune titles, the speed of performance, and even of the 'ornament' of a given style, the women and men who used them are rarely named. The two major exceptions to this rule are interesting, because not only was 'mussel-mou'd Charlie'[96] an itinerant ballad-seller in Aberdeen, and Mrs Betty Cameron of Lochaber a 'well-known character over a great part of the Lowlands, especially for her Jacobite songs, and her attachment to Prince Charles', but both remained staunch political reactionaries as well as being culturally conservative to the end, and so could have their songs 'copied verbatim' for Hogg's 'betters', without benefit of further mediation.

One of those 'betters', Sharpe, was reduced to using his own childhood experience as a source of song. One was 'taught me by a nursery-maid' and was 'so great a favourite that I committed it to paper as soon as I was able to write'. Almost all of Sharpe's oral sources were economically dependent on the country gentry from which he sprang. They were, therefore, already highly-selected, and so only partly representative of the culture in which they moved:

> These have been mostly gathered from the mouths of nurses, wet and dry, singing to their babes and sucklings, dairy-maids pursuing their vocation in the cow-house, and tenants' daughters, while giving the Lady (as every Laird's wife was once called,) a spinning day, whilom an anniversary tribute in Annandale. Several, too, were picked up from tailors, who were wont to reside in my father's castle, while mis-shaping clothes for the children and servants.[97]

From that perspective, 'an Old Woman in Perthshire' or the 'peasantry of Annandale' no doubt contrasted sharply with his other sources, the 'Old Gentleman', a 'gentleman, very eminent in the Scottish Bar', Mr Douglas of Fingland, Charles Lord Binning, Anne, daughter of Sir James Mackenzie, and Lady Dick. Other genteel people — including Scott and Mr Skene of Rubislaw, who got him the Old Lady's MS.[98] — acted as cultural brokers; and his printer, David Webster, later got hold of a transcript of James Nichol's manuscript collection.[99] Sharpe had access not only to song-books such as Jamieson's and Ramsay's, and to some broadsides, but also to at least one seventeenth century French jest-book, which he characterizes as a work whose 'extreme wit is at least equalled by its beastliness'. Songs from humble sources, however, are treated with almost uniform contempt, and described as a 'strange folly', a 'gross old ditty' or even a 'stupid ballad'; though he went on to pursue 'high-kilted' oral and manuscript texts right through the 1820s, with the fascination we would now associate with that of a voyeur, which, in terms of workers' culture, he had always been.

Working men and women went on making and singing erotic and other songs, of course, independently of such genteel amateurs, and items found their way into Scott's circle through Webster's brokerage. Maidment uses four texts from James Nichol, for example, in his *North Countrie Garland*, and said they 'had long been preserved by tradition in Ayrshire'. But the 'intelligent individual' from whom they came was not only a farmer at Strichen, but also a 'disciple of Tom Paine, and the author of some pamphlets which set forth views quite advanced for his time', on issues like infant education, feeing markets and philosophy.[100] The inevitable conclusion is that 'tradition', to men like Maidment and Sharpe, was essentially *nothing to do with most people*, but was, instead, associated with people like themselves. This suspicion is confirmed when we note that Maidment got material from his friend, Robert Pitcairn Esq., who got them in turn 'from the recitation of a female relative' who had heard one song 'frequently sung in her childhood' — we are not told by whom — around 1760. Other items he gets from 'an Old Lady', who is perhaps the 'Miss K.' he cites as a source elsewhere, and from Lord

Binning (via *The Charmer*, a 1750s Edinburgh song-book). This general tendency is followed through in Kinloch's *The Ballad Book* of 1827, which is devoted to the life and work of the wholly untypical 'Mussel Mou'd' Charles Lesly,[101] the Aberdeen ballad-singer who had the support of the city fathers up to his death in 1782, allegedly at the age of 105. To Kinloch, while the versifying of a 'friend' is to be commended, and the opinion of 'Mr Sharpe' is 'deserving of the highest regard', a 'proverbial expression' found amongst the 'vulgar' is an item fit merely for genteel curiosity. Charlie's appeal is based firmly on the fact that he was not only a 'living antiquity' in his own day, but that he had been dead for over 30 years, and could be offered as the kind of workers' culture acceptable to and assimilable by the Edinburgh bourgeoisie.

Even in Cunningham's *Songs of Scotland*, workers' songs derive from 'invisible spirits', while those from King James V, Sir Robert Aytoun and Francis Semple are named — though Cunningham could not gain access to the manuscripts and had to rely on 'traditionary remembrance'. Even after years in London, through Scott's patronage he had access to most printed song-books from Watson and Thomson to his own day. He cites Scott and Jamieson as *equivalent* to 'tradition', and praises Percy as one of the most 'distinguished among all our ballad poets'. His print-orientedness seems to have stopped Cunningham from collecting from oral sources, other than from his own memory, his wife's, and such manuscripts or texts as were passed on by Scott, Hogg, Laing and (through them) Peter Buchan. Indeed, though he recognized that it would be an 'acceptable labour to all who are curious in the history of national song to collect the innumerable fragments of ancient and modern verse still current among the peasantry', he wanted someone else to do it:

> Scotland is fruitful at present in men with learning, and leisure, and genius for such a task: to their nod the spell-bound doors of noble libraries would have flown open, and to their wish all the oral lyric riches of Scotland would have been gathered together ... I had no such aid.[101]

So, while he knew 'good songs are still abundant, and lyric fragments of great beauty are yet plentiful enough for those who have skill and leisure to render them worthy of public acceptance', Cunningham's modest means and comparatively low social status effectively debarred him from pursuing what had become a gentleman's patriotic hobby, to the products of which he had access only so far as they — people like the Scott circle — saw fit.

Motherwell had access to more esoteric printed sources than did Cunningham, but the important sources for his *Minstrelsy* were those of 'oral tradition'. By 1827, he pronounced it 'of the first importance to collect these songs with scrupulous and unshrinking fidelity'. He had shared the 'pleasant drudgery' of collecting, noted matters of performance style, and seen the importance of particular texts to particular singers. But this was *before* the structure of his book had been settled by the privileging of printed material, to which 'traditional' texts were accreted in the form of footnotes, as sources of 'variants' or as a test of others' editing. Thus, while he might note the oral source for a text recorded by Lord Hailes,[103] or mention that another was 'a favourite of the stalls', the very sequence of his song-texts was based on the chronology of the kind of song-books analysed in this book, together with one or two primarily commercial compilations, such as *The New British Songster* and *Albyn's Anthology*. In the earlier parts of his work, he might mention that a song is 'known to nurses', or that he had (somehow) 'heard a copy'. Occasionally, he mentions that a printed text is 'not so perfect as can be obtained from recitation', but his attitude to working people remains patronizing — he waxes sarcastic about the 'two *ladies*' David Webster collected from, 'One of whom is his own mother, and the other an honest fishwife of Musselburgh'. He had a 'host of friends' who had been 'most unremitting in their endeavours' to get him material, but it is not until Dr Andrew Crawfurd of Lochwinnoch began collecting songs for his friend in 1826 that Motherwell's view of oral sources changed.

Crawfurd was the son of a partner in a Renfrewshire cotton-spinning mill, and of a local landowner's daughter. After school, he clerked for a while, and then entered Glasgow College. He took a diploma as a physician and surgeon in 1818, but he contracted typhus and palsy, lost a leg, and was confined to his bed, hardly able to talk. He shared Motherwell's interest in 'everything old and Scottish', and had singers come to him with their 'Auld Ballads' and 'Scots Songs', which he 'copied after the[ir] recitation'. One of these 'various Persons' who got songs 'by Oral or Traditional Communication' was the poet Thomas Macqueen, who not only collected songs from his sister Mary, but was sent by Crawfurd 'to Ayr in quest of Ballads', with half a guinea for expenses, and then 'thro' Ayr & Galloway on the old quest', with two guineas, during 1827. This payment-by-results system worked: Mrs Storie got a guinea for her songs, and another 17 shillings for going to Paisley so that Motherwell could hear her singing *Bob Norice* at first hand and correct Crawfurd's transcription. (Crawfurd tended to affect a 'deliberately antique way of spelling' as compared to Macqueen's 'normal Scots' orthography.[104]) The tunes were frequently taken down by Andrew Blaikie, a protégé of Scott, member of the Abbey Session and not only a keen musical antiquarian, but also, conveniently, a musical engraver.[105] In the *Minstrelsy*, most of Crawfurd's sources remain unrecognized, or merely recorded as an 'old woman' of Kilbarchan or of Bonhill in Dumbartonshire. Other texts are said to be from 'recitation', from 'old people', 'a lady', or simply 'copies' gathered in Renfrew, Dumbarton, the 'southern parishes of Perthshire' or Stirling; while Motherwell scorns 'some wretched stuff, still preserved by tradition in Paisley'. Texts from his 'ingenious friend', or from Mrs Brown — 'a lady to whom much of the traditionary poetry of Scotland is mainly indebted for preservation', no less — indicate his acceptance of the primacy of mediators' instincts, and of the centrality of print and manuscript, for all his apparent deference to oral sources. Like the rest of his contemporary mediators, he felt people like himself really embodied 'tradition', and able to read the 'Universal mind' most accurately.

As it happens, we know a little about the people from whom Crawfurd took songs.[106] Mary Macqueen was the daughter of a 'travelling or some such tinkler family', and worked for a Boghill 'portioner', whose addresses she spurned in favour of a tailor called Willie Storie. Before the couple and their relatives emigrated to Canada in 1828, Crawfurd 'fished out of her' songs she had learned from her mother (and thus from her grandmother and great-grandmother), from her brothers Thomas and Hamilton, and from people in Galloway and Ayr, including a Mrs Smith, whose song resembles an Ayr chapbook version. (Other songs echo broadside and chapbook texts printed at Kilmarnock, Edinburgh and Glasgow, underlining what Cunningham knew of the importance to workers' song culture of the 'stall copies' Motherwell sought to downgrade.) Margaret Walker came from Ayrshire, married a Lochwinnoch servant, and ended a widow. Not only did she sing versions of Mary Macqueen's songs, but she had a song known to James Telfer on the eastern English Border, and some texts deriving from a 'book'. William Gemmel, a Lochwinnoch tailor who also hailed from Ayrshire, had a song composed by his father expressly for the Earl of Dumfries, which later found its way into a lady's song-book, then to William Macmath and so to Child. John Smith, another tailor, brought his repertoire from Stranraer to Lochwinnoch, including texts found by Buchan and Kinloch elsewhere. One song came from a chapbook, another from an Irish boy, and one deriving from a seventeenth century broadside. This, then, was the complex and print-oriented 'tradition' in which Crawfurd 'fished', from which he selected texts he felt good for Motherwell — some were too 'baudie' or 'modern' or both — who then suppressed the names of the real people who provided the songs, while at the same time foregrounding the genteel individuals who were happily caricaturing and appropriating workers' song-culture under cover of pretending to preserve it.

Peter Buchan employed James Rankin on a straightforward commercial basis to collect songs, though he later exaggerated the cost:

> I sent for and brought an old blind man from a great distance, kept him at Peterhead for upwards of four weeks, and paid all expenses, besides his own charges, which were not inconsiderable ...He was, however, worthy of his reward, great as it was, if I could have afforded it, for he was without doubt, a second Homer. He was possessed of the best memory I ever knew, and had been travelling through the north of Scotland, as an itinerant singer and beggar for the last fifty years. I got many pieces from him which I had not seen before, and many older sets of what I had seen.[107]

Rankin was in a way an 1820s version of Charles Lesly, and Buchan's use of him signals how crucial the cultural guide and explorer's role had become for song-editors in order to gain access to a culture from which Buchan was trying desperately to distance himself in his own career. Between 1827 and 1829, Rankin 'scoured the country clean'[108] of songs. Some of them, Buchan knew, would 'not suit our present hypocrites — they are too *high-kilted*',[109] and these were reserved for private delectation.[110] It is unlikely that Rankin invented anything, or that he cared whether a given song was from 'tradition' or from one of the many Scots chapbooks and broadsides which had been published so close as Aberdeen — some of them by Buchan himself — for decades. Scott, Laing and Sharpe found his texts 'obviously genuine'.[111]

When he published *Ancient Ballads* in 1828, Buchan exerted his property-right so far as to claim that the 'greater part' of the texts was 'taken down by myself during the last ten or twelve years, from the singing and recitation of old men and women, in various parts of Scotland, but chiefly in Aberdeenshire'.[112] To him, then, Rankin was not a collector at all, but a *source* in his own right: the editor acknowledged he was 'much indebted to the recitation' of his 'second Homer'. Other items were sent to Buchan 'by ladies and gentlemen of the highest quality', including Hugh Irvine Esq. of Drum, 'Malvina' (a young lady in Aberdeen) and 'Mr James Nicol, Strichen'; and he is punctilious to the point of servility in his acknowledgements to people of higher social standing. John Richardson of Pitfour Castle is warmly thanked for the loan of a manuscript which was barely used. Sharpe, one of the 'many gentlemen of rank and respectability' in Edinburgh who helped, is thanked for correcting the proofs. Scott, who saw the work through the press, Percy, and his 'worthy friend' Motherwell are credited, with varying degrees of obsequiousness. Even the Mr Smith who served as a musician to the Pretender up to Culloden, and who then settled in Peterhead as a violin player, receives formal notice. Yet the men and women who took an active part in handing down songs 'by oral tradition' remain, for Buchan, unnamed and unimportant. Rankin himself is referred to obliquely in the notes, as a 'wight of Homer's craft' who chanced to learn a version of *Sir Patrick Spens* 'in his youth from a very old person'. For the rest, working people are present only as inhabitants of the 'straw thatched cottages that abound in Aberdeenshire', where Buchan pursued his 'pleasant researches' from time to time. Once they had parted with their cultural property, Buchan didn't want to know.

Chambers' idea of a 'Collected' song-book was one culled from other people's work. The 'whole mass of published ballads', done by 'recent compilers', is laid under contribution for *The Scottish Ballads*. His knowledge of older editions was evidently slight — some are mis-dated and their titles wrongly-spelled — and he was totally dependent for information on sources to mediators such as Caw, Scott, Maidment and even Cromek. His own experience of hearing songs was evidently limited. One piece he had 'heard sung by the common people'. Another he mentions as being used by 'the Highland people'. A third was said to be sung 'by nurses' in Peeblesshire, and a fourth was 'partly taken from the recitation of a lady resident at Peebles', who was perhaps his own grandmother. All the same, Chambers had no hesitation in pronouncing a Buchan text 'the least meritorious from a literary point of view', and continually stressed any novelty, however slight, in the shape of a verse or two 'here printed for the first time', whether taken from new manuscript or oral sources, sent by a Mr J H Burton of Aberdeen, picked up by the editor in broadside-form at 'a stall', or produced by Scott, Cunningham, Sharpe and others as 'Imitations of the Ancient Ballads'. The idea of naming humble singers next to literary figures and antiquarians of this standing probably never even occurred to Chambers, given the appropriation of their songs to polite literature was nearing completion. His role was to retail the best wares — old, refurbished or invented — and not to probe the culture of those working people from whom the raw materials had many of them come.

* * * * *

(iv) Their editing

Scott's editorial practices in the *Minstrelsy* were governed by his sense of *literary* value. Thus, when faced with differing copies, he 'uniformly preserved what seemed to him the best or most poetical reading of the passage', 'in justice to the author'. He rearranged what he took to be transposed rhymes, and 'restored' 'obvious corruptions', to 'fit the ballads for the press'. Texts had to conform to his idea of the 'common ballad stanza', and have the allegedly characteristic subject-matter or use of language, but he offered no serious theoretical distinctions, and even changed his mind as to what was 'Historical' and what 'Romantic' from edition to edition. He admitted to having 'restored' part of a text, made 'conjectural emendations', 'supplied' verses, 'corrected' one version from another, and 'collated' two variants according to his notions of 'merit'. Elsewhere, he noted 'many apparent corruptions', adopted 'modern spelling', and referred to a 'more correct and ancient copy'. He hinted at expurgations, and singled out other mediators' inventions by using square brackets; but his claim (in later editions) to having used 'Much information' to 'correct and enlarge' texts was not backed up with the proper citation of sources. Only one text was described as 'copied verbatim' from 'an old woman's recitation'.

Later editors have been able to pinpoint his practices because he left his manuscripts behind. Child found 'not quite forty petty alterations' in one piece, and 'numerous alterations' in another.[113] He discovered verses left out or inserted with no authority, 'many editorial improvements, besides Scotticising of the spelling', and he concluded that Scott's 'variations, the contrary not being alleged, must be supposed to be his own'.[114] Child thought *Lady Anne* was a 'modern composition', *The Young Tamlane* a 'grossly modern invention', part of *Jellon Grame* not simply 'apparently modernized' but 'modern', and sections of *Kinmont Willie* the result of a 'great deal more emendation' than was 'absolutely necessary'.[115] Even his use of Herd's MS. was 'very far from precisely accurate': 'many lines' were not to be found there, though the results were redolent of 'much good taste'![116] Not long before he died, Scott confessed privately to Motherwell:

> In fact I think I did wrong in endeavouring to make the best possible set of an ancient ballad out of several copies obtained from different quarters, and that, in many respects, if I improved the poetry, I spoiled the simplicity of the old song.[117]

Perhaps he had learned more respect for the culture he raided. Hogg's mother told him to his face:

> ye hae spoilt them awthegither. They were made for singin' an' no for readin'; but ye hae broken the charm noo, an' they'll bever [be] sung mair. An' the worst thing of a', they're nouther richt spell'd nor richt setten down.[118]

Mrs Hogg's songs never were 'sung more', and it was Scott's responsibility (in her eyes at least), however much he may have exploited her songs for the benefit of his own class's literary culture.

Jamieson originally planned to use 'interpolated stanzas written by himself, wherever he conceives the narrations defective, or the transitions abrupt, obscure, etc.', but Scott's circle found him out, advertised the proposed policy discreetly, and changed his mind.[119] Scott himself noted a text of his ready for the press 'containing some modern stanzas',[120] but in *Popular Ballads* Jamieson was able to boast that his texts were 'much more perfect' even than those of Herd, and a Mrs Brown text was given 'almost exactly' according to the manuscript. His Scots parallels of Danish pieces were said to be authentic, but few turned out to be 'beyond the possibility of suspicion'. The original of *Clerk Saunders* was never produced to allow scrutiny, while Hecht found one item published with 'arbitrary alterations' from the Herd MS., and at least one other changed even from Herd's published text.[121] Jamieson's editing followed from his theory about 'ballads' being the residue of broken-down romances, which to his mind legitimized the habit of constructing versions of his own from those got from recitation. Nobody in Scott's circle could afford to challenge another's editing practices publicly, without damaging their own credibility. So, while Jamieson admitted to collating some texts, he waxed sarcastic about other unnamed mediators' 'very considerable liberties', including his 'good countrymen who can forge with address'. Only one or two coded allusions to Scott appear, along with pious apologies for having 'studiously copied from the originals' himself, in spite of 'irregularities of measure, and inaccuracies of the rhymes'. Such studied duplicity, allied to what we know of his aims, makes his texts of doubtful value.

Cunningham may have heard 'objectionable verses' when 'the drink was abounding, the mirth loud, and the humour far from select',[122] but he and Cromek did not print them in the *Remains*. Other mediators' distortions were, however, criticized trenchantly. Ramsay is denounced for having 'trimmed' texts, and 'laced' them 'with the golden thread of metaphysic foppery, over the coarse and homely hoddingray of rural industry'. Even Scott is implicitly criticized for being one of those 'heaping on their materials a mass of extraneous lumber in the shape of facts and dates, of minute discussions and conjectural emendations'; and he and Jamieson must be meant when Mrs Brown's texts are cited as having 'all the courtly magnificence of some of your 'Falkland-bred', 'gloved-handed bards' with their 'larded' verses. Cromek and Cunningham claimed their own texts were published with 'a sole regard to fidelity and truth'; but they exempted Burns from their criticism since he 'purified and washed from their olden stains many of the exquisite of past ages', and thus legitimized their own practices. They used 'the best', taken on 'merit', from parallel texts, and collated these elements so as to approximate to what is held to be the 'perfect form'. One source, Mrs Copland, is adjudged to have the same notions of 'perfect form' as the editors, but when Cromek meets a 'deal of unseemly chaff' 'intermixed with the heavy grain', the unworthy material had to go, through the process of a 'little winnowing and sieving'. They defended the fact that some songs dealt openly with what they coyly termed the 'short arm-grips of love', but they had qualms about publishing *Lassie, lie near me*, lest unwedded bliss should be suspected!

Later editors noted a lack of squeamishness in other matters. Hogg found some 'Jacobite' pieces to be 'evidently of modern manufacture', and suspected that more than one song bore 'strong marks of the hand of the ingenious Allan Cunninghame', his friend.[123] Hecht found unacknowledged 'close coincidences' between texts in Herd's MS. and the *Remains*.[124] Dick found 'an additional stanza of palpable modern construction' which was passed off as 'old and part of the song', and believed that the whole work was a 'spurious *antique*': 'All the mischief done by "Honest Allan" as a literary forger will never be discovered.'[125] Motherwell was even harder:

> there never was, and never can be, a more bare-faced attempt to gull ignorance than what this work exhibits. It professes to give as ancient ballads and songs, things which must have been written under the nose of its Editor. It alters and disguises others ... More pretention, downright impudence, and literary falsehood, seldom or ever come into conjunction.[126]

In fact, though Cromek protested that he had been told all the songs were 'traditional',[127] Cunningham later claimed that all but two 'little scraps ... both of poetry and prose' were his own invention.[128] They invented no music because they published none.

John Bell was no poet, and wished only to keep his *Rhymes* 'free from personal allusions' to living people. He had no theoretical contribution to make, and uses terms like 'Songs', 'Ballads' and 'Poems' almost interchangeably. More importantly, he seems to have printed his texts almost exactly as he found them. For example, Ritson pieces appear with only minor changes, such as the use of 's' rather than the old style 'ſ'. Punctuation is made orthodox, abbreviations are reinstated and obvious printer's errors are corrected. Only a very occasional phoneticizing of a spelling is allowed to creep in, some italics are added, missed-out names are inserted, presentation is usually improved and a few notes are added where absolutely necessary.[129] Borrowings are acknowledged, and tunes named where they are known. Without doubt, Bell was the most reliable textual editor before Child, and he expressly questions the wisdom of other mediators' collations. The *Rhymes* can therefore be taken to contain some of the earliest reliable song-texts taken from, amongst other sources, workers' culture. It is a pity that he did not print the tunes he collected, though that task could be accomplished today. On the other hand, Bell left us an enormous mass of information relative to workers' culture which could, if fully exploited, still give us a remarkable understanding of its history, as seen from the perspective of north-east England.

Hogg confessed himself 'so little of a musician' that he could 'scarcely be said to understand the first principles of the art'. That job, for the *Relics*, was subcontracted to William Stenhouse, an Edinburgh accountant, whose scrupulousness kept Hogg in check. Both were critical of previous editors of printed collections of music:

> the modern fashion of changing the name and style of these old tunes has been the cause of much perplexity and confusion of ideas to me. I look upon this as extremely reprehensible, if not disgraceful, in the collectors of our national airs.[130]

Since Hogg knew from experience that practising country musicians had no notion of a fixed tune for a certain text, and that broadside and chapbook publishers had time out of mind affixed the title of different tunes to sets of the same words, this yearning after an 'original name' relates to that for the 'perfect form' of the text, and thus to the expectations of the mediators' prospective market, not to those of the culture from which tunes and texts came. In fact, Hogg gave his tunes 'in their most naked and primitive style', and published the 'most ancient and original one extant' whatever its quality, precisely so that they could act as 'skeletons' which could be fleshed out 'by accompaniments, and set upon proper keys' by a fashionable 'public' and their musical entertainers. His policy in editing song-texts was breathtakingly honest:

> I have in no instance puzzled myself in deciding what reading of each song is the most genuine and original, but have constantly taken the one that I thought the best; judging, that in ten instances that the song loses by abridgements and interpolations of those who sing it, for once that it is improven. For that reason, though I have often got a great many copies of the same song, I have not only always taken the best, but the best verses of each, as far as I could judge.[131]

He admits to having collated, 'patched up', and even 'made up' one text out of several, 'leaving out a number of stanzas' of what he felt was 'extraneous matter'. Occasionally, he includes a 'modern song' out of 'a whim', prints some of his own versifying, and admits to expurgation (on grounds of a text being either 'too unpolished' or simply 'rude'). He sticks more or less to a chronological arrangement. Gaelic translations he has to take on trust. Later editors have come to see the *Relics* as a 'marvellous patchwork' of texts, some of which were 'merely parody', while others owed 'most of their finest poetic qualities to Hogg himself'. This 'rustic Sir Walter Scott', while he knew workers' culture at first hand, did not deign to notice it, let alone allow its songs and music to appear unmediated.[132] Even some of his 'Scottish' tunes have been found to have earlier counterparts in manuscripts from English sources.[133]

One of the texts which Sharpe sent for the *Minstrelsy* was later suspected of having received 'some modern corrections',[134] but his *A Ballad Book* — which contains no tunes, though titles are sometimes cited — not only used items from the more erotic elements of song-culture, but does so with apparent zest and accuracy. Some texts Sharpe 'suppressed on account of their grossness', but those he prints were 'not over delicate', though he claimed that 'little will be found to corrupt the imagination, and nothing to inflame the passions'. Since the booklet was privately-printed, he was able to keep editorial interventions to a minimum; but the Scott circle seems to have demanded helpful glossings, notes, citations or variants, and a rough sort of format. Later editors have found Sharpe to have given his text 'Printed as it was Sung'. The same is true (and for the same reasons) of Maidment's *North Countrie Garland* and Kinloch's *Ballad Book*, though Child doubted some of the latter's texts, while Legman hails him as the 'most trustworthy' collector after Herd.[135] Certainly, these three men helped open up workers' erotic songs to a tiny bourgeois audience, and to this extent reversed the previous tendency to suppress that vital part of their culture.

Cunningham continued to be squeamish into the 1820s, though in *The Songs of Scotland* he recognized that post-Bowdler readers 'blush at the indelicate ballads which delighted our grandmothers' only 50 years before. He published nothing which might give 'offence against propriety and decorum'. That might be done only for 'private perusal', if the bawdy songs were to appear 'without change or augmentation'. Yet he hints obsessively about erotic originals to the texts he rewrote, at the same time as blackguarding the 'leprosy of licentiousness', and lets his readers know that Scots singers display an 'occasional trespass against outward decorum', and were capable of 'going higher kilted at times than even the tolerant may think discreet'. Contemporaries found Cunningham's 'cure' morally worse than the cause:

> to engraft on some ancient loose ditty, a modern composition which, so far as words go, offers no outrage to the delicately sensitive ear; but in its spirit and covert allusion, smacks of the elder devil which it has supplanted; and, under a veil of snowy whiteness, dallies with wantonness in clean, nice, and well-picked phrase, is positively doing more substantial harm to sound morality, than ever its rude prototype in the unvarnished grossness of its strains, could, under any circumstances, have effected.[136]

To speak plainly, Motherwell knew Cunningham to be a hypocrite, and found not one text reliable enough — even from printed sources — to reproduce in his own collection,[137] because of the 'wholesale mode of hacking, and hewing, and breaking the joints of ancient and traditionary song' which he detected.[138] Instead of the 'standard collection' which had been anticipated, albeit for 'the tastes of the many' and not 'the sober approbation of the few',[139] Motherwell looked on the four volumes as the product of 'an unholy and abhorrent lust which … ransacks the tomb, and rifles the calm beauty of the mute and unresisting dead', before tearing away 'the ancient cerements in which they were swathed, for the purpose of tricking them forth in the garish garments of the living and the walking flesh.[140] Barely two of the four volumes of *The Songs of Scotland* were full of songs from other than recent sources. There is not one tune — Cunningham blamed 'history' for that! He cared far more about the texts as *poetry*, than about songs for singing, and especially perhaps the bawdy ones, which cost him 'a labour equal to original composition' to 'restore' to their 'uncorrupted purity' and to recall 'to something like modesty and discretion'. He saw himself as a Ramsay, if not a Burns, making songs 'more pure and passable for good company'; and as for scholarship, he actually boasted he could 'cheat a whole General Assembly of Antiquarians' with his 'original manner of writing and forging ballads'.[141] Fortunately, many of the forgeries were published in more reliable versions elsewhere.

Motherwell was obsessively accurate, compared to Cunningham, and used a chronology not of texts but of sources for the structure of his *Minstrelsy*. Editorial 'liberties of the most exceptionable and flagrant description' were anathema to him by 1827, though he seems to have begun the work in Scott's fashion before he was recalled to his sense of duty by the latter's confession.[142] Motherwell insisted that every song preserved by 'oral transmission' was of 'equal authenticity', which made careful collation a regrettable necessity, since it meant 'effectually marring the venerable simplicity of early song' and conveying 'very inaccurate impressions of the state in which these compositions are actually extant among us'. Instead, he contented himself with 'selecting that one of his copies which appears the most complete and least vitiated', and then giving it 'purely and simply as he obtained it', without hazarding any emendation whatsoever. Where a text was bawdy, the reader was referred to an unexpurgated source. Yet Motherwell's editing was no innocent process: his conception of 'Narrative Ballads', and his ideas about the 'Romantick' and the 'Ancient', helped delimit the range of texts from which he could select. His contempt for the various shady practices of 'old song editors' — the hypocritical expurgators who hung onto their originals, the failed poets — did not prevent him exercising his own 'intuitive and auxiliary sense' of what was a 'genuine' 'ballad' and what a 'forgery'. Likely, this 'sense' was deduced from the texts he chose to admit, as did his ideas about the 'mechanism of the ancient ballad'. On the other hand, Motherwell took scrupulous care with his notes — tracing a day of the week back to 1282 — and noted a comprehensive list of other mediators' sins. Ramsay's 'liberties' and the 'alembic established at Abbotsford' rate less blameworthy than Percy's 'delinquencies', and Kinloch, Buchan and Ritson merit praise. Texts first published are proudly described as being 'precisely in the form in which they were remembered by the several individuals who sung or recited them'. The few tunes were 'noted down and engraved' by Mr Blaikie apparently with similar accuracy,[143] unlike those which had already appeared in print, which had 'too often passed through a process of refinement, which has militated against their individuality and primitive character'. And yet, in spite of his massive superiority as an editor, Motherwell did collate and 'amend' many of his texts, but he did so, whenever he could, 'by the assistance of other recited copies' rather than trusting to his own judgement. Of course, it was *precisely* that judgement which preferred one reading to another.

Buchan did not discriminate between 'Ballads' and 'Songs', but he complained sadly in *Ancient Ballads* about the 'mountains of difficulties' an editor had to overcome, the 'hosts of enemies he has to encounter', and the 'myriad of little-minded quibblers he has to silence'. He maintained his texts were accurate, and 'faithfully and honestly transcribed', many of them from 'the mouths of the reciters', though some were variants of texts already in print. He congratulated himself that he had been able to 'complete many of the very best pieces hitherto only found in mutilated fragments', to give 'perfect copies' resonant with 'all the characteristics of antiquity'. He noted parallel texts, where he knew of any. Items which had 'suffered greatly in the hands of ballad collectors' and editors like Burns and Cunningham are noted and condemned as being 'deprived of their original beauty ... by the too officious, and sacrilegious hands of our wise-headed modern reciters and interpolaters'. But what constitutes a 'very old' or 'genuine' piece is never spelled out, and this gave an excuse for later editors to distrust Buchan's texts for appearing to be too perfect. Later collectors attested his trustworthiness, including the bawdy items which were preserved in manuscript while they could not yet be published openly. Scott believed Buchan's texts to be genuine,[144] yet only Sharpe's consistent efforts prevented Laing from altering the texts when they were being remedied for the press. (If Laing could not '*Polish* and *condense*',[145] he did change the northern to the southern Scots vernacular.) Buchan's own few editorial interventions are certainly no worse than those of his 'worthy Friend', Motherwell,[146] and his published texts of what David Buchan terms 'transitional'[147] versions can be relied on far more than those of mediators praised by smug editors like Child, Henderson and Hecht.

Chambers' *Scottish Ballads* hardly touched on theoretical issues. Its few ideas were often based, as the editor admits, on 'conjecture instead of fact'. 'Historical' and 'Romantic' items are separated out, yet the former is admitted to overlap with the clumsy category of 'Ballads supposed to refer to real circumstances in Private Life'. 'Imitations of the Ancient Ballads' is a logical enough category, and refers to the source of such items, whereas the other three categories are concerned with content, itself predetermined by the processes of selection from what Chambers understood to be 'the best' of 'the diffused merit of so many different and expensive books':

> by a more daring exertion of taste, I have, in a great many instances, associated what seemed to me the best stanzas, and the best lines, nay even the best words, of the various copies extant; thus producing something considerably different, it is true, from what is to be found in any particular part of the country, and therefore not correctly a representation of the condition of Scottish ballad poetry anywhere.[148]

Though 'deprecated by the antiquary', this process is deemed 'unquestionably better, at least in a literary point of view' in spite of the fact that Chambers' reliance on the editorial practices of other mediators means that in many cases he was compounding the acts of commission and omission they perpetrated, in the name of 'purifying' for the 'public'. The very first song is a composite from Herd's text and four others. Buchan's texts are downgraded because of the lack of 'literary' quality, while Scott's and even Cromek's versions are preferred. Verses are composed by the editor to 'connect' the 'disjointed portions' of a story cobbled together from three disparate sources. Tunes are never printed, and rarely referred to. Notes are relatively sparse and often lifted verbatim from Scott; and, in general, this mediation of others' mediating represents a wholly unreliable source for understanding the song-culture it seeks to exploit.[149]

* * * * *

With the exception of John Bell, the song-mediators in this period were remarkable for their reactionary political and cultural beliefs, and they were most of them prepared to go to considerable lengths not only to expropriate workers' culture, but to alter what they found so as to fit their own class-based preconceptions, prejudices and needs. On the other hand, we have to acknowledge that, through the work of John Bell and William Motherwell, the scholarly standards set by Ritson were not only continued, but in some ways improved upon. Bell, especially, was keen to get everything he could find, from the widest range of sources, and then to put what he found into print. He left enough material for another volume unpublished, because he could not afford to print it privately. However, even the most manipulative and shady mediators and pretentious poets managed to record and to transmit some aspects of workers' culture with apparent accuracy. And though not one of their books was free of internal contradictions, sometimes massive ones, taken as a whole these collections represent a positive gain for our own understanding of workers' culture — the very culture against which Scott, Motherwell and their associates reacted so violently, as it became ever more obviously the culture of the emergent working class. Opportunism played its part, as well as Romantic mysticism and idealism. Cromek and Chambers saw the way to make a few hundred pounds profit, both in the literary-antiquarian market, and also with commercial products aimed, now, at the increasingly literate working class, and the aspiring petty-bourgeoisie. Not only could song-books of material deriving (some of it) from workers' culture be treated as a commodity, but wholesaling was now possible too. What is particularly interesting, however, is the way in which in order to try to escape from giving a representative selection from the song-culture of the real people of their own day, many of these mediators set about constructing an 'alternative' 'people'. The 'peasantry' could then be offered as the legitimate inheritors of 'national' cultures which had once been, allegedly, much more homogeneous. Instead of coping with the realities of a *class* society, Scott and his coadjutors — and the considerable bourgeois market for literary products of the kind he and they produced — tried to immerse themselves in a much more straightforward past. Their problem was that not only did their 'past' never exist, but that the working-class they hated and feared refused to accept its previous servile status, to sing to their masters' tune.

4   From Thomas Wright to John Harland

English and Scots working class people did not go away after 1830. Instead, they began to organize themselves very effectively, first at a trade union and then at a political level. It would be difficult to overestimate the extent to which the British ruling class and the entire bourgeoisie were *terrified* by Chartism. Until 1832, it had been possible for the progressive bourgeoisie to maintain something like a united front with the leadership of unions and the various political organizations which had a substantial working-class membership. But once the Reform settlement was found out to be little more than a fraud, from the workers' point of view, the issue of separate political organization came more urgently onto the agenda. Of course, workers' consciousness develops unevenly under capitalism, so there were problems in achieving a national working-class political organization capable of taking on the ruling class. 'Moral Force' and 'Physical Force' Chartists demanded radically different tactics. Religion, craft trade unionism and sectionalism of all kinds helped to keep workers apart, then as now; and while workers had their own newspapers, clubs, societies, unions and so on, capital survived the crisis of the later 1830s and 1840s, and the Year of Revolutions in Europe left Britain comparatively unscathed. The skilled workers in the workshop of the world even went on to begin to enjoy a modest share of the fruits of Imperialism, and this led to the development of forms of working-class nationalism. Of course, this was an extremely contradictory and complex process; and, as ever, combined and uneven development played a crucial role. What was clear, however, was that there was an enormous working class market for cultural products as for every other commodity, and entrepreneurs were not slow to identify it and to seek to exploit it. There was obviously no way in which a person with the leisure and the inclination to collect and publish workers songs could offer what they found as the basis of any future national song-culture. By and large, the bourgeoisie had their own identifiable musical culture. By the 1850s and 1860s, the concert hall and then the music-hall developed into a key element in the culture of the urban petty-bourgeoisie, and of a sizeable section of better-off workers.

Only a died-in-the-wool antiquarian, and preferably one imbued with Romanticism, would want to gather songs from country workers now.

* * * * *

(i) The people

John Broadwood[1] was born in 1798, the son of James Shudi Broadwood, High Sheriff of Surrey, and grandson of the founder of the firm of Broadwood & Sons, pianoforte manufacturers. In 1799, the family acquired a thirteenth century 'seat' at Lyne, on the Sussex-Surrey border, where the father acted out the role of a benevolent landowner, with a fondness for bell-ringers. Though there is no account of John's childhood or education he took orders for the Church of England, and seems never to have needed to earn his living, even as a priest. Robert Bell was born in 1800 at Cork, where his father was a magistrate. Robert had schooling enough to be able to enter Trinity College, Dublin, and in 1828 he moved to London, where he earned a living with his pen. James Henry Dixon[2] was born in London in 1803, but went to Skipton Grammar School in Yorkshire, and was an articled clerk to a firm of Durham solicitors, before settling down in his profession at Grassington in Yorkshire, and then at Hornsey in Middlesex in the early 1840s. John Harland[3] was the son of a Hull watchmaker and jeweller, and was born in Hull in 1806. When he was 14, he was apprenticed to the trade of printing at the *Hull Packet* newspaper, but 'rose' to become a reader, and then a reporter. In 1830, he was employed by the *Manchester Guardian*, moved to Lancashire, and eventually became a partner. William Chappell[4] was born in London in 1809. His father owned a fashionable song- and music-publishing business which William managed for nine years on behalf of his mother, before his first retirement in 1843, at the age of 34. Two years later he bought a share in a similar firm, then retired altogether in 1861. Thomas Wright's[5] father came from a Bradford broadcloth manufacturing family, but moved to Tenbury in Shropshire and struggled to make a living as a bookseller and printer. Thomas was born in 1810, went to King Edward's Grammar School at Ludlow, and then on to Cambridge. For the next 40 years he made a bare living with his scholarship and his pen. James Halliwell (later Halliwell-Phillips)[6] one of Wright's patrons, was born in Chelsea, London, in 1820. His father came from Lancashire to the capital and prospered in business. James went to private schools, and then up to Cambridge, where he could afford to ignore 'ordinary academic studies' and to concentrate on his literary and antiquarian pursuits, which he did for the rest of his life, especially after 1867 when he inherited his late wife's name and fortune. These men's material security is clear enough (with the exception of Wright, to some extent), and all had adequate leisure-time for literary and antiquarian pursuits. Indeed, such interests sometimes became a full-time occupation for them, or a significant element in their way of making a living for those who had to do so. Why did they interest themselves in songs?

* * *

Wright's career at Cambridge — where he met Halliwell — was partly subsidized by a history book which he wrote for a London publisher, and his later life in London was sustained by fees from the three works a year he published on average for 40 years. There were few full-time university posts available to a man of such modest background and connections, so he relied substantially on the sponsorship of a range of learned societies set up by the literary and antiquarian members of the capital's bourgeoisie. (These institutions were established or revived during the Chartist years of the late 1830s and 1840s as part of a search for a unifying 'national' cultural heritage in the face of an obvious political polarization.) He got involved with Early English and Latin manuscripts, produced volumes on poetry and song from the period *before* the Civil War, produced at least one work for Bohn's Library — a commercial series — and cultivated wealthy patrons amongst his acquaintances, which included the members of the London Society of Antiquaries, and individuals like Chappell and Halliwell. In 1865 he was awarded a meagre Civil List pension of £65 a year, which was raised to £100 in 1872, but his health gave way under the stress of making a poor living in this fashion. Halliwell-Phillips (as he had become) helped his colleague with a dole during his last years, but Wright died in 'imbecility' in 1877.

By contrast, we know very little about Broadwood, precisely because what was to Wright a living was to him a hobby. Broadwood married in 1825, and between 1841 and 1847 he lived by the sea at Worthing, where he acted as Warden to the Chapel of Ease. There he met G.A. Dusart, who harmonized the songs he collected. Broadwood moved to Wigginholt in 1848, and by 1851, he was resident squire at Lyne, succeeding his father who died that year. In 1854, he and his three brothers rebuilt the nearby Rusper church in memory of their father, and though the living was in the gift of John's wife's aunt, he seems not to have wanted to do the job, preferring instead his activities as a member of the Sussex Archaeological Society, Trustee of the Newdigate village school and self-styled 'Clerk and Landowner', up to his death in 1864. Dixon was given the job of editing several volumes of poetry and song for the Percy Society in the 1840s, and in later life produced a 'chatty volume of antiquarian stories and historical sketches, embracing a number of his charming verses.' But though he was awarded the degree of LL.D., contributed bits and pieces to antiquarian compilations and was wealthy enough to go to Lausanne (where he died in 1876), his life remains remarkably obscure.

Halliwell is somewhat better-known, but was equally as secure, materially. He was elected fellow of the London Society of Antiquaries and the Royal Society in 1839, at the age of 18, and by 1840 he described himself as a member of the Astronomical Society, and of ten antiquarian societies in Europe and America. In 1840 he projected the Cambridge Antiquarian Society, and became its first Secretary, but he left Cambridge without a degree and settled in London, living off his father. He used his leisure in making books — he prepared ten for the press in 1840, and a further 13 in 1841, including one for the Percy Society — and by collecting early manuscripts. His book on *The Nursery Rhymes of England*, 'collected principally from oral tradition', was 'met at once with popular success' when it appeared in 1842. His work for the Shakespeare Society (founded in 1841) and for a journal he edited with Thomas Wright, *The Archaeologist*, brought him to the attention of leading antiquarians, including Sir Thomas Phillips, whose daughter Halliwell married in 1842, in spite of her father's opposition. The couple lived with his father in London, and then moved to Islip, Oxfordshire. In 1844, a scandal over a set of manuscripts bought by the British Museum led to Halliwell's being barred from that institution — not a small matter when he was in 'straitened circumstances' for a man of his background — because they had passed through his hands on their way from Trinity College Library, Cambridge. Writs flew, but Halliwell was let off the hook, and the profits of his dealings in old manuscripts and whatever he got from his father seem to have been enough to keep him afloat, and to allow him to publish catalogues of his possessions. In the early 1850s he moved to Brixton Hill, nearer London, and then to West Brompton. With Wright and Robert Bell, he started a publishing society, the Wharton Club, in 1855, but the project failed, and he lived by selling his manuscripts at enormous profits until his wife's inheritance made him totally independent in 1867. When she became seriously ill, Halliwell assumed her name by royal letters patent, took over the management of her estates in Worcestershire, and built himself a strange bungalow at Brighton. For the rest of his life he bought rare manuscripts, gave away his various private publications to fellow enthusiasts, planned to leave his valuable collection to various academic institutions in Britain and the United States, and was granted the honorary degree of LL.D by Edinburgh University in 1883. He died in 1889, an orthodox and rich Christian.

Chappell became a fellow of the London Society of Antiquaries in 1840, helped to found the Percy Society in 1841, and projected the Musical Antiquaries Society that same year. He also became treasurer of both the Camden Society (founded in 1838) and the Ballad Society, and ended up as vice-president of the Musical Association in 1874. Both as a young man of independent means, and in the 27 years of his second retirement, he combined his friendship with gentry and nobility — Queen Victoria was one of his shop's customers — with that of full-time professional musical academics and scholars. These included the child prodigy, William Crotch,[7] who went to Percy's, Surtees' and Sharpe's old college, Christ Church, Oxford, and became Principal of the Royal Academy of Music in 1822; George Macfarren,[8] who went on from Cambridge to be first a professor and then Principal of the Royal

Academy, and Edward Rimbault,[9] who turned down the chair of music at Harvard. Macfarren and Crotch helped him produce *A Collection of National English Airs*, 'consisting of Ancient Song, Ballad, and Dance Tunes', which was published in 1838, but their harmonies were either too elaborate or barely adequate.[10] However, Chappell was well placed to discover how at least metropolitan bourgeois musical taste was moving during the 1840s and 1850s, by what was selling at the New Bond Street shop, and he was also able to get access to 'new' musical material through his antiquarian, academic and society connections. Thus, while the publication of his major musical work still needed the financial security given by a subscription list, that list shows how the market for such a work had shifted since Thomson's *Orpheus*.[11] True, there is still an occasional Earl, Lord and Right Honourable, but they are vastly outnumbered by Esquires, Misses and a large number of church organists and professional music-teachers not only from Britain, but even from the colonies and dominions. Chappell's fervent English nationalism — he is said to have been provoked into publication by a Scotsman who worked in his shop, who 'frequently boasted' of Scottish music, and 'sneered' at the English equivalent as 'non-existent or unimportant'[12] — clearly fitted very well with that of the increasing number of people whose prosperity was bound up with the growing Empire, or whose livelihood depended on being professional ideologues and cultural practitioners in the 'colonies' of working-class England. Home or abroad, these people's job was to perpetuate ideas about 'national' unity from key positions in churches, schools or universities, in the face of working-class restiveness at home or commercial and political competition overseas. Chappell provided some of the cultural ammunition.

Robert Bell had put his pen at the service of the British state even before he left Ireland. In Dublin he edited a government-controlled newspaper, and helped in the general cultural and political offensive against Irish nationalism by organizing the Dublin Historical Society, which sought to take the place of an institution of that kind which had been officially suppressed. In London he exploited his proven loyalty to those in power and his journalistic contacts. He made a living as a freelance journalist and as an editor of 'popular' biographies of eminent people for the developing petty-bourgeois market, and he produced editions of plays, novels and miscellanies. Later, he edited the *Monthly Chronicle*, and then *Home News*, a periodical which was aimed specifically at the Indian and Far Eastern parts of the Empire. He dabbled in spiritualism for a while; but material pressures encouraged him to project a series of 24 volumes of an 'Annotated Edition' of the bourgeois-approved 'English Poets', designed for the aspiring 'Student of our National Literature', and modestly priced at half a crown apiece. Two of these volumes dealt with songs, and were produced with the cooperation of Dixon — and, possibly, Wright and Halliwell. This, and his literary and political connections, helped Bell to a seat on the committee which allocated state patronage to suitably deserving literary figures, under the title of the Royal Literary Fund; and there he came into contact with eminent literary people like the novelists Thackeray and Bulwer Lytton. So, though the making of song-books was not a major source of Bell's economic activity, it gave him — just like Robert Chambers, who also had a hand in the Fund — a handy legitimization over and above his journalism in literary circles, which helped sustain him until his death in 1867.

John Harland began to record tales and ballads, customs and beliefs in his adopted county of Lancashire during the 1830s and 1840s, perhaps using the refined shorthand which helped to get him his job. In his spare time he read the growing number of publications, in English and German, of the subject which after Thoms' *Athenaum* article of 1846 was known as 'folk-lore'.[13] He could not afford private publication, but he used features in the *Manchester Guardian* to investigate local history, was elected a member of the Historic Society in 1849, and edited documents for the local Chetham Society. He contributed brief items to *Notes and Queries*, Thoms' 'folk-lore' journal, during the 1850s, and eventually became not only a Fellow of the Society of Antiquaries but a Council member of the Chetham Society. He was also the secretary of the Manchester Rosicrucians, 'a society that did much to elucidate local history and antiquities'.[14] These connections gave him access to the work of men like Halliwell, Wright, and his collaborator Thomas Turner Wilkinson of Blackburn. Harland used his retirement after 1860 exclusively for scholarly projects, in imitation of pioneer 'regional' 'folk-lore' work produced by Richardson for the north-east counties in the 1840s, Sternberg for Northamptonshire in 1850,[16] and Halliwell's *Yorkshire Anthology*[17] of songs of 1851. After Harland's death in 1868, Wilkinson helped revise and publish the fruits of his and their labours. This 'sincere and single-minded Christian gentleman', who had been born a Churchman but became a Unitarian by conviction, was proud of the letters F.S.A. after his name, and helped link the work of Grimm and Scott not only to the Folk-Lore Society of 1876, but also to the late nineteenth century collections of 'county' songs which were later characterized as works on 'folk song'.

* * * * *

(ii) Their aims

Wright's 1839 edition of *The Political Songs of England, from the reign of John to that of Edward II* was the sixth publication of the Camden Society, founded the year before in London by members of the Society of Antiquaries. These members of the nobility and gentry, and amateur and professional scholars with historical interests, provided Wright's book with a ready-made audience. He did not have to cope with market considerations, so his definition of what constituted the 'political' is, like

Scott's,[18] notably crude. Politics was what was done by kings, knightly warriors and churchmen of high rank, while the extremely nebulous 'people' stand in the wings, or are visible in the distance on a battlefield, suffering the consequences of others' decisions and actions. More often, the individual people are absent, but the 'popular' is invoked to modify words such as outcry, party, declaration, cause, discontent, dissatisfaction or heroes, and its opposite, 'unpopular', is used with equal arbitrariness. The 'people' — sometimes, 'The English' — are characterized rather vaguely as 'the English peasantry', 'the middle or lower ranks', or 'the poor', in contrast to 'the rich'. This lack of theoretical and historical clarity disappears, however, when Wright wishes to distinguish what he terms the 'minstrels' and the poets who he believed made the songs he prints, from the working people who may have listened to them, or found them in manuscript form on 'the high road'. What Wright wanted was to hang on to the legitimacy of invoking the 'people' while discounting the merely 'popular', and to privilege the role of the artist over that of the audience, by assuming that those songs which he took to be the 'monuments of popular feeling' were produced on behalf of the 'oppressed people' by persons who just happened to write and sing in a foreign language. This passive role for most English people, who needed others to channel 'popular opinion' and give it 'vent', contradicts Wright's statement that 'the commons of England began to assume a more active part on the stage of history' at the start of the thirteenth-century. It is interesting that the historical period he chooses to cover ends at the Wars of the Roses, immediately before the Reformation put an end to what he terms 'barbarism'. Given his captive readership, his dependence on patronage, his essentially craft-worker's role, and the fact that this book was produced by Wright during the major upheavals of Chartism, it seems likely that the political settlement with the British bourgeoisie and part of the petty-bourgeoisie which took place in 1832 and 1835 (and excluded the overwhelming majority of the population) encouraged the likes of the Camden Society and its cultural artisans to consider the past more carefully. The political 'Reformation' of 1832 had not ended a period of working-class 'barbarism', but had accentuated the struggle, as the Chartist movement split into Physical and Moral Force factions, both of which were united on the issue of the moral bankruptcy of the British ruling class.

Broadwood's *Old English Songs* was published in 1843 in London 'for private Circulation', and had what was virtually a short essay for its title page. Dusart is credited with having all 16 songs 'Harmonized for the Collector', whose name does not appear; but it was probably Broadwood who claimed that the pieces were published

> as now Sung by the Peasantry of the Weald of Surrey and Sussex, and collected by one who has learnt them by hearing them Sung every Christmas from early Childhood, by The Country People, who go about

to the Neighbouring Houses, Singing, "Wassailing" as it is called, at that Season. The Airs are set to Music exactly as they are now Sung, to rescue them from oblivion, and to afford a specimen of genuine Old English Melody: and the words are given in their original rough state, with an occasional slight alteration to render the sense intelligible.[19]

Though Broadwood was credited with having produced one of the first collections of 'folksong airs for their own sake',[20] and an article in a recent 'journal of socialist historians' pronounces his slim book the 'earliest collection of folk songs in England',[21] this choosing of 'folksong' ancestors tells us more about the Folksong Revival in this century than about what Broadwood aimed to do. As Gammon notes, the compound 'folk-song' was not used before 1870 in England, and 'did not become common usage until the 1880s'.[22] Evidently, Broadwood sang the songs at home 'exactly as the smocked labourers sang', and was received with 'polite boredom'[23] by his friends and relations, who probably went away giggling at his eccentricity. The truth is that Broadwood would not have heard these songs had there not been a precise set of class-based social relationships involved in the cash-raising activity of Wassailing, since not every one of the 'Neighbouring Houses' would contain a person of private means with a strong sense of English nationalism and an interest in antiquities. He referred to the singers with class-bound condescension as memebers of the 'Peasantry'. In fact, the appearance (and the ideology implicit in) Broadwood's little publication were remarkably similar to the production of his contemporary, Dixon.

Dixon did not have to resort to private publication, since the market for literary-antiquarianism had, by the 1840s, become institutionalized, in London at any rate, and thus shielded editors of songs from the sharpening commercial pressures to which Chambers and Chappell had to adapt. The Percy Society took on responsibility for publication of 'British' songs between 1840 and 1852, sponsoring Dixon's *Scottish Traditional Versions of Ancient Ballads* in 1845, and his *Ancient Poems, Ballads, and Songs of the Peasantry of England* in 1846. Five of the Percy Society Council members of 1845 had been on the Council of the Camden Society in 1839, so this was an extremely small coterie. Dixon's ability to concentrate on what he took to be 'genuine traditionary relics'[24] did not jar with his belief, following Motherwell,[25] that authenticity was underwritten by texts being in the language 'as it is spoken at present',[26] that is, the 'dialect of a particular district, or, to speak more correctly, in the ancient language of the country'.[26] Following Cunningham,[27] Dixon credited country workers with having their own 'minstrels', a 'class of men' he knew to be 'still in existence, pursuing their calling, who are the regular descendants and representatives of the minstrels of old';[28]

In his rambles amongst the hills of the North, and especially in the wild and romantic dales of Yorkshire, the editor has met with several of these characters — they are not idle vagabonds who have no other calling, but, in general, are honest and industrious though poor men, having a "local habitation" as well as a "name", and engaged in some calling, pastoral and manual. It is only at certain periods, such as Christmas, or some other of the great festal seasons of the ancient Church, that they take up the minstrel life, and levy contributions in the hall of the peer or squire, and in the cottage of the farmer or peasant. They are in general well-behaved, and often very witty fellows, and therefore their visits are always welcome.[29]

In spite of his patronizing tone, Dixon recognized the independent existence of country-based worker-singers and musicians, with their own repertoires: they 'do not sing modern songs, but, like their brethren of a by-gone age, they keep to the ballads'.[30] Yet Dixon's own cultural perspective made parts of this culture opaque. He could not understand why performers held each other in contempt, and why they stuck to a given 'walk' or district,[31] because he ignored the importance of the marginal income such work represented. Moreover, he seems to have swallowed the singers' propaganda whole, when it fitted *his* view of history:

> these singers will tell you that they are the grandsons and great-grandsons of minstrels, and that they sing the ballads as they have come down to them from their illustrious progenitors.[32]

No doubt some of these people really were the descendants of gypsy-entertainers; but it is difficult not to suspect that Dixon's own ideas about culture were imposed onto the country culture he saw from outside, perhaps with the calculating cooperation of the performers themselves.

When Dixon does not like a given text he labels it as deriving from commercially-oriented print. One broadside is said to have been 'made from the oral recitation of some ignorant minstrel'.[33] He also believed that all songs 'suffered by oral transmission', when they were 'orally handed down'.[34] On occasion, the process of transmission is removed even from the anachronistic category of the 'peasantry',[35] and placed in a totally unhistorical 'stream of time' where their quality is somehow 'corrupted' by persons unknown.[36] In the end, Dixon had no qualms in arrogating to himself the role of quality controller for his colleagues in the Society, pronouncing contemporary texts and tunes 'very popular'[37] or even 'common'[38] and offering to differentiate between 'very unequal'[39] texts and parts of texts. This is the less surprising when we note that he was doing precisely the same in his *Ancient Ballads*, which separate out tracts of the 'West-country', the 'Northern Dales' of Cumbria and Yorkshire, and some other 'rural districts' where the genteel traveller might yet — even in the mid-1840s — light upon a 'peasantry' whose culture was assumed to be not only different from that of 'the masses' of the towns and industrial districts, but essentially *separate* from it. This 'peasantry', though it might take up 'popular modern compositions' would do so only for a while, before going back to their 'antiquated favourites', which it was the task of the 'antiquarian world' to preserve from the dangers of contemporary workers' 'Utilitarian spirit' and 'cold Saducean philosophy'.[40] Thus, while he highlighted the vitality of aspects of country workers' musical culture, his professed ability to distinguish 'ancient' originals from more recent 'traditional' versions fitted in with his framework of bourgeois literary and antiquarian values. He understood that there was, however regrettably, a two-way relationship between country and town-workers' culture, and between oral and printed texts. Contradictorily, though he took his ideas and values to workers' culture, and sought to legitimize them, Dixon helped open up that culture to more systematic study at a county level by later generations of song-collectors.

The song-collections which appeared during the 1850s and contain some songs from workers' culture illustrate some of the problems of publication, once the learned societies had declined. Patronage or commerce beckoned. Halliwell published *The Yorkshire Anthology*, 'A Collection of Ancient and Modern Ballads, Poems and Songs, Relating to the County of Yorkshire' in London in 1851, 'for Private Circulation only'. It was dedicated to Lord Londesborough, 'As a Slight Testimony of Gratitude for Many Considerate Kindnesses', while the 'Distribution of Copies' included the Duke of Buccleuch, a couple of Lords, two Subscription Libraries, and around 20 gentlefolk, including a few vicars and one woman. In attempting to do for a county, however large, what had formerly been done for regions or whole nations, Halliwell suffered the usual problems faced by pioneers. Robert Bell, on the other hand, used the legitimacy of his series to issue *Early Ballads illustrative of History Traditions and Customs* and *Ancient Poems, Ballads and Songs of the Peasantry of England*, 'taken down from oral recitation and transcribed from private manuscripts, rare broadsides and scarce publications. Both were published in London, in 1856 and 1857 respectively. Not only had Dixon road-tested most of both products in the previous decade, but Bell was also well-placed to benefit from the decline of society publishing, and from the reviving interest in English (as opposed to British) 'national' culture. That stress on 'oral' culture even caught the modern trend towards exploiting material still sung (and out of copyright) by working-class people who chanced to live in the countryside.

Chappell's *The Ballad Literature and Popular Music of the Old Time* of 1855-9 was not only an updated version of his *Collection of National English Airs*, but was specifically designed to counter the claim that the English had no 'national music'. Curiously, the 1838-40 work had relied heavily on the Oxford lectures of William Crotch, themselves based on the song-collecting work of Malchair, a Music Room band leader of the 1760s;[42] but for the new publication Chappell could rely on the custom of the clientele at his up-market London shop. He was profoundly suspicious of any song-mediator who denied the existence of English 'national' music, or who sought to lay claim for Scotland to material which Chappell had found in an English context. He produced what he believed was 'A History of Ancient Songs, Ballads and Dance Tunes of England', but he evidently felt the time for collecting new material from oral sources had almost passed. He also suspected 'tradition' — 'I confess to small faith in anything of the kind'[43] — and above all in its commercial, broadside manifestation. He had been 'informed that they are frequently reprinted from the dictation of ballad-singers, who require a supply for sale', and so can be labelled 'very corrupt'.[44] What little he knew of workers' culture, first-hand, he systematically downgrades; and he was keen to increase the 'English' component in 'British' musical culture in relation to that of the Scots,[45] and thereby preparing the musical (and, in part, the literary) briefing he felt to be necessary for parsons and schoolteachers who wished to insert bourgeois values in the form of song into the working-class culture of mid-Victorian Britain and its Empire.

John Harland published his *Ballads & Songs of Lancashire Chiefly Older than the 19th Century* in London in 1865, as 'Collected, Compiled, and Edited, with Notes by a Fellow of the London Society of Antiquaries'. This product of a Yorkshireman was printed at Edinburgh, and his aim of wishing to 'collect and perpetuate the fleeting, because oral, ballads and songs' of his adopted county, and those of the 'other five northern counties', has about it something of John Bell's earlier project. But whereas commercial publications of locally-made songs had been shown to be possible, in the north-east, for half a century, culminating in Thomas Allan's *Tyneside Songs*[46] of 1862, Harland's project could rely on a reservoir of material which had yet to find its way into the antiquarians' note-book or the commercial publishers' broadsides or song-books. Poems and songs, sometimes written in the 'dialect', had been the recipients of noble and bourgeois patronage for decades in certain parts of England. Stephen Duck,[47] the 'thresher poet' of Wiltshire had been patronized in the 1720s: Thomas Whittell, the Northumberland freemason-poet, had written for north-eastern merchants and gentry in the same period, and had his work published eventually;[48] Anne Yearsley[49] and J. F. Bryant[50] had received attention in the Bristol of the 1780s, and John Clare[51] had been recognized in Northamptonshire after the 1810s. But these were the exceptions. What Harland did, whether it was his intention or not, was to provide Lancashire writers with an anthology of locally-used if not always locally-made song and verse to serve both as a model and an inspiration; and as the successive editions of his work came out, after his death, in 1875 and 1882, they got larger and larger. English 'regional' culture and above all regional patriotism were clearly supported by his book of songs, and, in turn, those with an interest in 'regional' affairs bought out the three editions.

* * * * *

(iii) Their sources

The 'greater part' of Wright's *Political Songs* had necessarily to be 'printed from unique copies', given its aims and its antiquarian-scholarly readership. Wright points out that these 'copies' were the products of early English antiquaries who acted as 'clerk' to the nobility or gentry, or of the 'minstrel' who used the small rolls of parchment in entertaining that same stratum of society. Such people understood Latin or the Courtier's Anglo-Norman. They were the 'scholastic part of the people' as opposed to the majority 'with their good old English'; so it was futile, Wright believed, to expect such songs to exist in 'people's memory' over centuries if they were not retained there in the first place. In a way, Wright's collecting mirrored the practices of the clerkly antiquaries who committed the songs (for whatever motive) to writing. He successfully sought the Auchinleck MS. from the Advocates' Library in Edinburgh, had the cooperation of a surviving member of Scott's circle, David Laing, and even had contact with M. D'Avezac in Paris, from whom he got copies of material in Royal Library manuscripts and rare printed books. In England, Wright used his academic and antiquarian contacts to the full — people like Sir Frederick Madden, John Gough Nichols and his patron-to-be, James Orchard Halliwell. The Council and members of the newly-formed Camden Society no doubt helped him gain access to Clare College Library, the Bodleian, Cambridge 'Public Library', the British Museum, Trinity College Library and even Leyden Public Library, and to some private libraries and collections. Wright was able to use the Harleian MS., Cotton MS., Rawlinson MS. and Sloan MS., to accrete material from authorities like Percy and Ritson around this solid scholarly core, and to make reference to equally worthy publications produced by and for the Camden Society itself. What Wright's book signalled, then, was not only the earliest phase of the academic annexation of elements of British song-culture (and the consequent improvement in scholarly research), but also the conscious break with the culture of working people in past time, through the limitation of sources, and in his own day, even as potential sources, *by definition*.

Broadwood's sources may well have been 'Country People': he is usually credited with having 'noted down the songs and tunes traditionally sung by farm hands and others at harvest homes and similar rustic festivities in Sussex and Surrey'.[51] The Rev. John is also said to have had an accurate ear, but he chose to rely on the local village organist — probably Dusart — to write down the tunes just as they were sung, in spite of the professional musician's protests that a given detail 'can't be right, sir'.[52] Given the relationship between them — Broadwood appeared in the 'Gentry' in the local Directory, but Dusart, as a 'professor of music', was listed under 'Traders'[53] — the 'Gentry' prevailed, and appeared (albeit anonymously in print) as sole 'Collector'. At least Broadwood was *present* when the songs were sung. Dixon's *Scottish Traditional Versions of Ancient Ballads* was based on the use of Peter Buchan's collection, which had been on approval at the Percy Society since 1843. In 1844 £10 changed hands for the privilege of making a 'selection' — Buchan claimed the manuscript had cost him £350 all told![54] According to Dixon, the texts he published had been 'taken down' by Buchan, 'solely for the amusement of the transcriber', 'from the oral recitation of the peasantry' of Aberdeenshire and Banffshire, a district 'comparatively fresh and untrod by ballad gatherers'. Yet the greater part of the 'ballad' texts had been published by Buchan in 1828, 17 years before.[55] Either Dixon and the Society were remarkably careless, or Buchan was crafty. Perhaps neither party cared a great deal; but it took the threat of legal action to get the original manuscript back into Buchan's hands in 1847.[56] Unpublished manuscript material, or even scarce publications, had achieved an increased value as commodities because they were thought to be a finite source of raw material for 'new' song-books. When it came to selection, Dixon was little different from his predecessors, preferring manuscript authority to that of a singer, as a rule, but using an 'oral version' as a touchstone of authenticity for a 'genuine relic of antiquity' when it suited his purpose. He fell back on previously-printed song-books (to which he had adequate access) from time to time.

For his *Ancient Poems*, however, the scarcity of unpublished manuscript material seems to have encouraged Dixon to concentrate on the culture of the 'Peasantry of England', and to use items 'taken down from oral recitation' as well as those 'transcribed from private manuscripts, rare broadsides and scarce publications'. Some 'minstrel lays' he got himself, but others came from contacts in the Antiquaries, the Camden Society and the Percy Society — people like Chappell, Wright, Rimbault, William Sandys, Crofton Croker and W.H. Ainsworth. These genteel individuals are thanked with conspicuous politeness in the Preface, but 'several correspondents moving in a humbler sphere' are often mentioned only in the notes, including not only Davies Gilbert and Thomas Lyle, who had published *Christmas Carols*[57] and *Ancient Ballads and Songs*[58] in the 1820s, but also the 'peasant' poet John Clare, the Border poet James Telfer, and the Newcastle antiquarian, bibliophile and minor poet, Robert White, for whom Telfer and his brother had collected songs.[59] Like Percy before him,[60] Dixon was glad of the services of a contemporary broadside-printer, Mr Swindells of Manchester; and he had no scruples about using seventeenth century (or even modern) broadsides, chapbooks and song-books.

For at least four of his orally-collected texts, Dixon relied on William Sandys, editor of a book of west-country *Christmas Carols*,[61] and a man who associated himself with Dixon's growing interest in people the 'blind old fiddler', the 'leader of a parish choir', and the anonymous 'country people' of the county of Somerset. Dixon had occasionally collected material from events such as the harvest-home feast at Selbourne in Hampshire, where two 'country-men' recited a dialogue-style poem; and he seems to have had some acquaintance with the culture of the people he saw as 'the peasants of Devonshire', though perhaps largely through printed texts. In Skipton, Yorkshire, he collected from Francis King, who was locally famous as the 'Skipton Minstrel' and who died in 1844. King's fame rested on his skills as an entertainer, and he used mime, jokes, the composing and playing of dance tunes, and the singing of 'older songs and ballads' to this end. To Dixon, this was enough to make this 'eccentric character' and his texts and tunes 'traditional'; but the 'aged female in Bermondsey, Surrey', from whose 'oral recitation' he took one text is not accorded 'minstrel' status, any more than his aged and respected friend, Tommy Atkinson of Linton in Craven, a 'genuine Yorkshire yeoman', who was known for his 'excellent and humorous singing', but who insisted that he be not described as Esquire or Mr. Elsewhere, Dixon is extremely vague in his location of texts, noting that a piece is 'very popular on the border, and in the dales of Cumberland, Westmoreland and Craven', or linking a text to a given kind of occasion, such as the country merry-makings and feasts at which *John Barleycorn* is said to be sung. Certainly, he had access to such occasions, like the Craven churn suppers he attended, but he went along with the masters and not the employees.

His correspondents had similar forms of access. Sandys could give a first-hand account of Furry-day celebrations at Helstone in Cornwall, and of the fishermen's dances on Midsummer-eve at Penzance; while Mr Holmes, the Grassington surgeon, could collect the text and the major actions of a 'troop of rustic practitioners' of the sword-dance in Craven. Dixon knew the 'pace-egg' drama through the mediation of a young besom-maker, and collected at least one song from Willy Bolton, 'an old Dales'-minstrel, who accompanied himself on the union-pipes'. His brother sent him material from Seaton Carew in Durham. Dixon himself recollected a piece he had heard in his youth amongst 'aged people resident in the North of England', and recalls with pleasure how he found half a dozen New Forest charcoal-burners singing in a small inn, when he was 'tired with pedestrianing' on a sultry summer's day. Therefore, while he continued to trust some song-mediators implicitly, his knowledge of country song-culture made him distrust others, and to rate them less reliable than a 'modern broadside, or even ... a traditional version'. Dixon seems to have made some effort to cultivate his connections as a solicitor with well-to-do farmers, professional people and gentry but, like Broadwood, his relationships with those people ensured that what he was shown was workers' culture on high days and holidays. He understood the importance of broadside and chapbook texts, knew of the occasional manuscript collection made by a worker like Clare, had looked through windows in labourers' white-washed cottages, could tell a working-class Freemason when he saw one, and recognized that cultural exchange went both ways, since a professional stage singer like Emery (who left his native north-east to make his name in London) had learned songs from a 'country minstrel'. His work may well have inspired the generation of genteel amateur collectors who made the 'country' collections in the decades which followed.

The sources of Halliwell's *Yorkshire Anthology* were eclectic. He used broadsides by William Elderton, staged 'Yorkshire' dialogues, bits and pieces of quaint speech (with 'The Translation'), conscious 'Yorkshire' verse like the Rev. T. Brown's *Awd Daisy. An Eclogue*, 'a Collection of Significant and Useful Proverbs', '*A Yorkshire Pastoral*', a 'Ballad' from *Notes and Queries*, a broadside from Wood's collection in the Ashmolean, pieces from the Cotton MSS., Latin Verses from the Library of Trinity College Cambridge, contemporary 'Yorkshire' skits on 'low-life', the *History of Mother Shipton*, and a Freemason song. Only one text is said to have been 'obtained from oral tradition' and 'Kindly communicated by Henry Jackson, esq. of Sheffield', who copied it from '*a copy* written by an old gentelman who died in 1782'. Some items are dragged by main force into the collection, but have minimal reference to Yorkshire; and this underlines the problems of the non-native anthologizer who lives at a distance, relies on correspondents, doesn't have access to orally-collected material (or doesn't look for it), and can rely on a fair amount of toleration from people getting a free book.

Chappell was not only in less of a hurry but, paradoxically, his 'national' pretentions made his job easier, especially since he could exploit institutional collections, and a wide range of literary, antiquarian and society contacts. He did so with some thoroughness, but noted the beginnings of a disturbing tendency for items to disappear and resurface in 'some library in the United States'.[62] His attitude towards orally-collected material was deeply sceptical and was tinged with a fatalistic notion that the days for collecting had largely passed. He regretted not having noted down the considerable store of 'traditional songs' learned by a newspaper editor from 'one old sailor'; yet he knew of Broadwood and Dusart's 1843 collection, and made occasional references (amidst the welter of citation of print and manuscript sources) to songs 'still sung at harvest-homes' in the west of England. He included items collected by Mr Jennings, a Maidstone church organist, from 'wandering hop-pickers so recently as the summer of 1855', by Mr Barrett[63] 'in the North of England', by Mr Macfarren 'from hearing an old ballad-singer in Lancashire' in the late 1830s, and another from Mr J H Dixon in Yorkshire. He also knew of Dixon's network of correspondents from the 1840s. Sandys sent him a piece taken from 'a hale and hearty septuagenarian friend, Mr J C Schetky', and Chappell expanded that network to include Mr Durant Cooper, who sent a song taken from 'an old seaman, at Corson Bay, Devon'. Lord Vernon and Thomas Dibdin both supplied orally-collected material. Evidently, workers and some collectors were not totally happy with the idea that non-commercial song-culture was dead or dying, that the working-class of the 1850s could be written off, culturally, or that a reliance of non-oral sources even for the song-culture of 'Olden Time' was necessarily rational or scholarly.

Robert Bell was more libertarian, in that broadside and chapbook texts are accorded equal status with those 'derived solely from tradition in districts where they have been orally transmitted from generation to generation, time out of mind',[64] as part of the culture of 'the people'.[65] Sometimes, he tells us, transmission was affected by a 'collision of dialects', at others by the 'ignorance of scribes and the carelessness of printers';[66] yet his 1856 *Early Ballads* contained items from older collections such as Percy, Ritson and Scott, from Richardson's *Table Book* (itself highly derivative), and substantial sections of Dixon's two works. Not a single item appears to have been taken down by Bell at first-hand from singers. His *Ancient Poems* of 1857 virtually reprints what had been left over from Dixon's 1846 book of the same name, including most of the title page verbatim; but a handful of Dixon's texts were rejected, and nearly 40 pieces 'noted down from tradition, or gathered from sources not generally accessible' are added. These came from the Roxburghe collection, friends' libraries, and a broadside pasted on a Gloucestershire country inn, but also from 'an old Yorkshire yeoman', the singing of Richmond 'Mummers', people at Greenside 'wakes', a nameless 'young gipsy girl' and an 'old fiddler in Northumberland'. Most of these songs seem to have been recorded by Dixon, who had 'amassed additional materials of great value' since 1846, or by *his* contacts, including Sandys, Chambers, W H Longstaffe, the historian of Darlington, and Mr Denham of Piersebridge the collector of rhymes, stories and sayings. Like Chambers, Bell was acting as mediator of others' mediations, sometimes at more than one remove from any live sources; and his popularizing work confirmed the division of labour that was now established even in the commercially-oriented mediation of songs from workers' culture, reaching back, through Chambers, to Scott's circle. The products of that older workers' song-culture had now become the property of literary-antiquarian people of a different class, and could be bought, rented or exchanged in ways they saw fit, before being published for the bourgeois market.

John Harland used texts collected around Bleasdale by John Hill. He himself collected songs from Job Knight of Swinton, and was sent others by John Grimshaw of Gorton, John Higson of Droylesden, and by some fellow journalists and antiquarians. Chetham's Library was conveniently close: Halliwell's publications were to hand; *Notes and Queries* was too useful to pass over. A gentleman and a doctor from Warrington received his thanks. Roby's *Traditions of Lancashire*, scarce books published by subscription 'many years ago', the treasures of the Harleian and Ashmolean MSS., the 'muniments' of Lyme, the publications of Dixon, Percy's *Reliques*, local history books, one of Shenstone's poems, a Salford clergyman's wife's manuscript, a 'party of waitts' who came into his garden at Swinton in 1861, the *Ashton Reporter*, Hone's *Every Day Book*, his future collaborator, T.T. Wilkinson, local broadsides and chapbooks, old and new, Byron's *Miscellaneous Poems*, a Manchester literary Journal, the *Phoenix, Gentleman's Magazine, Elegant Extracts*, and one or two uncited sources are all laid under contribution. In a way, Harland benefited from the absence of both amateur and commercial precedents, and from his high visibility to potential correspondents both as a newspaper-reporter and a noted antiquarian.

* * * * *

(iv) Their editing

The editing practices of the period 1830–65 demonstrate how market considerations (or their absence) affected the mediating of songs. Wright attempted a strict chronological order, gave sources and detailed head-notes, translated Latin, French and Middle English, specified when a 'composite' text was being offered, noted variants, gave a full Index of historical, biographical and other matters. He recorded misgivings about his own ability to read a particular manuscript, though he hoped 'the texts will be found as correct as the manuscripts would allow', given the 'numerous corruptions' he assumed had been 'introduced by the scribes'. In other words, he did a thoroughly scholarly job, according to his lights and contemporary standards, partly, no doubt, because others could check his transcriptions; but he published no tunes in what was essentially a literary undertaking. Broadwood did: in fact, the tunes were more important to him than the words, because he felt that the latter were sometimes 'rough'.[67] According to family tradition, he insisted on the modality of the tunes:

> when the organist cried out against a flattened seventh Mr Broadwood, who had an accurate memory and a good ear, confirmed his vocal intervals by violent blasts on the flute and replied "Musically it may be wrong, but I *will* have it exactly as my singers sang it."[68]

Howes claims this as the first example of 'scientific method applied editorially to the oral tradition of English folk-song';[69] but Broadwood does not use the term. Nor does he give notes, sources, names, dates or places: the songs were 'his' just as much as were their singers, in his mind.

Dixon's 'Scotish' volume naturally finds Buchan's texts to be '*decidedly* and *indubitably original*', but some were too original to be printed, because of their 'highly objectionable' contents. Dixon was quick to note other mediators' handiwork, including Percy's '*made-up*' pieces; and he tries to trace historical and other relevant information, as well as variants. He published no tunes. Nor did he in *Ancient Poems*, which was overtly a 'selection' from a wider range of material, including 'every variety' of content and of form which Dixon recognized. He defined none of these varieties, though he singled out pieces characterized by 'profanity'. Variants are collated occasionally, and a 'conjectural emendation' and 'one or two verbal corrections' are admitted to. His preference for pieces 'in the rough', collected orally or from older broadsides, is clear. The latter are given complete with prose headings and tune names as in the original, and even the printer's colophon. Stage directions are given for the songs taken from dancers. Dixon's stress on using orally-collected and broadside texts to supplement those derived from other song-books, gives his work — and Robert Bell's which relied on it — considerable credibility in so far as they appear to be accurately transcribed, in spite of his patronizing attitude towards the culture they came from and in which they continued to circulate. Halliwell seems to follow a similar pattern, though he includes very few notes, does not hazard an introduction, prints no tunes, and cites names of tunes and even sources sparingly.

Chappell's scholarly motives not only encouraged him to attempt a chronological order for his tunes, but prompted him to present the reader with the evidence upon which his classification was founded. For the earlier periods, his assured sale allowed him to be exhaustive in his coverage, and give a 'collection' of the material he had come across; but for his second volume a 'selection' was necessary, sometimes citing only one or two verses (for items held to be well known), expurgating one or two texts, and using short sets. He applied the criterion of singability throughout, including the extraction of a simple tune from the ornament of a particular arrangement, a task usually performed by one or other of his professional musical advisers. His treatment of texts was, however, no less cavalier than other mediators', but his presentation of tunes — even though they came from largely manuscript and printed sources — represented a significant gain for scholarship. His willingness to include tunes from 'live' sources complemented the growing cultural liberalism towards orally-collected texts exemplified in the work of Dixon. In some ways, Chappell prefigured the tendency towards the scientific collection of both texts and tunes which was to emerge towards the end of the nineteenth century. But like many mediators, his unwillingness to theorize his editing and collecting practices not only signalled confidence in the universality of his own cultural assumptions and attitudes, but also, and paradoxically, allowed him to widen his range of potential sources. Similarly, his genuinely scholarly and antiquarian methods helped him preserve the products of workers' song- and musical-culture, even though he, like many others, saw fit to patronize the people, to underestimate their creativity and that of their ancestors.

Harland's book represents something of a step back in its form and method of editing, since he followed what had been the best practice of the 1830s and 1840s, and probably used Halliwell's works as a model. His was essentially a literary offering, and contains no music, or even many names of tunes. Harland tries to maintain a chronological order. He notes how 'Love, War, and Murder' characterize many of his more modern pieces, but does not advance any theoretical distinctions between the 'Songs' and the 'Ballads'. He modernizes spellings, glosses ancient and idiomatic words, notes when parts of a text are 'wanting' in a manuscript, and relates stories and curious information associated with particular texts. He comments on other mediators' errors — not only local historians', but also Robert Bell's — picks out portions of longer pieces which refer to 'Lancashire men and their acts', refers to variants occasionally, acknowledges correspondents and debts in head-notes, cites Rimbault, Dixon, Halliwell and even Percy as authorities, and claims (probably with justification) not to have 'ventured to alter' his originals 'in any way'. Of course, with so many correspondents and authorities, Harland like previous anthologizers was heavily dependent on other mediators' trustworthiness, though he notes curious correspondences between some texts sent to him from local people, and decides to omit verses which are 'almost identical' to those already used. Actual or putative authors, for once including many working-class people, are given without any of the patronage of other mediators; and this matter-of-fact approach encouraged later 'folk-song' writers to miss out Harland from their carefully-chosen 'ancestors' when they sifted old song-books for 'early' examples of what they did themselves. (They treated John Bell in much the same way.) To historians of workers' culture, of course, Harland's book is of great use and interest precisely because it *does* contain such information!

* * * * *

Song-mediating had become a genteel hobby, an antiquarian pastime, and had been all but removed from the constraints of capitalist production and of the market-place. It no longer represented a serious intervention in the politics of culture, if it ever really had been, and yet there was still the motivation of cultural nationalism, this time most notably amongst English mediators. The Scots had proven their credentials, they had recorded songs in something like a thorough fashion for a century; and it evidently irked people like Chappell to be taunted about the English having no 'national music' of their own. The claim could hardly be made about English literary culture, of course, though as yet there were no signs of *this* kind of literature being taken up by universities, let alone by state-sponsored schools. To some extent, the interest in 'county' and 'regional' song-culture might be taken to indicate a resurgence of the experience of the earlier provincial song-mediators who moved into the towns and cities of late eighteenth century England and Scotland,[70] especially since a whole range of material and cultural factors were beginning to obliterate or to absorb such regional culture as remained. At this crucial period for cultural change, much of the innovatory work was done by provincial bourgeois people. Almost all of the earlier 'county' song-books were based on material drawn from the north, where only vernacular speech (wrongly called 'dialect', since there was no separate grammar) remained to symbolize what had once been considerable cultural variations. Possibly, also, literary-antiquarians in the more remote English counties were experiencing something like the sense of loss of cultural identity felt by the Scots a century before. They too did not feel the need to collect and publish the songs until they had all but disappeared — as they thought. Whatever is the truth, it is certainly the case that the song-mediators of the mid nineteenth century felt they were dealing not simply with 'remains' or 'relics', like their immediate predecessors, but with remnants of a culture which was going for good. The working class had decisively rejected that culture, they believed, and it was up to antiquarians to do what they could to collect what they could. No doubt they subscribed to the myth of the 'Golden Age', and were on the escalator back in time in search of an 'organic' past culture.[71] Certainly, they had next to no grasp of the importance of broadsides and chapbooks to workers' culture, even in their own period, and they didn't like what little they knew of concert hall and music hall song. Above all, they liked workers only when they knew their place, and they preferred instead to contemplate the comfortable abstraction of 'the people' or 'the peasant'.

PART 2

Francis James Child and the 'Ballad' Consensus

The methods of formal analysis are necessary, but
insufficient. You may count up the alliterations
in popular proverbs, classify metaphors, count up
the number of vowels and consonants in a wedding
song. It will undoubtedly enrich our knowledge of
folk art, in one way or another: but if you don't
know the peasant system of sowing, and the life
that is based on it, if you don't know the part
the scythe plays, and if you have not mastered the
meaning of the church calendar to the peasant, of
the time when the peasant marries, or when the
peasant women give birth, you will have only
understood the outer shell of folk art, but the
kernel will not have been reached.

Leon Trotsky, *Literature and Revolution*, 1924

By the later 1850s and the 1860s, the study of workers' songs and of 'ballads' had simply declined to the status of a genteel pastime in England, and the generation of men who had worked alongside Scott was dying out. A person who wished to get involved in workers' culture could, however, participate in the activities of the various organizations concerned to 'improve' the condition of the working class. In terms of music and song, the state had begun to take a serious interest in working-class childrens' training after 1840, and particularly after John Hullah developed and applied *Wilhelm's Method of Teaching Singing*.[1] His example permeated teacher-training colleges, and by 1872 Hullah was a government inspector for musical subjects. Within a decade, the Tonic Sol-Fa method had won favour in the schools, supported by the exertions of John Curwen, and then his son, John Spencer Curwen, who was a music-publisher. The reasons for the state's interest in working-class education after the 1840s hardly needs spelling out. But the intervention was not only in the form of injecting 'old English' songs into classrooms: substantial *capital* went into the training of teachers, buying of instruments and the purchase of suitable music and songs. The interests of the ruling class and the ideas and publications of a person like William Chappell neatly coincided, and there developed a substantial market for comparatively cheap pianos, sheet-music and manuals of one kind or another for training both pupils and teachers of music, especially after 1870, when state-sponsored mass education really got going. If a song-mediator could work for this market, and fit in with its ideology, fortunes were to be made. Of course, working-class music-making, singing and song-writing went on outside the schools as well, in spite of employers' paternalistic subsidies for brass bands and choirs. But one of the consequences of the state's near annexation of 'old English' songs was the further marginalization of the work of song-collectors and song-publishers who were interested in working-class songs which could neither be sold as commodities nor used in schools. The logical home for such activities was perhaps the universities, but literary dons didn't care; and in any case the institutions were in great need of reform to widen social representation from the 'prospective parsons, prospective lawyers, [and] young men of rank and fortune' who were catered for at Oxford and Cambridge. In the USA, however, the class-system in education was not yet so rigid, and the study of 'ballads' at last found a home in the interstices of the curriculum.

* * * * *

5 *Francis James Child*

My copy of Child's major work, *The English and Scottish Popular Ballads*, weighs over 6 lbs. Its sheer bulk, wealth of detail, and apparently exhaustive critical apparatus present a formidable appearance. It is no wonder that generations of literary scholars and folklorists have regarded it with awe, and have used it as an effective definition of what a 'ballad' was in English and Scots culture. Yet Child was far from being the first to use the term, or to invoke the 'popular'; so before we go on to see how and why his conception of a 'ballad' came to have such significance, we need to put his *magnum opus* and Child himself in the context of the historical circumstances which produced both him and it.[2]

(i) The person

Child was a citizen of Boston in the USA.[3] He was born in 1825, the third child of eight. His father was a sailmaker, 'one of that class of intelligent and independent mechanics, which has had a large share in determining the character of our democratic community',[4] according to one of his biographers. But the truth is that Boston was characterized by social divisions along class lines. The town had a Latin School, for those boys who were able, intellectually and materially, to go on to higher education, and an English High School, for those who were destined to fill jobs which demanded more mundane skills. Child went to the English High School, where he took first place in his studies, but he was fortunate enough to be noticed by the headmaster of the Latin School for his 'extraordinary mental ability', and to benefit from a form of patronage based on meritocratic ideas. He was transferred to the Latin School, 'entered upon the regular preparation for admission to Harvard College', and soon won first place in Greek and Latin. The headmaster persuaded Child's parents to allow him to continue his studies rather than going out to work to help support the family, largely by making 'arrangements by which his college expenses should be provided for' in the form of a loan, which Child later paid back, with interest. In 1842, at the age of 17, Child entered Harvard; and he was based there until he died. Harvard was not yet a University, and Child's 'class' numbered only 60 students; but ideals of public service, patriotism and suchlike permeated the place, and the whole method of learning was structured on competitive 'recitations', and on individualism. Child 'at once took the lead and kept it', not only in classics, but in mathematics and English; and though he was a swot, his 'manliness of spirit' evidently won the respect of his classmates.

Immediately after he graduated, in 1846, he was appointed as a college tutor in mathematics. In 1848, the year of revolutions in Europe, he asked to be transferred to tutor in history and political economy, with some 'duties of instructions in English', and between 1849 and 1851 he obtained leave of absence (and, presumably, financial assistance) for travel and study in Europe. Partly, he went on medical grounds: he had suffered from 'close application to work', not surprisingly when even his leisure hours were spent in formidable productivity, like the *Four Old Plays* he published in a scholarly edition when he was only 23. At Berlin and Göttingen, he devoted himself to Germanic philology, which had passed from the romantic dilletantism of the early nineteenth century to a discipline with 'strenuous scientific' pretensions:

> Scholars, however severe, looked through the form and strove to comprehend the spirit. The ideals of erudition and of a large humanity were not even suspected of incompatibility. The imagination was still invoked as the guide and illuminator of learning. The bond between antiquity and mediaevalism and between the Middle Ages and our own century was never lost from sight.[5]

European literary scholarship was compatible with that in North America, but — especially in Germany — it was significantly more advanced. So, while Child wrote no doctoral dissertation, his experience helped qualify him for further promotion on his return to the USA. He was awarded the Harvard Chair of Rhetoric and Oratory in 1851; and thee years later his high standing was confirmed by the award of an honorary doctorate from Göttingen University. That link with German literary scholarship remained important throughout his life, and was symbolized by the picture of William and James Grimm which he kept on his study mantelpiece. Child held this chair for 25 years, supervising and criticizing undergraduates' work, and tackling a massive editorial project for a 150-volume series of 'British Poets' almost simultaneously with Robert Bell's,[6] but at a more high-powered level of scholarship. For that series, he produced an edition of Spenser's poetical works in 1855, and the first edition (as it turned out) of *English and Scottish Ballads* in 1857–8, which soon reached a second edition and was published both in the USA and in London.

This eight-volume work represented a natural development for a professional academic in the USA, if not in Britain, in that it took over where genteel literary antiquarians had left off. Child knew of Wright's work, plugged into what remained of the network of the various learned societies in London, and was contacted in turn by the Danish scholar,

Grundtvig,[7] who was also editing a 'national' collection of 'ballads'. Attracted by the material, and recognizing the atrophy of serious 'ballad' scholarship in Britain, Child was able to integrate his interest with the development of Harvard, which was being transformed by the demands of the US economy into a university with genuinely national pretensions. In turn, this expansion permitted a further specialization by its teachers and researchers, and part of this developing academic division of labour led to the founding of a new chair of English, to which Child was appointed in 1876, and which he held until his death. Not only did the material security afforded by this post enable Child to undertake massive correspondence and several trips to Europe in search of manuscript sources, but it also allowed him to integrate what had been a marginal academic interest into his development of 'English' as a discipline in an important institution. On the other hand, his powerful position obliged him to devote time and energy to routine duties: he remained secretary of the Library Council for 30 years; but that key position also helped him amass the considerable holdings of printed and manuscript material on which his own research depended, and which Chappell had noted disappearing across the Atlantic so early as the 1850s.[8]

The third edition of Child's work on 'ballads' began appearing in 1882; and because of that work he received honorary degrees from both Harvard and Columbia during the 1880s. But he went on collecting and encouraging others to collect, and was proud to have missed not a single lecture even in his fiftieth year of teaching. During his seventy-first year, Child continued to work on the last part of his edition, with 'scarcely any respite'. In August 1896, he discovered he was seriously ill; and within a month he was dead. After his death, Child was canonized by certain interested parties, both as a teacher and a scholar.[9] Yet in his letters to Grundtvig, for example, we can note not only how marginal his work on 'ballads' really was to his academic career and his material interests, but also how he felt about the duties he is said to have performed so selflessly and enthusiastically. Time and again he writes to Grundtvig about being 'so encumbered with a barren kind of work in the college',[10] and about having passed all his adult life at Harvard' where existence is not so favourable as it might be to literary or scientific productiveness.' By 1877, even lectures had become a 'burden' to him.[11] He envies Grundtvig his military experience, claiming that only a 'long and painful sickness of my wife' prevented him from offering his life 'in our great war', which had ended only a few years before he wrote,[12] and stresses his wish 'to do something now which shall be useful in its way', in spite of his work, his "languor and low spirits' and his premature gout.[13] It was the 'fear of dying with nothing done'[14] which seems to have prompted him from the 1860s onwards: even his trips to Europe for convalescence were used to gather material. Once, his and Grundtvig's paths almost crossed: but they never met. The American's overwhelmingly superior material security was constantly clear to both men. Child had no qualms in doling out cash for Grundtvig's knowledge and labour. He claimed that 'University professors all the world over are for the most part far from independent in their circumstances', and he 'belonged to the great majority'; but they both knew that Child was 'much better paid than much superior men at Copenhagen'.[15] He set himself to earn $800 or $1000 on one occasion over and above his salary[16]. Child had *got on* in what was to be a classic US fashion, the archetypal product of an allegedly meritocratic system and his own competitive individualism. By the 1870s he was unhappy about having been 'turned out' of his study 'by mechanics engaged in enlarging my house'[17]. People like his parents were now to some extent alien to his comfortable Harvard existence, and Child was totally integrated into the liberal component of East Coast bourgeois intellectual culture.

*   *   *   *   *

(ii) His aims

Because we have three editions of Child's 'ballad' collection,[18] it is possible to show not only how his ideas related to those of his British predecessors, but also how they changed through time. When the first volumes of the first edition began to appear, in 1857, Sharpe and Buchan had not long been dead. In Scotland, Laing, Maidment and Kinloch were still alive, as were John and Robert Bell, Chappell, Wright, Chambers and Dixon in England. Their successors, Hales and Furnivall — who edited the Percy MS. in the 1860s[19] — were 'dilletantes, not scholars',[20] according to Grundtvig; so if English people 'in the political sense of the word' refused to take a serious interest in 'Anglo-Scottish' 'ballads', it seemed to him that an 'English Scholar' from the USA should go ahead and execute the task in 'a scholarlike and rational manner',[21] according to Germanic principles, on the basis of Child's slightly revised second edition of 1860. After all, the USA was beginning to ready itself to give economic leadership at an international level, just as Germany was giving scholarly leadership in many fields; and the class-ridden British intellectual culture was evidently not interested or not capable of carrying out the task. For the proposed third edition, Child had the material security of his professorship (unlike, say, Wright[22]), the effective patronage of his university (without the strings of learned societies or of commercial publication), and the ability to build on whatever he found to be sound in the tradition of song-editing of over a century and a half. United States literary and general intellectual culture was, in any case, more concerned with the heterogeneity of the 'national' cultures of migrants from all over Europe, and, at least since the War of Independence, had been characterized by populist tendencies. In some ways, then, it is possible to see the production of *The English and Scottish Popular Ballads* as a part of a natural process of annexation of wider cultural responsibilities in the

English-speaking world, corresponding to the growing economic and political power which, not long after Child's death, challenged that of British Imperialism.

The first edition of *English and Scottish Ballads*, published at Boston in 1857 – 9, was 'part of one of those senseless huge collections of *British Poets*', as Child confessed to Grundtvig, and was 'made as a sort of *job*'.[23] It was done through a commercial publisher, was aimed at 'the "benevolent reader"' and 'readers for pleasure',[24] and so had to be made 'tolerably saleable'[25] by making concessions to bourgeois ideas of what constituted 'English Poetry'. This meant that Child 'felt obliged to include' everything that 'the English [sic] had been accustomed to call *Ballad*, at least in specimens',[26] in what he later termed an 'unconsidered collection'.[27] He apologized about this edition to Grundtvig for years afterwards, pleading he had been 'in great haste, being driven on by the publishers, who wished to finish their collection of 125 vols. within two or three years'.[28] Research time had been limited: he had insufficient access even to printed works in the USA; but he did try to make the texts accessible to non-specialist readers by the inclusion of a substantial glossary, and he made some effort to take into account texts from cultures other than the British. (He seems not to have considered patronage publishing, even through a learned society, and this first edition contained no dedication.) His aim was to publish 'all but two or three of the *ancient* ballads of England and Scotland', and, following Motherwell, 'nearly all those ballads which, in either country, have been gathered from oral tradition, whether ancient or not'.[29] He used as many texts from broadsides and garlands as 'might be wished for, perhaps I should say tolerated';[30] and when a text is 'extant in a variety of forms, all the most important versions are given', since 'Less than this would have seemed insufficient for a collection intended as a complement to an extensive series of the British Poets.'[31] There is no justification, however, for excluding Wales and Ireland from the collection of 'British' material; and Child writes of himself as an 'English editor'[32] of 'English Ballads'[33] on occasion. He was relating to the 'literary world',[34] to that part of the 'English and American public'[35] with an interest in 'English Ballad-literature':[36] and this Anglo-centredness clearly related to his and Grundtvig's shared sense of the primacy of English culture within the 'northern' or 'Gothic' nations of Europe.[37] Denmark, after all, had had to fight for centuries to maintain some sense of 'national' culture, and the United States had yet to develop anything like such a thing, given the cultural internationalism so obviously present in its cities and country-side. Danish cultural 'parallels' with British 'ballads', and the need in US culture for cultural roots in the country of its dominant language, neatly coincided in the cooperation which developed between the Danish and US scholars.

Child's experience with the first and second editions of his 'ballad' work hardened his resolve to see a 'proper'[38] edition produced, and this necessarily raised material questions. Initially, he used his 'enthusiastic friend' Furnivall's good offices to see whether the 'English Ballad Society' might sponsor the work, so as to help 'escape all control from publishers, both as to the extent of the work and the rate of publication'.[39] After Grundtvig's cooperation was offered, he decided to 'drop' the Ballad Society 'at once', because it was 'so ill supported that it could not afford any expenses beyond printing and copying, and the circulation of its books is and must be limited'.[40] Grundtvig had also opened the 'painful and very disgusting topic' of pay:

> Though my assistance is not to be bought, yet it must be paid for, or else, I am sorry to say, it cannot be given. The fact is, that as a professor of the university I have only a small salary, and all my spare hours therefore must be turned to profit, not only in an ideal, but also in a material point of view. Now, my dear Sir, you must judge for yourself, whether the assistance here offered would be of that importance to you, and even to the booksellers, that the enterprize could and should be encumbered with a moderate salary to me. To speak plainly, I must value the time it would take me to give you all the information I could wish, to the sum of 500 American dollars.[41]

To Child, this was a 'very small sum' which he could advance out of his own pocket, 'in expectation of receiving it back finally from the profits of the work'.[42] But it took him five years to send the cash;[43] and the relationship which grew up must have been materially affected by this transaction, though Child professed the cooperation was 'beyond any money value'.[44] (He even suggested using his influence to get Grundtvig over $1000 clear for a US lecture-tour, but this promised exertion of patronage-power came to nothing.[45])

Child hoped to see the first volume in the bookshops by 1877, and was 'always in fear of dying before completing the work'.[46] He tried to get a publisher to 'issue the English ballads' in part-form, 'which the English have a prejudice for',[47] but it was 1879 before even one sample text was set up in print, and 1881 before final 'arrangements' were completed.[48] In 1882, the first volume appeared, 35 years after the first volume of the first edition. It was in the form of 'an edition de luxe, a heavy quarto, I fear, such as none of us could afford to buy'. The publishers, Houghton, Mifflin and Company, had decided to 'fortify themselves by subscribers', but Child pronounced himself 'indifferent as long as they reserve me copies enough for friends and helpers'.[49] Evidently, he cared more about academic respect and fame than cash or the wider bourgeois market, and the potentially profitable idea for a 'selection for schools' was first postponed,[50] and then left to his literary executors. Child dedicated his work to Furnivall, and set out his most important scholarly aim in the Advertisement to Part I:

> It was my wish not to begin to print The English and Scottish Popular Ballads until this unrestricted title should be justified by my having at command every valuable copy of every known ballad.[51]

Most of the previous decade's leisure-time had been dedicated to this purpose, as was the remaining 14 years of Child's life; so he could not easily complain that he had been rushed in his research, or that his ideas and assumptions had not had time to mature.

* * * * *

(iii) His ideas

Leaving aside questions of value which usually coincide with British bourgeois standards, and the English or Scots origins of the texts he chooses for both editions, Child seems to have had a clear idea about what was and was not a 'ballad' from at least 1860. The 1857 edition had contained items 'not of the nature of ballads'; but the second edition was altered, so that certain 'short romances which formerly stood in the First Book' were 'dropped' 'in order to give the collection a homogeneous character'.[52] The 'popular ballads' remained, though

> Many of the older ones are mutilated, many more are miserably corrupted, but as long as any traces of their originals are left, they are worthy of attention and have received it.[53]

Child claimed to know what a 'ballad' was, when it was 'original' and 'popular', and what it had been 'corrupted' from. Moreover, he had a hierarchy of 'important versions',[54] and a perception of what constituted an 'authentic' text.[55] He recognized when a 'commonplace' was 'familiar'[56] or not, and when a text was or was not '*ancient*'.[57] The 'true popular ballads' were, evidently, the 'spontaneous products of nature',[58] unlike texts which 'can be called a ballad only by an objectionable, though common, extension of the term'[59] to include

> the works of the professional ballad-maker, which make up the bulk of the Garlands and Broadsides. These, though sometimes not without grace, more frequently not lacking in humour, belong to artificial literature — of course to an humble department.[60]

For Child, 'No words could express the dulness and inutility of a collection which should embrace all the Roxburghe and Pepys broadsides';[61] yet he already knew that the distinction was not absolute, 'for several of the ancient ballads have a sort of literary character, and many broadsides were printed from oral tradition'.[62] He later regretted that he had not 'separated the proper Volksballade from the others'[63] in his first edition. However, the couplets of popular/professional, spontaneous/artificial, nature/art were allowed to re-appear and beg the key issues. Did broadside-makers really try to make 'art' and fail? Or were their criteria different? Was there only one literary tradition, the current custodians of which include Harvard professors, or were there several?

Of course, as we have seen, there was no theory of 'the ballad' in British culture worthy of the name. What little theoretical rigour existed, as in Motherwell, derived in large measure from German Romanticism, with slightly more of a debt to the Enlightenment and to elements of Darwin's ideas. Child's appropriation of these ideas led him to accept the notion of there being a 'pure original' for every text, usually with 'ancient' Danish or Swedish roots.[64] He believed in the existence of an 'author'[65] at some remote period, but 'the unconscious poet of the real *traditional* ballad' was quite unlike the artist of recent literary tradition.[66] The 'people' who lived 'in those retired nooks where tradition longest lingers'[67] — the sources from who Grundtvig's schoolmaster and clergymen correspondents had collected texts[68] — were decidely not the same as the contemporary 'vulgar'.[69] Instead, they and their British counterparts were part of an 'ignorant peasantry', which did not exist in the USA, and was moribund in Britain:[70] 'Civilization has made too great strides in the island of Great Britain for us to expect much more from tradition.'[71] So, 'tradition' seemed capable of preserving only 'vulgar' versions of 'the residuum' of older texts, from which 'all the beauty and spirit have been exhaled';[72] and when Child disagrees, for example, with Scott over *The Outlaw Murray*, he does so on the issue of literary quality as perceived by bourgeois culture on both sides of the Atlantic.[73] The essentially *literary* nature of Child's intervention in 'ballad' study leads him, in spite of his challenges of some other editors' dubieties, to underpin many of their value-judgements and assumptions about literary value, though they were most of them as innocent of theorizing as could well be. In turn, underpinning Child's own apparently objective empirical scholarship, and making his 1857–9 edition possible, is the prior *assumption* that there are 'permanent' literary forms like 'ballads', 'epic' and 'romance'. It follows that, to adapt Raymond Williams' ideas on literature, all the mediator's

> active study is of variations within them, variations that may be admitted to have proximate causes, even a social history, but that in their essential features are taken in practice as autonomous, with internal laws.[74]

So, as in normative bourgeois literary criticism, 'tradition'

> is seen not as it is, an active and continuous selection and re-selection, which even at its latest point in time is always a specific choice, but now more conveniently as an object, a projected reality, with which we have to come to terms on its terms, even though those terms are always and must be the valuations, the selections and omissions, of other men.[75]

To Child and to Scott, Mrs Brown the professor's daughter was as 'traditional'[76] a source as any 'peasant'; and even after the first two editions of his work, Child's notions of what might pass as 'ballad' theory and social history were markedly idealist and unhistorical.

In his later article on 'Ballad Poetry' for Johnson's *Universal Cyclopaedia*,[77] which Child soon wished 'to be neither quoted nor regarded as final',[78] we can note a decisive extension of the negative criteria which Motherwell had begun to develop,[79] and only one positive statement, that a 'ballad' was 'a narrative song, a short tale in lyric verse',[80] a definition which had become established in the dictionaries. Other than that, Child adds a Social Darwinist gloss to the fundamentally idealist assessment of the place of 'popular' 'ballads' in cultural history, and of the 'people' in history in general. This 'distinct and very important species of poetry' has a 'historical and natural place',

> anterior to the appearance of the poetry of art, to which it has formed a step, and by which it has been regularly displaced, and, in some cases, all but extinguished.[81]

In order to legitimize his assumptions, Child resorts to the authority of the brothers Grimm, or to Motherwell's romanticism:

> Whenever a people in the course of its development reaches a certain intellectual and moral stage, it will feel an impulse to express itself.... The condition of society in which a truly national or popular poetry appears explains the character of such poetry. It is a condition in which the people are not divided by political organization and book-culture into markedly distinct classes, in which consequently there is such community of ideas and feelings that the whole people form an individual. Such poetry...will always be an expression of the heart and mind of the people as an individual, and never of the personality of individual men. The fundamental characteristic of popular ballads is therefore the absence of subjectivity and self-consciousness. Though they do not 'write themselves', as William Grimm has said, though a man and not a people has composed them, still the author counts for nothing, and it is not by mere accident, but with the best reason, that they have come down to us anonymous.[82]

However much such ideas represent a longing for a society without classes, and without the worst aspects of the industry which fostered them, they do considerable violence to the real history of English and Scottish people.

Lousie Pound was surely correct when she traced Child's ideological links with the period of intellectual ferment in both Europe and North America following the French revolution, when the intelligentsia were

> deeply interested in "the people" as a mass conception, in all that belonged to them and all that they created. It was in this period that theorists...liked to advocate the doctrine of spontaneous, unconscious growth "from the heart of the people", as the phrase went....[82]

From this derived Grimm's ideas about the supposed distinction between the 'artificial' products of the individual and the 'spontaneous creation of the people',[83] which fitted with Herder's collectivist conception of the origin of popular poetry':[84]

For literature, too, communal inspiration was advocated....Just as for language, a distinction was insisted upon between "art" poetry, coming from the individual, and "folk poetry", arising from the people.[86]

This tradition was helped to persist in the USA by Child even when it had been largely abandoned in Europe. Consciously or otherwise, it functioned as a way of coping with the increasingly divisive effects of the capitalist mode of production. Yet, in truth, Child's own class-based interests led him to minimize the role of contemporary workers even in the transmission of what he called 'ballads':

> The primitive ballad, then, is not popular in the sense of something arising from and suited to the lower orders of a people. As yet, no sharp distinction of high and low exists, in respect to knowledge, desires, and tastes. An increased civilization, and especially the introduction of book-culture, gradually gives rise to such a division; the poetry of art appears; the popular poetry is no longer relished by a portion of the people, and is abandoned to an uncultivated or not over-cultivated class... a constantly diminishing number.... The popular ballad is not originally the product or the property of the lower orders of the people. Nothing, in fact, is more obvious than that many of the ballads of the now most refined nations had their origin in that class whose acts and fortunes they depict — the upper class.[86]

The role of the 'lower orders' is instrumental, and yet, in terms of Child's own class-culture (in one of its romantic, populist modes), what remains of that 'popular poetry' is a positive acquisition for its 'national' attributes and associations, as well as for its literary value in bourgeois terms. The historical fact that many English and Scots people chose to buy and use songs in broadside forms from the sixteenth to the nineteenth centuries means that such cultural products have to be stigmatized as 'a different genus'. They are, to Child, 'products of a low kind of *art*, and most of them are, from a literary point of view, thoroughly despicable and worthless'.[87] In these kinds of ways, Child seeks to impose onto cultural history his own class's concept of linear cultural development leading to what was worthy from a bourgeois-literary point of view. The residue was a sort of fossilized remnant of a 'species' which had reached its Darwinian apogee and then stuck, becoming liable to damage:

> ballads which have been handed down by long-repeated tradition have always departed considerably from their original form. If the transmission has been purely through the mouths of unlearned people, there is less probability of wilful change, but once in the hands of professional singers there is no amount of change which they may not undergo.[88]

Change *equals* corruption. Professionalization of a social role *equals* individualism and art. The absence of formal education is all but a precondition of accurate transmission, and the only effect of working people on song is a deleterious one. Having read the minds of the makers of the 'original form', discounted the possibility of songs passing through (let alone being created by) the brains and the imaginations of the 'unlearned' majority, and being, like Motherwell, familiar with the minds of the unindividuated 'people', Child has no need of any further research into the complexities of medieval culture.

By the 1880s, Child's theoretical development had been modest, and instead of the 'elaborate introduction'[89] he promised but never delivered, all we have are some scribbled notes, a set of extracts of other mediators' work, and comments scattered throughout the 1882–98 edition. 'Tradition' remained a central concept, qualified by the addition of the term 'Popular' to the work's title, and supplemented by the notion of 'oral transmission', at every stage of which

> we must suppose that some accidental variations from what was delivered would be introduced, and occasionally some wilful variations. Memory will fail at times; at times the listener will hear amiss, or will not understand, and a perversion of sense will ensue, or absolute nonsense, — nonsense which will be servilely repeated, and which repetition makes more gross.[90]

Contradictorily, Child claims elsewhere that the wilful, servile, forgetful and generally unintelligent people who sustained this process often transmitted accurately, and that the 'ballad' was 'at its best'

> when it has come down by a purely domestic tradition, yet even so it is influenced by printed literature; and much depends on the experience and selection of the reciters, and on their varying memory, which is, however, ordinarily remarkable for its tenacity.[91]

He now understood that a broadside might 'become tradition'[92] in so literate and print-oriented a culture as Britain's, and that 'old tradition does not come to a stop when a ballad gets into print'.[93] One version of *Queen Eleanor's Confession* was probably one of the 'traditional variations of printed copies', and Child believed it 'got into print in the latter part of the seventeenth century, but was no doubt circulating orally sometimes before that, for it is in the truly popular tone'.[94] He now believed that because a song 'suffers in transmission', it will be 'at its best when it is early caught and fixed in print',[95] simply because of the minimization of human beings in the process. *Hind Etin* 'has been not simply damaged by passing through low mouths, but has been worked over by low hands'.[96] Richard Sheale's claims, as a Tamworth minstrel, to have written *The Hunting of the Cheviot*, and not simply to have used it as 'part of his stock as minstrel', is 'preposterous in the extreme'.[97] In other words, Child's assessment of 'tradition' is privileged without historical or scientific justification above the statements and claims of the very agents in the process, for whom he feels uninhibited contempt, even though he seems to have used three pieces written in the mid-seventeenth century by one professional ballad-maker, Laurence Price.

Other acts of faith in his judgement are required. Evidently, the 'lyrical quality' of a piece 'is to be regarded as no less significant than plot as the trait of a true ballad'.[98] Romances have a 'simple but life-like story, supported by the burden and the air'[99] and *Johnie Cock* is a 'precious specimen of the unspoiled traditional ballad'.[100] He does not deign to argue. Instead, his readers have to subscribe to a long list of supposed criteria for Child's ballad 'idea':

> Necessary as the story is ... it is seldom completely told.... Transitions are usually abrupt.... These abrupt transitions do not, then, result ... in incoherence, which accompanies corruption and is a sign of degeneracy.... Coherence, on the contrary, is a characteristic of the true ballad, an important phase of ballad excellence.[101]

Brevity, apparently, *is* a characteristic of the 'ballad', but then come more negatives:

> Introductions, not closely connected with the ballad story, are not characteristic.... The action is seldom carefully localized.... In dealing with the supernatural the way of the true ballad is to omit description or explanation.... Ghosts, though not sufficiently strange to demand special treatment, should, nevertheless, "have fair reason for walking".[102]

Chipping and peeling away at the whole body of song, so as to get at or near the kernel of the 'true ballad', Child feels confident in making an imaginative leap ahead of the evidence, operating on the principle that, as Hart terms it, there are 'degrees of departure from the popular style', and 'degrees of departure from the popular matter'.[103] Child felt himself possessed of the 'idea' of the 'ballad', and builds up a kind of photo-fit picture by blotting out the surrounding to the 'face', and occasionally pointing out a detail on it. The 'English ballad', aparently, is characterized by 'innocuous humour'.[104] A change of nationality is 'accompanied by change of the scene of action'.[105] Ballads have a tendency to 'combine'.[106] 'Ballad' style is 'artless and homely';[107] and 'ballads' have their own conventions, the most striking of which is the use of 'commonplaces'.[108] But then we return to the shadows around the 'face', to the things which a 'ballad' is not. 'Learned words do *not* occur in ballads'.[109] Extravagance, exaggeration, cynicism, sophistication, over-refinement, moralizing, and triteness of plot are 'not characteristic'.[110] Ballad' subject-matter is not 'horrible', and its style is not 'affected'.[111] Neither was a 'ballad' historically accurate: in fact, 'A strict accordance with history...would be almost a ground of suspicion.'[112] Such a web of arbitrary assertion indicates that Child was not only unwilling but *unable* to theorize his assumptions and practices, until death saved him, leaving executors awed by his labour and his scholarship, and without the 'hardihood' to do the job.

* * * * *

(iv) His sources

The 1857–9 edition was 'compiled from the numerous collections of Ballads printed since the beginning of the last century'.[113] What Child termed the 'Principal Collections' of 'Songs' as well as 'Ballads'[114] form an impressive list, and he rates their 'relative importance',[115] so that Phillips, Percy, Herd, Johnson, Ritson's *Robin Hood* and *Scotish Song*, Scott, Jamieson, Kinloch and Motherwell come out top. Percy Society publications are listed separately, and works from Denmark, Sweden and Germany are added. Child had established his hierarchy of sources, and felt confident that the 'few books' he had not found were 'all of slight or no importance'[116] — John Bell's *Rhymes* isn't there.[117] He relied on Scott and Percy for a quarter of his texts.[118] With Ritson and Buchan, the proportion rose to 40%, and with Motherwell, Jamieson and Kinloch, nearly 70% of the texts came from seven mediators. Child felt confident enough to accord praise and blame. Buchan's texts are criticized for not being 'purer and more ancient',[119] for being 'prolix and vulgar',[120] 'modernized',[121] 'twaddling',[122] 'modern',[123] 'entirely worthless'[124] or 'not worth reprinting',[125] because they had undergone 'successive corruptions'.[126] Cromek's material is noted for its 'suspicious character'.[127] Percy's 'undoubtedly spurious'[128] stanzas and his 'alterations and additions'[129] are indicated, as are Ramsay's imperfections'.[130] Child refers to an 'absurd'[131] verse in the *Museum*, and a 'modernized version'[132] in one of Dixon's works. Ritson's publication of Lambe's 'composition',[133] Pinkerton's 'composition'[134] and Cunningham's '*souvenirs*'[135] are slighted. On the other hand, Motherwell's notes are quoted at length, and only occasionally is a text of his relegated to an Appendix or said to be 'recast',[136] *Child Ether*, the text which was made up to fool Buchan, is published without any qualification! Broadsides are condemned out of hand, for having been 'worked over by some balladmonger of the sixteenth century, and of course reduced to dishwater',[137] though a chapbook or garland version may be used in an extremity.

Even in the 1850s, Child shared the pessimism of people like Chappell about collecting from oral sources: 'the material is not at hand',[138] he pronounced from a few thousand miles away, presumably on the advice of people like Halliwell and Collier, who supplied him with manuscript fragments and collations,[139] but not on that of Dixon or of Robert Bell. For the rest, Child printed variants taken from a Philadelphia magazine,[140] and offers the occasional reading from Percy — in fact, he used almost 50 *Reliques* texts, in spite of the editor's changes. Child condemned the 'dealer' who was understood to be keeping the

Percy MS. from the public, 'in order to enhance its value'[141] as a commodity; and he knew that though his own work was 'at once admitted to supercede all previous attempts in the field',[142] without the Percy MS. his edition would remain imperfect. First in 1860, again in 1864 and successfully in 1867–8, Child supported Professor Hales' and Dr Furnivall's efforts to publish the Percy MS., not only by adding a crucial £50 to their £100, but by giving moral support for a venture which incurred a debt of £800 on publication, and eventually cost Furnivall £400.[143] Once the edition was published, and all of Percy's misdeeds brought to light, Child was forced to reconsider his trust in all the song-book makers on whom he had relied.

It was Grundtvig's letter in 1872 which encouraged Child to make the massive effort which he knew would be involved in getting behind printed texts to manuscript and even oral sources: 'With your help' Child wrote 'I feel sure that I could do the work somewhat as it ought to be done.'[144] Child continuously placed himself in the role of Grundtvig's pupil, and accepted his estimate of 'the immense heap of rubbish' in the Percy MS. as well as his faith in 'much abused but very valuable collections'. Grundtvig wrote:

> what you term the "vulgarity" of the Buchan texts is to me the best proof of their material authenticity. For it must be remembered — and is well known to the ballad collectors of the old world, where the tradition of bygone days still lingers on, — that in the recent traditions of the common country people (peasantry) the old ballad cannot always appear in stately and knightly form and apparel, but must in many instances exhibit the traces of a long dwelling in a humble company.[145]

All Child could do was to rationalize his remaining prejudices and doubts:

> They exhibit an *artificial* vulgarity, it seems to me, and as I have said, there is no variety to this, which makes me fear that it comes from a man and not from a class of people.... The vulgarity that I mean consists in a tame, mean, unreal style of *expression*, far from *volksmassig*.[146]

How he could claim to understand the nuances of both medieval and contemporary workers' speech and syntax, on the basis of a limited knowledge of some of the products of medieval courtly culture, is not clear. An apparent humility barely hides a breathtaking pretentiousness, and in the end he had the sense to climb down. Buchan's texts were used over three times as often in the third edition as in the first.

Since he believed that the 'sources of English and Scotch ballads may be regarded as sealed or dried up for ever', Child's academic instinct led him to pin-point 'several manuscripts', which he assumed were 'lying *perdu* somewhere in Scotland and might be disinterred'. He did not think they would 'afford much', but 'we should be able to restore readings

altered by editors at any rate'.[147] Yet while he set Furnivall looking for
one collection, Child casually mentions that he had turned down
Buchan's 'relics' from the mediator's son.[148] Either he had second sight,
or his prejudices had already begun to erode his scholarship. Grundtvig
echoed Child's belief that Jamieson, Motherwell and Kinloch were
'honest people', but the Danish scholar doubted the 'genuineness' of
Scott's texts,[149] and passed on David Laing's name and address as a
potential middleman for Scottish MSS.[150] — the same person who had
dressed up Buchan's texts for the press![151] Meanwhile, Child tested his
mentor's opinions on orally-collected and broadside materials:

> We cannot of course exclude all ballads which have not been taken from
> the mouths of the people — nor perhaps include all such. The oldest Robin
> Hood ballads are derived from MS., and very many others of the best and
> oldest, and on the other hand some ballads written in comparatively recent
> times, especially historical ones, are found in the mouths of the people. The
> immense collection of Broadside ballads, the Roxburghe and Pepys, of
> which but a small part has been printed, doubtless contain some ballads
> which we should at once declare to possess the popular character, and yet
> on the whole they are veritable dung-hills, in which, only after a great deal
> of sickening grubbing, one finds a very moderate jewel. Some of the later
> Robin Hood ballads I have scarcely the patience to read: but the declension
> is so gradual from the freshest and raciest to the thoroughly *vulgar*, (by
> which I mean always the *essentially* vulgar, the absolutely mean and stupid)
> that it will be very hard, and to me at this moment looks impossible, to
> draw a line.[152]

Child had already warned Furnivall that 'not even the stolid patience of
a book-collector, a most useful though well nigh imbecile creature, would
suffice for twenty years of Roxburghe Ballads';[153] yet he used over 250
broadside and garland texts in his third edition.

Contact with Grundtvig encouraged Child to test his pessimism, and
to 'see if anything can be done in Scotland towards retrieving such ballads
as may be left with the people'.[154]

> I have endeavored by a considerable amount of correspondence — and by
> the circulation throughout Scotland of an 'Appeal', two thousand copies
> of which were dispersed, so that every clergyman and school-master in the
> country was reached, both to ascertain how much is left of traditional
> ballads in the memory of the people, and to get, whatever there is,
> collected. Several gentlemen have taken a warm interest in the matter and
> some have pushed their enquiries very zealously. The fruits, however, are
> small. I have not received *one* ballad that has not been before printed, and
> the copies taken down from recitation are in general much inferior to those
> that have already been printed.[155]

There is no hint that men in positions of authority in Scottish communities might not be able to discover new texts or many variants

because of their gender, status, abilities or access to potential sources, especially amongst working-class women. In any case, there was no question of waiting for the completion of his friends collecting in Aberdeenshire, since most of the texts they sent were pronounced to be 'recollections of *modern print*, a most undesirable aftergrowth of oral tradition'.[156] In order to appear to be thorough, however, Child unleashed another postal blitz amongst the 'gentlemen' of Shetland in 1880, with disturbing results:

> I had supposed that, as the Scotch had been 300 years in possession of the islands, enough of them might have gone there to plant Scottish ballads. But that seems doubtful; at any rate, an intelligent correspondent says that the Scotch clergy as *a class* have done their best to destroy any relic of antiquity in the shape of tradition or ballad. Some Norse traditions of value may remain, and the Norse population are said to be much more amenable to appeals in behalf of traditional remains.[157]

History, and bourgeois culture in one of its crudest class-based manifestations, at last reared themselves before Child's dismayed gaze; yet while he abandoned Great Britain as a lost cause, he persisted in using his genteel amateurs in the USA, even in 1881:

> I have issued circulars (there are to be 1000) inviting students throughout the country to unite in gathering ballads from the Irish American population.[158]

He gave instructions for the 'proper recording of ballads, burdens, and airs', but any pretence at objectivity is abandoned when he prints 'copies of *The Cruel Sister* and of *Sir Hugh* by way of specimens of the sort of thing desired'.[159] With this kind of prescriptive collecting, it is obvious that Child's ideas about the criteria for 'popular balladry' had shifted hardly at all since the 1850s. Only 100 or so texts in the third edition are credited to the genteel individuals who found what he wanted them to look for.

Much more important in Child's literary and scholarly practice were the manuscripts. Some he tracked down on his visits to Britain, in the British Museum or the hands of willing sellers. He gained access to most private collections: Abbotsford alone 'has given me trouble', he wrote in 1874,[160] but he lacked Tytler's MS. and one of the Glenriddell MSS. Two of Herd's MSS. he found in the British Museum 'by the merest accident',[161] and, in general, he found English and Scots people 'So *stolid*, absolutely stolid', that his idea for a new 'Ballad Society for the collecting and printing of all such remains of popular ballads as could be found in the memory of the people or manuscripts' fell on deaf ears.[162] Furnivall, his fingers burned by the Percy MS. enterprise, gave in and 'plunged into the Roxburghe broadsides'.[163] Child lived in hope of finding a new title in Kinloch's three manuscripts, which he had been promised, and he encouraged a man from Aberdeenshire 'to go out to

Scotland' in 1877 to collect, though with all his searching he had not 'found one unknown ballad since the *Percy MS.* was printed'.[164] By the early 1880s, apart from a correspondence with William Walker of Aberdeen in the 1890s, he was resigned to finding the occasional variant in a magazine,[165] and had come to see printing as a way of ending 'these vain outreachings', which cost him (or rather, his friends who gave money for the Harvard Library) £100 for 'three MSS. of no great value'.[166]

Child ranked Motherwell highest in his hierarchy of sources, followed by Kinloch and the various MSS. from Mrs Brown. Motherwell and Kinloch supplied almost 20% of the *main* texts in the third edition, Buchan provided more than Kinloch, and Scott was not very far behind. Percy was used for nearly 5%, Herd for over 3%, and Ritson's contribution was all but eliminated — a backhanded compliment to his accurate scholarship. From the top six contributors, manuscript texts were twice as numerous as printed ones. Manuscript and oral sources accounted for almost half the texts in the entire edition.[167] Why did this happen? James calculates that 115 texts from the first edition were omitted because they had been too highly 'edited', they were 'romances', had 'non-popular origins' (notably broadsides), were translations, or lacked a 'narrative element' or 'ballad style'.[168] Of the 90 texts included in the third edition for the first time, 37 were not available for the first, while 35 of the remainder were from Buchan, and 18 were fragments or unsatisfactory in some other way in the shape known to Child.[169] Yet Child had to rely not only on William Macmath[170] of Edinburgh, who acted as a transcriber and research assistant, but also on people like Robert White, the Newcastle litterateur, whose reliability has lately come into question[171]. In later Parts, some of the people we now know as 'folksong' collectors receive credits — Kidson, Baring-Gould, M. H. Mason, Broadwood, Fuller-Maitland, Bruce and Stokoe — but, once again, Child was relying on their collecting and publishing integrity to a degree which, as we shall see, it did not always merit.[172] In fact, Child used the apparent scarcity of songs in circulation to justify his own prejudices: 'gathering from tradition has been, as ought perhaps to have been seen at this late day, meagre, and generally of indifferent quality'.[173] The collectors' role seemed unproblematical to him, and their findings fitted in perfectly with his own conception of 'tradition' and his attitude towards workers' culture.

* * * * *

(v) His editing

Child came across Grundtvig's *Danmarks gamle Folkeviser* 'quite late',[174] but he imitated its formal structure and apparatus in 'nearly all respects'[175] in his third edition. In fact, Child spent the years after 1860 adapting his own ideas to those implicit in the Danish collection, and trying to fit his English and Scots material into a very similar structure, building on the aura of scientificity which emanates from his own second edition, where he admits an occasional collation and emendation:

> For the texts, the rule has been to select the most authentic copies, and to reprint them as they stand in the collections, restoring readings that had been changed without grounds, and noting all deviations from the originals, whether those of previous editors or of this edition, in the margin. Interpolations acknowledged by the editors have generally been dropped. In two instances only have previous texts been superceded or greatly improved.[176]

His criteria for the 'best', of course, were likely to coincide with those of a poet like Scott, and to clash with those of Buchan, from one of whose texts 'One uncommonly tasteless stanza, the interpolation of some nursery-maid, is here omitted.'[177] It followed that even if *Sir Patrick Spence* was 'not ancient', it had

> been always accepted as such by the most skilful judges, and is a solitary instance of successful imitation, in manner and spirit, of the best specimens of authentic minstrelsy.[178]

The literary standards of contemporary bourgeois taste could be assumed to be hegemonic, even in the construction of new 'authentic' texts; yet some items which were 'true' had to be suppressed because of the objectionable nature of their subject-matter. Following Motherwell's example, the reader was referred to the Index, where a reference gave the sources of five 'popular'[179] texts which had to do with sexual encounters. As Legman remarks, when we consider that Child's chosen texts silently condone sadism, butchery, murder and any amount of violence, it speaks volumes about the culture for which Child worked that sexual relations had to be apologized for or silently omitted.[180]

Child admitted to Grundtvig about his first edition that he 'never pretended that the arrangement was founded on a deeper principle than convenience'.[181] In general he 'suspected everything that was not vouched for by some other collector of credit',[181] but he agreed that he 'certainly ought to have proceeded upon a clearer principle'.[182] Grundtvig pressed for something 'more systematic' and 'without any appendices', while praising Child for his grasp of some European sources, for his grappling with 'the Angloscotic department of the common Gothic Middleage Ballad Poetry' and for his substantial notes.[183] Child remained uneasy about the 'compass' and the 'arrangement' of his third edition from 1872 onwards, worrying about his 'vague' reasons for omitting one text, and lamenting that he could not 'consistently insist on the lyrical, or singable, character as a criterion'.[184] From time to time he separated 'Outlaw' and '*Trylleviser*' texts from others as constituting a 'natural class';[185] but even so late as 1874 Grundtvig complained that he could not begin his own work until Child had sent a *'plan*, and a *list of contents'*.[186] To encourage his pupil, the Dane did send a list of items from the second edition which should be omitted from the third, and some ideas for new texts to be included. Grundtvig's views on 'immoral', 'irreligious', 'vulgar' and 'debased' items were shared by Child;[187] but so lacking in confidence was the American professor that even in 1874 he pleaded for an idea for the 'arrangement', and for

> the *criterion* of the popular ballad, the distinction between ballad and tale, *fabliau*, and between the genuine national or people's ballads and all varieties of a base kind. I think the distinction is easier to feel than to formulate. I should like to have you try to express the more subtle characteristics of an old popular ballad in words.[188]

Grundtvig refused to do all the work for him; and in 1875 Child contemplated using Scott's two categories, 'Romantic' and 'Historical',[189] while in other ways imitating Gruntvig's system of numbering different items and giving variants and notes. He professed himself unable to theorize his practice: 'the chemistry of the English and Scottish ballad seems to me, *mostly*, as indeterminable as Greek myths'.[190] Grundtvig concurred so far as to point out that differing materials made a common arrangement of *The Popular Ballads of the English Race* (as he wished Child's work to be called),[191] and those from other national literatures, impossible. The structure of the work would be 'quite arbitrary':

> there is no doubt that the ballad poetry of the Gothic nations is upon the whole contemporary and of a homogeneous character both with regard to its contents, treatment, style of poetry and form of verse, but nevertheless each department has its own peculiarities.[192]

He offered the notion of arrangement by *'the form'* or metre rather than by content;[193] and Child promptly followed this up by asking for him to 'go on with the arrangement, with a *reason* now and then in difficult cases'[194]. In 1877, Child had to ask for 'any opinion as to the time when the English ballads were produced',[195] and he admitted his dependence on the Danish scholar by writing, in 1880, that 'Every time you edit a ballad which occurs in English you do a large part of my work for me.'[196] Grundtvig's tongue must have been firmly in his cheek when he writes of his satisfaction that his 1850s plans had now been 'acknowledged and adopted by the very best men of the present day'.[197]

Finally, Grundtvig relented, and sent Child his own ideas for a structure of the edition based on the supposed chronology of verse-forms. Child found the proposal, unsurprisingly, a 'very convenient one', and adopted it immediately, even changing one text's form so as to fit the theory![198] But in the Advertisement to the third edition Child acknowledges Grundtvig's help sparingly.[199] Hustvedt believes, however, that not only the plan but even the choice of the contents of that work were Grundtvig's, based on the *Index* which he had kept and changed over the years. From the second version of this Index

> the following have been excluded, out of different reasons, partly because they were of too local a character, as the Border ballads, partly as decidedly political pieces, some also while they seemed to be of too recent date or were of doubtful antiquity.[200]

To the third version of the *Index* some items were restored, and this was the list which Hustvedt believed was crucial to the 'formation of the canon of English balladry',[201] though Child rejected Grundtvig's book-based chronology for one based on manuscripts.[202] So far back as 1850,[203] Motherwell's collection seems to have formed the basis of Grundtvig's current list, which fits in with Motherwell's status as Child's most trusted and major source. We have to acknowledge that *The English and Scottish Popular Ballads* of 1882–98, the result of a Dane supervising an American, and relying heavily on a violently reactionary Scots Tory who died in 1832, is not only a product of a particular stage of academic scholarship, but one which has deep roots in the culture and ideology of the English-speaking bourgeoisie on both sides of the Atlantic. About the lives, interest and culture of the people who made, re-made and used even these highly-selected kinds of songs, however, Child like his predecessors can tell us almost nothing.

6   The 'Ballad' Consensus

After Child's death, and when the last Part of *The English and Scottish Popular Ballads* had been seen through the press by his literary executors, peculiar things began to happen which the Harvard scholar probably never foresaw. His work, and the ideas implicit in it, were taken up by a fair number of professional academics, usually in university departments of English Literature, both in Britain and North America. The study of 'ballads' was established, above all in the USA, as a legitimate element in the curriculum; and several of the generation of literary academics who got jobs in the first two decades of the twentieth century in the USA, and later moved on to hold professorships, benefited materially from their association with the prestige in which Child's work was held. The paradox was that scholarly respect for Child's achievement was matched with an almost complete absence of rigorous theory in his work, so that in order to legitimize the emerging 'field', these young scholars had to set about trying to elaborate Child's *obiter dicta* into something which was academically presentable. They flirted with the developing discipline of anthropology, fought off attempts to annex 'folklore' to already-existing intellectual territories, and spent the first three decades of this century trying to cling on to Child's prestige *and* cope with all the contradictions in his practice. That struggle, in somewhat modified form, continues today[1]; and the kernel of Child's 'ballad' consensus lurches on, rather like a zombie, at the margins of academic endeavour. Though it has been savaged, partly destroyed and chopped in pieces, the consensus has managed to survive this long not simply because many people's material interests are involved, but because it has always been analaysed *piecemeal*, and because many of the ideas it contains continue to be of use to bourgeois ideology. This chapter seeks to trace the development of the 'ballad' consensus by showing what happened to the third edition of Child's work, and how his ideas on 'ballad' origins, transmission and change were taken up and amended. It also aims to show that this debate was firmly intellectualist for most of the period 1900–1940, and to suggest that ideas about the relationship between 'ballads' and 'workers' history and culture are hobbled by Child's assumptions and prejudices, even in our own time.

* * * * *

(i) The appeal to authority: 'Child ballads'

The appeal to Child's authority was almost uniform throughout the period 1900–1940 amongst literary figures. Courthope[2] and Henderson[3] in Britain, while distancing themselves from some of Child's ideas in the 1890s, paid tribute to his 'invaluable' edition. Ker[4] followed suit; Quiller-Couch part-dedicated his book to Child and claimed 'His work...left no room for follower or imitator'.[5] and Brimley-Johnson paid due homage to the 'monumental collections'.[6] Henderson, by 1912, was sure that Child's edition 'must ever remain the standard collection of British ballad versions', and adopted Child's numbering system.[7] Sidgwick in 1914 termed it 'the fountainhead of information on the 305 ballads included therein'.[8] In the USA, the appeals were positively fulsome. Kittredge was sycophantic:

> No possible source of information could elude him; no book or manuscript was too voluminous or too unpromising for him to examine on the chance of its containing some fact that might correct or supplement his material, even in the minutest point.[9]

Being one of the school of young specialists Child had fostered, Kittredge[10] was well-placed to bathe in the reflected glory of his master's 'rare faculty' and 'ready sympathy' in tackling editorial problems:

> Mere learning will not guide an editor through these perplexities. What is needed is, in addition, a complete understanding of the 'popular' genius, a sympathetic recognition of the traits that characterize oral literature wherever and in whatever degree they exist. This faculty, *which even the folk has not retained*, and which collectors living in ballad-singing and tale-telling times have often failed to acquire, was vouchsafed by nature herself to this sedentary scholar. In reality a kind of instinct, it had been so cultivated by long and loving study of the traditional literature of all nations that it had become wonderfully swift in its operations and almost infallible. A forged or retouched piece could not deceive him for a moment; he detected the slightest jar in the genuine ballad tone.[11]

From this position it was no great step to use Child's work as a *definition* in its own right. Gummere began to speak of the 'true ballad critic' who could recognize 'alien stuff' and 'traditional material', and who could do the 'comparative study of extensive material and patient scrutiny of details' in order to bring the study of poetry in general into the 'control of facts'.[12] Of course, Kittredge was quite right about the contrast between Child's work and that of his predecessors:

> In no field of literature have the forger and the manipulator worked with greater vigor and success. From Percy's day to our own it has been thought an innocent device to publish a bit of one's own versifying, now and then, as an 'old ballad' or an 'ancient song'.[13]

But instead of trying to situate Child in terms of the traditions of which he formed a part, people like Kittredge went on to canonize his work almost uncritically. It wasn't until the 1920s that Pound examined the role of 'specialists' in 'ballad' study, while a serious challenge to Child's concept of a 'satisfactory canon of specimens' had to wait until Gerould in the 1930s.

These post-Child academics wanted to present 'ballads' as a distinct 'formal literary type'[14] within bourgeois 'Poetry' and 'Literature'. Such debate as there was about definitions of 'ballads' hinged around the question of literary quality, and whether the so-called 'traditional ballad' was the same as the texts contained in Child's edition. Henderson characterized that work as 'a sort of library of the different versions, — good, indifferent, bad', and worse than bad', in which the 'chaff is out of all proportion to the wheat'.[15] Kittredge claimed that the 'great collection' comprised 'the whole extant mass of this material' except for a few variants remaining to be collected orally, and that it contained 'all the apparatus necessary for the study of this kind of literature', including texts of 'every grade of popularity'.[16] Ker was able to assume that 'no definition, even if it were perfect, would tell as much as a reference to the great collections of ballads made last century'[17] by Child and Grundtvig. Further, he asserted that not only were the 'ballads of the Teutonic languages' in 'three groups' — English Danish and German — but that 'The English [sic] are all together in Child's five volumes'.[18] This habit of using Child's edition as the definition continued in Britain through the 1910s, and Child's 'gallant 305'[19] remained as bed-rock even for field-collectors like Barry in 1929:

> This collection of ballads builds a New England superstructure upon Professor Child's well-laid foundations. We do not ask why he accepted or rejected his titles, but we try to square our work to his lines and to agree with his conclusions wherever possible. Sound critical work upon Child's own lines has been the objective.[20]

Given that it was Hustvedt who published the correspondence which highlighted Child's reliance on Grundtvig's ideas and his lack of self-confidence, his continued faith in the 'popular ballad' being defined as 'the sort of verse so named by Child, in whatever dialect it may happen to have been recorded'[21] is remarkable indeed. Even Gerould, who acknowledged that 'harm has been done by too rigid an insistence on the authoritative completeness of Child's collection',[22] and wrote that 'nothing like an exact census of English and Scottish ballads can be made',[23] hedged his bets:

> He brought together, however, so large and so representative a collection of texts that the student requires no further illustration either of the subjects treated or the manner in which the stories are told.[24]

Child's 'instinct' is smuggled in by the back door. How did Gerould know how 'representative' Child's texts were, other than by making the same set of assumptions and the same literary-critical judgements?

* * * * *

(ii) The 'marks' of the 'ballad'

When we examine the earlier writers, we find that they had the same contradictory attitude. Gummere, in his literary Social-Darwinistic search for the 'ballad' in a 'clearly-defined curve of evolution in the life-history of literary forms in English',[25] wrote of the 'normal type'[26] of the 'ballad' which the 'true ballad critic'[27] had to 'make up, as a composite photograph, from the best old manuscript versions of soundest oral tradition'.[28] Child happened to qualify as sifter and tester, and so other critics, like Quiller-Couch in Britain, could confidently use Child's texts as raw material for 'one form' of the 'ballad', the 'best according to his judgement and feeling' in 'firm black and white' sometimes removing a 'coarse or brutal phrase' for the benefit of 'boy or maid'.[29] Such people knew they were being irrational and idealist but felt no shame. Ker proclaimed:

> In spite of Socrates and his logic we may venture to say, in answer to the question 'What is a ballad?' — 'A ballad is *The Milldams of Binnorie* and *Sir Patrick Spens* and *The Douglas Tragedy* and *Lord Randal* and *Child Maurice*, and things of that sort,[30]

all of which chanced to be in Child's collection. Brimley-Johnson 'demanded no more of a ballad than that it should be a simple spirited narrative', but confessed to having been 'guided in doubtful cases rather by intuition than by rule' and by his own 'judgement of their artistic merits'.[31] The essential continuity, as Gerould noted, was through the 'ballad'-mediators themselves:

> The plain fact is that collectors and students of ballads ... somehow recognize that they are dealing with the same kind of thing....[32]

And given this was the case, theoretical development was limited to the elaboration of ideas *implicit* in Child's collection.

Kittredge noted that 'impersonality' was 'one of the marked tendencies of popular narrative poetry', along with the tendency to 'alter or eliminate specific names of persons and places'.[33] Gummere added to the 'Specific Marks of the Ballad'[34] the concept of 'incremental repetition', which was when 'each stanza repeats the substance of the preceding, but with some variation which enhances the story'.[35] Ker found that 'ballads keep to their point, and that is generally a definite tragic problem' or 'error' or 'conflict of affections or duties';[36] while Sidgwick believed 'you never know what a ballad will say next, though *do* do know how it is going to say it!'.[37] Pound, using a somewhat broader definition of 'popular poetry', discovered certain traits such as a liking for the 'extraordinary, not the near at hand', the 'unusual not the usual person', the 'strange, the sensational, the tragic, or at the other extreme, the comic'.[38] She found that 'repetition, structural or stanzaic, verbal, of the refrain type, or consisting of interweaving lines, may be found in all popular poetry';[39] but by stretching 'marks' of the 'ballad' out to embrace 'popular poetry', she was not so much expanding the range of the consensus as supporting the assumptions on which it was based. Gerould does the same by enumerating 'ballad' 'constants' like the 'stress on situation', action being 'focussed on a single episode' while 'the past is ignored altogether, or is implied rather darkly'.[40] There is even a 'way of telling a story' by 'permitting the action to interpret itself with the minimum of comment and descriptive setting';[41] but the crucial element in this 'refining definition' is the cultural otherness which Gerould and his predecessors thought they perceived:

> there is frequently displayed an insensitiveness to suffering that appals nerves more finely drawn, an impassivity in the face of life's worst outrages that reveals the equilibrium of a childlike and healthy race. Vices and virtues, in so far as they motivated ballad stories, are the vices and virtues of a rather primitive folk.[42]

Given that these theorists were content to *deduce* their 'definition' from Child's texts, it followed that they had to go on to deduce something like a social psychology of historic communities, and a cultural history to match. The 'elements' of the 'ballads', and ideas about the 'folk' who made or at least transmitted them, get blended into what is essentially an aesthetic analysis based on contemporary academic-literary values, in order to seek to explain the absence of motivation from 'Filial ingratitude', 'the jealousy that age feels of youth', 'avarice' or 'vaulting ambition':

> The folk who have sung ballads for a long while past, at least, have been simple of mind and station. Action, for them, has been limited by circumstance, but it has not been inhibited by "thinking too precisely on the event." Apparently they have seldom been moved to envy of their betters, since envy is not a motive used. Personal jealousy, like personal pride, is common enough; but dissatisfaction with the scheme of things does not appear. Even the outlaws object only to injustices of administration. Similarly absent are tales of discouragement and failure.... Sloth, which gave the mediaeval church such concern, does not trouble the ballad-singer.... Another conspicuous omission is of stories that turn on sacrifice for the sake of persons outside family or clan ... they show men acting either individually or in small groups — seldom with consciousness of anything beyond. The range of their themes reveals to us the preoccupations, emotional and intellectual, of common folk during the past centuries.[43]

This breathtakingly confident caricature of 'common folk' and their culture rested entirely on what Gerould deduced from Child's texts, and that deduction was used, in turn, to seek to legitimise Child's *prescription* of what consituted a 'ballad'.

The other definition of the 'ballad' was that by *form*. Courthope believed that

> The English ballads that have come down to us fall naturally into three classes: those which reflect the characteristics of the ancient *chansons de geste*; those which combine the features of the *chanson de geste* and the literary romance, and those which have a purely literary origin in the romance, lay or *fabliau*. [44]

Of course, these ideas stem from a particular set of assumptions about authorship and transmission, not to mention those about literature. Without proof, and knowing that proof was hard to find, Courthope develops the notion that a 'ballad' was 'usually a *precis* of a romance' which 'developed certain poetical features of its own, the most notable of which were abrupt transitions, repetitions of phrases, and conventional formulae'. [45] Kittredge's assertion that 'No one can read "The Hunting of the Cheviot", or "Mary Hamilton", and 'fail to recognize that, different as they are from each other in theme and effect, they belong together', [46] remained true, amongst 'ballad' theorists at any rate. Gummere, with his scientific pretensions, refuted the notion of 'defining' by Arnoldian 'touchstones' [47] in favour of learning to 'live one's way into balladry', to 'love it as a whole and not by elegant extracts'. [48] The solution to this problem, then, was a reversion to Motherwell's idealist conception. Ker wrote:

> The truth is that *Ballad* is an Idea, a poetical Form, which can take up any matter, and does not leave the matter as it was before.... [49]

Having established this notion, the 'Form' took on a life of its own, almost separate from human agency:

> "Ballad" is here taken as meaning a lyrical narrative poem ... either popular in its origin, or using the common forms of popular poetry, and fitted for oral circulation through the whole of a community. [50]

Logically, with this autonomy, 'form' could relate to 'form:

> As to the subjects there can be no doubt that there is freedom of communication — a free passage — between the popular tales (*Marchen*) and the ballads, with this most important condition, that nothing shall be taken up by a ballad except what is fit for the ballad form ... ballad poetry has a mind of its own...and will not take up a subject which is too complicated or too large.... [51]

From this idiosyncratic set of ideas, Ker is able to set himself up as a Motherwell-like 'universal mind'-reader:

> The essential thing .... is, first, the conception of the story, and next, the proportions of it. The story must be either tragic or, if not that, momentous in some way; it must have a situation, it must work to some point. This is what distinguishes these poems from the common rambling romances.... Again, they are all short poems, they rarely amplify or go into details, they have no digressions. This is what distinguishes them from epic.[52]

So, we return conveniently to the 'ballad' prescription, with the same assertions about literary quality and 'lyric beauty' from the same bourgeois perspective:

> Some ballads are derived from older narrative literature: of these, some are worth remembering and others not. Those that are not worth remembering are not worth calling ballads; those that are worth remembering are worth remembering *as ballads* and not as mere narrative poems.[53]

Quiller-Couch invoked Ker's ideas about the 'ballad', which 'would seem to have discovered, almost at the start, a very precise Platonic pattern of what its best should be'.[54] It followed, according to Sidgwick, that 'you cannot even write it down. At best you can but record a number of variants':[55]

> A ballad is, and always has been, so far from being a literary form that it is, in its essentials, not literary, and ... no single form. It is of a *genre* not only older than Epic, older than Tragedy, but older than literature, older than the alphabet. It is *lore*, and belongs to the illiterate.[56]

Who could then guide people into this time-warp of pre-literary culture? Clearly, only the enlightened. The *Idea* had to be swallowed whole.

* * * * *

(iii) 'Ballads' and 'common sense'

What confused literary academics was that real living people were still singing what they understood to be 'ballads'.[57] Evidently, the theory had to be made to fit; and by 1913 Barry had produced an essentially dynamic conception of the 'ballad', which he believed referred 'not to an event, but to a process', by which 'a simple event in human experience, of subjective interest, narrated in simple language, set to a simple melody is progressively objectivated'.[58] So, not only is 'the ballad' an *idea*, but any given text of a 'ballad' is an illustration of that *idea*, a phenomenon in its own right whose structure and style could be referred to the process of singing. This partially empiricist approach eventually became dominant, but its idealist content was eroded by the experience of field-collecting.

In the 1920s Pound had to fight against the hegemony of Child-based ideas and assumptions, noting the intellectual tradition which lay behind the use of the term 'ballad',[59] and the arbitrary linking of that term with the texts in Child's edition. Pound believed that Child had wanted to 'make for English a distinction similar to that afforded by Franz Bohme's ideas about *volkslieder* and *volksthümliche lieder*';[60] and though she still believed that the 'epic in little' was a 'literary species' which was 'exemplified in the conventional ballad collections',[61] she problematicized the concept of 'ballad' enough to sap the confidence of even the most abject supporter of Child. In the 1930s, Hustvedt went on to note how 'popular and non-popular elements have been strangely intermingled during the whole period of ballad history', though there remained 'substantial agreement that popular ballads, taken in the mass without distinction of nationality, constitute a unified body of data'.[62] Hustvedt conceded that 'folksong' and 'popularesque lyric'[63] — a song by a 'relatively recent individual author which has been received by the people and thus has taken on a popular character which it did not originally possess'[64] — and the whole range of 'non-popular' pieces would be of the utmost consequence in determining the true metes and bounds of what we now designate by the somewhat fluid term popular'.[65] Gerould went further, and admitted that it was 'not easy to establish a definition of what we call nowadays the popular or traditional ballad'.[66] He offered the minimal explanation that it was 'always a narrative', and 'always sung to a rounded melody'.[67] He agreed that 'we have no right to rule out narrative songs the words of which do not make good literature, and then base theories of origin and development on the residue';[68] but his starting-point remained that the 'ballad' was 'a distinct species of poetry and music', a pre-literary *genre*.[69] Such an idea presupposed an understanding of where 'ballads' came from, who made them, and when.

The debate over 'ballad' origins went back, in England at any rate, to Percy and Ritson;[70] but by the 1890s, academics in Britain were clear that they were dealing with what Courthope wrote off in a chapter as 'The Decay of English Minstrelsy':[71] 'ballads' were made by particular individuals in particular ways. Henderson dissociated himself from the uncritical and unhistorical undertow of Child's assumptions about 'communal' origins; though he was Social-Darwinist enough to see the 'romance ballad' taking over from the metrical romance.[72] Child's followers were forced to rationalize their acts of faith. Gummere propounded the view that

the way to treat the ballad for historic, comparative and genetic purposes is to separate it into its elements, and to follow these elements back to the point where they vanish in the mists of unrecorded time. Such elements —

and unlike the ballad itself they can be traced — are the fact of singing, the fact of dancing, the fact of universal improvisation, the fact of predominant chorus or refrain.[73]

Instead of following Henderson and making the imaginative leap to what 'the author of the Death of Byrhtnoth must have felt',[74] and seeing 'traditional poetry' as having 'intimate relations with other forms of literature, some of which have now perished',[75] Kittredge started from the premise that the 'poetry of the folk' is 'different from the "poetry of art"', even from 'minstrel poetry,' though 'it often happens that the truth lies too far back for us to discover'.[76] This is why Gummere's superficially scientific method appealed to those fighting to get 'popular balladry' assigned 'a specific and clearly bounded portion of the poetic globe',[77] and of the academic curriculum. Gummere wrote:

> For these three-hundred-odd ballads are either the surviving specimens of a genre, a literary species, which is called popular because in its main qualities it is derived from the 'people', or else they are the somewhat arbitrary collection of poems which had in some way become favorite and even traditional apart from print, with mainly unlettered folk.[78]

'Popular' and 'folk' were being used interchangeably and with extreme vagueness, and 'the people' and 'the folk' likewise. At the same time some critics were associating the study of 'ballads' with the 'youthful sciences of anthropology and psychology' which, according to Sidgwick, were

> sciences of the inexact type in their nature, at present consisting of little more than attempts to find truth by the balancing of probabilities and the elimination of improbabilities. Such elusiveness is to some minds anathema; to others it forms the whole charm of the quest.[79]

Such 'charm' underlines the real marginality of the study of 'ballads', in Britain, at any rate. In the USA, Gummere's 'communalist' view of origins hung on in 'ballad' circles for over two decades, and its ghost still walks.

Eventually, Pound exploded the strange idea that 'ballads' had their origins in dancing. Dance songs of the Middle Ages were called 'carols' in England, while the 'narrative songs which the eighteenth century collected were not dance songs' at all.[80] In order to try to explain why such ideas had any purchase amongst supposedly intelligent people, she began to *historicize* the tradition in which she stood, but only so far, and stopping well short of her own day!

> Belief in the origin of the mediaeval ballads by communal improvisation in the dance, and belief in the extinction, with mediaeval conditions, of the ballad as a literary type, seem to the present writer to have emerged from

and belong to a period of criticism which deliberately preferred the vague and the mystical for all problems of literary and linguistic theory.[81]

Her empiricism rejected the 'romantic enterprise' of those sociologists 'who thought to write a psychology of men *en masse* apart from any sane reliance upon the analysis of individual minds';[82] but in order to reject any one element of the 'communalist' position, Pound had to argue against all the others:

> the following assumptions which have long dominated our thought upon the subject of poetic origins and the ballads should be given up, or at least be seriously qualified; namely, belief in the 'communal' authorship and ownership of primitive poetry, disbelief in the primitive artist; reference to the ballad as the earliest and most universal poetic form; belief in the origin of narrative songs in the dance, especially definition of the English and Scottish traditional ballad type as of dance origin; belief in the emergence of traditional ballads from the illiterate, that is, belief in the communal creation rather than *re*-creation of ballads; belief in the special powers of folk improvisation; and belief that the making of traditional ballads is a "closed account."[83]

A decade later, she had won the argument so conclusively that Gerould pronounced it 'still harder' to find out how a 'ballad' ever 'came into being', since he believed all of them to have 'developed orally', making any effort 'to recover an "original" or "authentic" version' quite 'fruitless'.

* * * * *

(iv) 'Ballads' and 'the people'

Quite why critics like Pound should have had to argue positions like this 150 years after the War of Independence and the French Revolution is a curious question, especially since, in Britain, the contempt for 'the people' amongst 'ballad' editors remained remarkably uniform. In the 1890s, Professor Courthope dismissed the 'style' of 'ballads' as simply reflecting 'the tastes of those for whom they were composed',[84] an essentially passive bunch of consumers: 'What the people contributed to the making of the ballads was no more than the sentiment and taste which characterise them.'[85] When a given text did not fit contemporary bourgeois ideas about literary quality, the solution was simply to blame the artist — 'though the genius of this ballad-maker was considerable', he wrote of *Mary Hamilton's* putative male author, 'his taste was vulgar'.[86] By contrast, Gummere had a naive faith in the creativity of 'the people', and stretched his mind and what little evidence he had to claim that:

> poetry made by a throng, or in a throng, or made for a throng, or made

in whatever fashion but finding its way, as favourite expression, to a throng
— and every theory of communal verse may be referred to one of these
cases — is a quite disinct kind of poetry from that which is made by the
solitary poet for the solitary reader.[87]

To Kittredge, also, this stress on 'the people' underwrote his own
preferences for 'mind'-reading idealism:

> A ballad has no author. At all events, it appears to have none. The teller
> of the story for the time being is as much the author as the unknown (*and
> for our purposes unimportant*) person who first put it into shape.[88]

In this sense, Grimm's dictum of 'das Volk dichtet' could be allowed to
stand, at an unspecified historical period when 'a small tribal gathering',
living under 'very simple conditions of life', had 'no such diversity of intellectual interests as characterizes even the smallest company of civilized
men':[89]

> Here, now, we have the 'folk' of our discussion, reduced, as it were, to its
> lowest terms — a singing, dancing throng subjected as a unit to a mental
> and emotional stimulus which is not only favorable to the production of
> poetry, but is almost certain to result in such production.[90]

The same populist romanticism had penetrated 'civilized' American
ideology thus far; but the very literary quality of Child's texts forced
Kittredge to retreat a little on the question of origin:

> It makes no difference whether a given ballad was in fact composed in the
> manner described, or whether it was composed (or even written) in
> solitude, provided the author belonged to the folk, derived his material
> from popular sources, made his ballad under the inherited influence of the
> method described, and gave it to the folk as soon as he had made it, —
> and provided, moreover, the folk accepted the gift....[91]

Gummere's problem with this bet-hedging was that there was

> nothing but the law of copyright and the personal fame of Mr Kipling
> which could serve at some future day to exclude his 'Danny Deever' from
> a collection of English popular ballads or to differentiate it from 'Hobbie
> Noble' and 'Jock o' the Side'.[92]

On the other side of the argument, Henderson openly asserted that
the author 'must count ... for everything',[93] though he believed such a
person to be a 'merely mechanical maker'[94] rather than a creator of art.
He and the communalists agreed (for different reasons) that the 'proper
destiny' of that author was 'inglorious obscurity', while the 'appropriate
place' for the 'ballad' is 'enshrinement in the hearts and memories of the

people'.[95] However, Henderson's attitude to 'the people' at any historical period was one of outright contempt:

> unlearned people have limited powers of invention; unlearned tradition is
> also sometimes tenacious of the general gist of the story; for it is the story
> which appeals to it ... unlettered tradition evidently indulges in invention
> of a sort ... [but is] very careless as to expression and rhyme, and rather
> tends to make the ballad "popular", in the sense of being mean and com-
> mon and rude in style, and "impersonal", destitute of the traces of in-
> dividual authorship, for the simple reason that it has been gradually
> remoulded by the processes of instinctively stupid interference with the
> original text, by the ignorant touches of those by whom it has during many
> generations been preserved, by their inevitable preference for their own
> colloquial and, in a literary sense, obtuse method of expression, and often
> confused character of their notions and sentiments.[96]

Henderson claimed, then, that the 'popular' of his putative 'original'
was quite different from the 'popular' of particular texts found in
'tradition'.[97]

Sidgwick was more open in 1914, when he spoke about 'English
peasants' in general and the 'illiterate rustic'[98] of his own day, and
postulated the existence of some 'Aryan bard'[99] as being the fountain of
the 'ballad' in Europe, rather than some ancient community of adults
'with the minds of modern babies'.[100] This race-conscious élitism — they
wrote blandly of 'the older Teutonic poetry'[101] and the 'Anglo-Saxon'[102]
— underpinned British imperialism and ruling class ideology in general,
on both sides of the Atlantic. To Gummere, the real issue was whether
'ballad' themes were 'borrowed from our neighbours', or from 'a
common European or Aryan fund of popular poetry'.[103] Pound believed
that 'the development of the child mirrors that of the race',[104] but she
was also more anthropological, and tackled the communalists head-on:
'Did primitive man sing, dance, and compose in a throng, while he was
yet unable to do so as an individual?'[105] The rhetorical question led her
towards a belief in an 'older singer' who 'composed for the ear; otherwise
his work was vain',[106] in a period before printing became important. She
found that collective improvization, amongst workers, produced 'crude,
structureless, incoherent'[107] songs; and this led Gerould to a belief that,
though 'the art of the folk has been a somewhat ragged thing',[108]

> It seems to me that we are forced to accept belief in a tradition of artistry
> current at least in certain groups or families and in certain regions, and
> probably continuing from century to century....[109]

This helped explain the quality of those 'parallel versions of considerable
merit'[110] which Gerould wanted to locate in the culture of 'the people';
but to make his assumptions stick he had to postulate a time when

a large number of individuals were so affected by a sound tradition of music and verse that they could compose or adapt ballads in such a way as to make what was worthy of remembrance ... some of them may have been middle-class folk rather than peasants, and ... some of them were certainly "minstrels" — professionals of a sort. The art they practised, however, was beyond all doubt distinguishable from that by which the higher classes were beguiled, a popular if not a rustic art.[111]

From questions of origin dominating the debate, those of 'sound tradition' and processes of transmission had come to dominate intellectual concern with the 'ballad'. In the 1930s, Pound patronized 'the crude pieces that the "people"' sometimes improvize.[112] Gerould was élitest enough to deny the very agents of that 'tradition' any consciousness of their artistic role:

> the persons who have made these varying forms that we admire must always have been trained musicians, just as they have been far from unskilled in verse; but they have acquired their knowledge with so little effort, being in the tradition of it, as to be almost unconscious of artistry.[113]

In over a century, such leading ideas about the makers and bearers of 'tradition' had changed hardly at all. The 'minstrel' had simply been assimilated into 'the people' by a process of downward social and cultural mobility, and 'the tradition' included the work of these 'professional vagabonds'.

If the 'people' had relatively little to do, collectively, with the making of the texts these academics called 'ballads', what did they still sometimes sing them for? Courthope thought they simply 'preserved them' in 'their memories after they had been composed'.[114] Henderson noted that:

> Many of the traditional ballads are strangely unequal, and at a later period they tended to become a kind of patchwork in which stanzas of startling poetic beauty are occasionally to be found side by side with mere tawdry vulgarity or hopeless bathos.[115]

To his way of seeing,

> Much of the original beauty and accuracy of the alliteration and rhythm of *Chevy Chase* has plainly been lost, and it may therefore be inferred that both in it and in the English and Scottish versions of Otterbourne alteration and interpolation have wrought sad havoc on the unity and force of the original.[116]

He went on to exonerate the 'minstrel' from much of the blame, since 'he had been superceded by the hack balladist and the ragged ballad singer':[117]

> ballads, fallen from their high estate, were preserved, now, mainly, in the

confused memories of the lower classes; feudalism had vanished, and the conditions of society had completely changed; England had become a humdrum land of peace and plenty....[118]

Quite what ragged people were doing in apparently so comfortable a land isn't explained; but Henderson is quite confident in attributing to 'the people' the responsibility for overlaying the 'essential utterance'[119] of the ideal original with grime from their hands:

> We must make allowance for the deterioration effected by possibly some centuries of mangling by reciters; for tradition, contact with the natural man, contagion from the 'heart of the people' — which heart, however sincere and strong in its emotions, is now, and probably ever was, wholly untrained in the art of poetic expression — does not tend ... towards the elaboration of the consummate qualities of the ballad, but rather, as hundreds of instances could be adduced to prove, towards their obscuration, defilement, and final effacement.[120]

Hundreds of such instances are not adduced: 'the people' are *defined* as inept; while the broadsides they bought in their thousands are written off as 'merely vulgar, sometimes ferociously vulgar, travesties of the old ballad' which is known only to insiders like Henderson. Ker noted how Grundtvig's collection, for example, had come down through 'courtly'[121] cultural processes, and termed the construct of 'the people' as 'dogma'.[122] Sidgwick openly characterized 'the people' as an 'undistinguished many-headed common herd', in which 'folk-singers' were merely 'genuinely illiterate store-houses of folk-lore'.[123] These 'few old villagers' could be likened to a 'disused machine' which 'only needs a little coaxing and perhaps a little oil'.[124] They were the last representatives of that 'Germanic ring which surrounds the north of Europe', and were 'dying out.'[125] These were the people amongst whose forbears the 'ballad', 'having exhausted itself', 'declined (through a crab-apple stage of Broadsides) into sterility'.[126] The task of the mediator was to understand the 'mischances that attend the solidification of the fluid'[127] 'ballad' Idea in the 'golden age'[128] of c.1550–1700, before 'ballad' texts were deformed, debased and vulgarized by working people.

The American mediators' ideas about transmission were similar. Kittredge adopted Gummere's notion of a 'curve of evolution'[129] in literary history, with occasional texts representing a 'survival of an archaic type-specimen, in full vigor of traditional life, at a very late date'.[130] Gummere postulated 'ballads' as a 'closed literary account',[131] in order to rule out the 'daily production of ballads which may become in time as popular as any in our collections'.[131] This in turn meant that Kittredge had to assume that any contemporary 'teller of the tale has no role in it':[132] 'there are no comments or reflections by the narrator. He does not dissect or psychologize. He does not take sides.'[133] Kittredge retained some faith in the artistic abilities of the process of 'oral tradition', so long as the 'simple folk'[134] from whom songs were taken had no professional status. Ideally, they should be women:

> the most stationary part of the community and the farthest removed, by every instinct and habit, from the roving and irresponsible professionalism which characterizes the minstrel.[135]

Yet when he came to give some proof of these assertions, Kittredge blandly ignores the fact that the professor's daughter, Mrs Brown, was a key singer in his tracing *The Cruel Brother* back from 1860 to 1776,[136] and that the seventeenth century text of *Johnie Armstrong* was from print.[137] Kittredge is reduced, in the end, to the breathtakingly illogical claim that

> It is capable of practically formal proof, that for the last two or three centuries the English and Scottish popular ballads have not, as a general thing, been sung and transmitted by professional minstrels or their representatives. There is no reason whatever for believing that the state of things between 1300 and 1600 was different, in this regard, from that between 1600 and 1900....[138]

There is no evidence presented about the people who are supposed to have contributed to the 'tradition' Kittredge postulates, for 'every student of popular literature' was assumed to know intuitively that 'corruptions' always 'amount to a distinct kind of authorship', sometimes 'a second act of composition'.[139] With Gummere, he believed that only the 'community' in its 'unconscious' and 'primitive'[140] state *could* produce 'ballads', and once they found their way 'into the singer's basket and into the stalls' as broadsides, they were liable to be 'corrupted' by the 'rabble of the street'.[141] The attraction of these texts was precisely their supposed independence of 'art' and of workers' culture:

> Art can create far beyond the beauty of sea-shells, and on occasion can exactly reproduce them; but it cannot fashion or imitate their murmur of the sea.[142]

Pound rejected the idea that 'the making of traditional ballads is a "closed account"',[143] but accepted the concept of communal '*re*-creation':

> it should not be a test of genuineness of a piece as folk-song that it continues the style of sixteenth or seventeenth century popular song.[144]

Moreover, she mocked Kittredge's ideas about the period 1300–1600,[145] since the minstrels' status had changed after the 'introduction of printing and the disappearance of mediaeval conditions', leading to the break-up of the 'mediaeval form of minstrelsy' in the period 1400–1600.[146] She acknowledged that 'songs have been preserved in remote districts and among the humble',[147] but denied that was any proof of their origins, and supported the notion of artist-involvement:

> by the time that new songs have won currency on the stage, or in the city, or let us say, in the castle, or the market-place, or the ale-house, or the fair — the old have found their way into remote places and are likely to persist there, especially among that more fixed and sheltered element of the population, the women.[148]

Using material gathered by Cecil Sharp in the Appalachians, Pound generalized this one-way idea of cultural transmission:

> The folk improvise largely to familiar airs. They do not create their own melodies, and especially not on the spur of the moment. They make over, or add stanzas to, or somehow manipulate, something already in existence.[149]

When 'typical ballads' were 'recovered from oral tradition', Pound noted that they tended to come from 'special individuals' rather than from 'the most unlettered or even from people of average gifts'.[150] Therefore, while not denying 'Folk re-creation of traditional ballads',[151] the product of this transforming process was 'the work of and the property of the people';[152] but that did not mean that the same piece 'might not have been a ballad before the illiterate ever touched it in a modifying way'.[153] In general, she believed that the 'typical process, for the great majority of traditional ballads, is a process of decay'[154] in 'oral transmission', and this legitimized Alexander Keith's procedure of going to 'select people for his best texts'.[155] From holding a concept of 'ballad' and developing a theory of its origin and transmission, mediators like Pound now felt it necessary to go further and to prescribe the kind of people amongst a given population who should be chosen to deliver the best texts! Her definition rested on the mode of transmission:

> They are folk-songs if the people have remembered them and sung them, if they have an existence apart from written sources, and if they have been given oral preservation through a fair period of years.[156]

Contrary to Child's disciples, Pound had to agree that 'print does not "kill" good ballads, but helps to keep them alive',[157] and that to insist upon 'oral tradition' as the sole defining factor 'would have barred the majority of Professor Child's best texts'.[158]

After Pound's erosion of the communalists' case, such theoretical interest as remained was to be found amongst the people involved in collecting. Phillips Barry claimed that to find out what a 'folksong' was, you had to discover 'What are the folk singing?'.[159] Given that rational critics now accepted the dictum of 'individual invention plus communal re-creation' as the contemporary rendering of 'das Volk dichtet',[160]

Barry was able to show that 'the voice of the folksinger may yet be heard, as well in the heart of the great city as on the lonely hillside'.[161] No ballad ever 'died of printer's ink',[162] he maintained, and 'illiteracy is not a necessary factor in traditional balladry'.[163] What he now preferred to call 'folksong' was 'song alive, a living organism, subjected to all the conditions, and manifesting all the phenomena of growth and change',[164] an 'organic whole',[165] 'every available version' of which 'however imperfect or fragmentary, has the right to be recorded'.[166] Yet Barry downgraded a well-known piece such as *Lord Lovell*, sometimes declining to record variants 'if time was short, and anything of more value seemed possible to obtain'.[167] On the other hand, as his history of the piece's 'tradition' shows, Barry understood the importance of institutions such as the 'comic stage' in the transmission and diffusion of even 'ballad' texts, though he writes them off as 'early evil associations'.[168] These were the *'alien'*[169] influences still anathematized in the 1930s by Gerould, as distinct from the creativity of 'folk' artists, many of whom he believed to have been 'first and last, well trained in the music and poetry they have loved and perpetuated',[170] and 'not without some contact with their superiors in the social and educational scale'.[171] To Gerould the 'central problem' which remained was the understanding of the 'processes by which both words and melodies keep continually changing', so that 'we can find out why the ballads and other folk-songs have qualities of their own'.[172]

From this point, apart from a handful of recidivists amongst US literary academics, and even fewer British scholars who wanted to hedge their bets for doubtlessly sound material reasons, the concept of 'ballad' was largely abandoned in favour of the wider debate on the issue of 'folksong'. A. L. Lloyd was one of the first to challenge the notion of an 'unquestioned aristocracy' of so-called 'Child ballads' by placing the debate firmly in a historical context:

> whatever the literature dons might think, not all of these nobles are in Francis J. Child's *English and Scottish Popular Ballads*, nor can all the items in that great compilation be numbered among the peers of the folk song realm. The majority of Child's selection represents but one stage of the ballad, a middle stage lying between the old form of the epic song and the newer form of domestic ballad, journalistic ballad, street song and the like.[173]

But we are jumping ahead when we need to be jumping back. During the period that Child was developing his third edition, and especially in the years when it was being published, in the 1880s and 1890s, the concept of 'folksong' was being taken up and elaborated in Britain, and above all in England. In order to understand how and why Lloyd could make his judgement on Child we have first to analyse what came to be known as the 'Folksong Revival', central to which was the work of Cecil James Sharp.

PART 3

Cecil James Sharp and the 'Folksong' Consensus

A part of the bourgeoisie is desirous of redressing
social grievances, in order to secure the continued
existence of bourgeois society.
To this section belong economists, philanthropists,
humanitarians, improvers of the condition of the
working class, organisers of charity, members of
societies for the prevention of cruelty to animals,
temperance fanatics, hole-and-corner reformers of
every imaginable kind.

Karl Marx and Frederick Engels, *Manifesto of the Communist Party*, 1848.

Writers about 'folksong' have a strange way of choosing their ancestors. Some collectors and editors of songs are admitted to the family tree, while others who played a significant role are not. What this section of the book tries to show is how and why the concept of 'folksong' was constructed, predominantly in an English context, in the period c. 1870–1900, before the advent of the key figure of Cecil James Sharp. As before, we will concentrate on people who wrote theoretically about the 'folk' and 'folksong', asking what kinds of people they were — their class position, their ideology, their way of making a living and so on — up to the founding of the Folk Song Society. The concentration on England is not the product of my own chauvinism, but of the fact that collecting and editing songs in Ireland, Scotland and Wales followed significantly different paths, which deserve to be analysed in their own right. And though the history of the development of 'ballad' and 'folksong' theory has had to be separated out for the purposes of making something like an intelligible narrative, we have always to remember that what the English Ballad Society, Child and his followers were doing in relation to the 'ballad' was in practice closely related to the treatment of 'folksong'.

* * * * *

7 The Strong Men and Women before Agamemnon

After the bourgeoning of song-book making by English learned societies in the 1830s and 1840s, and the first attempts at 'county' collections in the period leading up to the 1860s, there was something of a lull. A similar pattern of production and consumption appears to have taken place in the commercial publication of broadsides and chapbooks for a working-class market;[1] and while railways, newspapers without prohibitive taxes, the onset of systematic state education and suchlike factors obviously had a bearing on this process, it was also true that the major political and economic upheavals of the Chartist 1830s and 1840s no longer haunted the British bourgeoisie with the same ferocity. There had, after all, been no revolution in Britain in 1848, as there had been in many countries of Europe, and the 1850s seemed to bring comparative prosperity to the most advanced capitalist economy in the world. The integration of the economy at a national level also related to the ways in which British — and especially English — culture was being made more 'national'; but while the capitalist mode of production and bourgeois ideology became dominant, neither was totally triumphant. There was combined and uneven development in culture just as much as there was in agriculture, yet Britain was, *par excellence*, a *class* society. The same economically progressive forces which made British industry the workshop of the world and led to Imperialism also gave opportunities for organization amongst the working class, massed together by urbanization, industrialization, the factory system and access to channels of communication unknown only half a century before. After passing through a sometimes hearty phase of regionalism — earlier in the north-east, later in the north-west — commercial songs aimed at workers began to develop marked London-oriented characteristics with the emergence of the early concert hall in the 1850s and 1860s,[2] and its transformation into the music hall of the 1880s and 1890s.[3] In turn, these complex processes sparked off provincial bourgeois interest in 'regional', 'county' and especially 'country' song-culture at the same time as arousing questions about the possibility of 'English' music at a national level.

* * * * *

(i) Carl Engel and 'National Music'

It is curious that when English bourgeois interest in workers' song-culture was reactivated in the later 1860s and 1870s, part of the impetus came from the work of a German émigré, Carl Engel.[4] While the Scots had simply to reissue dozens of reprints of their older song-books, which they proceeded to do during the 1870s and after, the problem of what was *really* 'English' music and song remained unresolved. Engel was a professional musician and music-writer who left Germany in the mid-1840s, and settled first in Manchester and then in London. Coming from a highly-developed German musical and literary culture, he seems to have been genuinely surprised at the absence of research and original composition in his adopted country. In 1866 he wrote a substantial *Introduction to the Study of National Music*.[5] 'comprising researches into popular songs, traditions and customs', and with a bulky bibliography covering dozens of 'national' cultures. His ideas and proposals seem to have lain dormant, however, until a revised series of articles appeared in the London *Musical Times* of 1878-9, which he subsequently republished as *The Literature of National Music*.[6]

Apart from his bibliographical aims, Engel also wished to influence the 'intelligent musician' in England to think of 'National Music' as a 'science', and as a recognizable category which included:

> any music which, being composed in the peculiar taste of the nation to which it appertains, appeals more powerfully than other music to the feelings of that nation, and is consequently pre-eminently cultivated in a certain country.... The peculiar characteristics of the music of the nation are therefore more strongly exhibited in the popular songs and dance-tunes traditionally preserved by the country-people and the lower classes of society, which form the great majority of the nation.[7]

Engel was in the tradition of the 'ballad' mediators of an earlier generation in his attitudes towards what he termed the 'generally simple and unpretending' musical culture of the 'uneducated or simple-minded man', which was to be found especially among the 'rural population', which was evidently 'less subjected to external influences'. He acknowledged that tunes changed in the course of time, but found it

> surprising that their alteration is not very great, considering that they have been preserved traditionally from mouth to mouth, at least only so by the country-people who own them.[8]

He felt such musical material was worthy of study by 'Professional musicians' not only because of its great 'originality', 'variety' and 'beauty', but because of its usefulness in 'ethnological researches',

> as it gives us an insight into the inward man, reveals the character and

temperament of different races, and the degree of affinity which exists between the different human families.[9]

Following the literary-Darwinian model, Engel also believed that 'National Music' was

> useful in an historical point of view, because it affords us an insight into the different stages of development of the art music in different countries.[10]

Above all, however, this music was useful as *raw material:*

> Professional musicians have many inducements to compose or perform music which they do not feel, while the untaught peasant will sing when his heart's emotions impel him to it.[11]

In an age when commercialism and utilitarianism seemed to have triumphed in the musical culture of the English bourgeoisie, and when the Empire provided raw material on a spectacular scale for British industry, Engel recommended students and professionals to exploit workers' musical culture in order to convert a cosmopolitan bourgeois musical culture into a recognisably 'national' one.

In a way, Engel was imitating the Romantic poets' rush to 'nature' and 'peasant' simplicity of a century before. He castigated the harmonizations of 'national songs', which he found 'too elaborate, and anything but tasteful', and noted that

> a harmonized national tune conveys not unfrequently a ludicrous impression, somewhat similar to that which might be conveyed by the sight of a peasant attired in a fashionable evening dress behaving awkwardly in a drawing-room party.[12]

What was needed was more work like that done in Silesia in the 1840s by Hoffmann von Fallersleben and E. Richter, who published 300 songs of the 'country-people'.

> The tunes are written down as they were gathered from the mouths of the singers, without any additions. The place where each tune was obtained is mentioned. Deviations in the tunes, or what may be called different readings, preferred in certain places, are indicated with small notes. The poetry likewise is carefully treated; and frequent references to other well-known collections ... greatly enhance the value of the book for study.[13]

However, when his critical bibliography discussed the British Isles, Engel was obliged to note that, though Scottish music had been fairly thoroughly published (however disfigured with harmonies), and Irish and music was available in print,

> It seems rather singular that England should not possess any printed collection of its national songs with the airs as they are sung at the present day; while almost every other European nation possesses several comprehensive works of this kind.[14]

Engel had discovered a couple of early regional publications, 'too insignificant to supply the desideratum', and he acknowledged the work of Playford, D'Urfey and Ritson; but found their tunes not to be 'national airs in the strict sense of the term, although the tunes may have been for some time in popular favour'. In 'almost all the English collections of old songs'

> The distinction between a national song (German, *Volkslied*) and a merely popular song (German, *Volkstumliches Lied*) is not always distinctly observed by the English musicians, and the two terms are often used indiscriminately.[15]

The same lack of scientific rigour, from a German perspective, Engel discovered in the treatment of the texts:

> it seems strange that English musicians do not make a distinction between the designation of *song* and *ballad*, but use the terms indiscriminately. At all events, many so-called ballads in English music-books are not ballads artistically speaking, but are lyric songs of the kind which the Germans call *Lied*.[16]

It is ironic that, in supporting the notion of 'English national music', Engel has to attack the sloppy genteel-amateur mediators of previous generations with imported theoretical distinctions!

One influential contemporary view was that English workers had no songs and music of their own:

> Some musical inquirers have expressed the opinion that the country-people in England are not in the habit of singing while at their work in the fields, or when towards evening they are returning to their homes; and that those social gatherings during the long winter evenings, in which the Germans and other continental nations delight in singing their favourite songs, are unknown to the English rustics. However, this opinion would probably be found to be only partially correct if search were made in the proper places. Large towns are not the nurseries for the growth and preservation of national songs; and the circumstance of England possessing many large towns may be the chief cause of the apparent dearth of such songs in this country. Still, there are in some of the shires rather isolated districts, in which the exertions of a really musical collector would probably be not entirely resultless.[17]

Engel derived his confidence not only from the English 'county' collections, like Harland's, but also from a few examples of tune-collecting, including an unpublished hornpipe picked up by a 'foreigner, during a night's stay in a much-frequented Welsh town'. Engel threw down the gauntlet to 'English musicians':

> Pianoforte teachers, organists, and other musical professors living in the provincial towns, must often have excellent opportunities of collecting airs from the lips of the peasantry. All that is required is that they take a real interest in the pursuit, not engaging in it as a troublesome business, but as a labour of love.[18]

Cornwall, Northumberland and 'other Northern districts of England' were pointed out as good places to start.

Engel found it 'singular' that, even though many 'intelligent musicians in England are foreigners, who cannot be expected to occupy themselves with collecting the songs of the English peasantry', the 'English musicians' should have

> neglected to investigate the national songs of the different provinces of their country, while much has been done by collectors in almost every other European country.[19]

He exhorted 'intelligent musicians' to begin:

> surely there are English musicians in London and in the large provincial towns who might achieve good results if they would spend their autumnal holidays in some rural district of the country, associate with the villagers, and listen to their songs. What change can be more desirable for a professional man, who during the greater part of his engagements moves in the fashionable circles of society, and is compelled to inhale the impure air of the concert-room — what can be more beneficial to him than an occasional abode among the peasantry in a village, where the pure and invigorating air, and the beautiful scenery, invite to rambles in the fields and woods, and chase away those morbid feelings and crazy notions which very likely have taken possession of the drawing-room musicians.[20]

This collecting could form the basis of musical lectures, which would supercede the unscientific mixture of gossip, singing and 'a stirring appeal to patriotism' which was currently prevailing. Such teaching would also perform the task of 'instructing the people' both in musical and ideological questions, notably the internationalism of musical development.

Engel could make assumptions about his *Musical Times* (and book) readership precisely because of the comparative homogeneity of professional musicians and music-teachers in mid-Victorian England in class terms.[21] He assumed, probably correctly, that they were mainly male town-dwellers, with petty-bourgeois if not bourgeois attitudes to country workers and their culture. Such people were usually reliant on church organist posts or the actual (or would-be) genteel drawing-room trade for a living; but their profession was currently experiencing something of a transformation. The growth of working-class and petty-bourgeois interest in choral singing and in brass bands, the English bourgeois musical culture centring on concerts, orchestras, opera and the legitimate theatre, and the opportunities offered by the development of state education, all contributed to the increased professionalization of the musicians' work. The National Training School for Music was founded in 1873, and succeeded by the Royal College in 1883. Commercial musical institutions were being transformed concurrently. The concert hall gradually changed from being a partly working-class and provincial phenomenon into a predominantly petty-bourgeois and national one; and these developments gave a further stimulus to the bourgeoisie to define their musical culture, as it were, *against* the culture perceived to belong to different (and lower) class of people. What all of these tendencies shared, however, was a strong sense of British (and especially English) nationalism, which corresponded to the rise of British Imperialism, of course, but which also, and paradoxically, enjoyed a love–hate relationship with the products especially of German musical culture. Crudely, what progressive people within the British bourgeoisie wished to do was to combine German standards of musical form, composition and execution with some species of indigenous musical and lyrical *content*. And by pointing to the untapped reservoir of 'national' musical culture which existed amongst the English working-class, Engel was leading the way for what turned out to be two generations of musical educators, collectors, practitioners and composers.

* * * * *

(ii) The early English 'field-collectors'

(a) The People
The people retrospectively acknowledged as early 'folksong' mediators were leisured gentlefolk, professionals and members of the bourgeoisie. John Collingwood Bruce[22] was a schoolmaster's son, became a clergyman, and took over the school, before retiring quite young to concentrate on his antiquarian hobbies. His co-editor, John Stokoe, was also a schoolteacher, and their early collaborators included the Town Clerk of Gateshead, a lawyer and a person who began life a farmer's son and ended it a man of independent means.[23] Lucy Broadwood, the first woman mediator we have met so far, was John's niece, and daughter of Broadwood & Son's owner. She had a private income, lived mostly in Lyne, Sussex, but used the family's London house, where people like Liszt came to visit. In 1899 she published an expanded edition of her uncle's 1843 collection.[24] Her collaborator, John Alexander Fuller-Maitland,[25] came

under the influence of C. V. Stanford and W. Barclay Squire at Cambridge, and acted as music-critic for various journals, enjoyed his archaeological pastimes and edited various works about music. When he was 55 he retired from Kensington to Borthwick Hall, near Carnforth. Sabine Baring-Gould[26] was a member of the 'old, privileged, land-owning class' of south-west England. He also went to Cambridge — where the Master's wife chanced to be a Gould — but left to become a priest. After working as a parson in the West Riding and East Anglia, he inherited his family's Devon estates, became a JP and appointed himself vicar of the parish, employing a curate to help him with a flock of only 200 souls, while he wrote books for money. His early collaborators included H. Fleetwood Sheppard, Precentor of Doncaster Choral Union and a Yorkshire rector, one of the pioneers of 'improved church music', and F. W. Bussell, Fellow (later Vice Principal) of Brasenose College, Oxford, whose mother and sister rented one of Baring-Gould's cottages as a holiday home. William Alexander Barrett[27] was a London choirboy, then a professional church singer at Oxford, before returning to sing at St Paul's. He took his degree, was appointed Assistant Inspector of Music in Government Training Colleges in 1881, and carried on being music critic of *The Morning Post*, and edited *The Monthly Musical Record* and *The Musical Times* for a period. He published books on old English and church music, and a *Dictionary of Musical Terms*. Frank Kidson[28] was the son of a Leeds rates clerk, who left him the makings of a library on antiquarian matters and a small private income. Kidson had no formal musical training, and only a rudimentary education at a 'somewhat rough local school', which taught him that 'no gentleman ever whistled'; but he built up his library into a remarkable collection, gave lectures and wrote about songs and pottery, as well as producing his own musical plays.

The noticeable concentration of people actively involved with church music and with education (formally, or through lecturing) and journalism indicates that Britain did not afford many full-time job opportunities even in the 1880s and 1890s for academics with an interest in the songs of working people. On the other hand, the people who did get involved were well placed to make an ideological intervention through publishing, newspapers, the church and schools. They were geographically rather more widely-spread than previous 'generations' of mediators, and they were all of them — even Kidson, who seems not to have gone to London any more than he had to — metropolitan-oriented intellectuals and musical antiquarians, usually with some musical training. Many of them were associated with academic musical professionals at Cambridge. Whether or not they had independent means, they all performed a significant ideological role in relation to the cultural needs of capital, at the heart of the British Empire. So when we examine their particular ideologies and aims we have to be clear that, while some of them were apparently radical, they were so within very narrow limits.

* * *

(b) Their aims

The idea for the 'regional' collection that was the *Northumbrian Minstrelsy*
came from the Duke of Northumberland, who expressed to the Newcastle
Society of Antiquaries 'a desire that the Society would turn its attention
to the collection and preservation of the old music and poetry of the North
of England'.[29] In 1855, an Ancient Melodies Committee was set up
(which excluded the Society's projector, John Bell, whom Bruce had only
recently worked out of the honorary Librarian's post).[30] The project
shuffled on throughout the 1860s and 1870s, as first one member died,
then another moved away.[31] Bruce and Stokoe revived the Committee in
the late 1870s, and Stokoe put a series of articles in the *Newcastle Courant*,
so as to make 'Northumbrian Pipe and Ballad Music' appear 'competent
to take a place at the poor man's piano',[32] in place of what he termed
'music hall vulgarities and drawing room inanities'.[33] Since he perceived
that tunes 'seized upon and extensively used by "patterers" and "street
singers" for their lugubriously pathetic productions' had 'nearly passed
with them into oblivion',[34] his duty was to help preserve such material,
and to rule out of account what he found by some unexplained process
to be 'Not Northumbrian'.[36] Stokoe also judged choral competitions, so
he was well placed to influence what 'respectable' workers and petty-
bourgeois people put into their repertoires.[37] Bruce gave a series of
lectures to the upper-crust Literary and Philosophical Society, and hoped
to draw on bourgeois regional patriotism in advocating the introduction
of the small-pipes as a cheap substitute for the piano in the most 'humble
dwellings'.[38]

These self-elected guardians of 'Northumbrian' musical culture
knew that tunes and texts had been written by professional musicians and
entertainers, and by amateurs of all classes; but they believed that they
themselves possessed the 'essence' of the region's musical culture, and
wished in their 1882 book to underwrite their ideas about a distinct
'Northumbrian' 'race' with a style of music 'peculiar to themselves'.
Their strategy was to influence the members of polite society who
belonged to the Antiquarians and who had power over some public as
well as private patronage. Their 'Collection of the Ballads, Melodies and
Small-Pipe Tunes of Northumbria' did not profess to be exhaustive, yet
the editors were confident that each tune at least was 'true Northumbrian', and many of them had never been published before. They wrote
of 'ballads' in the same sense as had Child in 1859, and were happy to
acknowledge a song was 'popular' when they had evidence; but they
remained in the tradition of mediators who wrote down the 'common
folk' — though they eschewed the term 'folksong'. This tradition included not only reactionaries, but even Thomas Doubleday, the old Radical
soap-boiler of the 1820s and 1830s, who had long been 'an enthusiastic
and eloquent advocate for the collection of old Northumbrian music'.
Amongst the bourgeoisie, as we have found already, regional patriotism
could be stronger than political differences, and the contributors to the

Minstrelsy all tended to share the same condescension towards people like the street singer from whom Doubleday collected a tune which he found to be 'full of mannerism, yet with a vein of unexpected feeling'. Such people, given their leisure and their access both to print and to an influential audience, had the power to weigh 'any claim for preservation from oblivion' according to its 'merit' in their own eyes, and to include (however patronizingly) the work of a man like Blind Willie Purvis. In fact, Purvis scraped a bare living by making music and playing up to his reputation of being an 'eccentric characer', and he succeeded sufficiently to take in sharper people than schoolteachers, who were anxious to stress the cultural and other values of a historical period they knew was gone for good:

> In these days of newspaper, railways, and cheap trips, we can scarcely conceive of the pleasure which fairs, harvest homes, and ploughing matches afforded the rural population of other times. To these meetings people of all degrees came. Class mingled with class, and friendly sympathies were awakened.[39]

Of course, this was a travesty of the experience of country workers in the 1830s and 1840s; but Bruce and Stokoe's essentially anachronistic perspective — their book could well have appeared 25 years before it did, any many of Bruce's ideas seem not to have changed much between his fifties and seventies — was meant to fit what was residually 'Northumbrian' into 'our oldest and best national melodies'. And while they claimed to have a broader cultural mission, they understood that it was to 'chamber music' of their own class that the tunes they preserved in print would be of most use.

*

Baring-Gould, who published another 'regional' collection, *Songs & Ballads of The West* in 1890, had a father who was a 'very prominent Liberal'[39] for his class. In between 'genteel vagabondage'[40] in Europe and his short spells as a boarder at English schools, the young Sabine experienced the fag-end of a period when 'labourers came to church in white smocks, beautifully giffered at the collar', and 'pretty milkmaids with their glittering cans went into the field or to the stable to drain the cows, and sang ballads as they pulled with two hands as though ringing a pair of bells'.[41] This was a time when 'every village goody and maiden dropped a curtsey to squire and squiress and to the parson, ay, and kissed his or her hand',[42] a time when country gentlefolk were accustomed to 'respectful service'.[43] Sabine formed what to his class were 'advanced political views'[44] in the slums of Europe, and found Prince Louis Napoleon Bonaparte a 'despised adventurer'.[45] When he went to Cambridge he went 'Ruskin-mad',[46] joined a Puseyite 'Holy Club', and professed himself a hater of 'Papal aggression' and bureaucracy.[47] Later, he became a believer in Darwin's theory of evolution.[48] When he came of age in 1855, he seems to have been able to combine his self-image of being a 'Zealous Radical'[49] with the customary 'dinner for the tenants and cottagers' in his native Devon;[50] but it is notable that it was the material sanctions threatened by his Low Church father — he paid Sabine an allowance — which forced him to move out of his 'strict adherence to the Catholic disciplines'[51] in his unpaid job at a Pimlico Choir School. Similarly, in spite of his evangelical hymn-writing in Yorkshire, Baring-Gould took up Gladstone's offer of a Crown living in Essex; and when his uncle died in 1881, he complacently presented himself to the family living of Lew Trenchard.

Baring-Gould saw himself as part of the 'old squirearchy' of England, whose 'sense of moral obligation'[52] was consciously different to that of contemporary German culture and politics. Thus, while he retained a life-long fascination for Norse Sagas, Germanic Legends and Wagner's music, and though he published an English version of Grimm's *Fairy Tales*,[53] he reacted strongly against what he termed the post-Lutheran 'sad defect in the German moral sense'.[54] He believed his own class's propaganda that 'the culture of the English landed gentleman has been progressive for many generations',[55] and that the local mansion had been a 'centre of culture whence it radiated throughout the parish'.[56] Therefore, his primary aim of looking after the 'moral and spiritual improvement of Lew Parish'[57] was part of that 'care for the tenants, the obligation of setting an example of justice, integrity, kindliness, religious observance', and so on, which had been 'bred' into him, and 'enforced through parental warning through three centuries at least'.[58] Yet farm rents on his estate were inadequate to support a family which eventually numbered 16 children, let alone the rebuilding of the manor house — complete with a stone dated 1620, *taken from a local cottage* — and the restoration of the church in Pugin and Morris style, in which local craftsmen had to be *retrained* from their customary methods. His immense literary output was produced largely for the money that his books brought in,[59] and while he believed his song-publishing was a 'great and important work', and the 'principal achievement of his life',[60] it has to be understood in terms of Baring-Gould's material as well as his ideological position.

He had heard 'old moormen' singing at country inns when, as a young man,[61] he had been exploring the archaeology of Dartmoor, and he continued to feel 'familiar with the minds, habits of thought, and prejudices of the agricultural and artisan class of Devon'.[62] He believed that he 'understood the people'.[63] So, when an after-dinner conversation at a friend's house in 1887 turned to 'Devonshire songs', Baring-Gould's genteel acquaintance immediately volunteered him as the fittest to 'undertake the job of collecting these songs and airs'.[64] The truth was that he took his ideas *to* the people, and did not learn from them. Even when he encountered the 'Song Men'[65] who had once performed an important function in the work of the farm, like the labourer Roger Luxton who was employed for his skills up to the 1850s, Baring-Gould still maintained that the tunes he collected 'sprang spontaneously from the joyous or sad hearts of the people',[66] who 'were like birds of the air'[67] and sang 'because it was a necessity to sing'.[68] Luxton knew otherwise:

> Ah, your honour ... in old times us used to be welcome in every farm-house at all shearing and haysel and harvest feasts.... All them things be given up.... The farmers be too grand to talk to us old chaps, and for certain they don't care to hear us zing. Why for nigh on forty years us old zingin-fellows have been drove to the public houses to zing.[69]

His 'honour' seems not to have heard and understood, though he recorded this important evidence about the growing class divisions in the countryside, and about the class-based attitudes to workers' culture which caused one farmer to laugh at the idea that his old labourers had any songs worth collecting.[70]

Baring-Gould agreed about the words being of little value, and 'soon came to mistrust'[71] them, since he thought they were 'often, but not always, corruptions of Broadside Ballads, transmitted orally'.[72] It became 'daily more evident' to him that 'the melodies were incomparably more valuable than the words',[73] and by 1895 he went so far as to state that a 'good many' of the tunes 'may have originated among the people themselves',[74] just as the 'peasant poet' was often responsible for words which were then taken up and 'grossly mutilated' by broadside publishers.[75] In the countryside, the older singers and Baring-Gould 'valued what they had once so prized, but which the present and rising generation regarded with scorn'.[76] The old people — like the man the parson termed an 'imbecile', who sat 'smiling and touching his forelock to every passer-by'[77] — had not lost the habit of deference; unlike the younger people, to whom 'a nod and jerk of the chin to one side suffices to show recognition' to the squire or clergyman, and who wore broadcloth while the parson had to make do with serge.[78] Baring-Gould wanted to use the songs he published to help turn the clock back, as though cultural products were any sort of a lever against the economic and political realities of a mature working class, the British state and Empire, and a capitalism which was internationalizing and moving steadily towards war. But when he looked for a way of getting his songs back into bourgeois, let along working-class culture, he immediately encountered several problems.

Professional musicians were not interested in what they perceived as technically inexpert performers, and in any case 'they themselves had been reared on music that was German, Italian or colourless English', made by composers who could no more create a living melody than they could create a flower of the field.[79] This, then, was the challenge which kept Baring-Gould going throughout the 1890s, as other collectors came to his support; and by 1895 he could attack with more confidence the 'received commonplace that the English have no folk music of their own':

> Nothing can be more erroneous. We have had our folk music as truly as the Scots, the Irish, the Welsh, the Germans. At present our children in Board and National schools are being taught German Volkslieder, adapted to English words, and our chimes ring out Scottish airs, as though, forsooth, we had nothing sound or tuneful of home growth.[80]

Baring-Gould believed that

> the gorge will rise and revolt before long against the sawny, sentimental stuff that is poured forth in floods to-day from the music printers, which is sung at our concerts and in our drawing-rooms; idealess, characterless stuff, whose only merit is in a certain skilfulness of accompaniment-writing. If so, let there be a reversion to some fresh English spring. We have imitated Italian, German, French masters long enough. To suit a degraded English taste, foreigners like the late Mr Lohr, had to write down to the level of the wish-wash drawing-room ballad. A revolt against musical vacuity is inevitable. Then the demand will come — Sing us in future some of the songs of our own dear English Zion. There is something even in music to be learned from our healthy English peasantry ... the finest people the world has ever seen....[81]

According to this view, 'our folk airs have not been printed, any more than have the songs of the thrush and black-bird and lark',[82] and even Scottish shepherds now knew only 'music-hall balderdash',[83] or other 'dilute treacle of modern song'.[84]

Working-class (and especially commercial) song-culture was seen to be a *problem*, and that problem could be solved only by a change of attitude towards their own training and practise amongst the professional musicians and singers, who could then aid the transformation of musical education for children of all classes. Baring-Gould began a modest programme of intervention at a local level, and while he enjoyed (in the 1890s at least) the reputation of being more of a populizer than a pedant,[85] his attempts to get the songs he thought highly of into the culture of those who came to his concert parties in the major Devon and Cornwall towns met with a lukewarm reception. The 'solos, duets, choruses, tableaux and dances, all in costume', performed by his relations and friends, left Baring-Gould considerably out of pocket.[86] The truth was that he did not understand the culture of his audience. He could not make out why they always laughed at a particular song, for example, until someone told him it had been taken over by local Methodist chapels.[87] As for the petty-bourgeois majority of his audience, they seem not to have understood why the Rev. Baring-Gould set such store by his old-fashioned songs.

*

Barrett's *English Folk-Songs* of 1891 was the first British song-book to contain the term 'Folk-Song' in its title. However, its tunes were 'arranged, and provided with Symphonies and Accompaniments for the Pianoforte' by the editor, who claimed to have 'collected' the songs 'during many years':

> A few of them are still sung, some have completely disappeared from among the people by whom they were once favoured.[88]

In almost every way, Barrett's book supported bourgeois ideas about 'obvious corruptions' of 'artless' music being found amongst 'unsophisticated English folk'; but he thought it possible that 'the melodies probably originated among the people themselves', even if the words of some were to be found on broadsides. He stressed the songs did not 'belong to any particular county', but hoped that the 'few specimens here given become as popular in the new sphere into which they are now qualified to enter as in that in which they have been the solace and delight of old and young for many years past'.[89] Barrett feels no compulsion to theorize 'folk-song'. Instead he usually uses 'tradition' in his foot-notes, or simply the adjective 'popular'; and in spite of his disclaimers, such detail as he cares to give often includes counties or even towns and districts in which a given piece is sung, including 'factory girls in the East of London'. Like some of his predecessors, he acknowledged the work of 'illiterate ballad poets', but presumed that it was the quality of tunes (in terms of his class's cultural values) which helped maintain the popularity of their texts. And since the term 'Folk-Song' appeared only in the book's title, and not once in the short Preface or shorter notes, it is possible that its use was simply a nod to a fashionable metropolitan term, perhaps suggested by the publishers.

*

Frank Kidson's *Traditional Tunes* was the improbable result of his being fired to collect after reading Marryat's novels,[90] and was published in a subscribers' edition by his Oxford friend and fellow musical antiquary, Charles Taphouse, in 1891. This 'Collection of Ballad Airs' was the outcome of 'much pleasant labour', and was intended to 'at least temporarily rescue from oblivion some few of the old airs, which, passing from mouth to mouth for generations, are fast disappearing before the modern effusions of the music hall and concert room'.[91] Both working-class commercial culture and bourgeois 'art' culture were squeezing out these 'simple homely ditties such as were sung by the humbler classes in England round the fireside of farm kitchens or at the plough tail';[92] and though Kidson agreed that 'the little wit or brilliancy they may possess must not be judged by a very high standard', yet he regrets that 'any young ploughboy who should sing the songs his father or grandfather sung, would be laughed to scorn' by those who took the 'cheap trips to the larger towns'. Such tunes and texts, apparently, 'remained unaltered for a great length of time' in the English countryside, and the tunes 'never got into print, for they were sung by a different class of people to those catered for by the music publisher'. The advent of cheap music-publishing, for at least the affluent or socially-aspiring sections of the English working class, in town and country, had led to a decisive and irreversible change:

> as printed music and musical instruments became more common, they were abandoned for newer and more fashionable music, till it was left for the cottage to preserve what the hall had cast aside.[93]

This familiar notion of cultural hand-me-down status for the songs is, however, qualified a little by admitting that 'rustic fiddlers or crowders', 'pedlars' and journeymen' had their place in the transmission of texts and tunes, sometimes resulting in 'wilful alterations', 'corruption' and 'unconsciously omitted' notes and words. There was also a regrettable tendency of singers to 'imperfectly acquire' a given tune, obscuring the supposed 'original structure'. Kidson believed that he could prove the 'tenacity with which certain tunes have held together while transmitted orally', and he also felt that 'the ballad sheets would give a certain stability' to the words, though 'the blunders of the reciter or the illiterateness of the printer have frequently turned a ballad, originally good, into an absurdity'.[94] He 'conceded that the rustic muse produced better melody than poetry or even rhyme'; but he firmly believed that their 'place in literature' was fixed by the 'simple audience to which they were originally addressed', and that working people made and transmitted the songs, however much the texts 'suffered by being handed down traditionally'.

This patronizing attitude towards working people and their culture is compounded by Kidson's apparent innocence of country workers' culture. A place ten miles from the centre of Sheffield he described as 'a remote village among the Derbyshire hills'. Versions of a song are 'so corrupted as to make a very doleful and pitiable story into that which might provoke more laughter than sympathy'; and a song described as being 'a great favourite with the old folk who still remember it' in the 1890s is dismissed as 'sublime doggrel'. Other texts, taken from working people, are labelled 'poor doggrel', sarcastically termed a 'delectable effusion', and 'a favourite song...though a very silly one'; but when a tune is judged to be 'pretty', Kidson assumes 'it is not much corrupted from its original form'. Underneath these subjective value-judgements, and sometimes poking through the patronage, is the real history which Kidson resented so much:

> Before railways and cheap trips acted as general diffusers of London music hall songs, such like ditties in country districts were common in the kitchens of quiet public houses, and were in general the exclusive copyright of the old fogies who gathered there.[95]

On a smaller scale, this culturally reactionary attitude, posing as anti-commercialism, was analogous to the 'made in Germany' taboo. Yet it cantained a keen eye for property-rights in culture — that 'copyright' implies that the 'old fogies' had some sort of financial interest before the song-collector came along and expropriated them — and ignores the fact that Kidson had no first-hand experience of pre-railway or even pre-music-hall England.

The invasiveness of commercially-oriented songs, and the rapid turnover of songs necessitated by the capital investment in institutions such as the music-halls, obviously produced a speed-up in the change of English country people's culture as well as that of urban workers. Kidson gives us some evidence for similar changes in generations before the supposed cultural watershed of the 1840s. He knows that the older inhabitants of Leeds' heard a certain song, it produced 'a recollection of a street singer with a Cockney accent, singing through his nose'. He sometimes refers to a garland, broadside, chapbook or hymnbook, which will have been 'new' in its own day; and he actually records the names of several of them. He refers carefully to the work of previous generations of 'ballad' mediators, and he acknowledges the songs of Sam Cowell, the London concert-hall singer. He also admits that a song may have been made by one 'Spencer, some wandering ballad singer, who has not been endowed with much poetical genius', and underwrites the importance of amateur and professional singers and song-writers, and the centuries-old importance of printed texts. Like Baring-Gould — whose work he knew and refers to in his book — Kidson had no use in the 1890s for the term 'folksong', and when he uses 'folk' it is the familiar way of referring, in polite company, to people of lower social status.

In later years, Kidson looked back on his original motivation for collecting songs, and cites the 'absurd cry, "*The English have no national music!*"'[96] as a major part of it. In the later 1870s, when he began,

> there was a great boom in German music — I mean of the second rate as well as of the greater composers' work, and we had plenty of fat, solid, German *Volksleider* [sic] in evidence. We considered these the model of what a people's music should be, therefore we sang, in translation, of the beauty of our Gretchen, of the happiness resulting from a never ending drinking of lager beer and Rhenish wine, and of our devotion to the German Fatherland. It didn't then occur to us, that we had songs about our own English Fatherland ... so we further discarded our old English rounds, glees, catches and part songs for weak translations of German ones the music of which was the production of Teutonic composers....

Kidson blamed influential figures like Sir George Grove for encouraging this 'German fever', and for ignoring the fact that 'an undercurrent of quaint National Melody existed, worthy to rank with any Nation's folk music and having characteristics all its own'. This idea of 'National Melody' brought no reference to the German critic, Engel, and was loosely characterized as having 'grown out of British brain to amuse British people'. It was distinct from internationally-renowned master-pieces, and its strength of melody alone qualified it for the role of 'substitute' for comic and sentimental songs of a 'clap trap character'. In the absence of 'modern songs of good quality which are suitable, by simplicity of idea, and directness of melody to replace these for modern Street Singing', something else was needed to give to 'horrid midnight parties of rollicking youths' who 'scream forth any music-hall ditty that comes into their brains.[97] Gilbert and Sullivan songs may have 'ousted a good deal of the trash under which we now suffer', but what was needed was 'old stuff' gathered by his 'friends and fellow collectors', characteriz-ed by 'earnestness' of lyric and 'pure' melody, and, like 'our folk lore', worthy of preservation 'if only to be pleasantly laughed at' by the provin-cial bourgeoisie who listened to Kidson's lectures, bought his publica-tions, and sent him songs through the post.

*

Lucy Broadwood and Fuller-Maitland's *English County Songs* of 1893 not only eschewed the term 'folksong', but sniped a little at Barrett's book. (According to Vaughan Williams, she 'never, if she could help it, used the word "folk song"', and she wavered between the fear of 'vulgarisa-tion' of the songs she collected and her feeling of duty as a self-appointed 'trustee' of them.[98]) They found that the number of existing 'collections of English songs' was 'comparatively small, and those which are of real value are either difficult to procure, or they refer only to one district or county'. Moreover, the 'ordinary albums of English ditties contain but a very small proportion of songs which are strictly speaking traditional', in spite of the fact that tunes 'remain among the English peasantry', many of which 'seem to have sprung up, no one knows how, within the last century or century and a half'. Later in their Preface, the editors and arrangers refer to 'the people' as the bearers of 'traditional songs', and while they assert that certain songs were 'undoubtedly characteristic of one part of England rather than another', against Barrett, they carefully disclaim any pretensions to having produced a 'scientific treatise'. The reader is referred to Baring-Gould and William Chappell for a discussion of song origins. However, the editors agreed with the concept of an 'original form' to every song, and they stressed that their work was mere-ly part of the 'groundwork' necessary before theorizing could begin.

This Leadenhall Press 'Copyright' publication is especially interesting in that its editors explicitly regarded the materials they published as 'no one's property' until they took them over in what they quaintly characterized as the 'most engaging pursuit' of 'getting the old-fashioned songs out of the people'. The persons who sent them songs also lamented the 'advance of so-called education', and the 'modern civilization which has spoiled these happy hunting grounds for the musical antiquary'. Of the 50 or so people listed as having helped, over two-thirds were women, and almost one-half were politely referred to as 'Miss' — only one had the title of Lady, and another that of The Hon. Of the men, there was one military officer, seven Mr's, eight Esq.'s and three clergymen, while collectors like the Rev. S. Baring-Gould and Messrs Kidson, Sumner and Bower were singled out for special mention. That network of leisured gentlewomen, clergymen and professionals associated with music and music education, was evidently firmly in place, well before the foundation of the Folk Song Society. Such people could be comfortably addressed as 'educated singers', would be assumed to accept Baring-Gould's statement that the words of songs were 'usually rubbish', and had no difficulty in taking the editors' word that 'outway songsters', 'not only sang favourite songs, but actually invented new ones themselves', and could make a given piece 'popular' in their neighbourhood, to add to those 'spread' by 'pedlars' who sold ballad-sheets. The editors protested that 'interesting discoveries' were possible even in districts not seen by gentlefolk to be particularly musical, though, 'strange as it may appear, the districts in which music is largely cultivated among the poorer classes are not those in which the old tunes are most carefully preserved and handed down'.[99] The explanation appeared to be in the nature of state education:

> It is perhaps natural, after all, that young people brought up on the Tonic Sol-fa system, with all that it involves in the way of fatuous part-songs and non-alcoholic reveries, should turn up their noses at the long-winded ballads or the roystering ale-house songs beloved of their grandparents.[100]

But time and again, even in their sparing footnotes, the editors are enticed back 20 and more years to the rural customs of harvest suppers, to what appeared to be a more comfortable if less 'civilised' England, before music halls — which Broadwood dated back to the 1820s! — before compulsory education, agricultural trade unions, the decline of deference and the rise of a restive proletariat partly imbued with socialistic ideas.

* * *

(c) Their sources
Bruce and Stokoe seem to have done hardly any collecting of their own from oral sources. They got John Bell's manuscript tune collection from him for 25 shillings when he was old, ill and needed the cash, and that formed the backbone of 'their' publication.[101] Thomas Doubleday, the

radical soap-boiler and playwright, had done a little collecting in Newcastle's streets during the 1820s. Robert Bewick, the small-pipe playing
son of the great engraver, had a manuscript tunebook to which they
secured access. In print they had Bell's *Rhymes* and John Peacock's
Favourite Collection of Tunes with 'Variations Adapted for the Northumberland Small Pipes, Violin or Flute' published about 1800. (His
tunes were indeed 'Adapted' to suit drawing-room tastes. Later, he
adapted the pipes themselves, so as to give a bigger range.) Robert
Topliff's 1815 *Selection of the most popular Melodies of the Tyne and Wear*
contained tunes harmonized for the piano by this expatriate north-
easterner, who made a living by playing a church organ in London, but
who occasionally returned to the north-east to produce a 'New Musical
Entertainment' in the assembly rooms of genteel inns, right up until the
1840s. Dixon's *Ancient Poems* contained a few locally-collected texts, and
the ropemaker Joseph Crawhall's 1877 *Tunes for the Northumbrian small
pipes, violin or Flute* had a little new material, as did Stokoe's newspaper
articles. The editors had little faith in being able to collect, but they
decided to try when the Duke offered cash prizes for the 'best and second
best collection of ancient Border tunes' which might be sent to the committee. Bruce hinted to his friend White that £5 might find its way to
James Telfer, if the Border poet 'would give us assistance in gathering the
old North [umberlan] d Music'; and this Telfer did, going back to people
who had given him song-texts in the 1840s, taking along a musically-
literate friend. His manuscript collection of 'genuine Border tunes' taken
from the 'mouth of the common people' — evidently, they only had one
between them — contained items from Teviotdale, Redesdale and North
Tynedale. The Committee promptly had the collection bound, embell-
ished with ornamental margins, and presented to the Duke.

The Committee believed that their enquiry was 'half a century too
late'; and yet they had received correspondence from the old Morpeth
piper, William Green, who had known not only the itinerant piper, Jamie
Allan,[102] and William Lamshaw, the Duke's piper, but had also made
the acquaintance of the famous fidler, Neil Gow in Edinburgh (then
ignorant of the small-pipes) earlier in the century. Green also knew of
William Cant, the Newcastle publican who was appointed piper to the
Northumberland Militia and had been Lamshaw's father's pupil. The
Committee were also contacted by Thomas Hepple of Kirkwhelpington,
who sent to Mr Gibson 'some old Ballads & have put the music to them
as I Have had off by the ear since boyhood'.[103] Hepple 'could have
wrote out in score many of the pieces such as "Derwentwater's Farewell,"
"Hexhamshire Lass," "Ther[e']s five Wives o Acomb &c," but he felt
it was 'likely you may be now have received them'.[104] They had not,
and they seem not to have troubled to ask for them. Hepple also put the
Committee in touch with his cousin, the piper John Baty of Wark, who
had a massive tune-book originally belonging to William Vickers in 1770.
The Committee had routes open to them to explore the real musical tradi-

tions of Northumberland especially, but they chose not to do so, presumably since they believed they knew what was 'Northumbrian' better than mere country singers and players.

*

Baring-Gould did go out to collect from oral sources, but there existed a great cultural distance between the squarson-magistrate and those country people he still called 'peasants' well into the 1890s. In front of his own drawing-room fire, or that of a neighbouring vicar or gentleman, with Baring-Gould at the piano, differences of social status, comparative affluence and the fact of class must have operated to affect any relationship which the clergyman thought he might be establishing:

> I had in old Hard. Then and there I obtained from him a further crop of ballads. That was the last reaping, for in the ensuing bitter frost the aged man was found dead, frozen on a heap of stones by the roadside,[104]

'I had in old Hard.' It's as though the crippled ex-stone-breaker, living with his wife on £4 a year, was rather like a dumb animal in Baring-Gould's eyes, or even the inanimate natural force, the 'field', which that image of 'reaping' a 'crop' implies. What the tenant or landowner had to do, presumably was to extract all that was left of Hard's cultural property, and then let the forces of nature do their worst, while parsons and gentlefolk sat round their blazing fires enjoying the 'treasure' that had been preserved for their own kind. Baring-Gould really regarded the songs as property, as the 'treasure' which people like the 'Singing Machine', James Parsons, could not be allowed to carry 'into the churchyard'. Parsons 'trembled with fright' the first time he was 'sent for' to the parson's house, but seems to have mellowed a little with the spice wine. When he cut into his knee while making 'spears' for thatching, while the doctor despaired for his life, Baring-Gould did so for his songs, and rushed to his bedside to offer money for each song he sang, piece-rate.[105]

Baring-Gould clearly did not transcend class relationships. Like Scott, a century before, he reinforced them; and now and again we glimpse working people's resentment piercing the 'respectful service', as with the angry woman at Prince Town, who told the parson she wanted 'nother you, nor nothin' of yours here'.[106] Such experiences were sometimes turned to the collector's advantage. He pointed out to his readers how hard it was to 'hunt after old singers', since they were 'few and far between', and only to be heard of after a diligent search'.[107] Not only

> is this difficult and a matter of much time and tact, but it is expensive work, requiring long journeys and lodging at inns, entertainment of the singers,

and also much disappointment. I venture to think that such work as the collection of folk airs from the old singers would be impossible, or nearly so, to a man who had not lived the greater portion of his time in the country, and who did not know the ins and outs of the countryman's mind. I myself find that, though I can rapidly unlock the hearts of our Devon and Cornish singers, I find more difficulty elsewhere — I do not understand the peasant in other parts so thoroughly as I do in the West....[108]

For all the world like a new-fangled anthropologist, or an Indian Trader with beads, Baring-Gould wrang all he could out of his privileged contact with country people, exploiting them and the curiosity-value they engendered in the book-buying bourgeois public, and talking up his worth as one able to chase after people like the 'aged grandmother on Dartmoor', who made him go 'from the kitchen to the pig-sty, or to the well-head and back, pencil and music-book in hand'.[109]

There was one part of collecting which presented particular problems. Baring-Gould and his collaborator once accepted a South Brent dentist's invitation to hear two 'notable song-men':

After dinner we adjourned to the kitchen, where was a roaring fire, and the old men were set up with jugs and tankards of ale. But some neighbouring gentlemen and ladies, notably the latter, had been invited to be present at the performance. This I saw at once would never do. Tunes have to be repeated several times to be noted with accuracy, as peasant singers are disposed to embroider them with twirls and flourishes of their own device; and further, I was not at all sure that the words of the ballads would in all cases be fit for ladies' ears. And so it proved. For after the singing of 'The Mole-Catcher' by John Helmore, the aged miller, there ensued a rapid dissolution of the company.[110]

In male company, Baring-Gould evidently took delight in such 'very interesting pieces',[111] and wrote with glee of a clergyman colleague who took one such song down as a kindness — 'It was begun in a firm hand, but after a few verses, the writing became shaky, and the final stanzas were quite illegible.'[112] The problem was that 'some of the most exquisite melodies were coupled to either foul or silly words', and while he seems to have been scrupulous enough to present Plymouth Public Free Library with what *may* be accurate fair copies of his original notes,[113] we cannot be sure how much editing went on in the transcription, let alone in the collecting itself. We do know that, like Scott, Baring-Gould sometimes memorized whole songs, repeating them to himself as he made his way home, before writing down what he remembered with the aid of his piano.[114]

He later remarked that he had not heard 'any songs or ballads expressing discontent at the life led by the country labourer',[115] but this is hardly surprising given that he exercised power over people at Lew in several ways, as priest. JP and landlord or master. But he did understand that 'to work the country properly' he would have to visit cottages and taverns, and not farmhouses and yeomanry, in order to get 'material of any value' for his purpose.[116] He knew what he did not want:

> One day Mr Bussell and I had been sitting in a little thatched cottage listening to two aged song-men, one nearly blind, the other childish with age, and had reverently and lovingly noted down their ballads and melodies. Then we went into a farmhouse, and there asked our direction across the moors; we told the farmer and his wife what we had been doing. They laughed till the tears ran down their cheeks at the bare idea of anything worth while being obtained from old Gerard and Stoneman. 'Ah', said the farmer's son, 'come in. I'll sing you a song, a first-rate one. "What a shocking bad hat". That is something worth your having.'[117]

Commercially-made music-hall material like that was common enough, and only one 'yeoman' farmer, Jimmy F—— of Chaddlehanger, gave him pieces other than from the early nineteenth century 'Vocal Charmers' or 'Appollo's Cabinets' favoured by that stratum of country people. Baring-Gould found he had to 'drop to a lower level' if he was to 'tap the spring of traditional folk music':

> I speedily discovered that what I wanted was to be obtained mainly from such men as could neither read nor write. At the outset we did not attempt to extort songs from the old women; in fact, we worked that field very little, and very inadequately.[118]

He collected 'as many variants as possible' of tunes to discover their 'original form' which was, evidently, not to be found in the early nineteenth century broadside publications of 'Such, Fortey, Ryle, Catnash [sic] and others' whose texts were 'not trustworthy' in the first place.[119] Some texts 'were obviously more correct in diction than those produced by the publishers who furnished the sheets that were hawked about at fairs',[120] though according to what criteria he does not say. Baring-Gould discovered more than one working-class 'poet' who could knock a set of verses together almost to order,[121] and yet, after a considerable outlay on printed and manuscript music, he found that 'village organists and conductors of village choirs' seemed incapable of writing melodies with the 'antique flavour' he liked.[122]

When we look at Baring-Gould's sources, we find that he seems not to have troubled to keep a record of the occupations of over half of them, and even the names of some.[123] Only three of the 56 we know are women, of whom one was a charwoman. Of the men, only six were described as 'labourer'; and even assuming these men worked on the land, that still leaves a considerable majority of skilled workers and small property-owners, including a farmer, an innkeeper, a coachman, a miller, a mine captain, a shoemaker, two tanners, two blacksmiths and three masons, to add to the roadmender, the 'cripple', the thatcher and the hedger. As to their mobility, this sample of what Baring-Gould termed 'peasantry' seems to have been capable of considerable movement. Samuel Fone went to London in a carrier's cart when he was 14.[124] Ginger Jack Woodrich ran away as a boy and as a married man with children;[125] and several of the men moved around the country to find work, notably on the railways during the 1840s boom. Illiteracy seems not to have been a common factor. One source proclaimed himself 'Poet of the Moor',[126] while another kept his relations up all night shouting out the words to the songs he knew in a collection of broadsides loaned to him by the collector.[127] Baring-Gould was not simply a second generation Puseyite gentleman, who recalled the pre-railway age from his youth. He clearly had an *idea* of song-culture which he imposed onto that which was alive in the 1880s and 1890s, even as he collected. And though he made the Buchan-like gesture of engaging a 'blind old fiddler to go round in South Devon collecting melodies', the man's increasing infirmities' slowed him down.[128] He also got 'Ginger Jack', his 'little man', to collect from navvies;[129] and had assembled enough material to produce *A Garland of Country Song* in 1895, with Novellos. But he used printed sources to help him pad out that 'National Monument of English Song' which was his eight-volume *English Minstrelsie*.[130] As far as he, and those who credited him, believed, Devon had been 'thoroughly investigated'.[131]

*

Barrett claimed that the majority of the songs in his collection had been

> noted down from the lips of singers in London streets, roadside inns, harvest homes, festivals on the occasion of sheep shearing, at Christmas time, at ploughing matches, rural entertainments of several kinds, and at the 'unbending' after choice suppers in country districts.[132]

In other words, his collecting was not unlike that of Dixon in the 1840s. But he leaves us little information to check his assertions in his footnotes, where notes of places take precedence over the people who did the singing. We are told of an unnamed Gloucestershire 'family', of 'village boys in Cheshire', of a 'group of the unemployed' who sang for money in the streets in the 1880s, and of 'girls engaged in making gloves, in the neighbourhood of Yeovil'. He also mentions 'factory girls in the East of London', 'girls and children employed in straw plaiting' in Bedfordshire, 'an old soldier', a farm labourer in Melksham, Wiltshire, a labourer met in a Slinfold tavern, and 'one of the crew of a schooner yacht' on a pleasure trip in 1877. Thus, while Barrett inadvertently links singing with work by these brief ascriptions, it is evident that he was not one of the yacht's crew, let alone an unemployed agricultural labourer. Booksources are scrupulously named, and even broadside and chapbook titles are mentioned. Respectful references to Chappell and Dixon are given prominence — though Barrett is careless of dating their work on occasion — and acknowledgement is made to a person of his own class, Mr Winholt, organist of St John's, Brixton, for a particular tune.

*

Kidson's collection of tunes had been 'chiefly obtained in Yorkshire and the south of Scotland', but he took his words both from broadsides and 'oral tradition'. (Less than a third of the songs in *Traditional Tunes* were published as they were collected.) To some extent, Kidson could relate to people like the railway pointsman from Goathland, Allan Wardell, and could stay in his cottage; yet the working man spoke to him formally as 'Mr Kidson', and acted as a kind of scout, getting people like 'Old Jack the fiddler' to come in one evening:

> Allan would recall an old song, Jack would catch up the tune on the fiddle and soon we would all be singing it together. Uncle would get me to sing it when we came to a piano. In this way he got many songs, for people in the village heard of him and would stop and say "Mr Kidson do you know an old song that goes like this?" Uncle felt they were giving him of their best and he took delight in their gifts.[133]

His niece, Ethel, 'was with him often when he collected', and he found her useful because of her 'retentive ear', which enabled her to 'give him the tune' if she had heard it only once.[134] What happened to the tunes sung by Kidson's original sources in this mediating process is now undiscoverable, of course; but if Old Jack[135] and the 'old fiddler in North Yorkshire, who played very nicely' were one and the same person, the cultural gap between the source and the collector becomes remarkably clear:

> he informed me that he could not play by note and "he didn't think any body was any use as a musician who could," thus sweeping away with one stroke the whole science of music. I could not agree with him and merely took down from his playing what I could gather of old stuff.[136]

If 'Jack and Uncle soon made friends',[137] as Ethel wrote many years later, it was evidently not on the same ground in terms of cultural values.

One-third of the texts and tunes in *Traditional Tunes* came from three people about whom Kidson tells us almost nothing — Mrs Holt, Benjamin Holgate and Charles Lolley. He was content, like Barrett, to locate particular pieces (presumably collected by himself) to geographical areas, notably the North and East Ridings, or to 'a ploughman', or 'fisher folk' at Flamborough or Whitby. Only once is a source labelled simply 'traditional'. His own grandfather is cited, as is his mother and a Whitby relative, and some of the Goathland people are dignified with names — including 'Mr A Wardill' and 'Mr Neswell Pennock', but not 'Old Jack'. One or two other individuals in Yorkshire and Scotland are cited, like Mrs Calvery of Gilnockie in Eskdale, probably because she was the grand-daughter of Walter Scott's friend, Tibbie Sheil. Kidson's 'habit of speaking to all street musicians'[138] produced a few more items from the streets of Whitby and Leeds, probably remembered from his youthful days in the 1860s and 1870s; and through his various other sources and correspondents he was able to reach back in time somewhat to Otley in the 1820s, Brough in the 1850s, Leeds and villages nearby in the early years of the century, Stockport in the 1830s and 1840s, Stoney Middleton in the 1820s, the border of Staffordshire, Cheshire and Shropshire in 1820–40, Lancashire in the 1850s and even across in Ghent in 1850 and India in the 1860s. Moreover, he possessed a Yorkshire performer's book of airs dating from 1825, and another small manuscript volume of airs from around 1800, plus all the broadside and chapbook sources he cites, which he had access to if he did not own. To *some* extent, this evidence contradicts Kidson's assertion that 'old traditional songs are fast dying out', since they were 'seldom or never sung, but rather *remembered*, by old people'.[139] He put down country singers' resistance to his collecting to 'shyness' or a 'difficulty of seeing the utility of collecting these old things', but with 'a little difficulty, by the judicious expenditure of tobacco'[140] or beer, he bought enough material from people who probably knew well enough that their cultural property had a market value for such as Mr. Kidson.

*

Lucy Broadwood had a problem which none of her male contemporaries faced.[141] Bourgeois proprieties dictated that she could not mix freely with working men and women, especially in pubs. She got over this difficulty by inviting singers to her own or her friends' houses for supper, singing a 'traditional ballad' to them, and then recording their songs. Sometimes, she issued them with penny exercise books with their names on, together with a list of the songs she required. Henry Burstow gave her a list of the 420 titles he could sing, and Broadwood asked for those she fancied, taking down the tunes (or getting a church organist to do it for her) and then having Burstow send on the texts by post. Samuel Willett was able to transcribe tunes himself, and so effectively collected from himself, sending Miss Broadwood the results, cutting out from his repertoire any which were 'adapted to a popular or well known tune'. Unsurprisingly, Willett became confused as to what she actually did want, and used 'rusticity' as a guideline, though he suspected his 'powers of discrimination are too limited to work out the process of winnowing you suggest in your letter'. In effect, Broadwood got singers to 'edit' their repertoires by remote control, and to guarantee that none of their material came from print. Between prohibitions and subjective criteria, it is clear that Broadwood was in the business of *prescribing* what a 'folk song' was and was not. Moreover, for her 1893 song-book, she seems to have cloned herself quite successfully.

In *English County Songs*, the editors claim that of those songs appearing in print for the first time, 'a large number have been taken down from the singers by the editors themselves', while many 'have been taken down by friends'. In fact, apart from the use of M.H. Mason's *Nursery Rhymes*, Charlotte Burne's *Shropshire Folk-Lore* and various other printed sources such as *The Musical Herald, Notes & Queries*, broadsides and garlands, very few of the orally-collected texts and tunes came from Broadwood's first-hand collecting, and even fewer from Fuller-Maitland's. The 50 and more individuals who gave 'help' made the 'most strenuous efforts', however, noting matters of performance, getting their servants to write down songs, describing any dancing or ceremonies associated with songs, acting as mediators with other collectors, or taking down words from 'a peasant', and having them 'disentangled and partly re-written' before sending them off. In effect, Broadwood was forming the network which became part of the cadre of the Folk Song Society; and she was able to bask in the approval of one of the Society's first Vice-Presidents, Hubert Parry, as one of those believed to have already 'practised the art' of collecting, and having 'developed a wonderful gift in this direction'. Parry, seemingly, swallowed the collectors' propaganda whole:

> Some people seem to think that they have but to walk out along the by-ways and hedges, and pick them up; but in reality, the collection of folk-songs requires the most extraordinary faculty of accurate retention, of self-criticism and practice as well, to distinguish what is genuine from what is emasculated.'[142]

The truth was that Baring-Gould, Kidson and Broadwood, above all, had been some of the earliest to get hold of this moveable property they called 'folk song', and, had, as it were, to some extent cornered the market. They were intent on hanging on to their lead in the retailing business, not so much for material gain and prestige as for the ability to intervene ideologically in their own bourgeois culture and, thereby, in the culture of the working-class.

* * *

(d) Their editing
Bruce and Stokoe imposed their class-bound values and assumptions onto the material available to them. They sifted through Hepple's songs, picked bits and pieces out of Bell's *Rhymes* (and often altered them to 'fit'

better), chose a tune or two from the repertoire of a 1770s piper and ignored hundreds of others, took much from Bell's tune book (but acknowledged his work hardly at all), preferred Percy's 'ballad' texts to Ritson's, and used Surtees' text of *Derwentwater's Farewell* in spite of his reputation as a forger. They relied heavily on Peacock's *Adapted* tunes, expunged erotic matter wherever they found it, excluded songs dealing with drink, and concentrated on 'Northumbrian' material almost all of which came from north of Durham City. They excised any piece which smacked of working-class struggle, downgraded worker-musicians at every opportunity and generally reconstructed a musical culture — according to Lloyd, they got one tune upside-down — from a very obviously ideological perspective, for the benefit of the Duke, members of the Society of Antiquaries, musical antiquarians elsewhere in the country, and all these people's connections in polite society.[143]

*

Baring-Gould chose to work with Sheppard because he was an accomplished musician, and 'not a formalist'. He could 'throw himself into a ballad air, make it his own and surround it with a flood of dainty harmony'; and he had a 'poetic faculty in music' which the squarson found 'so wanting in many who can write an accompaniment that is scientifically correct, but is void of feeling'.[144] The songs, in other words, had to be 'fit to be sung in a drawing room';[145] and Baring-Gould wrote 'fresh verses' to replace a 'great part of the words' that was 'obscene or indelicate'.[146] This was 'absolutely necessary', since some of the most dainty airs were 'wedded to the most indecorous words'.[147] He had the example of Burns to justify him, but he had none of Burns' talents, and while he might have made the texts 'tolerable to men and women of culture' in his own class, his assumptions about being 'imbued with the feeling of the folk poet' are staggeringly arrogant.[148] His chief aim was to 'rescue exquisite melodies from being killed by the words to which they are wedded'[148] — where death was apparently the result of remaining amongst working people. Tampering with the texts was totally in order. Sometimes, he got Sheppard to rewrite the words, 'softening down what was indecorous', as well as to harmonize the tunes, since 'a sympathetic accompaniment enhances their charm immensely'.[150] In fact, Sheppard would often change the rhythm of a piece, or invert a musical phrase.[151] 'Frequently the whole character of the original song was changed to what was practically his own invention in the style of his period';[152] and when he 'recast' a piece he did so often 'at the expense of the whole character of a song'.[153] What he was doing, of course, was to 're-write' a culture.

*

Barrett did not trouble to leave his manuscript songs for others to check;

but he did admit to having 'collated' oral and broadside texts 'in order to avoid obvious corruptions'. (That confident idea of an 'original' song was evidently still dominant). Barrett claimed that 'No other emendations have been made', and he implied that the tunes were printed as they were 'derived from the singers themselves', though with accompaniments done almost entirely by the Editor. As to notes, Barrett believed that the little he wrote told as much of the songs' 'history' as may 'interest the reader or singer'; and the entire format of the work was clearly designed for the latter, with words and music kept to one page or two, just right for the piano, and with such notes as there are stuck in any spare space at the foot of the page. For genteel singers, advice was offered on apparent mispronunciations, so as to aid the rhymes. Certain words are glossed, knowing comments about *The Masonic Hymn* appended, and tips are provided about pauses and incidental musical embellishments. Verses from several orally-collected texts and from various broadside versions are cobbled together with tunes sometimes not directly connected with precisely those words. Clearly, Barrett saw himself as supplying a marketable commodity; and he assumed that his potential buyers would accept his word for the authenticity of his songs, or not care too much about such an issue.

*

According to Lucy Broadwood, Kidson's *Traditional Tunes* was a 'turning-point in the history of folk-song, for its is the first book of English traditional songs in which tunes and texts, given in "undoctored" form, are accompanied by scholarly critical notes'.[154] Yet the book's title page announces that 'appropriate words' had been used from broadsides and 'oral tradition', and Green has shown that over two-thirds of the songs were composites of one kind or another.[155] For largely 'antiquarian' reasons, Kidson 'set down the airs as far as musical notes will permit with the utmost fidelity, scrupulously avoiding any attempt at arrangement or emendation'; but since the text was regarded simply as a 'vehicle' for the tune, Kidson did not scruple to use broadside texts to supplement (or put in place of) orally-collected ones, and to omit verses 'which are not essential to the story'. The reader sometimes had to be content with the first verse only because the 'whole song is poor doggrel'. Kidson also expurgated verses which he regretted were not 'equally meritorious and more suitable for this work'. Just as he held the customary view of there being a standardized tune, so there was also an 'ideal' text, which usually took the form of a broadside, whose words were 'often imperfectly remembered by old singers' (as he wrote later) and so needed to be restored by the editor of a song-book. Kidson's attitude towards workers and their culture was built-in to the way he collected, edited and published songs. No matter how erudite his notes, it is quite clear that a work entered at Stationer's Hall and privately published was oriented on the class culture to which Kidson aspired, and not that from which he expropriated musical ideas.

*

In more subtle ways, this is also what Broadwood and Fuller-Maitland did in *English County Songs*. Gammon has shown how, in addition to the mediating processes at work in selecting singers and collecting only segments of their repertoires, when it came to publishing, Broadwood selected out tunes which were in the simple major scale, and privileged those which were in other scales quite disproportionately, especially those which were 'modal'.[156] It would be surprising indeed if this predilection did not operate in collecting, and helped give Broadwood confidence that the 50 or 60 pieces she asked Burstow to sing from his repertoire of over 400 were in fact what she could easily recognize as the 'traditional type'. In any case, if the singers themselves refused or found it difficult to discriminate, the collector and editor would have to do it for them! A similar process seems to have taken place in her publishing of bowdlerized and otherwise edited texts; and she already had the problem of singers censoring themselves, because some of their songs were 'outway rude' and not fit to be sung 'even to a gentleman'. Burstow sent a text with a note which stated 'I dare say you can alter some of the words'; but in their book the editors claimed that only one text had been 'modernized', and that in 'all other cases, the words have been left absolutely unaltered, and the melodies have in no instance been tampered with'. In fact, the editors admit that their accompaniments have sometimes been 'treated' according to the styles of particular composers whose work 'shewed a very remarkable affinity' with an orally-collected tune; and all manner of liberties were taken with texts.

It's not simply that whole songs in *English County Songs* are ascribed to particular counties on the basis of the flimsiest association. A tune from the *Northumbrian Minstrelsy* is amended slightly; but no attempt was made to 'represent the dialect phonetically'. (It was assumed that singers would not speak the 'dialect', presumably.) Guidance for unison and even four-part choir singing is given, though there is no evidence of Broadwood having collected from choirs. Verses are 'restored' from published texts, or from other orally-collected texts; and other mediators' judgements on the omission of 'unimportant verses' are taken on trust. One set of words was known to have been 'disentangled and partly re-written' by a clergyman collector. Words are blandly described as being 'found on ballad sheets', but any tune which 'is interesting from its shewing traces of the Dorian mode' gets special treatment. (Broadwood once fooled Fuller-Maitland with a made-up tune![156]) While a text originating in a convivial society is printed, though 'strictly speaking' it was 'outside the scope of the collection since it is not in any sense traditional', its inclusion is legitimized by its 'pretty tune', for which 'No excuse need be offered.'

Indeed, it is astonishing how almost every song seems to fit the one or two-page format so convenient for accompanied singers, especially since Broadwood and Fuller-Maitland were strong believers in the idea of an 'original form', and understood that some singers took texts 'off a ballet' while others 'actually invented new ones themselves'. With such a stress on physically and typographically fitting songs to suit a culture for which they were destined, the real intentions of even the apparently most honest mediators stand out in stark relief, for all the pious 'patience and devotion' which they professed.

* * * * *

(iii) The formation of the Folk Song Society

The logical outcome of these tendencies in the mediation of workers' songs was the formation of the Folk Song Society in the summer of 1898, at 12 Hanover Square, London. The first meeting was an informal gathering, and included some people who had already published their collected material, including Fuller-Maitland and Laura Smith, plus a couple of musical knights, and assorted genteel women and men.[158] Kidson, Baring-Gould and Broadwood were not present, and neither was Cecil Sharp; but Broadwood and Kidson were appointed to the Committee not long after the society's formal inauguration in June.[159] Rules had been 'drawn up and approved' *before* the first General Meeting in February 1899:[160]

> At first the proceedings were rather of a dilettante and "tea-party" order. The members were largely professional singers, musical journalists and the official heads of the profession, most of them not distinguished for their knowledge of folk song, however eminent they might be as performers and composers.[161]

Yet the few members of 1898 understood how to legitimize their Society, and how to encourage people to join, especially those in London and the provinces who were interested in music, literature or the 'comparatively new science of anthropology', many of whom were 'later distinguished' in their fields.[162] They took care that leading musical academics and composers like Sir Hubert Parry, Sir Alexander Mackenzie, Sir John Stainer and Dr (later Sir) Charles Villiers Stanford, accepted Vice-Presidencies. The Society determined that its 'primary object' would be 'the collection and preservation of Folk Songs, Ballads and Tunes, and the publication of such of these as may be advisable';[163] though all contributions to the *Journal* were clearly understood to remain 'the property of the contributor', and this rule was later supported by the Copyright Act of 1911.[164] Within a year, this thoroughly bourgeois Mayfair-based institution numbered amongst its members composers like Elgar, Dvorak and Edward Grieg.[165]

Five years before the Society was founded, Parry had enunciated his Darwinian theory of the 'evolution' of music through history from 'folk-tunes' to the most elaborate symphony.[166] But whereas people in the Folk Lore Society, like Joseph Jacobs, had already admitted 'The Folk is simply a name for our ignorance',[167] no such qualms seem to have troubled the Society's membership, which included 'practically every worker in the field'[169]. Parry's Inaugural Address [168] lambasted an 'unregenerate public' and their fondness for the 'common popular songs of the day', those products of the cultural 'jerry-builder' and part of the 'boundless regions of sham' which he and his kind perceived when they looked at the outskirts of 'our terribly overgrown towns'. For that urban proletariat, 'modern popular music' was made 'with a commercial intention out of snippets of musical slang'; but Parry's contempt for the people who live in these 'unhealthy regions' is almost boundless, in spite of his evangelical tone. To him, they are people who 'for the most part, have the most false ideas, or none at all', who, while always 'struggling for existence' think that the 'commonest rowdyism is the highest expression of human emotion'. He and his class were therefore forced

> to comfort ourselves by the hope that at bottom, our puzzling friend, Democracy, has permanent qualities hidden away somewhere, which may yet bring it out of the slough which the scramble after false ideas, the strife between the heads that organise and the workmen who execute, and the sordid vulgarity of our great city populations, seem in our pessimistic moments to indicate as its inevitable destiny.[169]

What was needed, from the enlightened individuals who sat before him, was a 'wholesome and seasonable enterprise' like that of collecting 'folk-music'.

Parry and his audience found there was nothing in 'folk-music' 'common or unclean', 'no sham, no got-up glitter, and no vulgarity'. And if the songs were 'treasures' inscribed in the 'sensitive brain fibres of those who learn them and have but little idea of their value', where they were continually threatened by that 'most repulsive and most insidious' of enemies, music-hall songs, 'we' of the Folk Song Society could 'save it', even though 'the little urchins of distant villages catch the sound of a music-hall tune' and 'away goes the hope of troubling their heads with the old fashioned folk-songs'. The paradox which Parry attempts to smooth over was that the music which 'grew in the hearts of the people before they devoted themselves so assiduously to the making of quick returns' could plausibly be described as 'characteristic of the race, of the quiet reticence of our country folk, courageous and content, ready to meet what chance shall bring with a cheery heart':

> All the things that mark the folk-music of a race also betoken the qualities of the race, and, as a faithful reflection of ourselves, we needs must cherish it.[170]

Since 'style is ultimately national', in this way of seeing, 'the ultimate solution of the problem of characteristic national art' lay in the 'heritage' of folk-song', that quintessential product of 'crowds of fellow-workers', so apt for a period riven by class struggle brought about by the pursuit of 'money profits'. What was needful, in this anti-commercial and superficially anti-materialist perspective, was to get back somehow to a society which was said to be 'primitive', 'unsophisticated' and 'genuine', full of 'simple beauty' and 'emotions which are common to all men alike'. Yet it is perfectly clear that what Parry and the Folk Song Society feared was bound for 'extinction' was not only that idealized 'golden age' of pre-industrial rural bliss, but their very own material security which was being thoroughly tested by a 'Democracy' which they suspected was not their 'friend' at all. Whether they all fully recognized it or not, what the song-mediators of the Folk Song Society were now involved with was in fact the early stages of a new level of struggle to impose onto working-class people what was 'good' for them, from the standpoint of the ruling class, and of capital.

8 Cecil James Sharp

Friends, allies, supporters and apologists have usually tried to give the impression that Cecil Sharp[1] was somehow qualitatively different from his song-mediating predecessors, either in terms of his ideas, or in the way he did his collecting and publishing. The truth is that he was in many ways remarkably similar, and that what may appear, after over 80 years, to be significant differences between him and them can so easily mask the fact that what we are looking at is a struggle *within* English bourgeois culture, in its metropolitan and musical manifestation. By 1900, the facts of the British state and British Imperialism were not in doubt. The British working class had matured so far as to have established at least trade union consciousness and organization amongst significant sections not only of skilled workers, but also of manual and unskilled workers. For over half a century, most British people's experience had been an urban and an industrial one; and the ideas of socialism and of Marxism had taken some hold in the most advanced sections of the class. After 1909, exacerbated by the effects of the growing economic, political and military competition with the United States and, above all, Germany, there was a period of intense crisis and class struggle at an unprecedented level, which was only interrupted by The First World War. That war, and its attendant national chauvinism, to which all but a handful of revolutionaries capitulated in Britain, Germany and Russia, penetrated every aspect of British culture, and raised questions in the dominant bourgeois class about whole sets of relationships between their power and workers' demands, culminating in a series of 'reforms' of a political, economic and welfare nature, and in a radical review of the role of state education and of officially-approved culture. This, then, was the *general* historical context in which Sharp took up the question of 'folk song' in the period after 1903.

* * * * *

(i) Early life[2]

Sharp was a product of English metropolitan bourgeois culture. He was born at Denmark Hill, London, in 1859, the third child of nine born to a City slate merchant of antiquarian leanings, and the youngest daughter of a City lead-merchant, who may have had Italian forbears. At the age of eight Cecil was packed off to a private school in Brighton, where his parents usually spent the last three months of the year, 'being then in the fashion'. When he was ten, he was moved to Uppingham, the only English 'public' school with music on its formal curriculum. (His parents were fond of Handel and Mozart.) In 1874, perhaps because of ill-health, he was transferred to a Sharp family friend, George Heppel's 'coaching establishment for the University and the Army' — Cecil being intended for the latter[3] — at Weston-super-Mare. There, he passed the Cambridge local examination particularly well in mathematics, and was put under the tuition of the Rev. Sanderson at Royston, to be prepared for Cambridge. In 1879, when he was almost 20 years old, Sharp entered Clare College. He read mathematics, but also took the examinations for the first part of the Bachelor of Music degree. He rowed keenly in the second boat (for which there was little competition), took lodgings out of college in Tennis Court Road so as to be able to make as much noise with his piano as he wished, and became Secretary of the College Debating Society (at the third attempt), proposing annually, and unsuccessfully, that the House of Lords be abolished. From the first he became 'leader of the musical men' at Clare, was 'almost as enthusiastic about his mathematics as he was about Wagner', 'got up' People's Concerts with people like Fred. T. MacDonnel, W. H. Wing, Fred Bagnall and Oliver Puckridge, and sang in the Trinity Concordia. At Cambridge, and at Dr James Kingston Barton's Kensington 'At Homes' — a district where Sharp's parents had gone to live in 1870 — Cecil met those contacts in polite musical and literary society which were to help sustain his later campaigns, including Bernard Shaw, Henry J. Ford, Charles Hayden Coffin, Edward D. Rendall and Sir Owen Seaman. In this radical bourgeois society, Sharp was acknowledged to be a 'Freethinker' and a 'Radical', but distinctly lightweight. Ford thought Sharp's views 'to be founded not on the deeps but on the shallows'. His examiners agreed. Cecil took a Third Class Honours degree in 1882:[4] his father bought him a one-way ticket to Australia, and gave him a few pounds pocket-money.

He chose to go to Adelaide, reputedly because he admired Beethoven's song of that name; and though be began by cleaning cab-wheels, and then clerking in a bank, Sharp used the 'society' introductions he had carefully gathered together in England, and was rapidly assimilated to the lower levels of the expanding Colonial ruling class. In 1884, he left the bank, read law, and promptly landed the plum job of Associate to the Chief Justice of South Australia. All the while, he took care to ingratiate himself with the music-loving members of the expatriate English and German bourgeoisie; so while he became assistant organist at the Cathedral (where he also conducted the choir), and conducted the Government House Choral Society, he did not spurn the Directorship of the Adelaide String Quartet Club or that of the Philhar-

monic Society Choir. Though he paid a visit to his parents' newly-
acquired manor house at Weston Turville at Buckinghamshire, in 1886,
Sharp's chief hope of material success was amongst his studiously
cultivated 'connexion' in the colony. In England, though he wanted to
stay to study music, he got no work. When he returned to Adelaide, he
set up a commercial musical college, along with Herr Immanuel Gottfried
Reimann, the pianist he had appointed to the String Quartet Club.
Reimann supplied the cash, and Sharp the cultural 'capital' from the
pupils he taught music theory and practice, and his society 'connexion'.
Within a year, the venture proved a financial success; but when Sharp
returned from a trip to England (where he tried to get some of his compositions published) in 1891, he found that

> Reimann, my late partner, has turned out a scoundrel, and in league with
> the two men I brought from Germany has succeeded in ousting me from
> the College. Bang goes three years hard work and all my interest. It is hard
> as one grows old to preserve any faith in human nature. I have a sort of
> feeling that I should like to stay to oppose these German pigs and beat
> them, but after all such revenge is a poor sort of consolation, and really
> hardly worth a thought. I am not the man either to enjoy a fight of that
> kind. I will spend blood and money in the cause of an *idea* but to fight for
> personal and material superiority is not worth anything, and is repugnant
> to me in every way.[5]

From a man only recently reconverted to Christianity by seeing a young
Christian Socialist priest, Charles Marson, 'sitting on a fence telling fairy
stories to a lot of children', the brutal realities of commercial competition
would no doubt have come as a hard blow. He had not protected his
'capital', and it had been appropriated.

By January 1982 Sharp was living permanently in London, playing
for parties and musical evenings when he could get the work, and taking
private 'society' pupils, who treated him 'so unceremoniously' that he
wished to get 'as much lecturing, etc. in schools' as he possibly could. He
pestered Schott to publish his sonatas, part-songs of nursery rhymes,
instrumental pieces, songs and even an operetta, and managed to get two
songs (modelled on Schumann) into print. His experience with music
publishers was not a happy one, and he thought them wrong in believing
that

> the public, or a large and growing proportion of it, are unable to appreciate
> anything but the gutter garbage served up to them in such unwholesome
> quantities by the ballad ticklers of the day.[6]

The 'public', of course, was primarily the sheet-music-buying bourgeois
and petty-bourgeois variety; for though Sharp knew, and could occasionally allow himself to enjoy, a piece such as the music hall hit
TararaBoomdeay,[7] his knowledge of the culture of the remaining tens of

millions of English people was confined to a distant view from a railway-carriage window. When he visited a friend at Liverpool and was taken to see some beautiful pictures, he pronounced that

> Liverpool ... in other respects is the most saddening city I have ever visited. It was a good exemplification of the misery which the curse of competition can produce. Miles of sordid hovels housing myriads of dirty unwashed industrial slaves whose work forsooth is said to gain for England her supremacy in Commerce — the mighty boast of numskull statesmen! I wonder if the cost of such glory is ever counted and measured in the scales of human pity by those who so fully make use of it to gild the perorations of their speeches![8]

By this time, *Britain* and British capital was slipping behind both the USA and Germany in the international commerce league, and those 'dirty unwashed industrial slaves' were beginning to organize themselves into unions on a greater and greater scale, above all in the industrial cities.

Like many other members of the would-be bohemian element of the British bourgeoisie at this period, Sharp's ideology contained a bizarre mixture of radical and reactionary elements. He had an abhorrence for 'Girton and Newnham and the "mental loudness" they produce in girls', and yet his engagement to Constance Birch in 1893 called for a Wagner quotation: 'The love of the strong for the strong is *Love*, for it is the free surrender to one who cannot compel us'. (Two of their children were blessed with Wagnerian names!) He read Ibsen, Schopenhaur, Wagner of course, and studied elements of theosophy, spiritualism and Christian Socialism:

> the Christian Socialists are endeavouring to disseminate the grand ideal truths of Socialism very wisely, I think, leaving these principles to take concrete form themselves. Marson thinks you should begin by measures and work back to the underlying theories. We have had many arguments on the subject. To my mind the Fabians have lost all the power they had through tacking themselves on to the Liberal Party. Socialists should keep clear of politics for there is as much or as little Socialism in the Liberals as the Conservatives.[9]

Such a mixture of 'ideal truths' and political quietism kept Sharp clear of any kind of real commitment for several years, and characterizes his 'Radicalism', as much as his vegetarianism (which, in fact, was a result of his ill-health). On the other hand, he befriended Marson,[10] a staunch opponent of the 'wretched bourgeois church', and was not above propagandizing a friend who 'nearly got in at the last parliament':

> I do not think he is very sound on the question of socialism so I have just left a copy of the Fabian Essays in his bedroom![11]

Even when he landed a steady job as music-master at Ludgrove, the Eton prep school, in 1893, and cycled out from New Barnet on three or four days a week, he still liked to call himself a 'Conservative Socialist', 'air his Radical views and "pull the legs of the Tories"'.

Sharp was an ambitious man in his middle thirties when he married, and though he had £350–400 a year, and Constance had £100 a year of her own, his getting 'tired of these small societies' of musicians and singers and 'wanting something bigger' was not simply for an artistic challenge. He was appointed conductor of the Finsbury Choral Association by the father of the composer Benjamin Dale in 1893, and Sharp got 20 guineas a season until 1897. That honorarium was soon augmented by the income from a staff post at the Metropolitan College, Holloway, and the proceeds from taking a few private pupils. Ludgrove paid the rent, and the royalties from the piano compositions which he published occasionally helped him to live more easily, but his 'connexion' was worth more. In 1896, Sharp was appointed Principal of Hampstead Conservatoire of Music, a commercial music college, by a former Adelaide acquaintance, Arthur Blackwood. Within a year, he was castigating the Vice Principal of the Metropolitan College, Holloway, Sir Hubert Parry, over a star singer's double-booking; and when the committee truckled, Sharp not only resigned his post but published the correspondence, even though he was taking a serious financial risk at a time when his health was far from good and he and Constance had two children.

Right through this period, the publications of Baring-Gould, Kidson and Broadwood seem not to have diverted Sharp from his orthodox bourgeois musical tastes, and when the Folk Song Society was formed he did not join straight away.[12] His ideas of cultural intervention are highlighted by the way he brought Mattie Kay, a Lancashire contralto, to London in 1899 and 'put her under Medora Henson for singing', with a scholarship from the Conservatoire. That Christmas, however, Sharp heard and saw the Headington dancers, who were out unseasonally because of 'slackness of work'; but 'beyond harmonising and orchestrating the tunes' he hardly knew what to do with the material. He went through Chappell's work, and looked at Kidson's and Broadwood's 'traditional' material, but the idea of using a phonograph to record the tunes accurately seems not to have occurred to him. However, his reading did result, in 1902, in the production of a book of songs deemed to be suitable for the young gentlemen at Ludgrove. The book was disingenuously dedicated to the headmaster, and may have been designed to offset his apparently unpatriotic pro-Boer views, which had evidently upset his colleagues.

In the teacher's version of *A Book of British Song for Home and School*[13] Sharp tells his readers that the time was opportune for such a compilation, since educational authorities agreed that music was 'an influence of grave importance in the training of the young':

> It is in our power to bring out what is best and deepest in our children,

and to send them forth into the world with a standard of excellence that must have good results in the future, if we are careful to teach them only that which has indubitable merit. The safest way to secure this end, in the case of songs, is to teach none but those which have stood the test of time, and thus to put ourselves under the protection of the best of all critics. Therefore, in collecting these songs, I have confined myself to those which are traditional, and, being chiefly of folk origin, are of assured humanity. I have further selected only those which are British, believing that such will appeal more directly to boys and girls, and will form a better educational groundwork than those songs which reflect the customs and ideals of other nations.[14]

Even at this date, Sharp was quite clear about terms such as 'folk-song', 'traditional music', and the link with 'national song':

No nation has a richer store of traditional music than England [sic], and none is more prone to undervalue its heritage. It may be that we are too ready to accept the charge of being an unmusical race, but we certainly do show a strange incapacity of appreciating our own "folk-song", and not till the last fifty years have any serious attempts been made to collate and publish it.[15]

Chappell was evidently of little use, here, since he

had worked, in the main, among books only, and had made no serious effort to gather those innumerable songs and dances, which have been handed down among our peasantry from generation to generation, and are still to be heard in country places.[16]

This 'rich store of music' — Sharp takes little interest in the texts — 'was left unnoticed till recent years', when musicians began to 'collect, transcribe and publish it'. The 'Addition of this late but precious harvest to our garner' represented, to Sharp, 'a collection of national song such as any nation might be proud of'.[17]

His phraseology indicates that Sharp had been reading Engel; but there is no acknowledgement.[18] In restoring, as he saw it, 'part of our children's birthright', he had to reject not only German *Volkslieder* and 'German student-songs',[19] but also 'productions of the Dibdin type' which were 'far too artificial to rank with the ideal folk-song'.[20] Older 'patriotic' songs were contrasted with 'latter-day vehicles of patriotic sentiment'[21] — by which he must have meant music-hall songs — and in spite of the supposedly common factor of *popularity*, one whole section of the book consisted of 'many fine compositions, which from one cause or another have fallen into disuse'.[22] He took other mediators' texts and tunes on trust and presented them in their 'purest and most characteristic forms', with accompaniments which were 'simple *and* direct, avoiding over-elaborations'.[23] Most of the ideas which were to inform his later work were, then, in place; and this member of the Fabian Society *and* the chauvinist Navy League felt happy in passing off a selection of doctored texts and tunes, imbued with militaristic, patriotic, monarchistic and socially conservative values, as 'British', though most of them had an English provenance and all had been through the heads and hands of bourgeois mediators like Sharp himself, and had emerged as 'ideal'.

* * * * *

(ii) The 'discovery' of 'folksong'

In September 1903, Sharp heard his first live 'folksong' from the lips of John England, Charles Marson's vicarage gardener at Hambridge in Somerset. Though Sharp later claimed that it was 'Chance' which 'first guided my footsteps',[24] that was written after he and Marson had quarrelled. The vicar of Hambridge invited him specially, after hearing a song at a choir supper, and as soon as he heard *The Seeds of Love* Sharp

> whipped out his notebook, took down the tune; and afterwards persuaded John to give him the words. He went off and harmonized the song; and that same evening it was sung at a choir supper by Mattie Kay, Sharp accompanying. The audience was delighted; as one said, it was the first time that the song had been put into evening dress. John was proud, but doubtful about the 'evening dress'; there had been no piano to *his* song.[25]

At the age of 44, Sharp had found his 'idea',[26] his mission in life. By November, he was lecturing on the subject to an audience paying between a shilling and half-a-crown at his Hampstead Conservatoire;[27] and he used his extremely efficient connections (including Lord Roseberry's private secretary) to get publicity in the *Morning Post*. He suggested that if a government 'already overburdened with the cares of Empire' couldn't sponsor the collecting, then perhaps County Councils might take up this 'national duty' under the 'supervision of some central body'[28] — the Folk Song Society is not named directly — which might be 'prepared to undertake the sifting and arrangement of the material collected'.[28] Sharp was quite conscious that the way to recognition was through what singers termed 'the gentry',[29] people like the members of the Taunton Field Club and Conversazione who sponsored a meeting at Taunton Municipal Hall on New Year's Eve.[30] Leading members of the Folk Song Society took up the debate in the press, arguing about how important broadside texts had been, weighing the merits of the Musical Association (founded in 1874, and now the Royal Musical Association), the Folk Song Society and even the Folk-Lore Society in terms of their ability to do the work. Sharp characterized the Folk Song Society as 'moribund', suggested it 'put its house in order' or 'retire from the scene altogether', and enlisted the help of Baring-Gould and his friends Marson and Ford to attempt something like a *coup*. The Committee saw it coming, promptly invited Sharp to join them, and made Lucy Broadwood

Honorary Secretary! All this was effected with the support of the *Morning Post*, but with the added social and political weight of Sharp's appointment as music instructor to the children of the royal household at Marlborough House.

Throughout 1904 Sharp and Marson appealed for public support and tried to 'popularise the movement'. In May, Sharp lectured to the Society of Somerset Men in London, and next day he was mentioned in the *Somerset County Gazette*. Characteristically, he emphasized the waste of cultural resources represented by the singers, who, 'given the right environment, would not be making shirts at 2d a dozen or clearing out pig-styes', but 'would be singing in public-halls and ministering to the joys and needs of thousands of their fellow-creatures'. By so doing, he claimed, not only would 'Cider, churchwardens and "armory"' cease to prevail in rural song-culture, but the 'shouting of modern and vulgar music-hall songs' would be counteracted.[31] To the Fabians, Marson spoke of how

> nothing indicates more terribly the state to which the capitalist system has brought us than the contemptible, puerile and wearisome trash of our modern music-hall productions;[32]

and, after an aside about how the Germans had collected their *Volkslied* 'diligently and stupidly', he goes on to reinforce the 'socialist' myth of a past Merrie England:

> thanks to the stubborn conservatism of the English peasant, thanks to the tap-room, to the poaching, heathenish, Aspasian, Bohemian element in our villages, Folksong has eluded the massed armies of respectability.[33]

Those 'armies' were still legion, however, as Sharp and Marson found when Humphrey Milford of Oxford's Clarendon Press refused their first song-book which he had 'very carefully examined';[34] but their belief that 'the old tunes, wedded to suitable words', should be used 'in all the schools of the country'[35] kept them going. They eventually got a firm of Taunton publishers (who later chanced to get the job of printing the Society's *Journal*) to cooperate with a London firm on what was to be the first part of *Folk Songs from Somerset*, which was produced with the advice of Broadwood, Kidson and Baring-Gould, and was dedicated 'by permission to Her Royal Highness the Princess of Wales'.

After only one year of sporadic blitz collecting, Sharp and Marson had a very clear idea not only about the culture of country workers, but about 'folk song':

> The clapperings of the steam-binder have killed it from the harvest-field; the board school master, a perfect Herod among the Innocents, slays it in the children by his crusade against all dialect but his own, and all poems

except Casabianca (type of the legal spirit). The purveyors of cheap harmoniums, singing evangelists with their unspeakable songs and solos, choir-masters with their doggerel for Sunday and their clap-trap for the penny-reading, all prey upon the persecuted and forsaken remnant. Folk-song, unknown in the drawing-room, hunted out of the school, chased by the chapel deacons, derided by the middle classes, and despised by those who have been uneducated [sic] into the three R's, takes refuge in the fastnesses of tap-rooms, poor cottages and outlying hamlets. It harbours in the heathen kingdoms and the wilder parts. It comes out very shyly, late at night, and is heard when the gentry have gone home to bed, when the barrack-room has exhausted its Music-hall menu.[36]

For the assumed 'us' in their readership, Sharp and Marson waxed sarcastic about 'Hans of Hanover' and the 'heavy-footed peasants of the Fatherland', whose *Volkslieder* were imported by British people only because 'his *rulers* have had the sense to take them down reverently and to husband them carefully and to see that these songs should not be carried to the Churchyard with the old Crowders, who preserved them'.[37] Scotland had its Scott; but though Baring-Gould, Kidson and Fuller-Maitland had done some work, and the editors maintained that 'we do not rob the poor man when we take his song',[38] much more remained to be done, above all by those who wished to 'turn the hearts of children back to the fathers and knit past and present together in great and unaffected sympathy'.[39]

Marson and Sharp believed they had lit upon

the last lingering remnant of the old village life; a survival of the times when the village had a more or less independent existence, built its own church, hanged its rogues, made its own boots, shirts and wedding rings, and chanted its own tunes. All the rest is gone. We cannot call our souls our own now. We create nothing. We cannot even sell our trees without an auctioneer from a town. The people are going away fast, and in a couple of generations of such progress, there will be neither songs nor singers in the silent fields.[40]

You can almost *feel* itinerant church-masons, town-based hangmen, cobblers, tailors and goldsmiths gyrating in their graves, not to mention the travelling musicians, singers and broadside-sellers. Yet to those few people who had trees to sell in 1904, the real culture of the villages *was* essentially foreign. Marson admitted that 'folk-song is like the duck-billed platypus in this particular, you can live for years within a few yards of it and never suspect its existence'. Eight years 'constant residence' in Hambridge had left him 'in Stygian ignorance of the wealth of Art which that village contained'.[41] What these two self-styled socialists proposed, then, was a kind of cultural popular front with reactionary critics of industrialism and commercialism, and with the crasser elements in bourgeois culture — like the 'ladies in the suburban church of St. Jude the Economist' whose musical taste is sneered at[42]. Such people shared not only the editors' aspirations to cultural nationalism, but also their romanticized view of an English 'peasant folk'[43] whose culture could be used by this enlightened alliance in order to intervene in contemporary workers' culture.

By January 1905, Sharp had used the Folk Song Society *Journal* in order to get more tunes into print; and there he began to take notice of some of the realities of the culture from which his singers came. Thus, while he claims that people who were aged between 60 and 70 were the best sources for the kinds of songs he chose to collect,[44] and called 'genuine folk-made traditional ballad poetry',[45] he explains that many women learned their songs in Somerset cottage-industries such as shirt-making and glove-sewing, when it was the custom for such workers to 'congregate, for company's sake in one room; and this naturally led to the singing of songs'. In 1905, however, 'the sewing-machine ties each worker to her own cottage, and she must either sing without an audience, or not at all'.[46] Similarly, though he claimed that Lowland Scots songs were English pieces 'in northern dress',[47] in a *Bristol Times* article of the same month he noted how John England had learned *The Seeds of Love* from the 'next labourer to himself' not in a Somerset but in a *Dorset* turnip-field, when the gardener had travelled to get work hoeing.[48] Yet in spite of these intrusions of real history, Sharp spent 1905 thinking about using Child and Gummere's 'ballad' ideas on the question of 'folk-song'. 'Folk-songs' had been produced in 'that phase of society, where there existed no dividing line between the Artist and the Community in which he lived', and such songs express 'the ideals and aspirations, not of an individual, as in the case of a composed song, but of a class'. The absence of 'domestic songs' was seen as the result of the 'recent importation' of such things along with 'the Christmas tree and other German customs' by Prince Albert; and Sharp and Marson came to regard 'folk-song' primarily as what they termed 'raw material' rather than 'a finished product' from 'our modern standpoint'.[49]

By 1905, the state Board of Education had also cottoned on to the ideological uses of what they coyly termed 'national or folk songs', and ruled officially that the teaching of singing should be based on them, since they were

> the expression in the idiom of the people of their joys and sorrows, their unaffected patriotism, their zest for sport and the simple pleasures of country life. Such music is the early and spontaneous uprising of artistic power in a nation, and the ground on which all national music is built up; folk-songs are the true classics of a people, and their survival, so often by tradition alone, proves that their appeal is direct and lasting.[50]

Moreover, the Board assured teachers and 'others concerned in the Work of Public Elementary Schools' that the songs their largely working-class students learned should be 'musically as simple as possible',

> but it is not necessary that infants should understand all the words they
> sing, as the chief appeal is not to the intellect, the training of which is the
> purpose of almost every other subject in the curriculum, *but through the spirit
> of the song to the unconscious mind of the child.*[51]

Sharp entirely agreed: indeed, he remarked that a recent article on the
'Teaching of Patriotism' gave him 'the liveliest satisfaction, for it gives
expression to views which I have for years been doing my best to preach
in and out of season'.[52] He differed with the Board only on the best
means to achieve this form of indoctrination, and felt 'folk-songs' would
be far more effective than the 'Old English' pieces they had previously
favoured. Yet while he evidently saw himself as part of a modern brigade
of cultural fighters akin to Matthew Arnold's vanguard bourgeois
'remnant' of an earlier period,[53] Sharp did not have Arnold's materially
secure position. The struggle for hegemony in the state's official musical
culture meant that Sharp had to resign as Principal of Hampstead Conservatoire. The need to foster a born-again, 'national' musical culture,
and thus help to elevate and refine 'popular taste', would be a full-time
job.

To give his intervention historical as well as cultural legitimacy,
Sharp had to construct a model of why 'popular' taste had become so
unacceptable to advanced bourgeois opinion. Sometimes he did so in
opposition to what singers told him. For example, he placed the optimum
period for learning what he termed 'folk songs' in the 1850s and 1860s,[54]
and thus conveniently located their provenance after the first major
phases of railway building and the decline of the broadside trade, but
before the rise of the first generation of provincial concert-halls and
music-halls. He needed that distancing hiatus in order to explain the
survival of John England's 'only jewel' amongst dozens of music-hall
pieces, and of his best sources, Lucy White and Louie Hooper's larger
repertoire of 'folk-songs' among 'modern and worthless stuff, some of
which, to spare their feelings he 'actually noted down — something I
remember about a coal mine, dusty diamonds, England's boys, Union
Jack and so on'.[55] He acknowledged that the 'traditional singer' did not
'distinguish between folk songs and other songs in his repertoire',[56] and
so Sharp had to do it, not so much on their behalf, as on that of the potential bourgeois audience, which remained to some extent under the
hegemony of people like Parry. He claimed that the 'matter has nothing
to do with agriculture', 'not because the country is rural', but because the
people from whom he collected were 'out of touch with modern improvements' and 'untouched by modern civilisation'. In almost the next breath
he acknowledged the cultural importance of Louie and Lucy's mother,
Mrs England — possibly a relation of John England — to whom he
'traced many of the best songs of the district'.[57] Chances are that this

woman was a travelling singer, and she may even have been a professional ballad-seller; but to his metropolitan audience — which included
the music-publisher J. Spencer Curwen's Tonic Sol-Fa Association[58] —
Sharp could pass himself off as an expert on workers' culture and its
history. The truth was, as his comment on Catnach indicates ('Catnach
press the last — 1835'[59]) Sharp knew very little about the history of
workers' song-culture, even in its commercial manifestation. In spite of
Kidson's pioneering essay on broadsides in the *Journal* of the Folk Song
Society,[60] the fact that they went on being produced well into the twentieth century seems not to have registered with Sharp. (Sharp had his own
collection of older pieces, but Kidson bought up a Hull publisher's
redundant stock in the early 1900s.[61])

The year 1905 saw the republishing of the first part of *Folk Songs from
Somerset*, and the appearance of the second part, in which Marson and
Sharp sought to explode the notion of 'national' property in songs within
the British Isles. They claimed that 'each county so varies the scheme of
a tune that in time it develops racial traits, just as the county has
developed racial traits in the music of speech'.[62] Sharp, especially, felt he
could identify 'the characteristics' of a given tune 'in their purest
forms';[63] and when he came to revise Baring-Gould's early song-book,
he not only retitled it *Songs of the West* (leaving out the original '*&
Ballads*'), but made 'considerable changes' for the publishers, Methuens,
including particular judgements about what were and were not 'productions of the folk-muse'.[64] Whereas the 1890 edition had had to 'catch the
public taste, and humour it', the 1905 edition could rely on that taste
being 'a little healthier';[65] and yet Baring-Gould was most unhappy
about Sharp's editing out of songs like that of the 'Punch Bowl': I think
he erred, for it was a favourite in the public-houses, and the singers were
all country peasants.[66] Sharp's aim was to use 'our traditional songs' as
a 'great instrument for sweetening and purifying our national life and for
elevating and refining popular taste',[67] and he used his formidable
prestige as the most successful — if not the earliest — collector to add to
his power as a publicist and a professional mediator. He and Marson
could *tell* drawing-room and concert audiences not only what they should
sing, but how. They could deprecate 'individualist treatment', and the
imposition of the 'individual *ego*' on the product of 'many generations of
men in the long period of racial life'.[68] Moreover, they could feel some
confidence in taking on opposition in state educational policy even from
leading musical figures like Somervell, with whom Sharp's battle had
begun some time before: 'I know the man and have long realised that he
would do all in his power to spike my guns.'[69]

The military metaphor was apt, because Sharp had to fight the battle
over the difference between 'a people's song' and a 'folk-song' not only
with Somervell, Stanford and the musical establishment, but even with
the old guard of the Folk Song Society. While Sharp was pressing the
claims of songs 'made by the people as well as sung by them', as a

'communal and racial' product,[70] the Folk Song Society stabbed him in the back and approved the Board's *Suggestions for the Consideration of Teachers*. They also took their revenge for his asperity towards them in 1904 by endorsing Miss Broadwood's defence of the Committee's decision to side with the advocates of 'national' songs, rather than with Sharp and the supporters of 'folksong'. Sharp was almost completely isolated, and could only bemoan the fact that when the question of 'Songs for Soldiers' came 'on the tapis', in October 1906, as usual it was 'the National songs that its promoters look to, to counteract Music Hall influence and not the folk-song'. Sharp wrote to the Committee, as an individual, urging them to 'consider the claim of the peasant song for the peasant soldier', but he was not hopeful.[71] Even Marson had grown away from him, partly because of the pressures of collaboration and the problems of misunderstanding inherent in correspondence, but also because of what Sharp admitted was his own 'individual and autocratic' temper. However, Sharp had been able to get Curwen to publish his and Baring-Gould's *English Folk-Songs for Schools*,[72] which was made to meet the requirements of the Board of Education, but which resembled Sharp's own 1902 collection and contained 'folk-song' texts about which he was unhappy. In order to intervene at a national level, in state education, he had to win hegemony for his own ideas and assumptions; and it was this realization which led him to devote the next few months to the production of his first work of 'folksong' theory.[73]

* * * * *

(iii) 'English Folk-song: Some Conclusions'

Sharp's book appeared from the Taunton press of Barnicott & Pearce, and was published at his own risk. It is now hailed as an important theoretical intervention, but the truth is that he owed much to Parry, Engel and Gummere:

> The main thesis of this book is the evolutionary origin of the folk-song....The claims...made by those who advocate the re-introduction of folk-songs into our national life, all hinge upon this question of origin. They rest upon the assumption that folk-music is generically distinct from ordinary music; that the former is not the composition of an individual and, as such, limited in outlook and appeal, but a communal and racial product, the expression, in musical idiom, of aims and ideals that are primarily national in character.[74]

The stress on *race* characterizes the whole theory:

> The subjects of many of the folk-ballads, that are sung in different parts of Europe, are substantially the same. Some of them have been traced to

an Eastern origin, and they all appear to have been drawn from a common storehouse, the heritage, presumably, of the Arian race.[75]

And this emphasis links to Sharp's 'English' nationalism and sense of 'national' culture:

> Our system of education is, at present, too cosmopolitan; it is calculated to produce citizens of the world rather than Englishmen. And it is Englishmen, English citizens that we want. How can this be remedied? By taking care, I would suggest, that every child born of English parents is, in its earliest years, placed in possession of all those things which are the distinctive products of its race....
>
> If every English child be placed in possession of all these race-products, he will know and understand his country and his countrymen far better than he does at present; and knowing and understanding them he will love them the more, realize that he is united to them by the subtle bond of blood and kinship, and become, in the highest sense of the word, a better citizen, and a truer patriot.
>
> The discovery of English folk-song, therefore, places in the hands of the patriot, as well as of the educationalist, an instrument of great value. The introduction of folk-songs into our schools will not only affect the musical life of England; it will also tend to arouse that love of country and pride of race, the absence of which we now deplore.[76]

As to the adults and the 'uncritical' majority, what was needed was to

> Flood the streets...with folk-tunes, and those who now vulgarize themselves and others by singing coarse music-hall songs will soon drop them in favour of the equally attractive but far better tunes of the folk. This will make the streets a pleasanter place for those who have sensitive ears, and will do incalculable good in civilizing the masses.[77]

Such arrogant élitism squares oddly with Sharp's superficially democratic views, until we realize that his kind of politics were essentially those of a limited reform, from 'above', by a self-elected enlightened minority:

> When every English child is, as a matter of course, made acquainted with the folk-songs of his country, then, from whatever class the musician of the future may spring, he will speak in the national musical idiom.[78]

Meanwhile, Sharp's bourgeois acquaintance could work on the 'raw material':

> At the present day, there are several English musicians who, in musical ability, scholarship, and technical accomplishment, far outshine any of their predecessors of the previous century. But their warmest admirers must admit that they have as yet written nothing that can be called distinc-

tively English music. And this is, perhaps, natural enough, when it is remembered that, in the absence of an English tradition, they have been compelled to seek their inspiration from abroad, and to mould their styles upon those of their foreign contemporaries.[79]

But, by working on 'folk-song', such people could develop a 'National School of Music',[80] and imitate the poetic revival towards which Percy's *Reliques* made a significant contribution. Knowing what we do of Percy's methods, such a comparison is not without irony;[81] but when we come to look at the other ideas which underpinned Sharp's thesis and interventionist intentions, the comparison with Percy becomes ever more apt.

His ideas about history and cultural change were close to those which were to prove useful to maintaining the dominance of bourgeois culture in the period 1909–14, and after The First World War.

> In bygone days, the 'common people' formed no inconsiderable part of the population, and were fairly evenly distributed between urban and country districts. Nowadays, however, they form an exceedingly small class — if, indeed, they can be called a class at all — and are to be found only in those country districts, which, by reason of their remoteness, have escaped the infection of modern ideas. They are the remnants of the peasantry, which originally consisted of those of the 'common people', who resided in the country and subsisted on the land.[82]

Sharp felt he was using 'the expression "common people"'

> strictly in its scientific sense, to connote those whose mental development has not been due to any formal system of training or education, but solely to environment, communal association, and direct contact with the ups and downs of life. It is necessary that a sharp [sic] distinction be drawn between the *un*-educated and the *non*-educated. The former are the half or partially educated, *i.e.* the illiterate. Whereas the non-educated, or the 'common people' are the unlettered whose faculties have undergone no formal training whatsover, and who have never been brought into close enough contact with educated people to be influenced by them.[83]

Quite when such a clear cultural distinction actually existed, Sharp doesn't say; but he does claim that 'folk singers' stopped being born 'not later than sixty or seventy years ago — say 1840'.[84] They represented the 'great tradition that stretches back into the mists of the past in one long, unbroken chain, of which the last link is now, alas, being forged':[85]

> The evidence is overwhelming that, as recently as thirty or forty years ago, every country village in England was a nest of singing birds.[86]

Basing his account on what he believed to be the culture of the 'native and aboriginal inhabitants' of 'remote country districts',[87] Sharp went on to propound a 'scientific' definition of 'folk-song', which he uses

> exclusively to denote the song which has been created by the common
> people in contradistinction to the song, popular or otherwise, which has
> been composed by the educated.[88]

In the light of some criticism from the composer and song-collector,
Vaughan-Williams, this notion was qualified:

> Strictly speaking, however, the real antithesis is not between the music of
> the town and that of the country, but between that which is the product
> of the spontaneous and intuitive exercise of untrained faculties, and that
> which is due to the conscious and intentional use of faculties which have
> been especially cultivated and developed for the purpose.[89]

He poured scorn on the 'uncritical', who

> confound the common language of the illiterate with the dialect of the
> unlettered, and refuse to distinguish between the instinctive music of the
> common people and the debased street-music of the vulgar.[90]

And when he did encounter really creative country musicians, he used
Baring-Gould's experience and his own prestige as a collector to underpin
his customary dismissive tone:

> In some parts of England, especially in the West, almost every hamlet had,
> and in some cases still has, its own carols, which were highly prized and
> jealously guarded from appropriation by neighbouring villages. But these,
> as far as my personal experience goes, were always 'composed' carols,
> often harmonized, and obviously the productions of the 17th and 18th
> century village musicians, possessing no great musical or literary value.[91]

In part, no doubt, Sharp was a victim of his own and his sources'
nostalgia:

> Everyone sang in their young days, they will tell you; they went to their
> work in the mornings singing; they sang in the fields, and they trudged
> home in the evenings to the accompaniment of song.[92]

Treating his own experience as typical, he could make the preposterous
claim that 'The English Peasant still exists, although the peasantry as a
class is extinct'.[93]

So as to minimize human agency as much as possible in his
'scientific' definition, Sharp took over some of Gummere's idea about
'communal composition'[94] and elaborated three principles: *Continuity,
Variation* and *Selection.* He starts with the proposition that 'one man sings
a song, and then others sing it after him, *changing what they do not like*';[95]

and in order to counter the objection that this is how even 'new' songs
are produced he goes on:

> Insistence of type must be the rule, and variation the exception. Otherwise,
> types would be so quickly changed and multiplied that their relationships
> one to another would be obscured, their genealogies concealed, and order
> give place to chaos.[96]

Darwin's *Origin of Species* was exactly as old as Sharp himself, but in
transferring ideas derived from living organisms to cultural products
Sharp had to ask his readers to believe that songs had, as it were, not only
a life of their own, but that *he* could be trusted to recognize the 'type'.
In practice, he was given to autocratic pronouncements: 'We know a folk
tune when we hear it; — or we don't;[97] and the kernel of his theory
remains the anthropomorphic characterization of song. For him, two
examples of 'Continuity' suffice. The first involved the collection of two
versions of a tune (with very different words) from two women, both of
whom had heard the song sung by what was probably the same band of
travelling mummers some 30 years previously.[98] The second example
was of a set of words collected from a blind singer which were almost identical to those printed on a seventeenth century broadside.[99] No consideration is given to the idea that it was the mummers and the broadside
which were the essential elements of cultural continuity and dissemina-
tion. Professionalism and commercial song-culture were, evidently, to be
discounted.

As for the principle of *Variation*, Sharp insists that the singer of what
he (and not they) term 'folk-songs' 'regards it as a matter of honour to
pass on the tradition as nearly as possible as he received it'.[100] Therefore, what he saw as *Variation*, people like two of his best sources, Mrs
Overd and Henry Larcombe, would regard as *mistakes*. To Sharp, at any
rate, some mistakes were better than others; and, from his point of view,
the better singers 'aid very materially the evolution of folk-song', but
in an 'unconscious' way,[101] and with no sense of their own artistry,
creativity, innovations or even of their social role as singers. He
understood the 'mental qualities of the folk'[102] and their culture better
than they did themselves; and while he admitted his ideas about *Selection*
were 'highly speculative'[103] he insisted that the 'taste of the community'
was the determining factor,[104] with 'Celtic' and 'Anglo-Saxon' 'racial
characteristics' playing a crucial role.[105] At this point, Sharp's argument
slews across to a non-human analogy of a 'flock of starlings'[106] —

> Every now and again, however, it will be seen that one of the birds is
> followed by the rest, and the course of flight of the whole mass is
> immediately changed[107] —

and then is transferred back, characteristically, to a 'crowd of human
beings, in the absence of an acknowledged leader'.[108] The systematic

de-humanizing and de-individualizing of the process underlines Sharp's strategy of contrasting songs produced and used by working people with those from the 'civilised' and highly individualistic bourgeois culture of which he formed a part.

* * * * *

(iv) Song-collecting

When we look at Sharp's collecting up to the end of 1907, we find that most of it was done with the assistance of Rev. Marson, who helped secure the crucially important introductions to the vicars and squires who get thanked in the various parts of *Folk Songs from Somerset*. These people 'realized the need of dealing swiftly with this important matter', and introduced Sharp and Marson 'to singers in their districts'.[109] For a 'vigorous song hunt',[110]

> It is well to be introduced; to be a friend of the parson or of the publican or of someone who will pave the way by kind words, and convince the singer that one has no comic or sinister design, otherwise one will be directed to some red-faced and bulbous ancient who is said to be the life of all parties, the Meistersinger of the village and the inn, and that reverend Falstaff will gravely assure the enquirer that he has lost his voice these many years from holloaing of anthems; that his memory has clean forsaken him, and that his gouty foot is all that remains of his days of revelry. Believe him not. Only last night that now methodistical dumb ancient was leading a rousing chorus in the tap-room down the lane, and, if he knew you, could sing as the neighbours will tell you 'till his head be bawled off'; and what is more, there are several men as good as he.[111]

Both Marson and Sharp were *foreigners* in this culture; and pronounced 'that the home fields were reaped'[112] only to be put in touch by singers with other singers. The whole business, as Marson admitted, was carried out on the basis of a sometimes 'begrudged fee';[113] but so long as commodities came on the market, he and Sharp were in there bidding.

By 1905, Sharp had over 600 tunes, and was asking for other people to help in collecting under his guidance. By the end of 1907, he had collected 'fifteen hundred tunes. Between twelve and thirteen hundred of these ... in Somerset, or, more accurately, in about two-thirds of that county';[114] and he pronounced it 'unlikely that further research will yield sufficient new material to fill a fifth volume' of *Folk Songs from Somerset*'.[115] (He was wrong.) In fact, he had collected some 1450 tunes, only 1282 of which had a semblance of a text, and can be considered as *songs*. Of these, 1099 had been found in Somerset: 99 other songs came from north Devon; and the rest were found elsewhere or cannot be located or attributed.[116] Even in January 1905, Sharp recognized that

> with the exception of a few gleanings made during flying visits to Minehead, Holford, Ilchester, Clevedon, Bridgwater, and Lew Tren-

chard, all the tunes have been gathered in three small districts — in Hambridge and the villages hard by ... in Meshaw, north Devon ... and in East and West Harptree.[117]

Moreover, he had already formed an opinion similar to Baring-Gould's on questions of musical and literary quality:

> My own estimate is that the tunes are of the utmost value, but that the words are of less account. Indeed, so far as the words are concerned, I must reluctantly admit that the twentieth century collector is a hundred years too late. The English ballad if not dead, is at the last gasp: its account is well-nigh closed....[118]
>
> The case for the tunes is very different. Fortunately, they have survived the words, and, for a few years more, it will still be possible to recover many ancient folk-melodies in England, if search be made in the right way and in the right place.[119]

By late 1907, Sharp knew the 'right' places in Somerset. Of the 1099 *songs* from Somerset, 138 came from the small area bounded by Blagdon, Priddy, Farrington Gurney and Chew Magna: 231 came from the district enclosed by Bridgwater, Holford, Stogursey and Enmore; and 532 were found within six miles of Kingsbury Episcopi. In short, 82% of the songs from Somerset came from less than 10% of the county. Seventy per cent of all Sharp's songs came from these three patches of land, and, taken together with the small area enclosed by South Molton, West Worlington and Rackenford in north Devon, some 77% of all Sharp's songs came from just over 200 square miles of south-west England. Moreover, of the 1099 Somerset songs, 275 (or 25%) came from the village of Hambridge and the town of Bridgwater. With the small town of Langport, that proportion rises to 33½%; and, including the small town of Somerton, and the large villages of Cannington, East Harptree, Haselbury and Huish, we find that 52% of Sharp's Somerset songs came from eight settlements, most of them larger than average. From 16 places, he got 67%: from 26, 80%; from 42, 90%; and from 49, 96%. The towns of Taunton, Yeovil, Sherburne, Glastonbury, Street, Chard, Shepton Mallet, Weston-super-Mare, Clevedon, and Midsomer Norton, and the cities of Bath and Bristol, were left virtually untouched. Apart from Vaughan Williams' timely reminder — 'Take care that people do not say "this is an essay not on English Folksong but on Somerset Folksong"[120] — it is obvious that, by concentrating on smaller settlements, Sharp's notions of 'remoteness' were actually built-in to his collecting methods. Yet the importance to him of the larger rural settlements, and even of some small towns, gives the lie to his ideas about places which had 'escaped the infection of modern ideas'. Of the transformation of agriculture, which dated back to the Tudor enclosures, and which involved close contacts not only with local towns and cities on a day-to-day basis, but even with markets further afield, including London, he said (and probably knew) nothing.[121] At Harptree, the very house from which Sharp descended on the villagers had been built out of mine royalties.[122]

What of the 'remnants of the peasantry', who appeared to Sharp to have survived the capitalization of agriculture, state education, trades unionism and rural depopulation? In his introduction to *Conclusions*, Sharp mentions that his *tunes* came from over 350 people.[123] However, one-half of the *songs* from Somerset came from 32 human beings living in 18 towns and villages: one-third came from 13 people in ten different places; one-quarter from nine people in eight places; and one-eighth from three women, one living in Langport, and the other two in Hambridge. Louie Hooper alone contributed one-seventeenth. It is difficult to find any 'peasants' amongst these prolific sources, who are usually the only ones about whom Sharp recorded even their occupations. Louie Hooper was a shirt-maker for one of the town merchants. Mrs Overd was a town labourer's wife. William Nott (from Devon) and William King were both tenant farmers, and Mrs Lock was a tenant farmer's wife. Lucy White was the wife of an agricultural labourer. Tom Sprachlan was a retired soldier and a skilled dairyman. Lewis and Vickery were retired sea-going men; Robert Parrish was a sexton; and William Spearing was a miller. Not a male agricultural labourer among them. Partly, this was because of Sharp's own preferences:

> I find it easier to get on friendly terms with the women. They are — in Somerset at any rate — less taciturn than the men, and yield more readily to persuasion; they are available, too, in the day-time when the men are occupied in the fields.[124]

In fact, up to 1907, Sharp seems to have taken only about 25% more songs from women than from men, who would sing for him 'when things are convivial', and when the vicar or the man from London were buying the cider or the tobacco.[125]

Were these people 'unlettered'? Sharp does not tell us; but as to having 'undergone no formal training whatsoever' he and Marson provide evidence to the contrary. Farmer King was one of the well-known Mendip 'singing-men'; John England performed at choir suppers; and Louie Hooper and Lucy White were the daughters of the famous Mrs England, who, as we have noted, was almost certainly one of the many singers who attended fairs, merry-makings, markets, weddings, races and dances in Somerset towns and villages in the middle decades of the nineteenth century, selling broadsides and spreading words and tunes like seed-corn in the countryside. Such a one was the man Ruth Tongue wrote about elsewhere as Isaiah Sully, who was 'much in demand at every local fair in the south-western counties' during the 1840s and 1850s as 'a leading mummer, Morrisman or Singer, his powers respectfully acknowledged'.[126] Then there were the families of travelling people, the Locks, Hollands and Coopers from whom Sharp collected so many fine songs; and people like Aunt Loveday Blackmore, who for most of her life was in demand as a 'singer at supper parties', as well as being a 'fine leading diddler' at a dance, or in 'kitchens and barns and harvest fields where there were no musicians'. She learned a song or two from the 'ballad-singers at Taunton Market' in the 1830s and 1840s;[127] and even in the early twentieth century, Miss Tongue recalled a Mr Barry who sold songs printed on lavatory paper by an out-of-work type at the Tramps' Lodging House in East Road, Taunton, until his death in 1911.[128] Marson described the 'Village Musician' who was brought up as an orphan in the 1810s and 1820s, joined the village choir, saved up for a fiddle and learned to play it, was promoted to alto, led the waits at Christmas and made music for local parties. This man was driven by lack of work to Glastonbury during the 1830s, but the Hungry Forties forced him back to the village, where he survived by ploughing, while his wife and their children picked stones and scared birds in the fields. Eventually, the workhouse claimed him and his crippled legs, but he still taught the village children 'their notes' for a halfpenny a week apiece, and continued writing hymns and anthems, words and tunes, till his death in 1900.[129] Such people, as Sharp occasionally recognized, were *artists*, recognized by their own communities, and knowing each other's songs, tunes and abilities. There were no 'peasants', no '*un*educated' or '*non*-educated' people, but there *were* various ways of seeing country workers in such patronizing and unhistorical ways.

As to the 'instinctive' music such 'peasants' were said to have produced, it is interesting to look briefly at the real musical resources which were available to country workers in the south-west even before 1850. Robert Dyer recorded the travels made around and across Somerset and Devon by fit-up theatres and slightly grander companies. They played the sea-ports and major inland towns, and used songs in the various plays and between performances. Dyer sang what was to be a nationally-famous song, *Caleb Quotem*, at Taunton, before the stage-singer Colman made his name with it in London. (Similarly, Haynes Bayly's famous *I'd be a Butterfly* was first sung in his native Bath.[130]) It was recognized that every actor and actress had to undergo 'the usual provincial privations' on the Devonport circuit and those with which it melded, before London became a possibility. The capital's importance was obvious to Dyer, just as it was to an eighteenth century hawker like Bampfylde Moore Carew, who worked the south-west fairs and races, played the cripple or sold *Tom Thumb* and *Jack the Giant Killer* along the various 'walks' of the region, which included not only towns but some larger villages.[131] In Bristol, there was a recognized 'place of rendezvous' for the 'Brothers of the Mendicant Order', in a Temple Street Inn; and even mummers were town- and broadside-oriented for their material by the 1830s, like the group at Wincanton who sang *General Wolfe, Mistletoe Bough, John Riley, Villikens and Dinah, The Poacher's Song* and *We'll Chase the Buffalo* as part of their active repertoire.[132]

It seems never to have occurred to Sharp that to ask for old songs from old people in the early 1900s would necessarily result in the collection of items widely popular in a *commercial* context before 1850. His notebooks are full of songs about Boney and the French, Turpin, war at sea or on land, press-gangs, prostitutes and women in love with sailors. After all, there had been almost a quarter of a century of virtually constant war up to 1815. Thus, while Sharp did understand that the people he called 'folk-singers' knew 'a certain number of "composed" songs', and that these tended to be not 'the town songs of today, but of yesterday',[133] he still maintained that it was the 'peasants' who were

> singing the popular songs of the mid-Victorian era, such as 'Woodman, spare that tree', 'The Mistletoe Bough', 'Cheer boys, Cheer' etc., etc., rather than 'Daisy, Daisy', or 'The Bull and the Bush'.[134]

And while he never denied the influence of the broadside medium for song-texts, he insisted that though it 'aided the popularization of the ballad' it also 'tended to vulgarize it'.[135] An analysis of Sharp's notebooks of songs collected before *Conclusions* indicates how superficial his knowledge of pre-1850 south-west workers' song-culture really was.

Of the songs collected before the end of 1907, almost one-half were versions of 102 particular pieces, even counting similar songs such as *The True Lover's Farewell* and *Forty Long Miles* as distinct. Forty-nine songs accounted for 31% of his collection, 34 for 24½%, and 12 for 12½%. Of these 12, four have been found in similar shape on broadsides published in the south-west between 1780 and 1850, but chiefly in the 1810s and 1820s when the parents of Sharp's sources learned their songs. Kidson's reasonable advice, that a collector must know printed songs before he can pronounce on songs which appear to be 'folksongs', and his *Journal* article of 1905, were ignored by Sharp.[136] In fact, several printers were producing such material in the south-west at the key period: Elias Keys at Devonport (with retail outlets at Exeter, Truro, Newport in Wales, and Bristol), William Collard at Bristol (who also took in London sheets from Pitts and Catnach for distribution, and operated between 1807 and 1846), T. Willey at Cheltenham and W. Clift at Cirencester. Beyond these, perhaps the major suppliers, there were Besley at Exeter, Tucker at Bridport, Hurd at Shaftesbury, Bennett (1813-30), Bonner (1806-65), Clouter (1801-15), Major (1814-35), Shepherd (1823-5), Smith (1827-30), Storer (1805-19) and Taylor (1824-64) at Bristol, Shenton at Cheltenham, Porter at Wotton and Fowler at Salisbury. In the Madden broadside collection alone there are 29 sheets from these printers which give versions of songs which Sharp collected in 214 variants. Seventeen of the songs in *Folk Songs from Somerset* have local broadside equivalents. Singers told Sharp they had learned a song 'off a Ballet' or broadside.[137] One man had a collection of them, and another said it was easy to learn a song once he had the words, for he 'could always guess at the tunes'.[138] Sharp seems to have deliberately ignored the significance of their testimony, especially if it conflicted with his own values and assumptions. John England knew 'scores of music hall songs'.[139] Sharp's star singer, Henry Larcombe, felt that a broadside text was good enough for him — his version of *Lord Bateman* is almost identical with one printed by Keys of Devonport — but such matters were passed over by Sharp in silence, or written off in a sour aside on the many 'imperfectly remembered broadside versions' he claimed to have recognized.[140]

Censorship of a similar kind seems to have taken place with the tunes. By 1905, 125 out of the 500 or so airs Sharp had collected were 'modal', and he claimed not to have 'noted a single tune in the modern minor scale'.[141] He did not say how many he had heard but declined to note down. Both Sharp and Marson knew that many tunes and texts had been relegated to their sources' 'mental attics', since these singers 'far prefer the shoddy furniture which they show you to begin with'.[142] Such people were 'ready enough to sing music-hall ditties' for the 'gentry',[143] to learn songs from last week's paper,[144] or from the fly-leaf of an old book[145] — hardly evidence of a lack of formal education — and to give 'far more importance to the words of a song' than to the tune.[146] How could such people be trusted with the cultural products which they perpetuated? What was necessary was for parsons and squires to give Marson and Sharp 'further aid in the work' by 'making diligent and kindly enquiry after old songs, and when these are found by reporting their names and the general character of the tunes'.[147] At a distance of perhaps 100 miles, Sharp felt confident enough to plan his next 'song hunt'.

By 1907, Sharp had erected his preferred notion of what constituted 'folksong', singing *style* — that lynch-pin of much modern empiricist theory[148] — into a prescription:

> Attention must be drawn to the conventional method of singing adopted by folk-singers. During the performance the eyes are closed, the head upraised, and a rigid expression of countenance maintained until the song is finished. A short pause follows the conclusion, and then the singer relaxes his attitude and repeats in his ordinary voice the last line of the song, or its title.[149]

He conceded that 'Subtleties of intonation can best be noted and studied with the phonograph', since the 'attention of the collector is ordinarily occupied with other matters, many of which are at the moment of greater importance'. He also admitted that it was 'very difficult to record with scientific accuracy delicate shades of pitch variation'[150] as well as Grainger had done with his machine in Lincolnshire, but Sharp did not feel he had to follow suit.[151] He claimed that the phonograph made singers nervous, as though a London 'gent' armed with a local big-wig wasn't quite sufficient to do just that! The truth was that Sharp's role would then be shown to be unnecessary; and his power to edit repertoires, separate tunes from words — he always took down tunes first, and then recorded words only if he approved of their quality — and generally intervene in workers' culture *before* it became public would have been severely undermined.

* * * * *

(v) Song publishing

First of all, Sharp skewed his selection of texts for publication so as to favour songs taken from small villages rather than larger, and from both in preference to towns. In the first four parts of *Folk Songs from Somerset*, Sharp and Marson published 20% of the 146 songs collected in the village of Hambridge, but only 9% of the 129 from the town of Bridgwater. They used 10% of the songs collected in Somerton, but the only piece found in tiny High Ham. From the large village of Cannington they used 5% of the 43 pieces they had collected, while from the smaller East Harptree they used 17% of the 40 items they found. If the matter 'has nothing to do with agriculture',[152] then such a policy, consciously adopted or not, is curious, as is their treatment of repertoires. Sharp and Marson published 25% of Louie and Lucy's 100 songs, which were in any case only one-third of all they actually knew, but only one of Bill Bailey's 26. Five of William King's 11 songs went into print, but none of Eliza Small's 15. Yet again, the village singer takes precedence, even allowing a generous margin for aesthetic judgements. Similarly, on a wider scale, the editors reduced the proportion of songs published compared to those collected in both the industrial district of North Mendip and in the predominantly urban district of Bridgwater — from 12 to 8%, and 20 to 13% respectively — but they *increased* the proportion from the mainly agricultural area which included Hambridge and Kingsbury, from 50 to 67%. They did the same to women and men's repertoires, upping a collecting ratio of around 5:4 to a publishing one of 3:2; but this process does not tally with what Sharp claimed in the *Journal* about 'those singers who have given me the largest number of songs have also given me the best ones'.[153] In choosing what he thought were 'the best and most representative',[154] Sharp may have been oblivious of the real processes at work, but he cannot have been unaware of what happened to especially song-texts when they were being readied for publication.

In Part 1 of *Folk Songs from Somerset*, John England's *Seeds of Love* was tinkered with so that 'I was' becomes 'I were' for middle-class singers, and the tighter 'I'd stay' gets rendered by the pedestrian 'I would wait'. The fact that the text follows a Collard broadside goes unnoticed. However, there are disclaimers about editing out sexuality so as to conform to the bourgeois taste both Sharp and Marson affected to despise:

> In a few instances the sentiment of the song has been softened, because the conventions of our less delicate and more dishonest time demand such

treatment, but indication has been given, and we plead compulsion and not desire in these alterations.[155]

The editors claimed that the songs were 'presented to the public as nearly as possible just as...taken down from the lips of the singers', but certain unexplained shifts take place in the texts, even if the tunes are presented 'with exact fidelity'.[156] In Mrs Overd's version of *Geordie*, for example, it is the judge who looks down unpityingly on the horse-thief he is about to condemn, but in the published text it is 'the people' who take this attitude and are implicated in the condemnation made by the 'public' agent. 'Bohenny' is rendered as 'Bohemia', and her 'London' as 'Newcastle', presumably because the editors knew a similar (and probably a broadside) text was was located in the north-east. In the published text of *Wraggle Taggle Gipsies*, Sharp and Marson reduce the heroes of the title to mere 'ragged ragged rags', and de-lyricize 'Spanish livery' to 'hose of leather'. When Mrs Overd sang of the wife who was wholeheartedly sick of her lord and all his possessions, the editors convert her (with their customary masculinist bias) to a kind of unthinking, shameless hussy, particularly by the subtle change to 'I'll follow' from 'I'm off', when she decides to go with her chosen partner. Sometimes, it is admitted that 'Mr Marson has endeavoured to reconstruct'[157] a given song-text, like *Sweet Kitty*, which seems to have been patched up with bits of Mrs Overd's version; and broadside texts occasionally served as quarries for the same purpose. The mildly erotic implications of what had been the sixth verse of *Sign of the Bonny Blue Bell* are enough to ensure its excision, yet whole verses of *The Unquiet Grave* are evidently composed, and others are strangely jumbled, all for no other reason than to make this 'great favourite with Somerset singers'[158] conform to what Marson and Sharp felt was the 'ideal folk song'. Ironically, the new verses are laced with sensationalism and bourgeois sentimentality of the most vulgar kind.

Not one text in Part 1 of *Folk Songs from Somerset* went unaltered; and in Part 2 the editors admitted that 'The words in this series have been rather more freely dealt with'.[159] Anything approaching sexual connotation is ruthlessly excluded or changed so as to conform with normative bourgeois standards. The direct confrontation in *As I walked through the Meadows* is taken back into a passively-recorded verbal exchange, defusing the live conflict, and sentimentalizing it with parlour-ballad interpolations such as 'she pattered along on her dear little feet'. In *The Trees they do grow high*, the girl is deprived of her active part in putting an end to the boy's growing: the fulfilled relationship in the original text of *Foggy Dew* is scrupulously removed into a dream-world of adolescent wishfulfilment; and mawkish sentimentality replaces active physical love wherever necessary. Intercourse *means* marriage, even in the allegedly scientific work published in the *Journal* in 1905, while the cock which 'never trode no hen' in the collected version of *Blow away the Morning Dew* is emasculated so that his frustrated potency (and thus, by analogy, the man's) is said to make him 'cluck like any hen'. Marson's penchant for fairy-stories erupts gratuitously into *The Bank of Green Willow* — 'For O the ship was pixy-held' — and only occasionally does he acknowledge what he was actually doing to the song-culture from which parts of the texts had been extracted: 'Mr Marson has re-written the words, retaining as many lines of Mrs Hooper's song as were desirable.'[160]

There was no need to spell out who, precisely, would find such doctored texts 'desirable'. The hundreds of alterations, additions and omissions were, in any case, probably less significant than Sharp's overwhelming ignorance of the real processes of workers' cultural history. 'Child' ballads get disproportionate prominence: but on other texts he was less sure. To Sharp, *Dicky of Taunton Dean* had 'all the character of a genuine traditional ballad', whereas country people knew it to be a townsman's mickey-take of a caricatured yokel.[161] Though he knew *Green Bushes* was Louie Hooper's favourite, he gives little prominence to the play of that name which went the rounds in Somerset in 1845. If two of his women sources knew *The Keys of Heaven*, which they had learned, probably, from the same group of travelling mummers, Sharp preferred to supplement what they remembered with verses culled, apparently, from *English County Songs*. And if Sharp's source for *Early Early in the Spring* sang of a young man going off to 'serve the queen', Sharp published the line with 'king' instead, forcing the song back to the period before 1837, or perhaps forward to that after 1901, so as to make spurious links with his readers. Even in the 'scientific' work for the *Journal*, convenient emendations and interpolations made for the song-books get carried over, as did the doctored texts used by Baring-Gould in 1890, when Sharp re-edited *Songs of the West* in 1905. Baring-Gould and Sharp collaborated for *Folk Songs for Schools*, in 1906, where the liberties taken with song-texts were, even for them, unprecedented. Words which, in 1905, Sharp and Marson could pronounce as being 'mere doggerel or obscure'[162] did not deserve, presumably, to be linked to the 'purest forms' of tunes. By 1907, Sharp was calling unashamedly for an English Scott or Burns to rewrite song-texts so as to be suitable for the consumption of infants, according to the criteria of bourgeois taste.[163] No matter what working men and women sang, loved, or treasured, now that the products of their culture had been traded for a mug of cider, a quid of tobacco, a few pounds or some other trinket, they were Sharp's property, to do with as he thought fit. They were a commodity with a market-value, an ideological 'instrument' and cultural 'raw material' for the class of which Sharp was becoming, as we shall see, an increasingly less radical member. What Scott and Burns had done for bourgeois poetry, 100 years before, Sharp wished to help do for bourgeois music.

9 The 'Folksong' Consensus

Sharp's *Conclusions* was greeted with some scepticism by the literary and musical establishment; but part of his struggle within bourgeois culture involved the finding, recruiting and cadreization of a body of like-minded people, all of whom, in the later 1900s and early 1910s, were men.

* * * *

(i) Sharp's cadre

Vaughan Williams was collecting songs in 1903[1], even before Sharp. George Gardiner began collecting in Hampshire at Lucy Broadwood's suggestion in 1905[2]. The Hammond brothers began 'trying to collect some of the gleanings of Mr. Sharp's harvest', in the summer of 1905. The Hammonds lived at Clevedon, knew Sharp's wife's family, and met Marson there[3]. Percy Grainger's interest was initially awakened by contact with Grieg the composer, and then by a Lucy Broadwood lecture and a 'folksong' competition in North Lincolnshire judged by Kidson[4]. He, too, was soon in contact with Sharp. Another budding composer, George Butterworth, came into contact with Sharp and Vaughan Williams when he was a student at Oxford[5]; but by the end of The First World War, this male cadre had been decimated, and by 1930 the first two generations of 'folksong' collectors were all but extinct. Gardiner and Henry Hammond died in 1910, both of them in middle age. Butterworth was killed on the Somme in 1916. Sharp died in 1924, as did Baring-Gould. Kidson died in 1927, and Broadwood in 1929. Grainger left for the USA in 1914, and by that date Vaughan Williams had turned away from collecting songs towards using their musical ideas for bourgeois concert music. Sharp collected in the USA during the War; but Baring-Gould seems to have done little after 1900, and Broadwood and Kidson did hardly any more. They felt, by and large, that the job had been done[6], and no comparable generation of collectors came forward during the 1920s or 1930s to replace them. Part of the reason why will become clear when we see what kind of people they all were.

Gardiner was born in 1852 in Kincardine, the son of a Scots Presbyterian minister and of the sister of the founder of the Scots

Evangelical Church. After taking his M.A. at Edinburgh University, he went on to act as a Professor's assistant, and then to be Classics Master at Edinburgh Academy where he met Henry Hammond. He took the degree of D.Sc. in 1894, published various Latin translations, and spent a good deal of time in the early 1900s holidaying in Europe and convalescing in England or at Melrose[7]. Henry and Robert Hammond were the grandsons of a clergyman, and the sons of a member of the Indian Civil Service. Henry was born in 1866, was sent to Lancing College and took an open scholarship to Corpus Christi College, Oxford. He worked for a living for a year at Blairlodge school before going on to Edinburgh Academy. There, he met and befriended Gardiner, and wrote a report for the Education Department on Baden secondary schools. He was soon appointed Director of Education in Rhodesia, though his health broke down after only a year, and he retired to Clevedon to convalesce in 1899. During the 1900s, he seems to have lived on his own means[8]. Vaughan Williams was born in 1872, a vicar's son. His father's family had held legal positions and church livings for some generations. His mother was the great granddaughter of the potter, Josiah Wedgwood, and was closely related to Charles Darwin. Ralph went to Charterhouse, on to the Royal College of Music for a couple of years, then to Trinity College, Cambridge, where he took a history degree. After a further year at the RCM (where he became Professor of Composition after the War), he went off to Berlin to work with the composer, Max Bruch, and returned to marry Adeline Fisher in 1901. He also took his Mus. Doc. degree, supplemented his private income by teaching at a private school, and by the occasional fee from editing, conducting and arranging work. He also had a growing income from royalties from his published compositions. Though he saw himself as a 'Radical' at school, he got only so far as Fabian pamphlets at Cambridge, and was virulently anti-Soviet. In the late 1930s he accepted a prize from an institution in Nazi Germany, after overcoming his initial scruples, and during the Second World War he was deemed sufficiently reliable to chair a Home Office committee supervising alien musicians in Britain[9]. Grainger was born in Melbourne, Australia, in 1882; but his abilities as a pianist enabled him to make a European tour at the age of 12, and to stay on until 1900 in Frankfurt where he learned piano-playing and composition along with Balfour-Gardiner and other up-and-coming English composers. After 1900, Grainger moved to London and made a living as a professional pianist and concert performer for metropolitan bourgeois audiences. He was befriended by Grieg in 1904, mixed with Folk Song Society people of both factions — Sharp's 'folksong' cadre and the Broadwood–Kidson axis — and decamped to the USA in 1914[10]. George Butterworth was born in London in 1885, the son of a professional singer and of a solicitor who became general manager of the North Eastern Railway. He was sent to Aysgarth School in Yorkshire, won a foundation scholarship to Eton, and went up to Trinity College, Oxford in 1904. He did not read law, as his father hoped, but Mods. He also became president of the university Musical Club, took a degree, and decided on a career in music. He spent a year as a music critic on *The Times* in 1908, worked as a teacher at Radley College for another year, took a year's worth of an RCM course, and helped Sharp to found the English Folk Dance Society. He collaborated with Vaughan Williams at musical composition, had his own work played at the Leeds Festival and the Queen's Hall, but enlisted straight away as a private when war broke out, and was promptly transferred to be a second lieutenant in the Durham Light Infantry. He won the Military Cross in July 1916, one month before he was killed[11]. The class homogeneity of these men is striking indeed, as is their tendency towards making their name in the polite arts or the liberal professions.

* * * * *

(ii) The struggle for hegemony

After 1907, Sharp knew he had lost the battle for his 'scientific' ideas about 'folksong' with the leading members of the Folk Song Society, and amongst their allies in the educational and musical establishments. For a period, he concentrated on the dance, where he came up against Mary Neal, who was not only a suffragette sympathizer and Labour Party supporter, but also an effective propagandist.[12] Sharp was also worried about supplementing his Ludgrove income, but when he complained to his publisher, Curwen, he was advised to rob Baring-Gould:

> Your trouble comes from having to share the royalties. Why bring in Mr. Baring-Gould? You can easily revise the words yourself, and we feel sure he would not mind, as his disposition is so generous.[13]

When Curwen refused to double Sharp's royalties, the collector switched to Novello's, where he was well-placed to act as middleman between the commercial publishers and the collectors and arrangers who were interested in 'folksong'. All the same, material pressures remained a problem; in 1908 Sharp was writing that he was 'having a most miserable time, camping out absolutely alone with only one servant for several weeks.[14] He managed to ease Marson out of any involvement with the last two parts of *Folk Songs from Somerset*, however, and the fact that 'folksongs' had 'obtained a footing' in universities, several public schools, 'many elementary schools' and on London concert platforms — in suitably refined arrangements — meant that his editorship of Novello's School Songs gave him a strategic position outwith the control of the Folk Song Society. He maintained his 'connexion' with leading society figures and with the more liberal elements in the state, especially those involved with education. In 1909, he got himself appointed Director of the London Polytechnic School of Morris Dancing. By 1910, there was a Folk Dance Club; and by 1911 this had been transformed into the English Folk Dance

Society. Lady Mary Trefusis, Woman of the Bedchamber to Queen
Mary, was President, while Butterworth and many well-connected young
women formed its cadre. And yet, in spite of this progress, by July 1910
Sharp had resigned his post at Ludgrove and seriously considered 'throw-
ing everything up and emigrating to Australia'.

He was prevented from admitting total defeat by the appearance of
a Civil List pension of £100 a year, to add to the £500 he and his wife
received from other sources. A friend told him that 'the document we sent
to the Prime Minister ... was the most remarkable collection of distinguished names I have ever seen'. The recognition, rather than the cash,
seems to have spurred Sharp on, and up to 1914 he lectured on song and
dance in 'nearly every boys' public school in England'.[15] He did his
duty at the 1911 Festival of Empire, and kept up his work at the distinctly
upper-crust Shakespeare Festival at Stratford. Using that base and his
access to institutions like Chelsea College, he built up a dance cadre
amongst the elementary school teachers, the people best-placed to get
access to the children of working-class people. In 1914, he was involved
in Granville Barker's production of *A Midsummer Night's Dream* — for
£100 down, and £5 a week — and when the war broke out in August he
took the earliest opportunity to go to the USA with that company, cashing
in on his collecting experience amongst 'society' people like the members
of New York's Colony Club. He regretted that this 'social crowd' put him
off, because that ruined his chances of 'getting private drawing-room lectures which would pay me best'; but he managed to clear £400 in four
months, and knew he could get much more if he set up a 'really swagger
studio', and made a bid for 'social people and charge enormous fees'. In
the end, he decided not to do that, but on his annual visits he saw to it
that Carnegie was approached for funds, that CBS gave him a record
contract,[16] and that his collecting work was amply subsidized by lecturing work — so much so that he sent money home, and could afford to
employ Maud Karpeles as an amanuensis. He was still trying to pump
Rockefeller and Yale University for cash in 1917.[17] After the war, he
accepted the occasional inspectorship of state Training Colleges — which
was offered by Vaughan Williams' brother-in-law — took the £400 a year
salary as Director of the EFDS, honourably resigned his Civil List pension and allowed his old university to award him the degree of Master of
Music. Up to his death in 1924, Sharp's experience as a mediator, almost
as much as his society connection, was an asset which could be converted
into cash in both seemly and unseemly ways. His work fitted well into the
dominant bourgeois ideology on both sides of the Atlantic, and both sides
of the House of Commons, because it *sounded* radical and populist even
though it *was* essentially reactionary and élitist.

Given his central importance in the 'folksong' and 'folk dance' fields,
Sharp's rightward ideological drift during the period after 1907 assumes
disproportionate significance. *The Times Literary Supplement* review of
Conclusions of January 23 1908 charitably supposed that 'the printer was

responsible for the allusion to the 'Arian' race'; but Sharp's ideological tendency *was* towards those attitudes we would now characterize as 'hard' right. He had no sympathy for the Women's Suffrage movement — though a woman apologist later claimed it was their methods he disliked — and his struggle with Mary Neal must have had political as well as aesthetic components. He claimed that what he characterized as 'philanthropy' and 'art' had 'nothing in common, and to unite them spells disaster'. Neal was trying to disseminate dances amongst working-class women, and she vigorously resisted his élitist notions about his role, asserting that the only 'expert' on the dance was the 'traditional' dancer. Sharp, however, wanted to get his ideas 'to a small percentage of the population', usually the children of the bourgeoisie and the ruling class, 'in the right way'. In 1913, he resigned from the Fabians because of their alliance with the Labour Party; but he seems to have rejoined when Mrs Webb pointed out where his class duties lay — 'it was felt we had to take some part in the organisation of a Labour Party, as perhaps the most potent instrument for permeating working-class opinion'.[18] Certainly, he 'did not regard democracy as a fetish to be unreservedly worshipped',[19] even before 1914, and he complained bitterly at the way in which the 'infernal' US Musicians' Union insisted on getting a share of his profitable lectures and performances: 'How Music can flourish in a country such as this I do not know'. On the question of Russia, Sharp's changing reactions are quite revealing. In March 1914 he was apostrophizing about what he would not give to go there to see the dancers; and by early 1917 he was attending a lecture on the February Revolution. But after October he took to pointing to the Soviet state as a 'hideous example'. By then, he admitted to taking 'the conservative view in politics',[20] and to having a 'constant fear' about permanent revolution:

> the war will not reach a definate [sic] conclusion with a signed treaty of peace as wars in the past have done but .. will gradually assume a general revolution in this and any belligerent country ... War ... and [the] general dislike to return to the unfair almost savage economic conditions which existed in pre-war days will very likely lead to something of this kind — a world revolution following up on a world war.[21]

By September 1918 he was describing Winston Salem N.C. as 'a noisy place and the air impregnated with tobacco, molasses and nigger!'[22] His diary records his surprise when his liberal hosts resented his 'dubbing the negroes as of a lower race' and maintained that it was 'a mere lack of education etc!'.[23] Evidently, the racist residue of his mid-Victorian childhood had burst through the 'radical' veneer of 1899 so soon as Sharp came to believe that his own and his class's material interests were under threat from democracy. He wrote to his son that 'One of the evils of democracy is that it is liable to become ruled by a tyrannous majority', and that 'one of the problems that democracy will sooner or later have to solve will be how by majority rule to protect minorities'.[24] As a member of a privileged minority himself, Sharp evidently felt very vulnerable, even though he understood the pressures which were built-in to the capitalist social system –

> The Swedish and Holland thrones totter. Even Switzerland is threatened with a general strike. Will anything happen in England? God knows there are grievances enough to warrant an uprising — if that were the only way of removing them. And those who have suffered under them during the last generation might well be excused for thinking that was the only way![25]

Baring-Gould was later to sound off in his own racist fashion about the mistaken belief that Trozky Castle in Bohemia was the place from which 'the murderous Jew, one of the heads of the Bolsheviks in Russia, has taken his name';[26] but Sharp put his weight behind a rather more intelligent ruling-class strategy. While recognizing that the only long-term solution to class struggle was that 'the leisured class may become the whole community and not one small part of it', and that the 'future of art' was ultimately bound up with such a material improvement, Sharp also understood that, short-term, part of the ideological defense against socialism and revolution was 'Nationalism in art', which before the war had been merely an 'academic subject' but which, after 1917 and 1918 had 'become a vital one'. As one of the self-appointed 'guardians and disseminators' of mediated workers' culture, his job was to ensure that the songs and dances did not remain as a bourgeois 'cult', 'appropriated and patronised by a few choice spirits and protected from the common herd':

> it was the common herd from which they had proceeded and it was the common herd to which they belonged; and to whom it was my intention to restore their lost heritage.[27]

To 'restore' that 'heritage', of course, people like Sharp had first to appropriate it, sift and winnow, and then dole back as and when they thought fit.

Sharp's motives were not, of course, entirely altruistic. So early as 1912 he was asserting his faith in the existence of 'national' musical culture against the music critic, Ernest Newman[28] — 'as Lord Morley said of the elephant, that although we cannot define it we can recognize it when we come across it'[29] — and he was lamenting the lack of development of an English 'national style'.[30] Composers for bourgeois music still stood in need of the 'model' of 'folk-song', and by the start of the First World War Sharp's friends, like Holst and Vaughan Williams, had served their apprenticeship by arranging tunes already collected, and were fully launched on successful careers. Sharp now saw his own role as reassuring his well-to-do supporters that they had no need to fear the 'vulgarisation' of the 'folk songs which one loves':

> A lover of Beethoven's music must feel the same if ever he thought of the way his favourite composer's music is being rendered in Crouch End, Hornsey etc. If anything good is to be made popular, many things will happen which will shock the ears of the elect. This is inevitable and must be accepted.[31]

The tactical problem was how to get what the 'elect' liked and took from one group of workers 'made popular' amongst the majority. So when one of his dance cadre, Tiddy, wrote asking for 'some arrangements for his regimental band of some folk tunes for marching purposes' in France, in 1915, Sharp promptly obliged. The 'verdict was unfavourable', Sharp believed, chiefly because the 'average tommy' was 'too much of a townsman'.[32] So it was to the elementary schools that he turned, especially after 1916, when he lamented that he had 'lost all my pillars except one, Vaughan Williams'.[33] Before 1914, Sharp felt that the dance was intended for 'the recreation of the workers of the world, as it has the power like nothing else of taking their minds off the daily drudgery which must fall to their lot'. After the war, when the 'must' came under severe scrutiny right across Western Europe, Sharp's own class's need for believing and disseminating such propaganda with all available means became politically crucial.

* * * * *

(iii) The consensus

What is remarkable about the development of what passed for 'folksong' theory after 1907 is its Sharp-centredness. He had set the terms of debate even for those who disagreed with many of his particular ideas, and he had begun to identify many of the important issues so early as 1904. His importance to the history of 'folksong' rests on *Conclusions*, however, chiefly because it tried to present a relatively coherent set of ideas and assumptions, and forced others either to produce a full-blown alternative theory of their own, or to seek to modify this or that element of Sharp's argument. They chose the latter course, and nobody took on his theory as a whole — not only the older guard at the Folk Song Society, but even the younger people who collected, arranged and published songs in the later 1900s and the 1910s. They did not feel the need to construct an alternative theory because, though they represented a fairly wide spectrum of ideology within bourgeois culture, that culture was well able to contain what passed for 'socialist' belief in polite company, so long as it did not venture to combine an adherence to some socialist ideas with political *practice* of a genuinely socialist kind. In any case, the material well-being of even the more bohemian element amongst Sharp's younger musical friends ensured that they tended to restrict their intervention to the level of *épater le bourgeois* rather than attack the class basis of their own support. The old guard put up virtually no fight at all.

Lucy Broadwood was against Sharp's publicizing of 'folksong' and resented his generalizations about 'the peasant'.[34] She felt Sharp had the 'patronising attitude of the townsman towards the countryman', and felt it a 'betrayal of trust' to bring the songs 'into the glaring light of the concert room and theatre, or to make them a cog in the educational wheel'.[35] She continued to dominate the Folk Song Society and its *Journal*, and was stung into producing a book of material from her own collecting in 1908.[36] Sharp's EFDS did not get her support,[37] but in any case her collecting had shifted away from England towards Ireland and the so-called 'Celtic fringe' by 1911, where singers could be compared to 'peasants of southern Europe and of many Eastern races'.[38] In fact, she played a small role in the literary and musical components of the 'Celtic Renaissance', which was fostered by miscellaneous bourgeois nationalists and literati.[39] She seems to have rested content with taking part of the profits of the piano-making business, and she slipped quietly into Lord Tennyson's place as President of the Folk Song Society when he died in 1927.

Frank Kidson was dead by that time, but some of his ideas survived him, as when the publishers of a posthumous edition of part of his song-collection insisted that it be called *English Peasant Songs*, against Ethel Kidson's wishes,[40] in 1929, presumably because they felt that was what the book-buying public still wanted. The chief issue between Kidson and Sharp had been that of the importance of broadsides, with the former insisting that his assumption of cultural 'degeneration' made it logical that singers were garbling 'corrupt' versions of broadside texts produced by town-based professionals. Even in 1906, when he wrote to Sharp about 'Folk Song' in his capacity as a leading light in the FSS, Kidson insisted on 'tradition' being defined as being through 'nonprofessional' singers and musicians; though he gave credit to people 'who had a local reputation for skill in music and whose services were requisitioned at merry makings or at other gatherings'. He insisted on only 'a generation' of transmission before 'folk' status could be achieved, even with pieces where known composers were involved.[41] In his *Musical Times* review of *Conclusions*, Kidson took the opportunity of pinpointing the lack of specificity of Sharp's reliance on the notion of the 'common people' by observing that 'we are all mentally developed by environment, communal association, and we all have ups and downs in a greater or lesser degree'. A 'compact definition of "folksong" is still needed', he maintained;[42] and in 1915 he joined Sharp's dance opponent, Mary Neal, to produce a short work on *English Folk-Song and Dance* for Cambridge University Press.[43] But that slight work offers no consistent definition of 'folksong', and, instead, lurches from concepts such as 'people's song' to 'primitive song' to 'popular music' to 'national song', and makes rhetorical appeals to 'the bed-rock temperament of a people' as opposed to 'Artificial music', before alighting on the idea that it is 'a song born of the people and used by the people — practically exclusively used by them before being noted down by collectors and placed before a different class of singers'. As for the 'people', they are, much as with Sharp, 'a stratum of society where education of a literary kind is, in a greater or lesser degree, absent', and distinct from that 'certain class' identified as the bourgeois music composers and their audience. Apart from his stress on the importance of broadsides, Kidson's ideas on the 'degeneration' and 'corruption' of 'original' texts and tunes had barely changed since 1891. He might claim to speak for the 'chief collectors' and for the Folk Song Society — Sharp's contribution is placed chronologically last — but the book is adequate evidence of the Society's intellectual and methodological arrested development. So it is the less surprising, then, that the Folk Song Society failed to recruit and hold another generation of collectors, or that those who did join tended to look to Sharp and Vaughan Willams for their ideas.

The Hammonds and Gardiner made little or no original contribution to the debate. They simply took over the gist of *Conclusions*, and referred to 'peasant song' without a qualm,[44] noting apparent differences in culture between counties, and thanking Messrs Novello and Co. for permission to reprint their own collected material in the FSS *Journal*. Gardiner took care to plug the Novello 'county albums' in newspaper articles,[45] referred disingenuously to the 'nameless, hereditary English songs of the people' that were about to be copyrighted. He also advertised his membership of the Folk Song Society and canvassed a 'monumental national collection' of songs akin to Johnson's *Scots Musical Museum*. He was scathing on the 'ephemeral' 'modern ballad', characterized the 'music-hall ditty' as 'neither sense nor art', lamented that 'We have neglected our own music, and gone for that which is made in Germany', and yet cried 'Hands off' to composers and arrangers. In terms of what he sent to the *Journal*, however, Gardiner admits that he 'discarded' dozens of items even before the editor got to work on the 'best' variants; and the songs he collected which went into Novello's *Folk Songs from Hampshire*[46] passed not only through Sharp's hands, but also those of Vaughan Williams. Tunes were arranged, and sometimes altered, by Holst.

Willy nilly, the *Journal* tended to become tune-centred and to disregard matters of provenance. After 1914, its habit of categorizing songs into distinct 'types' meant that people like Hammond and Gardiner had songs expurgated, and their transcriptions 'corrected from a phonograph record'. Tunes were still reduced to a putative 'original' melody, which was usually a modal one. In such ways their intellectual weight and collecting experience marshalled behind the 'degeneration' theory in what we have come to look upon as the golden age of song-collection and publication. Broadwood's preferred method had been to sing the kind of song she wanted to collect, so as to try to put her sources at their ease.[47] Kidson disliked the phonograph because it preserved 'excessively elaborate rhythms', and thus made the discovery of the 'original structure of the tune' difficult to decipher — 'what the singer obviously means',[48] as mediated by the 'expert' collector. Compared to them, Hammond and Gardiner were scientific. And yet their cycle tours were compared to the 'arts of the chase', and Hammond acknowledged that he took down only those texts and tunes which 'impressed' him — this fact perhaps accounts for his having heard no minor tunes.[49] He and Gardiner used the same kind of networks of squires and parsons as Sharp preferred. They also elected to record from people over 70 when they could, and rejected tunes which they felt they had found already or which had been published elsewhere. Gardiner proudly announced that he had explored an 'agricultural district' 'remote from the railway', when it was 12 miles away at the furthest. He claimed that 'farmers' were the best sources, but collected from one retired sailor who had been so far as Japan; and he relied heavily on one 'old Lady' who put him in touch with other singers. Later, he used contacts in Hampshire Boards of Guardians to get at the older singers, since they could 'be had at any time', and were not otherwise engaged in haymaking or other country work. By 1909, he had visited every Hampshire Workhouse 'except two'. He seemed surprised to find so many apparently Irish songs being sung to him in the institutions' gardens, forgetting that, as with the various railway lines (and the seasonal agricultural labour), migrant Irish workers had been an important economic support to English industrialization since before the 1840s. He got many more songs from men than from women, paid for them with peppermints or cash, and noted with some surprise that one singer 'actually created' tunes 'in order to earn a small fee'. Though he took down what the singer gave him — eroticism, apparent nonsense and all — he or his 'musical colleague' filtered the body of the material as they collected from repertoires, and *before* it went off to Miss Broadwood. (Balfour Gardiner and Vaughan Williams, who acted as his assistants, were, of course, both composers too). This self-censored material, collected according to Sharp's methods, then altered musically for commercial publication after a further filtering and privileging of modal tunes, represented the highly-mediated product of the dominant cultural values acting through even the more enlightened collectors.

Though Grainger's use of the phonograph and his 1908 article in the *Journal* represent something of an innovation, it is important to remember that his ideas were otherwise not markedly different from those of the older collectors and fellow FSS Committee-members. Grainger referred to Mr. Joseph Taylor on the leaflet accompanying his record of 'English Traditional Folksongs' as a 'Genuine Peasant Folksinger'.[50] In fact, Taylor was a bailiff on a large estate, and Grainger's two other best singers were a retired lime-burner and a coal-shipper! In his notes, he refers to the songs being the 'most native and racial in the musical life of

Britain', the 'outcome of an unconscious inner activity', uninfluenced by the art music of this or other lands' and at the same time the basis of some future 'independent English music'. What Grainger was offering to 'otherwise excellent artists' and Folksong students, years hence, who had heard only folksongs sung at second hand', was the means to 'acquire the interpretive traditions and characteristics' of 'peasant' singing styles, simply by playing these 3/6d and 5/6d gramophone records on 50 guinea 'Sheraton Grand' players, 'as supplied to H.M. Queen Alexandra'. In his *Journal* article, Grainger bluntly refuted some of the Committee's assertions. The argument about upsetting singers was self-evidently nonsense, when they were already 'familiar with gramophones and phonographs in public-houses and elsewhere;'[51] and in any case pad and pencil recording was both inaccurate and a nuisance, since it required interruptions and repetitions which disturbed any singer. But Grainger's acknowledgement that comparisons between phonograph recordings and his own notes turn out 'sorely uncomplimentary'[52] to the manual methods did not remove the troubling fact that 'the phonograph puts valuable folk-song, sea-chanty, and morris-dance collecting within the reach of all possessed of the needful leisure and enthusiasm'.[53] The Editing Committee covered its daring publication of Grainger's article with an unprecedented collective disclaimer, denying any formal support for his methods and his views.[54] After all, what he proposed threatened not only their pleasant pastime, but also their monopoly control over the mediation of workers' songs. Anyone could use a phonograph, and self-styled experts were therefore redundant!

The eventual victory of Grainger's cause resulted from the way in which the phonograph helped give 'an enduring picture of the live art and *traditions* of peasant and sailor singing and fiddling'. It recorded 'dialect' and 'such entertaining accessories as the vocal quality, singing-habits, and other personal characteristics of singers'.[55] But this was not enough to outweigh the problems inherent in undermining the Society members' privileging their version of a 'normal tune'.[56] The truth was, as Grainger knew, that there was no such thing as a 'normal tune', outside the pages of the *Journal*:

> the more I hear talented traditional singers in the flesh, and study phonograph records of their singing, the stronger grows my *personal feeling* that any noting down of an *individually and creatively gifted* man's songs that does not give all possible details of all the different verses of his songs, and in certain cases, of his different renderings at different times ... cannot claim to be a representative picture of such a man's complete art and artistic culture, but only a portion of it.[57]

But however he wrapped it up — 'One is so distressingly liable to think one hears what one is expecting to hear'[58] — the implications of Grainger's acknowledgement of the artistic status of 'creatively gifted' singers were that the entire policy of the Folk Song Society, and its editorial conventions, would have to change. Once they admitted they were dealing with a real, live, creative culture — Grainger's insistence on class-based cultural appropriation by arrangers who have 'to fake',[59] and his Sharpian notions about 'unconscious' artistry notwithstanding — the dominant ideas about working-class song culture came under attack. Worse, the members' own relationship with the cultural products they had converted into property came into question. All the same, Grainger set about 'popularising' the tunes in the form of piano arrangements, chamber music and pastiches for orchestra. He may have believed part of the Committee's propaganda about 'folksong' being the 'traditional art of our races', and redolent of the 'throb of the communal pulse',[60] but his ideas were to some extent subversive of their general position, and distinct from Sharp's. Though the Society bought a phonograph, its use was deprecated, and Grainger left them in peace when he went to make his fortune in the USA in 1914.

Vaughan Williams did most of his collecting between 1903 and 1908. He had been in contact with the Broadwood family as a child, had lectured on 'English Folk-Songs' by 1902, and his ideas were settled before he presented the copyright of a pamphlet based on his usual lecture to the Folk Song Society in 1912. He was on Sharp's side, against Kidson, for example, and ridiculed the idea of 'corruption' — 'what must the original have been?' — but unfortunately he chanced to use as an example a song known to have been spread all over England in the 1840s by a travelling theatre company. He addressed those 'engaged either in teaching, performing or writing music', and his chief interest was in what could be done to 'purify' this musical 'raw material' by people like himself.[61] When he responded to *Conclusions* late in 1907, for example, apart from not liking Sharp's Antithesis between town and country — 'folk song belongs to the town just as much as to the country' — Vaughan Williams also wanted to clarify the point that the

> country people from whom we get these songs are only a small part of our population — why should *their* music be essentially our national music? Is it not because it is only *there* ... we can find music in its most *primitive* state and *this* is the reason, is it not, why we go to them to find out where our national music really is?[62]

The great-nephew of Charles Darwin, and the pupil of Parry and Stanford, was interested in 'unconscious', 'purely melodic' 'folksong' because he agreed with Sharp that it was

> a spontaneous, unself-conscious, unwritten musical utterance, limited in its scope, it is true, but, within its limits, often of supreme beauty, and containing in embryo all those principles which are at the basis of the fully developed art of music.[63]

It never troubled Vaughan Williams that this 'embryo' was to be transplanted into what he proudly characterized as 'bourgeois' music, especially since the practice of singing the songs appeared to him to have 'begun to die out about the year 1860', which marked 'the beginning of a great increase in the means of transport and of popular education', and the growth in 'ready-made' art being imported into the countryside from London.[64] Since the songs had 'ceased to grow' on their 'native soil', it was but a kindness on the part of 'native composers' to rescue them,[65] and only the bourgeoisie could perform this historic task on behalf of the nation, since the working-class had abandoned the 'embryo'. In a way, and in spite of his defeat in establishment quarters, Sharp had managed to win considerable support for most of his 'Conclusions'. The 'folksong' consensus was established.

10 Alfred Owen Williams and the Upper Thames

It comes as a surprise to many people interested in British working-class song culture that at least one working person, Alfred Williams, was involved with the collection and publication of such material at roughly the same period as Sharp and the other bourgeois collectors. Often, Williams' achievements are patronized as being less scientific or, more often, less discriminating than those of the better known collectors. His work is mentioned, if at all, by way of an aside, an aberration even, though interesting in its very lack of theoretical clarity. The truth is, however, that Williams' aims were somewhat different to those of Sharp and the Folk Song Society. His work cannot be understood without an analysis of his form of working-class consciousness, his relationship with literary elements in bourgeois culture, and his attitude towards country workers. But it is the contention of this chapter that Williams' achievement, for all its flaws, represents in certain important ways a qualitative advance in the study of aspects of English working-class culture.

* * * * *

(i) His life and ideas

Alfred Owen Williams was born into a downwardly-mobile family at South Marston, Wiltshire, in 1877.[1] His mother's people had been farmers and builders, and his father's had included lawyers and a doctor. Their marriage ended when Elias ran away in 1880, leaving Elizabeth to take in needlework, sell sweets and newspapers, glean corn from farmers' fields and try to pay off the debts her improvident husband had left behind. Alfred, the fifth child of eight and the last son to be born, had to go as a part-timer at school, and work as a houseboy on a local farm. He tried to enlist in the Navy, the Marine Artillery and the Metropolitan Police, as a young man, but failed because of his poor health. He left school altogether when he was 11, and after four years in agricultural work he went off to nearby Swindon, attracted by the much higher wages at the engineering works of the Great Western Railway. He was already considering marriage, and this gave him the greater incentive to get promotion, moving up from rivet-hotter to a hammerman, and then to a

chargeman. The urge for self-improvement also led to his taking a correspondence course with Ruskin College in the early 1900s, and he tried
to give himself a literary training in such leisure time as the forge allowed
him. He read and wrote poetry in the evenings and at week-ends, and
came under the notice of a local patrician Liberal, Lord Edmond Fitz-
maurice. During his late twenties, Williams' ideology changed. In 1899,
he had proclaimed himself a 'Radical in politics' and read the 'little
England' press, becoming 'captivated with its outcry against the im-
perialistic aims of the Government of the day'.[2] But by 1905 this early
radicalism had turned into a 'progressive conservatism'.[3] He had come
to accept, with extreme bitterness, that the most he could hope for was
a life as a hammerman, with his status as 'Hammerman Poet', in
between the bouts of hard physical labour.

During the early 1910s, a period of marked class struggle, Williams
began researching and writing books on the rural district of the White
Horse in the upper Thames Valley. He also wrote a book on his
experiences at work, but *Life in a Railway Factory* was not published until
1915, after he had left the GWR, because of his fear of retribution by his
employers, and his susceptibility to the pressure exerted on him by his
patron. That book shows how Williams was trapped, ideologically as well
as materially, in his job, between what he knew of managerial pettiness
and what he characterized as almost unrelieved working-class selfishness
and ignorance. It also demonstrates Williams' failure to grasp the full
reality of his own and his workmates' situation. He depicts the ways in
which worker was set against worker, showed how the GWR factory
dominated the life of workers for miles around Swindon, and criticized
the ruthlessness with which managers used stop-watches, work study and
lay-offs to discipline the workforce. Yet the book reads as though Williams
saw himself as somehow 'above' all that, looking down with god-like
disdain on the doings of intellectual pygmies. On the other hand, his own
23 years' continuous service and his steady promotion, indicate a high
level of acceptability to the works foremen and management. He felt no
confidence in the ability of most manual workers to organize at a trade
union level, let alone politically, and he held almost all of them in profound contempt for their lack of 'general culture'.[4] Of course, this intellectual superiority was no protection against the indignities heaped on all
GWR workers–

> The convenience consists of a long double row of seats, situated back to
> back, partly divided by brick walls, the whole constructed above a large pit
> that contains a foot of water which is changed once or twice a day. The
> seats themselves are merely an iron rail built upon the brickwork, and
> there is no protection.[5]

Added to this degradation was the danger to health, as when the night-
shift boss was ordered to 'send the men outside in the yard and keep them

there for two or three hours shifting scrap iron, in order that they might "catch cold and stop at home, and give the others a chance"'.[6] Accidents, particularly on nights, were frequent and nasty; while the damage done to mind and body by the shift-system was profound. The coming of 'scientific management', or Taylorism, made matters worse: jobs were speeded-up, piece-rates driven down, and men made to work much harder in order to earn something like a living wage.[7]

What, we might ask, did he *do* about this situation? Very little, it seems, because of his prickly individualism and his contemptuous attitude towards fellow-workers and their culture:

> The workmen do not think for themselves, and if you should be at the pains of pointing out anything for their benefit they will tell you that you are mad, or curse you for a Socialist. Anyone at the works who holds a view different from that expressed by the crowd is called a Socialist, rightly or wrongly; it would need an earthquake to rouse many of the men out of their apathy and indifference.[8]

Consistently, Williams seeks to gloss over class-struggle, the capitalist mode of production, the drive for profits and suchlike material factors by attributing the resulting conflicts to personal and even individual failings — 'pride', 'intolerance', and so on. His individualism, linked as it was to a profound respect for bourgeois literary culture and its essential individualistic ideology, seems to have been reinforced rather than undermined by the fact that his experience at the GWR works was gained during the last major transition in the British economy, in terms of industrial organization, and of the final establishment of a town-oriented working class. It wasn't that he didn't understand how capital and capitalist relations had penetrated even his beloved countryside. He knew how farmers exploited child-labour, and understood that labour was 'too cheap and machinery too plentiful' for the farmer to need to give factory workers a bit of evening work during harvest-time.[9] His profound alienation from his work and his workmates was symbolized by his retreat, at meal-times, to 'the field', a patch of overgrown wasteland attached to the works, where he could meditate alone, and imagine himself in 'some remote village corner, surrounded with fresh green foliage and drinking in the sweet breath of the open fields'.[10] This, of course, was an example of that individualism he saw fit to criticize in others; and his entire production of 'country' books in the period after 1911 has to be seen in this context. The only way 'out' of the factory was in the evenings, at week-ends, or in imagination; and, precisely because capital had penetrated social relations in the countryside, that 'country' and its culture had to be a deliberate construction (or, at least, a very careful selection) from the full reality of country life and work. He did not, for example, write a book like that on the GWR works about *Life on a Wiltshire Farm*.

Williams not only had to make sure that his books sold, but they had to make a profit on which he could live, once the regular wages from the GWR ceased. He had to steer a narrow course between those potential readers and purchasers associated with progressive, metropolitan-oriented bourgeois opinion, as typified by *The Nation*, which pronounced him a 'bigoted Tory',[11] and the reactionaries in the countryside, one of whom, a parson, was driven to burn copies of Williams' 'unvarnished' picture of Wiltshire country life.[12] It is not in question, however, that he became an unalloyed reactionary, believing in the 'great men' theory of history, advocating the primacy of 'will' over 'brains' in education, and lauding the least progressive aspects of country life over the culture of towns and working-class communities, even though he never lived in Swindon, or stayed there any longer than he had to after work. When the First World War began, he did not enlist, and in 1916 he was using his patron's good offices to try to extract a grant from the Royal Literary Fund to help him live. He had shown his loyalty to this imperialist war by producing *War Sonnets and Songs*, and had hopes of patronage at Prime Ministerial level; but the medical board passed him fit enough for garrison duty late in 1916 and this solved his dilemma about income. By 1917, he was posted to Ireland, and then to India, where his distance from the British working class seems to have accentuated his reactionary tendencies:

> When I consider all things in connection with the life of the masses, the crowd, or whatever one likes to call them, I become more and more convinced of my opinion so long held — namely, that I'll never be a *democrat* and that Democracy as a ruling power would be fatal to England, for when you give one of them an opportunity of showing what his rule would be, he is the most terrible tyrant and hog you could imagine. I am especially thinking of the manner in which they treat the poor natives here.[13]

What was apparently a humane statement, sparked off by a revulsion against racism — which had been built into working-class culture systematically for generations as an important component of British imperialism — ended in Williams' habitual deference to enlightened paternalism. No wonder that he could find 'no chums' in the army!

When Williams returned to England after demobilization he managed to eke out only a bare living, and he struggled throughout the 1920s. In 1924–5, his contempt for what he termed the 'materialism' of the urban working class helped persuade him to write a series of diatribes against socialism for *The Times*, though, thankfully, they were never used. *100 Letters from a Worker to Workers* are drivel, and rather nasty and hypocritical drivel at that. The example of the Russian Revolution clearly terrified him as much as it did Sharp or Baring-Gould, and he sought to trivialize socialists' demands by characterizing them as 'twopence a pound off sugar'.[14] Class struggle by workers, was unnecessary and misguided:

> An infuriated democracy is not an enlightened democracy. Hatred leads to murder; murder begets reprisals, and so one crime follows hard on the heels of another. Class hatred is foolish and fanatical, and I have too much confidence in the good sense of the majority of British working men ever to imagine that they will be converted by such a pernicious gospel.[15]

He made what turned out to be a partly accurate prophesy about the British Labour Party, arguing that it would replace the Liberals, undergoing 'considerable change and modification' in the process:

> It will attract the lawyers, professors, and intellectuals in plenty, who are out for office, and these will crowd out the working-men; but the masses, i.e. members of Unions, will never tolerate it for any length of time, because they want the power in their own hands. The result, I imagine, will be the growth of a third or fourth party, composed of more vigorous and violent elements; which will battle with and defeat the moderates and intellectuals, in the same way as Labour at this time has ousted the Liberals.[16]

Of course, the Communist Party of Great Britain had by this date not only been formed, but was attracting significant working-class support. In any case, the real basis of Williams' politics was his profound alienation from 'Trade Union Leaders' who, evidently, did 'not realise their limitations': Pure politics are for men of training and culture, and the workshop is certainly not the place for gaining the necessary experience.[17] Such an attitude is strange, given that the Letters were addressed to 'my old companions of the Forge' by one who had been out of the works for a decade; but no doubt the resiliance of the British ruling class would have surprised and gladdened Williams' heart. When CPGB activists were imprisoned during the General Strike, and the whole struggle was sold down the river by the 'leadership' of the Trades Union Congress — which included one railwayman, J.H. Thomas, who had been an engine-driver on the GWR and went on to become a Lord — no doubt Williams rejoiced. How he would have crowed at the disastrous mistakes forced onto the British Communist Party during Stalin's manipulations of the Comintern during the 1930s![18] But Williams was prevented from that joy by the fact that, in spite of his militarism, his thoroughly reactionary ideology, and his fetish of the men — never the women — of 'pure descent',[19] he was allowed to die, in poverty, at the age of 53, in 1930.

* * * * *

(ii) Song-collecting

Williams is known to have had some admiration for Sharp's collecting work,[20] but his own class-position and his ideology encouraged him to adopt notably different aims, methods and practices. He was constrained by the lack of leisure-time, for example, and by the distance it was possible for an unfit man to travel on a bicycle in a hilly district such as that on both sides of the Thames, between Oxford and Malmesbury, during the evenings and at week-ends. This material constraint largely accounts for the fact that, apart from David Sawyer at Ogbourne, Williams seems to have gone no further south than Wanborough.[21] Most of his 559 locatable texts — for he seems to have paid little attention to music — come from an area bordered by Cirencester, Tetbury, Brinkworth, Hinton Parva, Didcot, Eynsham, Burford and Winson. As with Sharp, we find that certain settlements appear to have been more productive than others. Four villages provided a quarter of Williams' locatable texts; with two more villages, the proportion goes up to one-third. One-half came from 13 places; two-thirds came from 26; and three-quarters from 33. Swindon was totally ignored; but apart from that prejudiced anomaly, the larger the settlement the more songs Williams seems to have found. Besides, within the geograpical pattern of his collecting, we find that 'remoteness' was far from being the key criterion Sharp maintained. Over half his songs came from under 80 square miles of country — the Inglesham-Aston-Winson triangle, plus the district enclosed by Purton, Stratton, Castle Eaton and South Cerney. Over a quarter came from the 20 square miles in the trinagle formed by Inglesham, Aston and Lechlade. And for all his 13 000 miles of cycling, nearly 300 of the songs came from within a mile of a turnpike road, and an overlapping 340 pieces came from within a mile of a canal or a railway. The main roads between Cirencester and Swindon, Lechlade and Oxford, and Burford and Witney, were especially productive.

Williams' song-collecting was begun, something like Sharp's almost accidentally, in that he came across them as a by-product of his research for material for his more general 'country' books:

> the existence of the songs if not obvious. You may pass through hundreds of villages, with eyes wide open and wits alert, without finding one. They are not on the main routes; they are hidden in the nooks and crannies...[22]

> The knowledge that many of them still existed dawned upon me gradually. At first I noted speech and story, local lore, and rhymes. And while I confined my attention to these, I got nothing else. A villager seldom, if ever, offers you a song.[23]

Part of the reason for this reticence — and apart from the fact that it was only in winter-time that agricultural workers were available to sing at a reasonable hour of night,[24] and then only for a short time, presumably — was Williams' own relationship with his potential sources. From the first he was referred to as 'sir' by all and sundry on his travels, not just out of the politeness he was fond of noting, but also out of deference.[25] His dress, bearing, and perhaps his speech persuaded Gramp Iles that

Williams was a curate when first he called;[26] and this can't have been an isolated example of the distance between the self-educated factory-worker and even the most self-confident country worker. Williams recognized that felt difference:

> Not the most intelligent sang. For the most highly intelligent is not commonly the most musical. Often the reverse obtains. Otherwise all the singing would have been done by tradespeople and schoolmasters. Generally speaking, it was the *middle class* of the working people who were most musical. At the same time, very many of the best singers I knew were quite illiterate, and some were incapable of much interest in matters of a more practical value. Still, they were never stupid. The absolutely stupid person never sang. Yet he appreciated the music and provided an audience.[27]

When we examine what Williams recorded of his chief sources, we find that it is precisely from this class fraction that he collected most of his songs. Carters, waggoners, shepherds, cowmen and stablemen — the skilled, relatively mobile and independent workers — had more opportunity for song acquisition and performance than the lesser-skilled farm workers, no doubt. A mat-maker, blacksmiths, gypsies, retired soldiers and sailors, a gardener-cum-gravedigger, a shoemaker and a thatcher provided more pieces; but the people Williams related to most of all were those he termed the 'Journeyman Farmer' type, who was not really a farmer at all, but a

> labourer, a "Jack of all Trades", that can turn his hand to ploughing, sowing, hoeing, reaping, mowing, theshing, shepherding, sheep-shearing, cartering, milking, hedge-cutting, draining, ditching, tree-felling, thatching, hurdle-making, faggoting, and anything else that may be needed of him, as well as being able to help the master with particular advice concerning the exact times for sowing and the quantities of seed required according to soil and the season, cutting and carrying crops, complaints in cattle, and being a reliable weather prophet into the bargain.[28]

These heroes of rural labour — the agricultural counterparts of the skilled fitters and engineers Williams admired at the GWR works — contained in their ranks not only Tom Hancock of Blunsdon Hill and Gabriel Zillard of Hannington, but the prolific Elijah Iles of Inglesham and 'Wassail' Harvey of Cricklade. Only Henry Serman appears to have been a life-long agricultural labourer.

The size of singers' repertoires seems to have been somewhat smaller than that found by Sharp. Three-quarters of the attributable texts came from 75 people; two-thirds came from 54; half came from 25; one-third came from ten; and one-quarter came from four men. David Sawyer, the downland shepherd of Ogbourne, who 'sang at the shearing feasts every year about the downside'[29] provided one-twelfth; Elijah Iles, the 'journeyman farmer'[30] of Inglesham, produced almost as many; and

'Wassail' Harvey of Cricklade (another farmer), and Charles Tanner (the Bampton morris dancer), provided four per cent apiece. Only five singers sang Williams more than ten songs; only 22 knew more than five; while 39 individuals gave him two songs; and 14 others only one. But this thinner spread does not seem to arise from Williams' restricted tastes. In fact, he paid little heed to the arbitrary criteria promulgated by the more pretentious collectors. He cheerfully admitted that 'Once or twice I have had to buy a song outright, as though it had been a saucepan or a kettle',[31] and, in general, he seems to have collected what singers sang. If Gramp Iles knew *The Jolly Tinker, Lord Bateman, The Banks of Sweet Dundee, Sweet Peggy O,* and *Blow the Candle Out* as well as *Paddle Your own Canoe, my Boys,* then so be it — that was the real rural culture Williams wished to show.[32] Implicitly, *folksongs* were those songs sung by the *folk*, and the latter category was much more liberal, and thus, more historically-specific than any of the contorted formulae produced by Sharp.

Who were the 'folk'? Though Williams remained susceptible to his habit of caricaturing country workers' culture and their supposed 'characteristics', when it came to songs he was usually more specific. 'Certain villages', he wrote,

> throughout the Upper Thames Valley, were celebrated above the rest for the number of their singers and the quality of their songs. In several of these about every other person you met with might have sung to you some piece.[33]

The kinds of live traditions noted by Sharp also came to his attention:

> As some individuals were more musical than others, so also were some families. Very often the entire members of a family, for generations, had been famed for singing, and their songs had usually belonged to a distinctive class or order. One of the most convincing illustrations of this is the case of the Kings, of Castle Eaton. They were a numerous family, and nearly all were good singers and possessed of fine voices. The entire choir at the church was composed of the Kings, male and female, and bands of them practised carol-singing at the farmhouses for miles around every Christmas-time.[34]

On the other hand, he believed that this was true only of the 'agricultural population':

> very few others, if we except stablemen at the inns, figured to any extent in the minstrelsy. Individuals had their favourite pieces. This one was popular with the ploughboys, who taught each other songs at the plough-tail, and in the stables. Another was the favourite of the women at work in the fields reaping, hoeing, or haymaking. This was commonly sung by the cowman to keep the cow quiet during milking; that was chanted by the

shearers as they clipped the fleeces from the sheep in the spring-time. The husbands and wives, sitting at home weaving and straw-plaiting, whiled away the hours with a song; the children learned the melodies and repeated them out of doors, or after they had gone to bed, and often sang themselves asleep. A few of the choicest were taught the children at school; this especially seems to have been the case at Lechlade. The servant girls and maids in the kitchen at the farms and country houses also regularly had musical evenings, and taught each other new melodies. In this manner the folk-songs of different counties and localities became interfused. When the young women left their situations and returned home, or married, they remembered the songs sung by their companions, or very often, by the farmer and his wife, and, in time, passed them on to their children, who treasured them for their mother's sake.[35]

This is a much more credible and realistic account of country culture than the romanticized notions propagated by Sharp and others. There is no attempt to seek to isolate particular songs, and then their singers, not only from the rest of cultural history, but also from the 'contamination' of formal education. Central to song-culture in Williams countryside was the practice of *work*, especially, of course, agricultural-oriented work, and the festivals, institutions, customs and traditions which had been developed in association with it. From the very beginning, then, Williams took that culture on as near to its own terms as he could manage; and, rather than pick and choose song material from his sources after the manner of a Sharp, he seems to have taken down almost everything that was offered. For this reason alone, as Frank Purslow notes, his collection is 'a much more human document'.[36] But that 'document' was not to be fully human, however, partly out of deference to the hypocrisies of bourgeois culture, but also because of Williams' uneasiness with his own sexuality. The 'fact of sex' was a 'greater mischief' than most, and though he conceded that the 'indulgence of the passion is not a crime, scarsely [sic] a fault', it 'must spoil purity'–

I have wished that I had never possessed the distinction of sex, and even as a boy the thought was present to me, and the inward revulsion. Yet, notwithstanding this, I rejoice in the knowledge that I am a man, and make light of my natural weakness and imperfection.[37]

Country workers, however, 'knew not shame as we do':

They were really very innocent compared with ourselves. We have had our eyes open, but at what a price! I have more than once, on being told an indelicate song, had great difficulty in persuading the rustic, my informant, that I could not show the piece, and therefore I should not write it. "But why not?" I have been asked. "There was nothing wrong with that". Neither was there, really, though the eagerly apprehensive minds of most people to-day would soon read wrong into it. The unsophisticated villagers feel hurt at the decision and often discover considerable embarrassment, though if I were to be candid, I should say that, upon such occasions, I myself have felt something of a hypocrite. Of a truth, the shame is on our side, and lies not with the rustics. And where the songs were professedly bad, this much might be said of them — they were so honestly. That is to say, they were simple, open, and natural. They were morally immoral, if I may say so, and not cunningly suggestive and damnably hypocritical, as are some of the modern music-hall pieces.[38]

Apart from the special pleading and the expurgation of repertoires, Williams' account of country culture in his various books represents a remarkable step forward on other mediators' accounts or assumptions. Although he doesn't systematize his description of country culture, he does provide us with some materials for the historical reconstruction of some of its key elements.

Central to rural song-culture was the inn. 'Most of the men sang at the inns, and their pieces were consequently more or less publicly known'.[39] Indeed, Williams came to believe that inns 'had more to do than anything else besides with the perpetuation of the folk-songs', since a 'few men never sang anywhere else' and their 'souls only expanded in society'. Moreover, he was quick to deny that the men 'only sang when they were half-drunk',[40] a slur sometimes made by those who were totally ignorant of the exigencies and opportunities of country labour:

> It was common, years ago, during wet weather, when labour out of doors was at a standstill, for the rustics to assemble at the inns and have singing matches, in order to see — not which could sing *best*, but which could sing *most*.[41]

There was a tendency he had noted for clubs and friendly societies to be based at the local inn, where, as at Aston, Coate and Shifford, the club festival provided yet another occasion for singing.[42] If club-members felt that *You Gentlemen of England* was appropriate, who was Williams to contradict them? And if Scamp, at a Harvest-Home, wanted to render *The Miner's Dream of Home*, Williams saw no occasion to patronize a culture he knew mostly from the outside.[43] Shearing feasts, farm festivals and suchlike not only punctuated the year's work, but they also provided opportunities for cultural interchange within relatively small areas. Thus, David Sawyer's *Shearer's Song* may have been unknown outside the North Wiltshire Downs, at the time Williams was collecting,[44] but the interlocking nature of agricultural and industrial work would not have precluded its eventual 'escape' from that district. The resilience of such cultural products, over time, was, of course, a common experience for collectors:

> Old Elijah Wheatley, nearly ninety, with shaggy, grey hair, and smiling face, still hums the airs played on the fiddles at the dancing when he was a young man.[45]

Songs travelled over time and distance in all sorts of ways. Robert Baxter learned a song as a by-product of his activity as 'one of the last of the Eastleach morris dancers'.[46] George Ash learned another from 'an aged morris dancer near Cirencester'.[47] Elijah Iles had a song from 'travelling navvies and drovers, who camped between Coleshill and Faringdon, when he was a boy';[48] while 'Wassail' Harvey, 'last of the band of Wassailers who performed their merry games at Cricklade every Christmas-time',[49] doubtless picked up tunes and songs on such visits. There were connections between older country customs and relatively new ones. Williams was told that the players in the game which gave rise to a song, *The Football Match*, were 'dressed with ribbons and caps, or hats, after the fashion of the morris dancers';[50] and he records that the village choir at Watchfield used to combine its other duties with 'going out "Christmasing" at the farmhouses',[51] like any other band of wassailers. On such occasions, choirs would bump into the bands of mummers, like those from St. Margaret, who would also be making the rounds;[52] and the plays of Robin Hood or St. George, 'with a collection of old and new songs', would serve to amuse both farm households and people in towns and villages.[53] In summer-time, Cricklade tan-yard workers would act out their own 'crude rustic play' (as Williams apologetically describes it),[54] to celebrate the end of the bark harvest, consciously paralleling the harvest-home of land-workers.[55]

Williams noted the subtle transformation of village culture and of that of town communities also. At Kingstone Lisle, for example, a brass band had been organized. The players, by and large, were farm-workmen — ploughmen and foggers — but the conductor was a carter from a farm 'under the downs'. Instead of the inn, the bandsmen used the local school for practice in the evening, and the old carter complained of his neighbours that: 'Ther's nob'dy yer to support a band, the fawks got nothin' to gie, tha be too poor; *us wants gentry to kip us agwain*'.[56] The absence of a squire's or a vicar's support, or the threat of its withdrawal, was evidently crucial to this element in rural culture. At Highworth, for example, the local church had been a vital centre of music:

> There were two wooden galleries in the church. In one of these, opposite the parson, sat the musicians...and provided harmony for the worshippers. Their instruments were — the violin, the key bugle, clarionette, baritone, bass viol, the "horse's leg", and the big wavy trumpet, commonly called "the Serpent".[57]

Thomas Hardy's *Under the Greenwood Tree* had, of course, recorded a nostalgic view of this rural institution, five years before Williams was born. But what Williams noted, and Hardy did not, was the impression that church musicianship was intimately connected with other country customs (as when the village bell-ringers struck work because their traditional, 'old time annual supper' was discontinued,[231]) and that there appeared to be a cultural hierarchy associated with church singing and playing. From the King family from Castle Eaton, for example, Williams collected *Here's a Health to all Good Lasses*, and noted that (allied to his other experience of glee-singing)

> Glees were usually sung by those having slightly superior tastes in music; that is, by those above the average intelligence among the villagers, or by such as had been trained at some time or other to play on an instrument, it may have been a fiddle or cornet in the local band, or in the choir on Sundays at the church.[59]

If this wasn't simply the product of Williams' intellectual snobbery, then his failure to comment adversely on the ruling-class penetration of aspects of rural working-class culture may be taken to indicate tacit approval, in contrast to the attitude of a 'folksong' collector like Cecil Sharp.

On other questions too, Williams was at variance with the more conservative collectors of 'folksong'. Out of the 600 separate pieces he had obtained he

> did not think there are above ten or twelve which were composed in the Thames Valley. There were local rhymes. There are also several inferior songs composed on local events, such as the one on Watkins, the Purton Stoke murderer, "The Wiltshire Labourers", and "The Poor Tradesman's Lamentation", printed at Wotton-under-Edge.[60]

Like Sharp, such aesthetic judgements are made without argument, even though Williams maintained that there was a recognizable difference between the products of the 'rural muse' and the 'common street ballad'.[61] *The Prize Shorthorn* was a local production, and was composed

> without pen or paper, as the herdsman went about his work in the yards and stalls, or as he lay a-bed at night, and was first of all communicated to old Shadrach and the shepherd, sitting in the small room at the little Axe and Compass Inn, at which they delight to meet now and then and talk over the day's experience, and see which can tell the quaintest item of news, jest or story.[62]

From his own experience as a poet in the traditions of bourgeois art, Williams knew that dialect-writing was 'a species of composition of rather recent introduction';[63] and, indeed, he frequently apologized to his bourgeois readership for the introduction of even prose dialect writing, knowing that it might 'appear a little barbarous to those of refined tastes'.[64] He was sure that, with the exception of *George Ridler's Oven*, dialect songs rarely dated back 'farther than about the middle of the nineteenth century' in South-west England,

> And they are never very good specimens. They are invariably comic, and

have for their subject the doings of clownish countrymen, farmers' daughters, and dairy-maids. "Dick of Taunton Dean" and "Zarey Zikes" are examples. One of the best known dialect songs around these parts is "The Vly be on the Turmut". This, too, is practically modern, and is claimed by several counties — Wiltshire, Somersetshire, and Gloucestershire. It really has little to boast of. It is the favourite, not of the rustics, but of the townsmen. The villagers will not sing it. That is a certain proof of its inferiority. The villagers speak dialect, but do not care to read it. They are shocked and offended when they see their own language written. The townspeople do not speak dialect, but like to read it. There is the difference. Clearly, then, our dialect, as we know it, was written by outsiders, not by those who spoke it. And that is why so very few of the regular folk-songs survive in the dialect form.[65]

Other 'dialect' forms were, however, imported into rural culture:

Certain forms of words used imparted an additional charm to the singing: such as *lov-yer* for lover, *air* for are, *breek* for break, and *coold* for could. Many old singers invariably said *chorius* for chorus, and substituted *v* for *w*, say *ven* and *Villiam* for when and William.[66]

Williams acknowledged the importance of the London-based broadside trade, and was not in the least disturbed by the adoption of part of the street-singer's 'cockney' style.

It was his firm belief, based on talking to many singers, that

The songs were mainly obtained at fairs. These were attended by the ballad-singers, who stood in the market-place and sang the new tunes and pieces, and at the same time sold the broadsides at a penny each. The most famous ballad-singers of the Thames Valley, in recent times, were a man and a woman, who travelled together, and each of whom had but one eye. They sang at all the local fairs, and the man sold the sheets, frequently wetting his thumb with his lips to detach a sheet from a bundle and hand it to the customer in the midst of the singing.[67]

Such people formed part of the retinue of travelling entertainers, which included players, wrestlers, back-sworders, cock-fighters, fiddlers and dancers.[68] And even outside fair-times 'any who could tell a good story and provide entertainment at the inns never failed to attend and were listened to by an appreciative audience'.[69] Songs like *The Struggle for the Breeches* could be disseminated quite rapidly through such channels of cultural exchange,[70] and were as much commodities as the cheaply produced 'images' of Tom King and Dick Turpin that found their way into country workers' cottages.[71] Illiteracy posed no real problem:

very few of the agricultural labourers of a hundred years ago could read or write. They consequently could not have learned the songs from the ballad-sheets. But though they could not read they had remarkable acquisitive faculties. If they chanced to hear a song sung several times they had it. I have heard old labourers say that if they could hear a song clearly once only they were able to remember it completely. And we must bear in mind the fact that they were not short pieces. One old labourer told me a song containing eight verses of eight lines each, and took his oath that he had heard it sung once — at Highworth Fair.[72]

These processes constituted the chief agency of change in songs, and had nothing mysterious or 'unconscious' about them. Professionals' canniness was a factor, when they 'substituted a fresh name to fit in with the locality' to help a song to 'catch on':

> And even though the printed sheet showed the original place-name, the local singers substituted one well known to them. And since one has, at this time, to depend entirely upon oral recitations, what he obtains will be, not the song as it originally stood on the ballad sheet, but as it has been altered and fitted into the local requirement.[73]

Unlike Sharp, Williams seems to have been prepared to listen to all that his singers told him, and to have believed them:

> The ballad-singers came regularly to the village, every Christmas, when Granny was a girl. There was a band of minstrels, and one preceded the others, carrying a great wooden bowl for the ale upon his head. As they walked they sang an ancient piece .... [74]

That song was a wassail, and the bowl went to every farmhouse, where it was dutifully replenished: 'all the company quaffed from it, and wished good health to the farmer and his wife,[75] as gypsy musicians had done for generations. No doubt times were leaner for the professionals in winter, and they had to eke out a living by relying on such old customs. On the other hand, such people came into their own in spring, summer and autumn, selling the ballad-sheets. Williams knew of ballad-printers at Wotton, Cirencester and Highworth, and had come across sheets from as far away as Bristol, Newport, Birmingham, Winchester and London.[76] Others, no doubt, would have come from presses at Oxford, Banbury, Gloucester and Salisbury, and, via such cultural staging-posts, from much further afield — Ireland, Scotland, Preston and Newcastle.[77] This is presumably how a song of American origin, *Old Bob Ridley O*, penetrated Thames Valley culture, unless it came through the music-hall.[78] Williams notes that he found the text of *The Recruiting Sergeant*, printed on 'an illustrated handbill' dating from around 1800, in the village of South Cerney.[79] The old carter of Woolstone declared that 'hundreds of these sheets were disposed of at a single fair time', and that while the singers worked in groups of two, three or four, one of the most common pairings was that of man and wife.[80] Some of their songs were 'grave, some sentimental, and others comic or satirical', and though Williams professed one particular fragment 'crude enough', he could believe that there was some 'good material' circulating:

> One can readily understand, from this, how it was that the countryside was vocal in the old days, since every cottage contained sheets of the ballads, the airs of which had been taught the people by the singers at the feasts: they could not fail to make a deep impression on the villagers.[81]

Nor was this professional link the only agency of transmission. A schoolmaster remembered 'when the ballad-singers went from village to village, singing their rhymes', and he stressed to Williams that '*he had helped to train them when he was a young man*'.[82] Another schoolmaster had 'taught the children pretty morris dances, and Maypole games';[83] and we are left to wonder whether this man had come under the influence of the bourgeois Folksong Revival, or whether he had in some way pre-empted that movement's policies on his own initiative.

Certainly, Williams was not hobbled by any of the Folk Song Society's attempts at theory, and did not indulge in any high-flown theorizing about the term 'folksong'. *The Downhill of Life* is characterized as a 'folksong' because it had been 'sung in Poulton for at least a hundred years by a family of blacksmiths'.[84] *Life let us Cherish* is accorded the same label on the basis of guilt by association: Williams had heard it 'sung with folk-songs at Latton and Cricklade'.[85] He recognized that since few of the songs he published figured in the bourgeois literature of their time, then they must have been 'perpetuated by means of the common broadside, or passed on from one generation to another by the process of oral tuition'.[86] Yet he subscribed to the Sharp view of a historical/cultural rupture:

> Before the middle of the nineteenth century the writing of even moderately good folk-songs had ceased; all that have been produced since then belong to another and inferior order, approaching to what is commonly known as the popular song of the day.[87]

He does not deign to argue or to give examples. Like Sharp, his attitude towards contemporary worker-made songs was dictated by his prejudice towards town-culture in general, and towards the music hall in particular, which had led to the displacement of 'folksongs' even in strongholds like The Blue Lion at Chiseldon:

> A good many of these old songs and chanties survived about the villages till late years, but they are fast dying out now, and are replaced by the idiotic airs of the music-hall, or the sound of music is heard no more.[88]

There were, however, other, more material reasons, for the decline in village singing:

> the most dull of all villages are those in which there is not and has not been an inn, and, consequently, no, or very limited means of association open to the inhabitants.[89]

Then again there was what he defined as the problem of social and cultural mobility:

> very often, when a villager who had been a singer left the farm and took up work of a more highly skilled nature, and mixed with other company, he felt ashamed of his songs and definitely relinquished the singing of them. The same thing happened in the case of one who, fond of singing, and gifted with a good voice, was tempted to learn music and join a choir, or play an instrument in the band. Thereafter he, too, neglected the pure folksong, and showed a preference for classical, or, at any rate, for standard pieces. He was under the impression that his taste had improved, whereas, in reality, the opposite had often taken place. Thus, the singing of the folksongs constantly and continually devolved upon the rank and file, the lower order, if you will, by which I merely mean the carters, waggoners, shepherds, cowmen, and other farm hands, and the stablemen at the inns.[90]

He believed that this change was particularly important in the early years of the century; and, in spite of what he had written elsewhere about the role of schoolteachers in the propagation and training processes, he claimed generally that

> The instruction given to the children at village schools proved antagonistic to the old minstrelsy. Dialect and homely language were discountenanced. Teachers were imported from the towns, and they had little sympathy with village life and customs. The words and spirit of the songs were misunderstood, and the tunes were counted too simple.[91]

Migration, emigration, and the opening up of railways tended to allow urban-oriented culture into the countryside and country workers out.[92] Industrialization processes gradually wreaked structural changes in the country economy, and then the country culture:

> The dearth, or, at any rate, the restricting of the fairs, and, consequently, of the opportunities of disseminating the ballad-sheets is one cause of decline. The closing of many of the old village inns, the discontinuance of the harvest-home and other farm feasts, the suspension and decay of May games, morris dancing, church festivals, wassailing, and mumming are other obvious reasons. Another factor was the advent of the church organ and the breaking-up of the old village bands of musicians. That dealt a smashing blow at music in the villages .... All the week they were free to

be used for the entertainment of the people. The musicians had to be continually practising, and much of it was done in public. As a matter of fact, the villages never were without music. And the *need* of the band kept the wits of the performers fully alive. They laboured to make and keep themselves proficient, and the training they took both educated them and exerted an unmistakable influence upon the everyday life of their fellows. But when the organ came, the village band was dismissed from the church; they were not wanted any more. Their music was despised. There was no further need of them, and the bands broke up. For a while the fiddle sounded at the inns and at the farm feast, and was soon heard no more.[93]

It is typical of Williams' romanticized view of the old, paternalistic village culture that he chose not to indicate the deeper economic changes that mid- and late-nineteenth century capitalism demanded from country workers. It seemed enought to point the figure at an unsympathetic schoolteacher, an absentee squire or a dismissive parson; and Williams' only idea for a solution was to shame such figures into reverting to what he took to be their former role. And yet, as the introduction of the church organ suggests, the role of Church and State was by no means unguided by the demands of capital accumulation, bourgeois Law 'n' Order, and the de-skilling and de-manning associated with the drive to maximize profits in industry and commerce. Williams, like Baring-Gould, notices aspects of this creeping imposition of bourgeois 'order' on country culture, but he does not pursue those insights very far, let alone systematize them:

> the singing of the old songs went on as long as the fairs and harvest-homes were held, and even after they were discontinued, till they began to be rigidly discountenanced, or altogether forbidden at the inns. This was the most unkind and fatal repulse of all. It was chiefly brought about, I am told, not by any desire of the landlord, but by the harsh and strict supervision of the police. They practically forbade singing. The houses at which it was held, *i.e.* those at which poor labourers commonly gathered, were marked as disorderly places; the police looked upon song-singing as a species of rowdyism. Their frequent complaints and threats to the landlords filled them with misgivings; the result was that they were forced, as a means of self-protection, to request their customers not to sing on the premises, or, at any rate, *not to allow themselves to be heard*. The crestfallen and disappointed labourers accordingly held their peace. The songs, since they could no longer be sung in public, were relegated to oblivion; hundreds have completely died out, and will be heard no more. The gramophone and the cinema have about completed the work of destruction, and finally sealed the doom of the folk-song and ballad as they were commonly known.[94]

So as with the fairs, travelling players and gypsies, an unsympathetic local lay and religious Establishment chipped away at traditional customs and rights, piecemeal, until they had succeeded not simply in closing down the old opportunities for public association (and so, amongst other things, singing), but also in driving working-class people into the arms of the commercial, town-oriented leisure industries, just then beginning to boom. Williams probably recognized most of this, but, because of his sentimental view of rural culture, and the way in which bourgeois ideology encourages the concentration on the individual rather than the collective, the surface appearances rather than the reality, he seems to have been incapable of making a thoroughgoing analysis of why this transformation was taking place. *Par excellence*, in this crucial instance, Williams demonstrated the truth of Marx's dictum that the dominant ideas in society are those of the ruling class.

* * * * *

(iii) Song-publishing

Williams' aim was to produce nothing more than 'a friendly collection of home songs, neither scientifically treated, nor intended to appeal to the cold specialist of such things'.[95] But his editing of *Folk Songs of the Upper Thames* resulted in what he said he did not want, that is a 'more or less undigested mass of materials',[96] like many of the already-existing collections. He was clear however that certain errors were to be avoided. In a draft noted, later crossed out, he insisted that

> A common one is that of imagining that the inhabitants of a locality are incapable of appreciating their ballads and songs. Consequently, the average collector, when he has obtained any pieces, never thinks of restoring them to the peasantry to whom they belong, but carries them off to a new atmosphere, exhibits them to a few intellectuals and is satisfied with that. In reality, the pieces are lost about as completely as they were before, and perhaps, relatively speaking, more so, since he who communicated them to the collector feels weakened by having parted with them and, thinking them safe, is himself now inclined to neglect them.[97]

In his song-book aimed at an essentially bourgeois market, he contents himself with the pious view that

> People would read them if they had them. One of the things most to be deplored, in my view, is the fact that so much that is good, beautiful, and *vital* should be kept locked up in books and libraries out of the sight and reach of all but a privileged few, while millions are languishing daily for the want of it.[98]

In another place he had been somewhat more firm:

> I always think it radically wrong to take from many thousands in order to give to several hundreds and probably less than that. And folk songs never

belonged to the intellectuals. They were the property of the people. And if they stand any chance of being remembered and held as cherished possessions it will be by the simple peasant folks, those who have not been educated out of their nature. We are all ready and eager to give a man that which belongs to another. But who will ever be so simple and ingenuous as to think of rendering him his own? That is what we want to do in the matter of folk songs. Give them back to the people. Schools and universities do not want them. They are lost amid our great towns and cities. They cannot live in the atmosphere. And the dwellers there have other compensations, poor ones though they be. It is in the villages and small country towns where they would be welcomed. If it were in my power I would see that there were not a cottage in the land but possessed a book of the ancient national folk songs and ballads, together with examples and summaries of other choice and useful literature.[99]

Probably out of this impulse, many of the texts which later formed his song-book first appeared in a Swindon newspaper in the early years of the war. They did not have published tunes any more than did the book, because Williams' purpose was overwhelmingly and unmistakably *literary*.

When the idea for the song-book was mooted, in the early 1920s, Williams was adamant that he should retain control of the project and its contents. He

> always privately considered the collection to be the one really important piece of work he had done, because, though he did not consider himself to be an expert, he was the first man to make any thorough attempt at collecting the folklore of the neighbourhood.[100]

He probably knew it was to be his last 'country' book, and it was dedicated to his mother, yet it sold slowly, and he was to receive a 10% royalty only after a thousand copies had been sold. In spite of all this, when Frank Kidson wrote to him in June 1923 on behalf of the Folk Song Society, offering help towards the publication of the rest of his song collection, Williams declined. According to his biographer, Clark, he was

> under the mistaken impression that Kidson merely wanted to choose two or three of the rarer examples for the Society's collection. As a matter of fact Williams was not greatly in sympathy with the aims of the Society, for he believed that the old songs should not be revived merely to become the fashion of the moment and the innocent victims of commercialism. He stated on several occasions that the desire and need for folk songs had passed; the singing of them had been the chief and often the only pleasure of the old people, but modern times had brought other interests and delights to them. His collection he regarded as a piece of reconstruction rather than propaganda.[101]

Reconstruction certainly there was. Though only one of his notebooks seems to have survived, on the basis of a study of texts which appear there and in print Frank Purslow concluded that Williams had 'indulged widely' in collating, editing and expurgating texts.[102] This is the less surprising, given the real nature of Williams' purpose in publishing the texts at all.

Though he claimed no right

> to condemn the taste exhibited in, or the imperfections of the old songs, and mutilate, patch, polish, or correct them in deference to the wishes of those trained exclusively according to the modern ideas of poetry and music,[103]

that is precisely what he did. He cheerfully confessed that he was 'old-fashioned', and that he had an affection for 'simple and elemental things':

> For the simple things are the great things, and the elemental are also the fundamental things, and they remain when every other part of the superstructure has been swept away. And it has always happened that when Art, in literature and poetry, as well as in sculpture, has become corrupt, obscured, or debased by a diversion from its true course, the process adopted for its recovery has been a total and unconditional surrender and repudiation of the means, and a return to and re-employment of the original and elemental forms. That is what needs to be done just now with much of our literature, and especially with our poetry, both lyric and epic. We want not to kill the new spirit, not suppress it, but to chasten and purify it. We want, as it were, new blood in the old veins, not old blood in the new veins. Things dead are dead, the good as well as the bad. But be sure a thing *is* dead before you heap Oblivion's dust upon it. I claim that the spirit of the old poetry, and even that which animated the ballads and folk-songs, is not, and cannot be dead, and that it might, in part, at least, be revived to advantage, not in the form, nor in the absolute spirit, but as a basis for future work.[104]

The correspondence with Sharp's advocacy of the music of 'folksong' as 'raw material' for bourgeois art-music, and as an 'instrument for civilizing the masses', is striking indeed. In that sense, and in spite of his pioneering attempts to give a rounded account of Upper Thames rural culture which included songs and singing, Williams remained substantially a prisoner of the 'folksong' consensus, just as he did of the bourgeois ideology on which it was based.

11 Albert Lancaster Lloyd: the one that got away?

If Sharp were alive today he would be a 'folklorist', dealing in what has been unhappily called 'folkloristics'. In other words, he would be wrapping up empiricism or even positivism with an aura of scientificity, like many other people involved in post-war social science, anthropology and cultural studies. Chances are, he would have a job in the USA, working as a professor of 'folklore' in a college or university, because if he remained in Britain he would have been placed outside the mainstream of bourgeois literary and musical education, at the margin of academic endeavour. He may even have remained part of the honourable tradition of serious 'folksong' amateurs, making a living doing something else, on a full-time or a freelance basis. Certainly, he would have to put up with being patted on the head by professors of established disciplines, and with being exhorted by those on the left to 'give the morris dancers a rest'. The serious study of 'folksong' has never won a firm institutional base in Britain, and this is remarkably contradictory, given the concept's history and its overwhelmingly bourgeois character. But what, at first blush, is even more peculiar is that when the first phase of the Folksong Revival had petered out into amiable irrelevance in the 1920s and 1930s, and the Folk Song Society had merged with Sharp's English Folk Dance Society in 1932 so as to secure a viable basis on which to survive, it should have been socialist intellectuals who put so much effort into reviving the Revival.[1]

The full story of this intervention is now being researched,[2] but what I want to show in this chapter is that while there appeared to be considerable ideological differences between the first and second phases of the Folksong Revival, the continuities are even more remarkable. The key figure, from the 1940s until his recent death was A.L. Lloyd. What was seemingly revolutionary in his early writing has become more or less axiomatic, now; but I want to argue that the links between Lloyd's and Sharp's ideas are stronger than the differences, and that Lloyd's challenge was more to the inanities perpetuated by Sharp's would-be followers than to the core of Sharp's ideas. I also want to argue, following from what I wrote almost a decade ago, that while Lloyd's work does represent something of a *rapprochement* between the serious study of 'folksong' and that of workers' history in England, it remains true that he was intellectually hobbled by the contradictions inherent in the 'folksong' consensus. Further, while Lloyd's work is undoubtedly informed by many marxist ideas, it would be inaccurate to characterize his analyses as marxist, not least because of his adherence to the intellectually-crippling deformations of both Marxism and Leninism loyally transmitted through the Communist Party of Great Britain from Moscow. Of course, this is not to be a moral critique, or an unsympathetic attempt to accord praise or blame. Lloyd, like all of us, was a product of a particular stage of historical development, and his achievement has to be analysed as such, not mindlessly dismissed by Cold Warriors, or mindlessly reverenced by self-appointed torch-bearers.

* * * * *

(i) His life and ideas

On the face of it, Albert Lancaster ('Bert') Lloyd could hardly have been more different to Sharp, both in terms of his experience and his ideology.[3] Lloyd was born into a working-class family in Streatham, London in 1908. His mother had been in service, and his father had worked as a draper's packer and as an Automobile Association patrolman. By 1913 the family was living in Sussex, and this was where Mabel Lloyd learned to give what have been called 'sympathetic parodies of the singing style of the local gypsy women'. Ernest Lloyd performed comic ditties and some 'traditional' pieces like *Barbara Allen*. When the First World War got underway, Ernest joined up. He survived, but he was badly wounded and lingered on until 1925 when he died as a result of his wartime injuries. By that date, Bert's mother and his sister had died of tuberculosis. At the age of 15 with a 'good basic education' including both Latin and Spanish from a north London Grammar School — even getting to such a place was an unusual achievement for a working-class child at that period — Bert accepted help from the British Legion, and went as an 'assisted migrant' to Sydney, Australia. The local labour exchange placed him at various small farms, but he eventually found himself a better job at a New South Wales sheep station, and became a member of the Agricultural Workers Union, where he got his first taste of politics. For nine years he worked as a stockman, but he used his leisure-time productively, getting 'progressive' novels through the Sydney Central Reference Library book-loan scheme, and buying 'classical' 78s for his gramophone through HMV and Columbia mail-order catalogues. Sometimes, he would amuse himself by taking down the words of songs he heard at work, and by memorizing the tunes, so that he could learn to sing them. Dissatisfaction with his prospects as a worker and with the limits of self-education, prompted him to return to England in the early or mid-1930s. He worked his passage on a liner, stopping off for six months in South Africa, but when he landed in London he found that the capitalist crisis was worldwide, and that he had returned half way round the world to a British labour exchange.

Undeterred, Lloyd got hold of a reader's ticket for the British Museum and set about reading in a more systematic way, including books of 'folksong' and 'ballads'. By this date he was a confirmed marxist, and he regularly attended Communist Party meetings in London. It is not clear whether he had a Party card at this period — likely, he did — but since the CPGB was the only organization of any size which a marxist could realistically join or work alongside in the 1930s, the formality of membership was much less significant than the fact that Lloyd took part in activities like the anti-fascist street demonstrations and fighting British nazis in the East End. Of course, the CPGB was umbilically linked with Stalin's Soviet Union, and Lloyd, like almost all other Party members and close contacts was 'very pro-Moscow'. It is easy for us, looking back, to point to the horrors and contradictions of the 'socialist' gulags, to Stalin's murders of Trotsky and many other old Bolsheviks, to the disastrous defeats of the German and Chinese revolutions brought about by Stalin's world-historic mistakes, and so on.[4] This must not be gainsaid. It is also easier for us to see how and why, at a period before the use of the Red Army and then nuclear weapons as key agents of Soviet foreign policy, Stalin turned what had been genuinely revolutionary Western European and other communist parties into line-toeing machines. Yet while at the level of the Party apparatuses these organizations refused to form an effective united front with European social-democratic parties against the Nazis, and thus made a significant contribution to Hitler's war effort in the name of the wholly non-marxist concept of 'socialism in one country', rank and file CP members saw principled anti-fascist activity to be not only possible but vital.

Whole layers of politically-aware workers and intellectuals were drawn to that activity, just as Lloyd was settling down in London, and by 1935 even the Comintern recognized that the Soviet Union would now need the protection of greater numbers than its constituent CPs could muster. The resulting 'popular front' strategy, which involved attempting to unify all 'progressive' forces against fascism, led to the courting not only of the British Labour Party but even of 'democratic' capitalists, and of entire capitalist states. But this historic compromise did little to help build a fight in the German or the Italian working-class against fascism, let alone to tackle the capitalist social relations which gave rise to nazism. In fact, members of European Communist Parties found themselves damping down workers' struggles from key positions in the trade union movement as in Britain, or from positions of political power, as in France, so as not to rupture the popular front. In Spain, CP members went so far as to murder revolutionaries who opposed them politically. Wherever they were argued with from the left, CPers felt it enough to denounce their opponents as 'Trotskyists';[5] and the bloody and bizarre political manoeuvring at a national and international level worked its way through to some extent even into leftist intellectual and artistic circles.

Lloyd's access to Party members, fellow-travellers and sympathizers in the London literary coteries meant that he could meet not only the CP historian, Leslie Morton, but also 'progressive' artists including the poet, Dylan Thomas and the sculptor, Henry Moore. In 1936, Lloyd managed to get his translation of Lorca's *Lament for the Death of a Bullfighter* published by Heinneman, and he continued to make contacts with 'progressive' individuals in journalism, publishing and radio. Lloyd had a job as a bookshop manager, but in 1937 he made one seven-month trip to the Antarctic on a whaling factory ship. The crew sang hymns and 'popular hits', by and large, not 'folksongs'; but this experience gave him the idea for a radio programme on the life of an ordinary seafarer. A BBC producer, Laurence Gilliam, took up the project, gave Lloyd a contract and 25 guineas, and let him get on with what turned out to be a drama-documentary. The audience success of 'The Voice of the Seaman' won Lloyd a six-month contract with the BBC's Features and Drama Department, during which he and Igor Vinogradoff produced a lengthy history of Nazism, *The Shadow of the Swastika*, which is said to have been listened to by 'three quarters of the population'. Lloyd's contract was, however, not renewed in 1940: the BBC thought he was 'too left-wing to be handling programmes during a war for democracy', which seems peculiar, now, even though Stalin was about to make a pact with Hitler. Tom Hopkinson of the populist *Picture Post* had no such qualms, however, and he hired Lloyd to write for the periodical as a 'social expert' on the war effort, in between his bouts of army training in the Tank Corps. When the Soviet state did its about-face and came into the war on the side of capitalist democracies like Britain and the United States, the British establishment followed suit. Lloyd was officially seconded to the Ministry of Information to work on a Russian language paper which sought to promote 'British culture' in the Soviet Union!

Towards the end of the war, Lloyd was commissioned by the Workers' Music Association to produce a short book on the British analogues of the 'people's songs' which had been of some use in the US labour movement, and had gained some footholds in leftish intellectual circles in places like New York's Greenwich Village. The WMA was an organization promoted by the CPGB in 1936, and while it numbered the composers Benjamin Britten and Aaron Copeland amongst its Vice-Presidents, as well as the singer Paul Robeson, it was effectively controlled by the Party. *The Singing Englishman* — its very title redolent of the Anglo-centred and masculinist attitudes still common on the British left — was put together, according to Lloyd, 'mainly in barrack-rooms, away from reference works, in between tank gunnery courses',[6] and it appeared in 1944, at the period of the Second Front in Europe. It was offered quite unambiguously as 'An Introduction to English Folksong'. This 'modest but influential'[7] work was followed by *Corn on the Cob*, containing 'Popular and Traditional Poetry of the USA', which was published by Fore Publications Ltd. in 1945. But such productions had to take second place to Lloyd's continued need to earn a living. After the war he returned to the 'progressive' *Picture Post*, along with people who were eventually to make a name for themselves in British television journalism — Robert Kee, James Cameron and Fife Robertson — so that before he was 40 Lloyd's contacts in the media, the CPGB, the left intelligentsia and artistic circles, especially in London, must have been formidable indeed.

In the late 1940s, Lloyd teamed up with 'Ewan MacColl'[8] — the stage-name of Jimmy Miller, who had been helping with Joan Little-wood's experimental Theatre Workshop — to 'promote British folksongs in the jazz cellars and skiffle clubs of London':

> Their reasons were twofold; firstly, they felt that a cultural product of the lower classes was being unjustly neglected and deserved an airing, and secondly, they felt that British popular music was being swamped by the American Corporations, a situation that needed to be resisted.[9]

This nationalist content to apparently progressive and anti-capitalist practices was, of course, fully in line with official Soviet propaganda, but it helped Lloyd and MacColl make links with the unlikely figure of Humphrey Lyttleton — an ex-Eton, ex-Guards cornet-player who played jazz — and to make a radio programme, 'Ballads and Blues', in 1951. In the USA, jazz and 'folk' had been accepted by the Communist Party and the Confederation of Industrial Organizations as a useful adjunct to political and trade union work, and the importation of jazz to Britain therefore had a radical as well as an anti-racist edge, which appealed to a wide spectrum of 'progressives' and liberal bourgeois people. In the USA, performers like Josh White, Hudie Ledbetter, Burl Ives, Woody Guthrie, the Almanacks and the Weavers had received some support from radicals and from the state-sponsored song-collecting activities of Alan Lomax, a person not noted for his progressive political views. In Britain there was only the English Folk Dance and Song Society. Lloyd had joined the EFDSS in 1948, and had won the solo sing-ing class in the Folk Music Festival Competition; but he seems to have had little impact on that institution until after he took the decision, possibly with encouragement from the CPGB, to resign from *Picture Post* and to become a freelance 'folklorist'. This was in 1950, and one of his first jobs was being appointed judge of the newly-nationalized National Coal Board's contribution to the Festival of Britain, which was to 'try to collect coalfield songs before they disappeared'. Using the management's magazine, *Coal*, and a cinema newsreel about 'colliery affairs' called *Mining Review*, Lloyd took the lead in running the competition. On behalf of the NCB, he awarded the prizes for the best 'finds' amongst the hundred or so entries; and one of the results was his first British song-book, *Come all ye bold miners*, published by the CP-linked house of Lawrence and Wishart in 1952. From this collection, the Workers Music Association (who had reissued *The Singing Englishman* in 1951) asked

Lloyd to compile a 2/6d 'copyright' booklet, *Coaldust Ballads*. This publication was intended principally for male voice choirs, and had musical arrangements done by Alan Bush, the President of the WMA and a CP member. Lloyd's reputation as an expert in 'industrial' song — if not his interest in it — stemmed from the reception of these two collections, and was sufficient to help get him elected to the Editorial Board of the EFDSS *Journal* in 1952. Probably, this election was not universally popular in the EFDSS: Lloyd's first published contributions were a few notes in the 1953 *Journal*, and a short article on the Copper family of Rottingdean in 1954, which he used to challenge discretely some of the more old-fashioned notions about the influence of print on 'folksong', the incidence of choral singing and the issue of musical literacy amongst singers. His first review had to wait until 1955; but by that date he had gained experience as a collector in his own right, some of it in Britain but mainly in Eastern Europe, where his CP connections eased his path considerably by setting up field trips with experts and translators. In Britain, even with his contacts, freelance journalism and professional 'folklorism' can hardly have been a profitable occupation. Who wanted articles written about Eastern Europe during the early stages of the Cold War?

From the early 1950s Lloyd's ability to promote his ideas about 'folksong' was enhanced by the development of the 'folk clubs'. The Scots Hoose in London's Cambridge Circus housed MacColl's Ballads and Blues Club from 1953, and it was managed by Bruce Dunnet, another CP member. In turn, many of the clubs growing up in various parts of London and then throughout the English provinces sustained the earliest 'folk' magazines, which were often controlled by CPers, fellow travellers or members of the YCL. These publications advertised not only CP events and Eastern European institutions — notably the World Federation of Democratic Youth — but also developed links with US magazines and 'folk' enthusiasts, and especially the Greenwich Village intellectuals around Pete Seeger. In fact, all and any international connections seem to have been made, using CP networks and front organizations, or those individuals within relatively autonomous institutions who were sympathetic. For the market identified by this cultural intervention the WMA began to make gramophone records, and TRL3, issued in 1955, found Lloyd and MacColl working alongside Harry Corbett, later star of *Steptoe and Son*, the TV comedy show. Lloyd also made an LP of *Australian Bush Songs*, which was edited by the American Kenneth S. Goldstein, in 1956, and followed this with other recordings for the US Riverside label, drawing on material extracted, apparently without acknowledgement, from the EFDSS *Journal*. Next year, Lloyd became Artistic Director of Topic Records and used this increasingly influential position not only to give an airing to the songs and music he had collected in Eastern Europe, but also to select what was suitable from his perspective for folk club performers in Britain. Lloyd exerted a strong influence in this way, at a period when the major record companies had yet to cash in on the 'folk' market, and he used his growing power within the EFDSS to stab people like the Australian, Anderson, ever so nicely, in reviews.[10] Not only did his collection of positions make him an obvious candidate for bodies like the International Folk Music Council — where he also became chairperson of the British National Committee — but it also gave him some more leverage at the BBC and with 'progressive' capitalist publishers. Penguin Books, for example, teamed Lloyd with the aged Vaughan Williams to produce *The Penguin Book of English Folk Songs* in 1959.[11] In the absence of any serious competition for a cheap source of songs to sing in folk clubs, this collection reached its third edition by 1968.

The very success of the folk clubs brought with it ideological and institutional struggles. Cash helped divide the movement, and then the issue of *control* came to the fore, notably in 1960–61. There will no doubt have been connections between this cultural struggle and the decline of the CPGB,[12] and with the splits over issues such as Berlin in 1953 and especially Hungary in 1956, when Soviet tanks crushed a rising in a 'socialist' country that had never had a socialist revolution. From a peak of over 55 000 members in 1942, CPGB membership had been dropping steadily for years, and any pretence at holding revolutionary marxist politics had finally gone overboard in the early 1950s. Ten thousand members left the CPGB in 1956. By that date, the organization was operating as a glorified ginger group in the trade unions, and it was losing members hand over fist to the bigger reformist party to its right. As the Labour Party itself moved further right, under the influence of its elec-toral defeat in 1951 — evidently, sending in troops to break strikes and the managerialist form of 'nationalisation' did not impress too many working-class voters — the CPGB trailed along after it, politically, instead of trying to get back to something like a real socialist alternative to parliamentary cretinism.[13] While this was happening at a general level in British politics, in the microcosm of the 'folksong' movement Lloyd seems to have remained loyal to the Party. In the June 1961 issue of the CP's journal, *Marxism Today*, for example, it was Lloyd[14] who was chosen to comment on the impotence or the indifference of the EFDSS, on the 'Left-Wing Colouring' (if not content) of the Revival, and on the heavy commitment to the collection and study of workers' songs in what he wittily describes as the 'People's Democracies'. He also made an appeal for serious support in this area of cultural struggle from institu-tions like the Labour Party and the Trades Union Congress. Evidently, the popular front strategy was still CPGB policy, after a quarter of a century of somewhat mixed success! Like many another loyal CPer in a union or other cultural organizations, Lloyd had to rest content with hanging on to his positions, and wait for the tanks. Meanwhile, he had to do what he could to retain some influence (if not control) over the folk clubs and the performers.

Topic Records limped through 1962, producing only EPs. There was some evidence of liberalization, however, and Moscow probably did not rejoice over the inclusion of a piece from Tito's partizans on the *Songs of Protest* record, alongside others from the International Brigade in Spain, from the prisoners in Hitler's concentration camps and from the US Civil Rights movement. When LPs were feasible once more, in 1963, *The Iron Muse* concentrated on the politically less contentious category of what Lloyd termed 'industrial folk song'. Probably, he was still feeling his way with this revisionist concept, but the songs on that record struck a chord in the burgeoning folk clubs, where Topic records were loyally sold and raffled, and where singers needed to build up their repertoires if they were to take advantage of the club circuits and the paid 'guest' spots. Lloyd was well placed to get articles in the folk magazines which proliferated after the mid-1960s, and to sing at the clubs for a fee plus expenses; so that when folk festivals got underway, following that at Sidmouth in 1964, he was in regular demand as a leader of workshops and lecturer, as well as a singer. Even though the CP contacts probably continued to do what they could to help him make a living, Lloyd seems by this time if not before to have become relatively autonomous of Party patronage, what with fees, royalties and above all his unrivalled access to the media. (His work for Topic was paid for by the job, and he got a retainer as Artistic Director for only one year.) Not only did he become involved in Charles Parker's epoch-making 'Radio Ballads', beginning with *The Ballad of John Axon* in 1957, but such contacts seem to have smoothed his way into television, especially after the mid-1960s.

Lloyd was probably never totally independent of CP patronage, however, and he was involved with the CPGB Cultural Committee for years. Though he refused to have *The Singing Englishman* reissued yet again, the WMA continued to press him to produce a new book on 'folksong', and doubtless his comrades agreed. In the end, this pressure and the support of the publishing house of Lawrence and Wishart combined to encourage Lloyd to write *Folk Song in England*, not least by helping feed him and his family while he did the research. Material support also came from establishment circles: the Arts Council floated him a 'maintenance grant' as he writes 'out of the blue', and 'all the more delightful for being unsolicited'.[15] Perhaps this was a little disingenuous: *somebody* must have done the soliciting; though Lloyd *was* considered respectable enough for the *Encyclopaedia Britannica* to ask him for contributions, including one on 'popular song', and he was in demand for 'countless reviews and articles for academic journals around the world'. He had won a formidable hegemony on 'English' 'folksong' on both sides of the Atlantic and of the Iron Curtain, not only in official bodies such as the European permanent Commission for the study of industrial folklore, but also amongst the thousands of singers and students to whom he spoke, and whose letters he seems always to have answered, in between what became frequent visits to hospital and intermittent collecting trips so far away as the East Indies.

After *Folk Song in England*, which was eventually paperbacked and reissued, Lloyd seems to have felt he had done what he could in that direction; though he did agree to revise the 'Bible'[16] of many early folk club singers, *Come all ye bold miners*, in 1978, for Lawrence and Wishart. (In fact, it was a significantly larger and less inaccurate work.) He was, after all, 70; yet he was delighted to accept an invitation from Goldsmith's College, London, to teach ethnomusicology towards the end of his life. By that date, material worries umbilically connected with freelance status may have become less of a problem. Perhaps the rates of a comparatively large house at Greenwich were a source of anxiety, in spite of the value of many of Lloyd's possessions, which included several hundred books and gifts of original work from people like Henry Moore. When he died, in 1982, even people on the right in politics had to admit that he had become the most important 'folksong' expert in England, and possibly in the world. For those on the left — and especially for members and ex-members of the CPGB — he was a real hero, a 'giant', and one in some danger of being placed in the communist mythology as a 'Completely self-educated' producer of 'unsuperceded' works.[17] Yet after the understandable loyalty to the man has been expressed and the unquestionably justified praise for his achievements acknowledged, it is crucially important for us all, and for socialists especially, to recognize the contradictions and problems which characterize Lloyd's work and ideas.

* * * * *

(ii) The Singing Englishman

The Singing Englishman presents history as the history of class struggle. It starts from the premise that 'the best way to understand these songs is to relate them to the times and circumstances they were made up in'. According to Lloyd, these 'songs of the common people' showed how they lived, thought, worked, got paid and had things happen to them in history, all of which was 'reflected' in what he still terms 'folksongs'. This 'reflectionist' view of history and culture relates to the 'vulgar' or 'mechanical' marxist conception of Marx's notion of the relationship between economic 'base' and legal, political and general culture 'superstructure' — as though culture were 'reflected' in a complex mirror from the economic element in social organization rather than having a dialectical relationship with economic and other forces.[18] But, of course, this model was hegemonic within the CPGB. It would have been very surprising if Lloyd had somehow transcended Party ideology,[19] even though this crucial element has been repeatedly analysed and rejected since. The difficulty is that Lloyd's use of the reflectionist model works its way through into his analysis of culture in general and of 'folksongs' in particular. The latter are *defined* as 'the peak of cultural achievement of the English lower classes'. They 'came out of social upheaval', and are the product of 'a class just establishing itself in society'. So, 'when that class declined, the folksong withered away and died'. Apart from the bourgeois ideology underpinning this conception of 'art' as the high-point of 'culture' — some might think that trade unions and socialist political parties had a claim to this honour, from a working-class perspective — Lloyd's way of arguing his position is no less ascriptive and logically incestuous than Sharp's had been. *The Cutty Wren*, for example, is blandly yoked to the Peasant's Revolt of 1381 with absolutely no hard evidence, and then, later in the narrative, the relationship between the song and the event is treated as though it were an established fact of history. It wasn't just that this was sloppy scholarship, or imaginative journalism: it gave Lloyd's ideological opponents inside the EFDSS an opportunity to challenge the important and new elements in his book, as Sharp's former amanuensis, Maud Karpeles, was quick to discover.[20]

Lloyd also had difficulty in defining the social class which made and used 'folksong'. From the invocation of the 'common people' he moves on to the even less clear category of 'ordinary and obscure labouring men'. (Here he gave away his masculinist tendencies, writing about how 'wife' and 'kids' were so often simply 'shackles' around men's feet!) For the Anglo-Saxon period he uses the term 'farm workers', and as history passes, the 'lower classes' become the 'peasantry', then the 'illiterate', the 'yeoman', the 'whole nameless and undistinguished mass of working people', the 'agricultural labourers' and finally the 'urban proletariat' — sometimes 'an overworked and undernourished slum proletariat'. Lloyd refers to 'the villagers' who were 'done for' as a 'vital class' by the 1830s, 'and as they went down they took their culture with them'. These 'villagers' 'still sang the old folksongs', but they 'had not the heart to make up new ones because somehow the old idiom no longer suited their outlook and the sad change that had come over their way of life'. Thus, 'the wave of folksong retired and the tide went away out and has not come back again'; so it is possible to claim that 'what we quickest recognise as folksong is the product of a social system that has come to an end'. In other words, it wasn't simply railways, or newspapers, or state education or any other single material change which killed 'folksong'-making, let alone Sharp's idea of the 'fundamental change in the outlook of the people themselves, arising from the attainment of a particular stage in their development', which Lloyd satirizes. The transformation was effected primarily by capitalism, culminating in the completion of the early stages of the industrial revolution. Over a century later, all that Lloyd can hope for is that a complete alteration of society will somehow lead to a situation where there is no longer 'any special distinction or variance between the composer and the rest of his fellowmen', when what he terms 'cultured music and popular music have become one and the same', and people can think and feel and sing 'without reference to class or colour or creed'. This idealism links to Lloyd's unreconstructed elitism: evidently 'great individuals' like the Scarlattis and the Stravinskys deserve their prominence in music books, so long as the 'very fine music' of working people got recognition alongside them. His aim, then, was to establish workers' culture as comparable to the best of past ruling class culture — feudal, bourgeois or state capitalist — rather than as *opposed* to that culture in the sense of being not only quite differently made and used, but also needing to be differently evaluated.

Lloyd was no less critical than Sharp of what he characterized as 'decadent' or 'sad and sickly' songs made for a 'slum proletariat', or any the less satirical of contemporary commercial songs and singers; but he took Sharp to task for his 'false and unrepresentative' arrangements of 'folksongs'. Lloyd shared with Sharp the belief that 'real folksong' could not be considered as individually-made 'art', but was essentially 'communal' and an 'unselfconscious mass thing'. As with Sharp this led to a thoroughly romantic view of history. For example, Lloyd celebrates late medieval Border life as 'heroic', and existence on the East Coast as 'bitter and hard without any illusions at all', when in fact both were brutalized, hand-to-mouth and verging on the barbarous for many ordinary women and men. Similarly, he finds 'life' for 'at least half the 18th century ... pretty plump and easy', but he doesn't say which half! And while he recognized, (using comrade A.L. Morton's popular history book[21] and having access to his advice) that class struggle characterized English history so far back as the Anglo-Saxon period, Lloyd's general thesis seems to be that 'folksongs' were the products of 'yeomen', 'agricultural labourers' and 'peasants'. The 'fagend of the folksong period' was in the 'early 19th century', and though shanties continued to be produced after mid-century, by and large 'folksong' culture was moribund by Sharp's time, and all but dead by the 1940s. In other words, in spite of the crucial recognition of class struggle, Lloyd's overall perspective on 'folksong' and workers' history and culture was otherwise remarkably similar to Sharp's.

The parallels between Lloyd and Sharp stand out more clearly when we examine how *The Singing Englishman* deals with the cultural processes of which 'folksong'-making and -singing were part. For example, Lloyd had a concept of the 'original' tune of a medieval song. The *Green Bushes* tune he prints with *The Cutty Wren* is 'surely too sophisticated to have been the original', though 'Pretty certainly' that song had a 'strong revolutionary meaning' and was 'pretty surely' sung by the 'secret political societies' labelled by the Church as 'witches' sabbaths' in the late fourteenth century. (All this in spite of the disclaimer that 'most kinds of culture do not reflect their history and their social upbringing directly or without distortion, and folksong is no exception in this respect'.) Like Sharp, Child and Gummere, Lloyd thought he knew what the position of 'the illiterate folksinger' was, and blandly asserts that 'he' was 'not interested in treating' his 'subject' in 'any startling or innovatory way':

He had no idea of impressing his personality on it, and unlike the cultured artist he did not see himself as an exceptional figure with a message either of substance or of form. What he was singing, he knew many of his neighbours could sing as well; and what his song was about was what everybody felt. Of course to suit his personal fancy he would alter the words here and there, and ornament the tune with turns and flourishes wherever he chose to put them, but in the usual run of folksong the phrases and the forms were something sanctioned by long tradition and within that tradition everybody knew just where they were.[22]

Lloyd felt he knew what the 'usual run of folksong' actually was, and that songs 'were always learned by ear' because they had 'no one author'. This last was a result of their mode of transmission:

> as they spread from village to village across the country and down the ages, they were changing all the time. Lapses of memory would leave gaps which needed new verses to fill them in; bits of other songs, words or tunes, would creep in by accident or intention; singer after singer would modify or embellish the song; till by the time it had spread two hundred miles and been sung for two hundred years, so much would be lost and so much would be added that often the original song would be impossible to distinguish among a thousand variants; and sometimes the variants were so different from the original that they were really quite new songs.[23]

From this borrowed theory passed off as historical fact it wasn't far to passing judgement on the qualities of the 'truly great ballads' and the 'best of the ballads and songs' which were characterized, evidently, by 'pride and commonsense', by 'looking reality dead in the eye'. It was plausible to postulate a 'common primitive source' for 'the English ballad', and to give an internationalist and non-sectarian flavour to this notion by showing how three tunes, 'not handpicked' — though one of them chanced to be a 'lament for the death of Lenin' — from the Soviet Far East, Piedmont Italy and England had a 'close inner similarity'. It is difficult not to draw a parallel, here, between the political undertow of the older English and Scots bourgeois mediators' attempt to re-homogenize 'the people', and that of a loyal CPGB member in the 1940s, who recognized the strategic importance of trying to demonstrate a link between the 'common people' of Britain and those of the Soviet Union, especially in the year of the Second Front in Normandy.

Lloyd builds on Sharp's ideas about 'the modes' being the 'natural idiom' of the 'English folksinger', and imitates his breathtaking pronouncements on singers' styles, telling us what singers would 'Commonly' do with a tune. He also claimed to know how this treatment changed with the end of feudalism, and how the 'strong unity between the emotional life of the merchants and the lower classes' was broken, once the merchants and gentry felt confident enough to develop their own distinct culture after 1600, leading to the gradual decay of the culture of the 'peasantry', and to what Lloyd believed was the characteristic 'melancholy' of the songs, which encapsulated the 'deep longing for a better life'. After this rupture, the songs of 'the English folksinger' 'wrapped up' the 'facts of life' in 'fantasy', and did not propose any strategy for changing them. These were the pieces which 'the persevering collectors of whom Sharp is justly enough the most respected' found lingering in the English countryside between 1890 and 1914. The rot set in, apparently, after 1815:

> As the rustic communities became demoralised and broken up, the old folksongs became decadent and almost depraved in style and full of new modern tricks that were no good for anything. The new urban proletariat was taking the country songs over and ridiculing them by absurd parodies. Already the representative folkmusic was the street song and not the country song.[24]

Many of these newer songs Lloyd judged to be 'so poor and so lacking in pride or passion or technique or beauty or even surprise' that they did not 'qualify as folksong at all but as something else', though he was 'not sure what'. He *was* sure that industrialization had put an end to the days 'when country labourers had only two or three ideas about livening a dull evening', one of which was by 'making up and singing songs around the kitchen fire'. This imaginative journalism squares oddly with the statement that 'many folksongs were closely related to a certain stage of technical development', 'and that when any given stage had passed' and the 'whole social thing [*sic*] that they reflect no longer obtains', they passed too. Lloyd's ideas in the mid-1940s were, then, a strange mixture of Sharpian assertion and romanticism, based on a model of history and of cultural change which was, formally if crudely, informed by elements of Marx's thought. Fundamentally, however, what he offered was an updated and radical-seeming variant of the 'folksong' consensus with unintegrated elements of marxism. His brand of communism in practice had about it more of Fabianism than of revolutionary struggle.

* * * * *

(iii) *Come all ye bold miners*

When Lloyd came to put together *Come all ye bold miners* in 1951–2, the ideas about 'folksongs' which he had largely taken over from Sharp came up against the fact that he was given 'parodies, literary recitations, parlour ballads' and 'stage songs of the past' by working miners, not to mention material from a wide range of ephemeral printed sources and from miners' own manuscripts. Only 'a few' could pass muster as 'folksongs' using Sharp's criteria, according to which the genuine articles had to be 'so shaped and eroded in passing from mouth to mouth that they acquire the smoothness, subtlety and surprise of a sea-pebble'. Lloyd's way round the problem was to apologize for the 'rough songs, mostly made by rough men' on which 'tradition has hardly got to work'. Yet he insists that what the songs represented was what he terms 'industrial folklore', which could be more or less near to 'tradition'. The contradiction he faced was that a given 'traditional' song might have to be 'learned from print and kept for formal occasions', whilst a 'stage song' could be 'passed on by word of mouth and brought out whenever spirits run high'. He was ready to concede, however, that the songs sung by miners might have been 'painfully evolved by the colliers themselves' *or* have been 'written by slick gentlemen who never wielded a pick, either wet or dry, in anger'. By sticking with the concept of 'folksong', in other words, Lloyd has to try to reconcile the theory with the fact that the 'folk' had changed. Yet in spite of his attempt to slant the evidence by gratuitous praise or blame, by his superficial knowledge particularly of north-east workers' history, or by ascribing particular songs wrongly to workers' culture (while ignoring or writing-down those which did not fit his preconceptions), Lloyd was puzzled to justify theoretically the distinction he thought he perceived between the 'homely ballads' and the

> moth-eaten stereotypes of the standard popular song, with its blubbering self-pity, its nostalgia for old wishing-wells or for tumbledown shacks in Athlone or Tennessee or some other region of the dream-world.[25]

The only hope from the USA was the 'American example' of the 'early days of the C.I.O' when 'miners began to make for themselves a number of vigorous songs very close to folk-song'. No wonder that Lloyd was surprised and delighted to discover the work of Thomas Armstrong, the 'Pitman Poet' of North-west Durham, who wrote for beer-money as well as for the union in the later nineteenth century, and that he offered him as an example to be followed in 'British mining balladry'.

The problem with *Come all ye bold miners* was that it was based on a fundamentally distorted view of north-east workers' culture in the nineteenth century;[26] and though Lloyd was to some extent dependent on his sources it is now clear that his preconceptions about 'folksong' undermined his strong sense of sympathy with miners' and coal-workers' culture. For example, he claims that three 'recitations' were favourites 'in the colliery cottages', *with no evidence*. In fact, Edward Chicken's *Collier's Wedding* of the 1720s was a townsman's *parody* of pit-village culture, printed in Newcastle for would-be superior townspeople and reprinted at periods of industrial struggle, presumably with the intention of bolstering well-to-do people's morale.[27] Henry Robson's *Colliers Pay Week* of 1800 was, indeed, written by an ex-pit-village man who became a skilled print-worker in Newcastle; but it, too, was aimed at an audience of petty-bourgeois and artisan people, who were close enough to the embryo working-class to feel threatened by its combativity during a period of labour-shortage, and especially by comparatively affluent pitmen's ability to court and marry much younger than those who believed and trusted in deferred gratification.[28] Skipsey's *Hartley Calamity* may have appealed to a minority of 'respectable' working-class readers in the 1860s; but it was the *concert-hall* songwriter Ned Corvan's *The Queen has sent a letter* which penetrated the working-class communities of the north-east along with his other locally famous songs. Not only that, but Lloyd was also at the mercy of his informants even when it came to the accurate transcription of manuscript texts.[29] As long as 'folksong' or the equally problematical notion of 'industrial folklore' remained an organizing principle of his work, it was probably inevitable that, like almost all of his song-mediating predecessors, the contradictions inherent in his theory should work their way through into his editing practices.

* * * * *

(iv) *Folk Song in England*

During the decade and a half after 1952 Lloyd's ideas and practices seem to have changed remarkably little. When he put together his first LP, *Australian Bush Songs*, in 1956, the Australian John Meredith 'doubted the authenticity of many songs' and wrote to Lloyd to tell him so:

> In his reply, he admitted making "settings" of the texts to other tunes, and further, stated that he had made so many alterations and additions to, and arrangements of, his original field notes that he no longer knew what was genuine and what concocted.[30]

According to Meredith, Lloyd made statements which could 'only have come from a "Stranger"' to Australia, and Alan Scott noted that all the songs on Lloyd's LP were 'available from published sources or from the archives of the Australian Folklore Society'.[31] Similarly, the 1959 *Penguin Book of English Folk Songs* was produced not from Lloyd's own field-collecting but from the *Journal* of the FSS and that of the EFDSS; and while tunes are said to be reproduced accurately, Lloyd and Vaughan Williams admit that in order to 'make the songs singable', they have not hesitated to 'complete' a song from 'other traditional sources', should the actual singer chance to have left out verses or lines, or have known the song 'only in imperfect form'. In other words, they used the same assumptions about 'original' form and 'tradition' as did Sharp. Unlike him, Lloyd and Vaughan Williams could hardly claim to be pioneers. Moreover they had the benefit of over half a century of the products of collectors' work to fall back on in order to supplement the broadside texts they admitted to having used. Even the tunes were subject to further mediation so as to 'preserve the collectors' impression of what their informants were actually singing', at a distance, in some cases, of 50 years![32]

By the 1960s, if not before, Lloyd had developed the concept of 'industrial folk songs', which, according to his notes on *The Iron Muse* LP, were

> created by industrial workers out of their own daily experience and were circulated, mainly by word of mouth to be used by the songwriters' workmates in mines, mills and foundries.[33]

The key to Lloyd's thesis was that while Sharp and others' 'confined themselves to the rural past and rather shunned the industrial present', the *creation* of folk song had passed almost entirely into the scope of the working class of the towns within the last century or so.[34] The 'folk', according to this conception, had *become* the working class, and had to be spoken up for by socialists. Consequently, the 'Panorama of Industrial Folk Song' which appeared as *The Iron Muse* LP, 'arranged by A.L. Lloyd' for Topic in 1963, was meant both as a source for singers' repertoires in the clubs, and one in the eye for those who believed that 'the cultural horizon of the working class is bounded by the bingo hall and the idiots' lantern'. Moreover, since the working class was held to be 'only dimly aware of its own self-made cultural heritage', this LP was intended as an intervention in the culture of the 'industrial community', especially if it encouraged the making of 'new industrial songs': 'The tradition is a fine one and worth preserving'. In fact, this LP and its sequels, *Tommy Armstrong of Tyneside* and *Leviathan*, seem to have inspired only a tiny handful of song-writers — who were often as not schoolteachers, people with university degrees, and assorted petty-bourgeois individuals — to write 'industrial' songs. Labouring women and men are conspicuous by their absence from the ranks of song-writers who gained access to Topic LPs.

Lloyd evidently regarded his theory of 'industrial folk song' as his major contribution to the work of the 'great collectors', and hoped that it helped to place him within the tradition which led back to Sharp. Probably, he saw the politics of his intervention, as a record-arranger, writer, journalist and theorist in line with the CPGB strategy of winning some sort of hegemony for what *were* comparatively progressive and historically-aware ideas amongst backwoodspersons in the English Folk Dance and Song Society and its international analogues. In other words, by occupying the positions he did he wanted to drag the 'folksong revival', still screaming, just a bit more to the left; but by so doing, I believe, he not only perpetuated Sharp's 'folksong' consensus, but allowed its contradictions to take a serious toll on his marxism. (Rather like those marxists who have recently entered the Labour Party, rather than changing it, it changed them.) In *Folk Song in England*, Lloyd maintained that Sharp's *Conclusions* was still a

> solitary beacon and a towering one, but it was lit sixty years ago and its glow is fading. It would be pleasant to think this book ... might help *Some Conclusions* to shine clearer, if only by putting a little fat on the fire.[35]

In that 1967 book, the concept of 'folklore proper' still existed, for Lloyd, and he like Sharp could recognize it when he saw it.

In his major work of theory, Lloyd wanted to show

> the continuity of folk song, from the 'classic' rural forms, through the urban industrial forms (those queer amalgams of the collective-folkloric and

the individual-'literary'), into that as yet vaguely-charted territory that lies between folklore proper and the realm of the commercial hit.[36]

But to try to prove this thesis Lloyd had to make generalizations about the 'makers and bearers' of the songs he selected from the period of industrialisation, who were, according to him, 'anonymous amateurs who earned their living, meagre as it often was, in other ways than entertainment'. In order to adapt the 'folksong' consensus to the more obvious historical and cultural facts Lloyd was forced to offer a highly romanticized account, often unsubstantiated by hard evidence and dependent for credence on his own authority. At the heart of Lloyd's mature theoretical position lies his support for the pronouncement of the International Folk Music Council, which is itself simply a more sophisticated version of Sharp's three principles of 1907, with one or two of the more obvious loopholes closed:

> Folk music is the product of a musical tradition that has been evolved through the process of oral transmission. The factors that shape the traditions are: (i) continuity which links the present with the past; (ii) variation which springs from the creative impulse of the individual or the group; and (iii) selection by the community, which determines the form or forms in which the music survives.
>
> The term can be applied to music that has been evolved from rudimentary beginnings by a community uninfluenced by popular and art music and it can likewise be applied to music which has originated with an individual composer and has subsequently been absorbed into the unwritten living tradition of a community.
>
> The term does not cover composed popular music that has been taken over ready-made by a community and remains unchanged, for it is the refashioning and re-creation of the music that gives it its folk character.[37]

As with Child and Sharp, this is not an analysis but a *prescription*, which depends on a whole range of assumptions about the role of the artist in any community, the artist's status and way of earning a living, definitions of what consitutes 'popular' and 'art' music, musicians and singers, and so on. In fact, Lloyd had to admit that the 'definition' didn't really fit British cultural history — 'we in Britain are still without a definition of folk song that really fits our local conditions'. But he still clings to the IFMC's authority, and finds its Sharpian dictum valuable because of what he terms its

> clear suggestion of the vital dialectic of folk song creation, that is, the perpetual struggle for synthesis between the collective and the individual, between tradition and innovation, between what is received from the community and what is supplied out of personal fantasy, in short, the blending of continuity and variation.[38]

Of course, this 'definition' is not clear, and begs all the important questions. We are left asking, what criteria are to be used for assessing any process of 'oral transmission'? Why do not continuity, variation and selection represent the conditioning factors for *all* artistic production, amateur or professional? How can any community remain uninfluenced by 'art' or 'popular' music, and what *are* they anyway? We could go on to enquire about how the 'taking over' of any performed art is different from what is supposed to happen in 'oral transmission', and what such a process signifies except one kind of popularity, given that any two performances of the same song (even by the same artist) produce variations in interpretation, style and suchlike. Where, in the twentieth century, and above all in England, is this postulated 'unwritten living tradition'? But Lloyd does not ask these questions, let alone seek to answer them. Yet again, we are obliged to take his detailed attributions and unsupported generalizations on trust and to accept his right of veto. As with Child, we are told what is *not* 'folksong', not what *is*; and we are advised as to which cultural processes do *not* produce 'folk' materials, as opposed to those which *do*. In short, Lloyd swallows the IFMC's arbitrary concept of 'tradition' whole, and, with some stretching on the issue of broadsides, that of the essential orality of transmission, thereby collapsing what he knew of workers' culture and history back into the conceptual trammels of the Sharpian consensus.

What was novel (and to some people, disturbing) about Lloyd's account of *Folk Song in England*, was not so much the megalomaniac breadth promised by the book's title, as the development of his theory about 'industrial folk song', which was, evidently, nothing less than 'the musical and poetic expression of the fantasy of the lower classes — and by no means exclusively the country workers'. Given the logical extension of this argument, which hinted that once the 'lower classes' became the working class, then 'folksong' had to be understood as working-class song, the outrage of the Cold Warriors in the English Folk Dance and Song Society was as inevitable as it was anti-intellectualist.[39] But as it happens Lloyd's assertions remained very little different to Sharp's, in that, after the 'Fall',

> when the mainly unwritten culture of the peasantry was reduced to rubble, the field was by no means left free to 'bourgeois' culture, that is to the fine arts and popular entertainments licensed and provided by the established order ..... As the old lyric of the countryside crumbled away, a new lyric of the industrial towns arose, frail at first but getting stronger, reflecting the life and aspirations of a raw class in the making, of men handling new-fashioned tools, thinking new thoughts, standing in a novel relationship to each other and to their masters.[40]

There then follows a sentimental glorification of what Lloyd pronounced to be the 'typical creator of industrial ballads', who made his song under a hedge perhaps, sheltering from the rain after a fruitless trudge round the mills for work, or who sat up all night by candle-light with a stub of pencil in his fist, writing an elegy on his neighbours killed in yesterday's pit-explosion.[41]

Not only that, but Lloyd seems to have been specially-gifted to read such people's minds. 'He'

> had a narrow political horizon as a rule, but he understood solidarity with his work-mates, could tell when he was hurt, and more and more in the nineteenth century he realized the need for fighting and said so in his songs.[42]

Leaving aside the masculinist attitudes, what was happening here was another kind of homogenizing process, similar to that carried through by Sharp on his 'peasants'. True, Lloyd feels keenly that workers had their own dignity, and some of them had developed class-consciousness; but the Worker as Hero (rarely Heroine) had still to be spoken *for* by the sympathetic mediator, and have even 'his' songs interpreted for the benefit of twentieth century counterparts. There is little sense, in Lloyd's writings, of the working-class being conscious of its own making, of a body of widely different women and men feeling and acting together, first at an economic and then at a political level, struggling to wrest control over their own lives from the ruling class. There is little sense, either, of the *positive* achievements of that formative working-class culture, of the institutions they built and maintained, their appropriation of aspects of the products of other class's culture, of their victories, creativity and self-reliance.

Unfortunately, as with Sharp, Lloyd may have allowed his theoretical assumptions to work their way through into his collecting and publishing activity.[43] It is not simply that he seems not to have known that a working-class family would not have been able to afford candles: rush-lights would have had to suffice. His understanding of the complex-ity and materiality of working-class culture remains superficial, and distorts his analysis. For example, during the great pitmen's strike in the north-east of England in 1844, we know that the Ranter Methodist preachers who controlled the union bureaucracy and its paper used religiose verse to bolster morale, and almost certainly sought to censor the songs which went into broadsides for the collection money. They could not control what rank-and-file pitmen and women sang, of course. When you compare the original manuscript of the pessimistic song which Lloyd decided to re-title as *The Coal Owner and the Pitman's Wife* with his own collected versions of the fiercely militant *Blackleg Miner*, it is easy to understand what the marxist conception of combined and uneven development can really mean! The problem is, however, that Lloyd thought fit to change the broadside text of the former piece, at times significantly, in his published work; and he confuses the reader by issuing varying versions of the latter, orally-transmitted piece. And while he might have pleaded singability as a key criterion in the first edition of *Come All Ye Bold Miners*, no such excuse can exist for the 1978 edition of that work, after the issue had been brought to his attention. Similarly, we are entitled to ask why the brutal class-hatred of the chorus of Tommy Armstrong's *Durham Strike*, which Lloyd rechristened *The Durham Lock-out*, was silently edited out in 1952, and returned only as another verse in 1978. Further detailed study might well reveal other anomalies elsewhere.

The problem was, and is, that very little sustained and detailed research has yet been done on the culture of the majority of English people.[44] This is hardly Lloyd's fault; but it does mean that his generalizations need careful scrutiny. For example, one study has shown that Lloyd had mistaken ideas about the differences between the early English concert hall[45] and what became the music hall, stemming from the same undialectical puritanism which characterizes many CP attitudes towards commercial institutions used by workers, and paralleling Sharp's own fervent anti-commercialism. Yet it ill-behoves a person unable to offer a scientific and non-contradictory definition of what he likes, and calls 'folksong', to castigate and smear the music and songs taken up and used by contemporary working-class people:

> Donkey and horse both have four legs and may pull carts but they are not the same beast; nor are the compositions of a Dylan or a Donovan folk songs by any workable definition.[46]

That the search for a 'workable definition' of 'folksong' is fundamentally incompatible with the materialist analysis of workers' culture and history seems never to have occurred to Lloyd. He, like Sharp, knew an elephant when he saw one; and if we choose to demur, then he seems content to rest on his authority. Any serious examination of this theoretical contradiction, of course, also represented a threat to Lloyd's hard-won position within the Second Folksong Revival.

Lloyd claimed the the Second Revival was not only based on the work of Sharp and other 'splendid pioneers', but was also in some mysterious way 'coming from below now'. This is disingenuous, at best. In fact, the history of the Second Folksong Revival as we have seen was closely involved with the cultural policy of the CPGB. The strategy was to popularize selected and modified elements of the musical culture of British workers in order to counterbalance the records from US industry, which were understood to be having deleterious effects on the culture of contemporary working-class youths. In order to side-step the worst problems posed by McCarthyism, CP intellectuals chose to emulate Fabian tactics and to permeate the clubs, at the same time as supporting institutions such as the Workers' Music Association and Topic Records. It is ironic that Lloyd should still be claiming in 1967 that 'folksong' had appealed 'for the most part' to 'young people searching for something more sustaining than the mumbled withdrawals or frantic despair of the pops', given the commercial success the Revival was currently enjoying. Lloyd, MacColl and others won a share of the 'financial reward' accruing from the 'folk' boom: after all, they had done much of the spade-work, and questions of professionalism, commercialism and the role of capital in workers' culture always have been much more problematical than Lloyd was prepared to concede.

Such minor contradictions give us a hint of more fundamental problems with what has to be seen as Lloyd's mechanistic conception of the relationship between cultural practice and capitalist social relations, whether in history or today. According to him, 'folksong' in England constituted a recognizable body of songs,

> evolved by labouring people to suit their ways and conditions of life, and they reflect the aspirations that rise from those ways and conditions. In the process of creating this fund of song, economic conditions are more decisive than any relative distance from formal culture, book education and the like, for our experience shows that, as elsewhere, the most inventive bearers of English folk song are likely to be the liveliest-minded, best-informed of their community, but among the poorest.[47]

It is pointless to blame Lloyd for not producing answers to questions which still trouble contemporary cultural theorists; but this does not mean that we have to be taken in by sweeping and unsubstantiated generalizations about 'the true laconically dramatic style' of the broadside balladeer, who, according to Lloyd, was 'no poet, but a craftsman of sorts, a humble journalist in verse'. This is Sharp-ing with a vengeance, as is Lloyd's use of the comparison of 'folksong' to a pebble, an inanimate object being worked over by unconscious natural forces, rather than a product of workers' conscious cultural practice. Time and time again Lloyd wrenches us back in his description from the brink of a materialist history, trailing a liberal-populist rhetoric. Thus, while admitting that song-origins and factors of song-development were 'as mixed as Psyche's seeds', he lapses into banalities in order to rationalize what are, fundamentally, assertions based on subjective value-judgements:

> It is a poor folklorist who is not also in part sociologist, and the sociologist in us must ask why should we be interested in folk poems of a certain quality (to our way of thinking), and not in other versions that may (to us) seem short of beauty but nevertheless reach a vast public and are accepted with pleasure, and even passion.[48]

Why could not the production of a Dylan (or even a Donovan), which also gave pleasure to working class-people, be included? For all the habit of self-deprecation, Lloyd knew his 'good-style folk singer' when he listened to one.

How did Lloyd argue that songs come to represent community, let alone class interests?

> The idividual creation, or creation-by-variation if you will, is only effective if the song-maker is expressing the thought and feelings of his community, for only then is his song taken up by his neighbours and passed into general currency.[49]

Thus far 'folksong' is no different to any other kind of song, so Lloyd has to continue his prescription:

> Among creators of folk song the desire to explore the obscure margins of private experience is always less than the wish to impose individual order on common experience. So before he starts composing the maker is affected by the outlook and aspirations of his community; in short, each folk song at its inception is at least partly a product of social determinism.[50]

Did not Brecht and many other artists do this? Which songs have *not* been subject to constraints imposed by material factors? Where is the evidence to support Lloyd's factitious generalization about the psychology of the largely anonymous authors of the songs he publishes? And it is of note that, while he does attempt to re-insert some materialist analysis into the flabby idealist ideology of the Second Revival, he does so not only in a vulgar marxist fashion, but as though in support of bourgeois pluralism. Surely, in composing a photo-fit picture of the 'typical' worker-songwriter, Lloyd was paralleling the production by the contemporary song-writer, MacColl, and various associated lefties, of that bizarre working-class myth, *The Big Hewer*.[51] The individual will to impose order on common experience is not that of any putative song-writer in history, but Lloyd's and MacColl's, just as Sharp constructed his mythical 'peasant'. Lloyd's appropriation of a selective version of workers' culture is just as culturally imperialist as Sharp's, and just as authoritarian, however well it fitted into the anachronistic attempt to foist a deformed version of 'socialist realism' onto English history.

Apart from the great respect in which Lloyd was (and is) held, not only on the left, but also amongst liberal intellectuals in Britain and elsewhere, one reason why he does not usually get tarred with Sharpism is his habitual self-effacement. *Folk Song in England,* the most important single book on English workers' songs ever written, is introduced by its author as 'a book for beginners and not specialists'. In spite of anything like adequate references to sources and suchlike scholarly apparatus, Lloyd nevertheless feels confident in making enormous claims and pronouncements:

> The folk songs are lower-class songs specifically in so far as they arise from

the common experience of labouring people and express the identity of interest of those people, very often in opposition to the interests of the master.[52]

This paraphrase of a key passage from Edward Thompson's *The Making of the English Working Class*[53] is alright so far as it goes, but unlike the historian's account of political organization, Lloyd fails to show how (or even if) the 'common experience' of an entire class is articulated through the songs he cites. The key theoretical issue is side-stepped by mere prescription, the appeal to authority, and suchlike disreputable manoeuvres; and thus the most difficult part of the emerging historical materialist theory of culture is short-circuited. 'Industrial folk song' *had* to be

> the kind of vernacular songs made by workers themselves directly out of their own experiences, expressing their own interests and aspirations, and incidentally passed on among themselves mainly by oral means, though this is no *sine qua non*. The kind of songs created from outside by learned writers, on behalf of the working class, is not our concern here.[54]

But what of that enormous body of songs written by non-learned writers, whose names are known to us, for use on broadsides bought by workers, and in concert halls, whose audiences were overwhelmingly working-class? What of the hymns, poems and anthems made and used by working women and men in chapels, pubs, clubs and union halls? To Lloyd, the matter is cut and dried: concert hall songs, for example, and other 'Productions of this stamp cannot be considered folk songs by any workable definition'. But, yet again, isn't that the point? Is the 'refining definition' by example and fiat offered by Lloyd workable at all? The historical fact is that many concert hall artists, like George Ridley and Ned Corvan in the north-east, were working-class, and worked and wrote for the working-class;[55] but instead of trying to make his definition fit the historical evidence, Lloyd adopts the reverse policy. What doesn't fit is left out or down-graded. Here, once again, the legacy of Sharp and Child vitiates one of our best mediator's work. In a sense, in its attempt to grasp the general historical and cultural processes, Lloyd's work represents something of a step back from the specificity of that of Alfred Williams. In the absence of adequate specific studies of English workers' culture on both a national and a regional basis, perhaps Lloyd had to take the risk. We have no such excuses; and in the concluding chapter I hope to point to some of the more obvious areas for research still waiting to be done.

12 Conclusion

> The *elements* of democratic and socialist culture are
> present, if only in rudimentary form, in *every*
> national culture, since in *every* nation there are
> toiling and exploited masses, whose conditions of
> life inevitably give rise to the ideology of democracy
> and socialism. But *every* nation also possesses a
> bourgeois culture (and most nations a reactionary
> and clerical culture as well) in the form, not merely
> of "elements", but of the *dominant* culture.
> Therefore, the general "national culture" *is* the
> culture of the landlords, the clergy and the
> bourgeoisie....
> In advancing the slogan of "the international
> culture of democracy and of the world working-class
> movement", we take *from each* national culture *only*
> its democratic and socialist elements; we take them
> *only* and absolutely in opposition to the bourgeois
> culture and the bourgeois nationalism of *each* nation.

> Vladimir Ilyich Lenin, *Critical Remarks on the National Question,* 1913

In so far as 'folksong' and 'ballad' retain any explanatory power, as concepts, they do so in relation to bourgeois culture. In relation to workers'
culture, they are simply a *problem*, and I can offer no hope of rehabilitating
them. We have to move on, and there is plenty of work waiting to be
done, not only in relation to songs, singers and singing, but in the much
wider field of the history of social life. For most workers, historically, the
biggest problem was not one of 'leisure', of course, so we have to try to
understand social life in relation to the opportunities for, and the
demands of, work. To understand work, we need to know how working
people related to employers, and to the changes in both technology and
the mode of production, through history. And to understand that, we
have to have a theory of history and of historical change which explains
the material transformation of society, and helps to explain how human
beings effected those changes and were affected by them. We have, in
other words, to understand history in a dialectical and a materialist way.
Moreover, it is not possible to understand workers' culture unless we
understand the culture of the ruling class. Which brings us back to

'folksong'. My contention is that unless we can locate cultural products and practices in history, we can understand neither culture nor history. More, unless we are prepared to learn to cope with cultural products, like songs, which derive from workers' culture, then hisotry will continue to be written from the 'top' down, whatever the 'top' happens to be at any given period, and we will *never* get anything like a history from the 'bottom' up, however provisional it may be at first.[1] This, then, is the general perspective which I believe is necessary to make progress, but there are many particular tasks which will need to be done before we can begin to write general histories of workers' culture.

Whole cultures remain to be examined in relation to how concepts like 'folksong' and 'ballad' or their equivalents were developed and applied, not only in what is now the United Kingdom, but in the USA, and in both Western and Eastern Europe. The history of institutions remains largely unwritten: where is the history of the Folk-Lore Society, of the English Folk Dance and Song Society, or of their analogues in other countries? We have no satisfactory book on the trade in cheap printed songs and music in Britain, few biographies of the key people involved, and not even a survey of what of their products survives. Biographies of key figures in the 'folksong' and 'ballad' movements remain unwritten, or unsatisfactory: Lucy Broadwood, Frank Kidson, A. L. Lloyd and many more. We need *critical* biographical studies of Sharp and Child, serious studies of the 'Folksong Revival', a history of the folk clubs and of the record companies who interested themselves in 'folk' songs and singers, and so on. The list is endless, and little enough progress seems to have been made since last I drew one up![2]

Beyond these, the particular research areas, we need dozens of studies of singing and music-making on a regional basis, not in the antiquarian or the anthropological mode, or in the spirit of bourgeois empiricism — which believes that by describing it is analysing — but, as Trotsky wrote 60 years ago, getting beyond the shell to the kernel of what *really* happened, and moving beyond the current boundaries of nation-states to examine what most people sang or listened to, and how that experience related to the rest of their lives, in the fullest possible way.[3] Nor must we concentrate on the past alone. As members of the International Association for the Study of Popular Music[4] have recognized, it is not possible to understand where culture is going until you know where you are, and you can't fully know where you are until you known where you came from, how and why. As Lenin would be the first to recognize, no nation-state in the 1980s has a monopoly on democratic, let alone socialist culture, and there is little enough apparent internationalism just now. And yet, not long before the Russian Revolution, Lenin feared he might not live to see workers take power. The contradictions in capitalism saw to it that he was not disappointed. Some day, given the right organisation and the right politics, we will be able to raise his slogan once again. Meanwhile, there is a lot of work to be done, and even intellectuals interested in culture have their modest part to play.

Appendix

Putting Harker in his place

Dave Harker's parents were both born, grew up and still live near the Durham–Yorkshire border. Bessie was the daughter of a tailoress and a locomotive-fitter. She went to a grammar school so long as her parents could afford it, and then worked as a typist before she married. Harry was the son of a woman who worked in the home to look after six men, and of a bricklayer-turned-house-repairer who was also a respected Primitive Methodist lay-preacher. He was apprenticed to an undertaker to learn carpentry, and worked for the basic union rate for his father, along with his three brothers, to help build up E. Harker & Sons, a firm of speculative builders which never employed more than a dozen or so other workers.

Dave was born in 1946, the younger of two brothers. After various infant and junior schools he, like his brother, 'won a scholarship' to Guisborough Grammar School. His parents' increasing affluence meant he could stay on to take 'A' levels, and then go to University. An early interest in 'folk' clubs remained with him through his time at Cambridge, where he came under the influence of Raymond Williams and Terry Eagleton, and was strongly drawn to A. L. Lloyd's *Folk Song in England* and Edward Thompson's *The Making of the English Working Class*. By the time he graduated Harker was a socialist; and his research work on north-east working-class culture, done under the supervison of David Craig, combined with the upturn in class struggle in the early 1970s to make him a marxist. He lived a year in Newcastle, and married a schoolteacher who also came from Cleveland.

In 1972, fed up with Cambridge and student grants, Harker took a job teaching 'Communication Studies' at Manchester Polytechnic. He joined the Labour Party, as he thought, without illusions; but he was wrong, and he left in 1975 to join the International Socialists, who later became the Socialist Workers Party. He worked in his union branch, began teaching TUC-sponsored shop stewards' courses, and by the early 1980s was doing that work full-time. Academic research took a back seat until 1982, when a set of political pressures and the public expenditure cuts combined with the contradictions of being a cheerful new middle-class traitor, and drove him to reading and writing so as to help keep his head together. How far he succeeded in doing so, and whether the effort was worth it, will be best judged by his comrades in the Gorton Branch of the SWP and those in other socialist parties.

Notes

The reader has no need to consult these notes, except to check a reference or a quotation or to find suggestions for further reading.

Two strategies for saving space have been adopted. Firstly, all references in these notes are in the author/date/page convention. Full details of particular works are given in the Bibliography. Secondly, because of the massive quotation from song-books and books of theory, it has not been possible to reference every short extract, except where confusion might arise, as when more than one work is being used in a given paragraph or sentence. All biographical information about a particular person is taken from the source first cited. Where no such source is cited, it may be understood that the source is the *Dictionary of National Biography*. Readers who care to check will discover that I have made nothing up.

* * * * *

Introduction

1. Halifax 1983.
2. Harris 1983.
3. Trotsky 1960:169.
4. Harker 1983 attempts to provide a working bibliography for the study of song and history in England.
5. See below, pp. 256–7.
6. E. P. Thompson 1968.
7. R. Williams 1963.
8. R. Williams 1973.
9. Cliff 1975–8.
10. See R. Williams 1983: 204–7 for a general discussion of the term.
11. R. Thomson 1975 contains some useful information.
12. Shepard 1973 is a general survey, based on Shepard 1962; and Shepard 1969 is a useful study of one London publisher. Other sources are cited in Harker 1983.
13. See Gammon 1980, and Gammon 1985.
14. See Dean-Smith 1957–8, Gammon 1980 and 1985.
15. Pickering 1982 is a pioneering attempt to situate Blunt's mediations.
16. Deacon 1983 contains some of the raw material for a full analysis.

17. See below, p. Dean-Smith 1954 is one influential listing.
18. Kinlock 1827b, P. Buchan 1825 and L. Broadwood 1908, for example, fall into the latter category.
19. R. Williams 1971 and 1977 sum up most of the key points about this debate.
20. Child 1965.
21. See Harker 1976:492–502 and Harker 1980:146–210.

Chapter 1

1. See E.P. Thompson 1968 for the period 1760-1830. Cherry 1981 is a useful short introduction to workers' history for the period after 1830, and contains a very good bibliography.
2. This account is based on Mackerness 1964:76-84, supplemented by Chappell 1965. Laurence Price, author of three songs canonized by Child and over fifty others, seems to have been the exception. The present writer is preparing an analysis of one of Price's songs, *A Warning for Married Women*, as part of a joint research project on 'Child 243', *James Harris* or *The Daemon Lover*.

3. Chappell 1965:2,481.
4. Welford 1895:3,610-614 gives a brief life of Whittell.
5. For D'Urfey, see also Day 1959 and Chappell 1965:2,261.
6. Day 1959:iv.
7. Hales and Furnivall 1867-8:2,xv note.
8. For Addison's intervention, see Hustvedt 1916:65ff.
9. The following account is based on Craig 1961, supplemented by T.F. Henderson 1910, R. Chambers 1835 and Smout 1972.
10. Chappell 1965:2,423.
11. Craig 1961:127.
12. R. Chambers 1835:4,127.
13. T.F. Henderson 1910:401-2.
14. T.F. Henderson 1910:401.
15. Craig 1961:130.
16. T.F. Henderson 1910:404.
17. T.F. Henderson 1910:404.
18. For Bannantyne and his MS., see T.F. Henderson 1910: 239 note.
19. For Lady Wardlaw's *Hardyknute*, see T.F.Henderson 1910:395-6. For Ramsay's use of the Bannantyne MS., see T.F. Henderson 1910:337 and Hecht 1904: 80 note 2.
20. See also Farmer 1962a.
21. Farmer 1962a:I.
22. Farmer 1962a:IV.
23. For the fashion for kilts and other hilarious examples of the inventions of 'tradition' in Scotland, see Trevor-Roper 1983.
24. See Fischer 1963 for a lengthy discussion of the history of this process in European bourgeois 'Art'.

Chapter 2

1. See also Gilfillan 1858, and Pickford 1867.
2. See also R. Chambers 1835:3,42, and Hecht 1904:30ff.
3. See also Plomer 1968:85.
4. See Bronson 1938, Fordyce 1857:2, 173 note.
5. See also R. Chambers 1835:4, 100-104.
6. See also R. Chambers 1835:1, 427-46,
7. See also Farmer 1962b: XIIIff.
8. Hecht 1904:34ff.
9. Bewick 1975:134. For Kemble, see Mackenzie 1827:593 note, and Oswald 1936.
10. Welford 1895:3,390-4.
11. Bronson 1938:144.
12. Bronson 1938:616.
13. Ritson 1884:9. For the market 'regulation', see Mackenzie 1827:72.
14. See below, pp.24-5, 32-3.
15. See below, Chapter 3.
16. Legman 1966:234.
17. R. Chambers 1835:1,430.
18. Barke and Smith 1965:39.
19. R. Chambers 1835:1,433.
20. Hecht 1904:34.
21. Craig 1961:115.
22. Craig 1961:115.
23. Craig 1961:119.
24. See below, pp.33-4.
25. Dick 1903:xiv.
26. Barke and Smith 1965:39.
27. Dick 1903:xvii.
28. Dick 1903:xv.
29. Dick 1903:xvii.
30. Dick 1903:xiii,385,429.
31. Hales and Furnivall 1867-8:1,ix.
32. Hales and Furnivall 1867-8:1,xii.
33. Hales and Furnivall 1867-8:1,xvi.
34. Hales and Furnivall 1867-8:1,xiii.
35. Percy 1858:1,xxv.
36. Hales and Furnivall 1867-8:1,xvi. For some of the songs Percy excised and Hales refused to have in the Victorian edition, see Furnivall 1868.
37. Shepard 1973: 113.
38. Montgomerie 1957:292.
39. Montgomerie 1957:292 and Montgomerie 1967:216.
40. Montgomerie 1967:225.
41. Montgomerie 1967:224 and Montgomerie 1957:293.
42. Montgomerie 1967:208.
43. Montgomerie 1967:223.
44. Montgomerie 1967:199.
45. Montgomerie 1967:199.
46. Montgomerie 1967:198.
47. See Bronson 1938:116-7.
48. Pinkerton 1783:2,185-6.
49. T.F. Henderson 1910:339. For Pinkerton's literary aims, see Craig 1961, and for an earlier version of his collection, see Pinkerton 1781.
50. Hustvedt 1916:252-3.
51. Bronson 1938:176.
52. Welford 1895:3,392.
53. Ritson 1791:1xxv.
54. Ritson 1791:1xxv-1xxvi.
55. Bronson 1938:197.
56. See Welford 1895:1,676-680 for John Cunningham.
57. See Welford 1895:3,1-6 for Lambe.
58. Hecht 1904:54-6, 74-5, and see also Walker 1915:71 note.
59. Craig 1961:104.
60. Dick 1903:xv.
61. Dick 1903:419. For Kirsty Flint, see Dick 1903:xi.
62. For Clarke, see Hecht 1904:38,51,284, and Legman 1966:164,218,229.
63. Lewis 1976:62.

64. Dick 1903:414,490,491.
65. Dick 1903:381,386,434,467.
66. Dick 1903:375,390,404,470. See also Hecht 1904:321.
67. Barke and Smith 1965:196.
68. Dick 1903:393.
69. Dick 1903:501.
70. Dick 1903:351,404,470,494.
71. Dick 1903:386,401,404,406,417,422,428,445, 491-2,500. See also Hecht 1904:334-5.
72. Hustvedt 1916:157-61.
73. Percy 1858:1;xxix.
74. Hales and Furnivall 1867-8:1,xi.
75. Hales and Furnivall 1867-8:1,xvi.
76. Hales and Furnivall 1867-8:1,xvii.
77. Hales and Furnivall 1867-8:1,xxii-xxiii.
78. Hales and Furnivall 1867-8:1,xvi.
79. Hales and Furnivall 1867-8:1,xvi.
80. Hales and Furnivall 1867-8:1,xvi.
81. T.F. Henderson 1910:338.
82. Herd 1776:xii.
83. Walker 1915:243.
84. T.F. Henderson 1910:338. See also Walker 1915:241.
85. Hecht 1904:20-21.
86. Hecht 1904:23-4.
87. Legman 1966:163-4, 177,182. Barke and Smith 1965:passim. Hecht 1904:34,37.
88. Hecht 1904:passim. Walker 1915:241.
89. Hecht 1904:52-3. Legman 1966:155.
90. Craig 1961:258,308.
91. Hustvedt 1916:252.
92. Fordyce 1857:2,173 note. Bronson 1938:44-7.
93. Ritson 1783:1,v. See also Legman 1966:343-4.
94. Ritson 1802:1,cix, quoted in Bronson 1938:568-571.
95. Barke and Smith 1965:73. See also Legman 1966:229-30.
96. Barke and Smith 1965:105,140.
97. Dick 1903:384,396,401,404,406,408,412,417,4 24,426,434-5,480.
98. Hecht 1904:319-20.
99. Dick 1903:356.
100. Legman 1966:234.
101. Laing 1853:viii. See also Dick 1903:395.
102. Dick 1903:369,449.

Chapter 3

1. For Scott, see Lockhart 1902. For the history of Scotland, see Smout 1972, and for the consequences of political and economic change on literature, see Craig 1961.
2. Lockhart 1902.
3. No relation to Dr Jamieson. See below, p.44.
4. Lockhart 1902:3,142-6.
5. D. Hogg 1875.
6. Walker 1915.
7. M'Conechy 1881. See also *Whistle-Binkie* 1878:16-23.
8. W. Chambers 1884.
9. Harker 1971. See also Harker and Rutherford 1985, and for the Bell Family, Lockey (n.d.)
10. Craig 1961:40,152.
11. W. Scott 1902:1,xi.
12. See above, p.20.
13. See above, p.17.
14. E.P. Thompson 1968:passim.
15. See also Craig 1961:154.
16. Craig 1961:12,150-1.
17. Craig 1961:154.
18. Craig 1961:120.
19. Craig 1961:114.
20. Hecht 1904:34.
21. Walker 1915:71 note,86,247. See also *Whistle-Binkie* 1878:1,20.
22. Quoted in Craig 1961:115.
23. Craig 1961:279-80.
24. Lockhart 1902:3,143-6.
25. Lockhart 1902:8,101-2.
26. See below, pp.50-1.
27. Quoted in Craig 1961:281.
28. It is not clear when this organization was founded — see Mackenzie 1827:598 note. Something of the kind was in existence in 1820 — see Sykes 1866:2,338-9.
29. W. Scott 1932:3,208.
30. See below, pp.89-90.
31. M'Conechy 1881:xi.
32. M'Conechy 1881:xi-xii.
33. *Whistle-Binkie* 1878:1,16.
34. *Whistle-Binkie* 1878:1,17.
35. *Whistle-Binkie* 1878:1,17.
36. *Whistle-Binkie* 1878:1,17.
37. M'Conechy 1881:xii.
38. M'Conechy 1881:xxi.
39. For these developments, see, for example, Craig 1961:299-300.
40. See also D. Hogg 1875:321-2.
41. See above, pp.24, 30-1.
42. Lockhart 1902:2,111-2.
43. See below, pp.58-60, 70.
44. Shortreed 1932:280.
45. Craig 1961:150-1.
46. See, for example, Jamieson 1806:2,175,367, Scott 1839:316 and the information in Lockhart 1902:2,223, Child 1965:1,81-2 and D. Buchan 1972:155,227.
47. Cromek 1810:ix.
48. See R. Williams 1963.

49. Quoted in R. Williams 1983:232.
50. Harker 1971 forms the basis of this paragraph.
51. Harker 1971:xii.
52. J. Hogg 1874:1,vii-viii.
53. J. Hogg 1874:1,212.
54. E.P. Thompson 1968 remains the best account of this period.
55. All three were reprinted in Stevenson 1868, along with Maidment 1844.
56. Motherwell 1827:xciii.
57. Sharpe 1868:v.
58. A. Cunningham 1825:1,67-8.
59. See below, pp.110-2.
60. E. Lyle 1975:xviii.
61. Motherwell 1827:ii-iv.
62. Motherwell 1827:x.
63. Motherwell 1827:cii.
64. Shortreed 1932:271-2,283.
65. Shortreed 1932:274.
66. Shortreed 1932:275.
67. Shortreed 1932:274.
68. Shortreed 1932:281.
69. Montgomerie 1956:159 note.
70. Raine 1852.
71. See Raine 1852:25, Walker 1915:13-14 and Reed 1973:4.
72. Child 1965: 1,88ff.,218 note, 227,253;3,497-8,4,454,5,432, queries most of Sharpe's texts.
73. See R. Chambers 1835:4,74-85.
74. Shortreed 1932:274.
75. See S. Tytler and J. Watson 1871:2,180ff.
76. Hecht 1904:60-1,117,138,184,207.
77. For Mrs Brown's Manuscripts, see Bronson 1945:131, D. Buchan 1972:6,278, and Montgomerie 1969-70:60-75,238-54. For Tytler's ideas, see Tytler 1783. For Riddell and the Glenriddell MS., see Montgomerie 1968-9:91-7. For the 'Old Lady's' collection, see Montgomerie 1968-9:97-104.
78. D. Buchan 1972:62-4,72-3.
79. Bronson 1945:131, Walker 1915:4-5,8, D. Buchan 1972:173.
80. Walker 1915:8.
81. See below, p.70.
82. See Walker 1915:5-6, Hecht 1904:61, Bronson 1945:130-1 and D. Buchan 1972:69-70,72,75.
83. Jamieson 1806:1,194-5
84. A. Cunningham 1825:1,26,54,70,162;4,60.
85. Cromek 1810:63. See also A. Cunningham 1825:1,245-6.
86. A. Cunningham 1825:1,126-7.
87. A. Cunningham 1825:2,73,124,243.
88. A. Cunningham 1825:2,222 — see also 2,246 and 3,132.
89. Whittell 1815 contains many of his pieces.
90. J. Cunningham 1766 is the fullest collection of his work. He was no relation to Allan Cunningham.
91. H. Robson 1814 contains some of his work. See also Allan 1891:106-15 for a short life and some of his poems.
92. See Allan 1891:54-8 for a short life and such poetry as survives. For Purvis's place in the history of north-east workers' songs, see Harker 1981:30-2.
93. Harker and Rutherford 1985 analyse how Bell put together the material for what was to have been the second volume of the *Rhymes*. Rutherford 1964 first brought attention to Bell's importance as a song-collector.
94. Hecht 1904:319,333.
95. Walker 1915:40.
96. See below, p.65.
97. Sharpe 1868:vi.
98. Child 1965:5,398.
99. D. Buchan 1972:225-7.
100. D. Buchan 1972:223-6.
101. See above, p.63.
102. A. Cunningham 1825:4,359-60.
103. See R. Chambers 1835:2,47-54, for Sir David Dalrymple, Lord Hailes, who also gave texts to Percy.
104. E. Lyle 1975:xiii-xxiv.
105. For Blaikie and his work on the tunes, see Lyle 1972. For Motherwell's links with R.A. Smith, see Montgomerie 1958.
106. E. Lyle 1975:xxv-liv.
107. Quoted in D. Buchan 1972:210.
108. Quoted in D. Buchan 1972:211.
109. Quoted in D. Buchan 1972:211.
110. This collection was later entitled *The Secret Songs of Silence* — see Legman 1966:139-40.
111. D. Buchan 1972:212.
112. P. Buchan 1875:1,xvi.
113. Child 1965:1,82; 2,269,415.
114. Child 1965:2,423;3,362,458,484.
115. Child 1965:1,218 note,335; 2,302; 3,469.
116. Child 1965:2,142,156. See also Hecht 1904:98,99,148,etc.
117. Walker 1915:3.
118. Montgomerie 1956:163. Lang 1910 is an interesting attempt to restore Scott's credibility. See Munro 1976 for an account of the Abbotsford Collection.
119. D. Buchan 1972:206. See also Reed 1973:184.
120. W. Scott 1839:316. See also Lockhart 1902:2,223. Dobie 1940 shows how the editions of the *Minstrelsey* changed, and the relationship between Scott and Jamieson.

121. Hecht 1904:62,325.
122. A. Cunningham 1825:**2**,286-see also **2**,246;**3**,132;**4**,177.
123. J. Hogg 1874:**1**,vii,292-see also **1**,294; **2**,274,355,356,371.
124. Hecht 1904:285,308
125. Dick 1903:421,469-see also 486-7,497.
126. Motherwell 1827:lxxxviii. Compare D. Hogg 1875:260.
127. Dorson 1968:120.
128. D. Hogg 1875:79.
129. Harker 1971:liii.
130. J. Hogg 1874:**1**,xiii.
131. J. Hogg 1874:**1**,xv.
132. T. F. Henderson 1910:382-3,454-5.
133. Chappell 1965:**2**,434,524,611,687,705.
134. W. Scott 1839: 244-see also 235, 237, 379.
135. Legman 1966:139.
136. Motherwell 1827:xcvii.
137. Motherwell 1827:xcviii.
138. Motherwell 1827:xcvii.
139. Motherwell 1827:xcv.
140. Motherwell 1827:xcvi-xcvii.
141. D. Hogg 1875:80.
142. D. Buchan 1972:205-6.
143. E. Lyle 1972.
144. See above, p.68. Buchan had already published P. Buchan 1825.
145. D. Buchan 1972:307 note 22.
146. See above, pp.74-5.
147. D. Buchan 1972:243.
148. R. Chambers 1829:ii.
149. Another example is R. Chambers 1826.

Chapter 4

1. Godman 1957 and Godman 1964 are the main sources for John Broadwood.
2. For Dixon, see Andrews 1885:61-2 and Boase 1965:**5**,115.
3. For Harland, see Green 1972:v-viii, Andrews 1885:27-8 and Dorson 1968: 319-327. Harland and Wilkinson 1870 and 1882 contain more of his ideas on songs.
4. For Chappell, see Sternfeld 1965:v-ix. Mair 1961 is a short and scrappy account of the firm.
5. See also Dorson 1968:61-6.
6. See also Dorson 1968:66-74.
7. See Grove 1954:**2**,544-5.
8. See Grove 1954:**5**,468-9.
9. See Grove 1954:**7**,171-2.
10. See Sternfeld 1965:ix.
11. See above, p.12.
12. *D.N.B.*
13. Thoms 1846. For Thoms, see Dorson 1968: 75-80.
14. Andrews 1885:28.
15. Richardson 1841-6.
16. Sternberg 1850.
17. See below, p.87.
18. See above, p.48.
19. Dusart 1843:1.
20. Godman 1964. See also Howes 1943.
21. Gammon 1980:62.
22. Gammon 1980:72.
23. Gammon 1980:64-5.
24. Dixon 1845:xi.
25. See above, p.55.
26. Dixon 1845:xii.
27. See above, p.54.
28. Dixon 1845:xiii.
29. Dixon 1845:xiii-xiv.
30. Dixon 1845:xiv.
31. Dixon 1845:xiv.
32. Dixon 1845:xiv-xv.
33. Dixon 1845:84.
34. Dixon 1845:93,98.
35. Dixon 1845:84.
36. Dixon 1846:81.
37. Dixon 1845:87.
38. Dixon 1845:85.
39. Dixon 1845:93.
40. Dixon 1846:vii-viii.
41. Crotch 1831. For examples of Crotch's ideas on 'National Music', see Crotch (n.d.).
42. Sternfeld 1965:vi. See also Chappell 1965:**1**,xv.
43. Chappell 1965:**2**,738-see also **1**,64 note.
44. Chappell 1965:**2**,522-see also **1**,145,160.
45. Chappell 1986:**1**,57-8, etc. Walker 1915:197ff. puts the Scottish case.
46. See Harker 1972b:passim.
47. See R. Williams 1973:87-90.
48. See above, p.62.
49. See Harker 1972b:228 note.
50. See Harker 1972b:228 note.
51. See R Williams 1973:132-41 for further references. Deacon 1983 seeks to claim Clare for the 'folk tradition'.
52. Howes 1943:159.
53. Godman 1957:107.
54. Walker 1915:100-103.
55. Walker 1915:101.
56. Walker 1915:102-4.
57. See Gilbert 1823.
58. See T. Lyle 1827.
59. For Telfer and White, see Harker and Rutherford 1985.
60. See above, p.28.
61. See Sandys (n.d.).
62. See below, p.103.
63. See below, pp.147,162-3
64. R. Bell 1856:5.
65. R. Bell 1856:6.
66. R. Bell 1856:6.
67. Dusart 1843:1.
68. Quoted in Howes 1943:159.

69. Howes 1943:160.
70. See above, pp.15-20.
71. R. Williams 1973:9-12,35-45.

Chapter 5

1. This paragraph is based on Mackerness 1964:154-95 and R. Williams 1965:155-65.
2. This analysis of Child first appeared in a somewhat different form in the *Folk Music Journal* — see Harker 1981. It was originally intended to be the first of three articles, the second of which covered the material set out in Chapter 6, and the third of which was planned to examine the work of Kenneth S. Goldstein, Albert Lancaster Lloyd and David Buchan in relation to the 'ballad'. I am grateful to the Editor of the *Folk Music Journal*, Ian Russell, for releasing me from the obligation. The proposed third article has now been overtaken by events, in that Michael Pickering and Anthony Green are currently editing a book for this series which aims to deal with contemporary theory and practice. My own response to Goldstein's work is set out, briefly, in Harker 1976:503-7.
3. All material on Child, except where specifically noted, is taken from Kittredge 1965, which was reproduced in Child 1965, and was based on Norton 1897 and Norton (n.d.). See also Gummere 1909.
4. Norton 1897:161.
5. Kittredge 1965:xxv.
6. See above, pp.82,87.
7. Hustvedt 1930 is the source of all material on Grundtvig throughout this chapter.
8. See below, p.92.
9. See below, pp.121-4.
10. Hustvedt 1930:246.
11. Hustvedt 1930:253.
12. Hustvedt 1930:253. See also Bradford 1969:208 — I would like to thank Charles Hamm for bringing this essay to my attention.
13. Hustvedt 1930:255,262.
14. Hustvedt 1930:246.
15. Hustvedt 1930:247.
16. Bradford 1969:217.
17. Hustvedt 1930:278.
18. Child 1857-9, Child 1861 and Child 1965 (the reissue of the 1882-98 edition).
19. Hales and Furnivall 1867-8.
20. Hustvedt 1930:243.
21. Hustvedt 1930:243.
22. See above, pp.79-80.

23. Hustvedt 1930:246.
24. Child 1861:1,viii.
25. Hustvedt 1930:255.
26. Hustvedt 1930:262.
27. Hustvedt 1930:283.
28. Hustvedt 1930:262.
29. Child 1861:1,vii.
30. Child 1861:1,viii.
31. Child 1861:1,viii.
32. Child 1861:1,xi.
33. Child 1861:1,xi.
34. Hustvedt 1930:279.
35. Hustvedt 1930:243.
36. Child 1861:1,xi.
37. Child 1861:2,244.
38. Hustvedt 1930:246.
39. Hustvedt 1930:246.
40. Hustvedt 1930:247.
41. Hustvedt 1930:245.
42. Hustvedt 1930:247.
43. Hustvedt 1930:272.
44. Hustvedt 1930:247.
45. Hustvedt 1930:247.
46. Hustvedt 1930:270.
47. Hustvedt 1930:282.
48. Hustvedt 1930:289.
49. Hustvedt 1930:292.
50. Hustvedt 1930:298.
51. Child 1965:1,vii.
52. Child 1861:1,xii.
53. Child 1861:1,viii.
54. Child 1861:1,viii.
55. Child 1861:1,x.
56. Child 1861:2,33 note.
57. Child 1861:1,vii.
58. Child 1861:1,vii.
59. Child 1861:1,68.
60. Child 1861:1,vii.
61. Child 1861:1,viii.
62. Child 1861:1,vii note.
63. Hustvedt 1930:262.
64. Child 1861:2,114 — see also 2,342, and Davison 1884.
65. Child 1861:1,40.
66. Child 1857:VI,22, quoted in Hart 1906:799.
67. Child 1861:1,xi.
68. Child 1861:1,xi. See Hustvedt 1930:245,249 for Grundtvig's collecting.
69. See, for example, Hustvedt 1930:278.
70. Child 1861:5,35.
71. Child 1861:1,11-2.
72. Child 1861:1,217.
73. Child 1857-9:6,22, quoted in Hart 1906:799.
74. R. Williams 1971:7. Williams' views have developed through R. Williams 1977 to R. Williams 1983.
75. R. Williams 1971:7.
76. Child 1861:1,109.
77. Child 1895.

78. Quoted in Hart 1906:756.
79. See above, p.55.
80. Quoted in Hart 1906:756.
81. Quoted in Hart 1906:756-7.
82. Pound 1924:440.
83. Pound 1924:441.
84. Pound 1924:443.
85. Pound 1924:443.
86. Quoted in Hart 1906:757
87. Quoted in Hart 1906:757.
88. Quoted in Hart 1906:757-8.
89. Kittredge 1965:xxix.
90. Child 1965:5,309.
91. Hart 1906:805.
92. Hart 1906:805.
93. Quoted in Hart 1906:760.
94. Child 1965:3,255.
95. Hart 1906:805-6.
96. Child 1965:1,360.
97. Child 1965:3,303.
98. Child 1965:2,204 note.
99. Child 1965:2,204 note.
100. Child 1965:3,1.
101. Hart 1906:782-3.
102. Hart 1906:783-5.
103. Hart 1906:766.
104. Child 1965:3,258.
105. Hart 1906:798.
106. Hart 1906:798.
107. Hart 1906:785.
108. Hart 1906:788.
109. Child 1965:5,309.
110. Hart 1906:779-781.
111. Hart 1906:800.
112. Child 1965:2,19.
113. Child 1861:1,vii.
114. Child 1861:1,xiii-xxxii.
115. Child 1861:1,xiii.
116. Child 1861:1,xiii.
117. See above, p.72.
118. This analysis was caried out before David Buchan kindly brought my attention to James 1933, which was also unknown to me when I wrote Harker 1981a.
119. Child 1861:1,171.
120. Child 1857:1,306 note, quoted in Hart 1906:798.
121. Child 1861:1,179.
122. Child 1861:6,40.
123. Child 1861:3,3.
124. Child 1861:2,46.
125. Child 1861:2,272.
126. Child 1861:1,190.
127. Child 1861:1,152.
128. Child 1861:2,30.
129. Child 1861:3,224.
130. Child 1861:2,145.
131. Child 1861:2,213.
132. Child 1861:4,261.
133. Child 1861:1,281.
134. Child 1861:2,231.
135. Child 1861:2,220.
136. Child 1861:3,59.
137. Child 1861:1,29.
138. Child 1861:1,xi.
139. Child 1861:1,x.
140. Child 1861:1,209 note.
141. Child 1861:1,xi.
142. Kittredge 1965:xxvii.
143. Hales and Furnivall 1867-8:1,x and Hustvedt 1930:262.
144. Hustvedt 1930:247.
145. Hustvedt 1930:249.
146. Hustvedt 1930:264.
147. Hustvedt 1930:248.
148. Hustvedt 1930:248.
149. Hustvedt 1930:249.
150. Hustvedt 1930:250.
151. See above, p.76.
152. Hustvedt 1930:254.
153. Hustvedt 1930:247.
154. Hustvedt 1930:255.
155. Hustvedt 1930:256. See also Child 1873.
156. Hustvedt 1930:263.
157. Hustvedt 1930:283.
158. Hustvedt 1930:288.
159. Hustvedt 1930:288 note.
160. Hustvedt 1930:263.
161. Hustvedt 1930:263.
162. Hustvedt 1930:263.
163. Hustvedt 1930:262-3.
164. Hustvedt 1930:274.
165. Walker 1930. Hustvedt 1930:283,286.
166. Hustvedt 1930:288-9.
167. This estimate is based on counting only Child's *major* sources, using the first-given source in any series — e.g. Aa, but not Ab etc. — and including texts in *Additions* and *Corrections*, but not those in *Appendices*.
168. James 1933:52.
169. James 1933:53ff.
170. For Macmath, see Montgomerie 1963.
171. Harker and Rutherford 1985.
172. See below, Chapter 7.
173. Child 1965:1,vi.
174. Hustvedt 1930:262.
175. Hustvedt 1930:275.
176. Child 1861:1,x.
177. Child 1857-9:1,306 note, quoted in Hart 1906:797-8.
178. Hart 1906:796-7.
179. Child 1861:1,vii-viii note.
180. Legman 1966:343-52.
181. Hustvedt 1930:254.
182. Hustvedt 1930:270.
183. Hustvedt 1930:249.
184. Hustvedt 1930:253-4.
185. Hustvedt 1930:254.
186. Hustvedt 1930:259.
187. Hustvedt 1930:264-5 note.

188. Hustvedt 1930:268.
189. Hustvedt 1930:269. See above, p.69.
190. Hustvedt 1930:272.
191. Hustvedt 1930:252.
192. Hustvedt 1930:276.
193. Hustvedt 1930:277.
194. Hustvedt 1930:278.
195. Hustvedt 1930:278.
196. Hustvedt 1930:282.
197. Hustvedt 1930:284.
198. Hustvedt 1930:292,193.
199. Child 1965:1,ix.
200. Hustvedt 1930:301.
201. Hustvedt 1930:303. Compare Child 1965:5,182.
202. Hustvedt 1930:303-4.
203. Hustvedt 1930:300.

Chapter 6

1. See Bynum 1974 for Child's 'Legacy'. Goldstein 1964, Legman 1966, and D. Buchan 1972 represent the best in this tradition, but see Harker 1976.
2. See Courthope 1895:446.
3. T.F. Henderson 1910:336.
4. Ker 1909:179.
5. Quiller-Couch 1910:v, ix.
6. Brimley-Johnson 1912:ix.
7. T.F. Henderson 1912:viii.
8. Sidgwick 1914:36 note.
9. Kittredge 1965:xxix.
10. For Kittredge, see Wilgus 1959, 32-5.
11. Kittredge 1965:xxx. My italics.
12. Gummere 1907:317, Gummere 1901:5.
13. Kittredge 1965:xxx. Compare Henderson 1912:56.
14. Gummere 1907:Preface.
15. T.F. Henderson 1910:336.
16. Kittredge 1904:v,xiii.
17. Ker 1909:179.
18. Ker 1909:179.
19. Sidgwick 1914:41.
20. Barry 1929:xvii. For his earlier published work and ideas, see Barry 1910, 1912, 1913 and 1914.
21. Hustvedt 1930:4.
22. Gerould 1932:30. For an early essay, see Gerould 1923, and the rejoinder by Pound in 1929.
23. Gerould 1932:30.
24. Gerould 1932:15.
25. W.A.Neilson, in Gummere 1907:xiii.
26. Gummere 1907:317.
27. Gummere 1907:317.
28. Gummere 1907:317.
29. Quiller-Couch 1910:x-xii.
30. Ker 1909:179.
31. Brimley-Johnson 1912:vii.
32. Gerould 1932:4. Compare Goldstein 1964:1 note, and Harker 1976:503-7.
33. Kittredge 1904:xvi.
34. Gummere 1907:61-71.
35. Kittredge 1965:xxii. See Gummere 1901:194ff. and Gummere 1907:90ff.
36. Ker 1909:203.
37. Sidgwick 1914:61.
38. Pound 1921:105.
39. Pound 1921:135.
40. Gerould 1932:4.
41. Gerould 1932:5.
42. Gerould 1932:36-see also 1932:57.
43. Gerould 1932:65-66.
44. Courthope 1895:445-6.
45. Courthope 1895:461.
46. Kittredge 1904:xii.
47. For Arnold and 'culture', see R. Williams 1963:120-36.
48. Gummere 1907:324-5.
49. Ker 1909:200.
50. Ker 1909:179.
51. Ker 1909:193.
52. Ker 1909:201.
53. Ker 1909:199.
54. Quiller-Couch 1910:vii.
55. Sidgwick 1914:39.
56. Sidgwick 1914:7-8.
57. See below, pp.136-7.
58. Barry, quoted in Wilgus 1959:72.
59. See above, pp. 109-10.
60. Pound 1924:447 note.
61. Pound 1921:34.
62. Hustvedt 1930:17.
63. Hustvedt 1930:viii.
64. Hustvedt 1930:10.
65. Hustvedt 1930:viii.
66. Gerould 1932:vii.
67. Gerould 1932:3.
68. Gerould 1932:31.
69. Gerould 1932:11-2.
70. See above, Chapter 2.
71. Courthope 1895:426ff.
72. Henderson 1910:78.
73. Gummere 1901:27-8.
74. Henderson 1910:64-5.
75. Henderson 1910:78.
76. Kittredge 1904:xvi.
77. Gummere 1907:2.
78. Gummere 1907:15-16.
79. Sidgwick 1914:8.
80. Pound 1921:45.
81. Pound 1921:236-see also 1921:235.
82. Pound 1924:444.
83. Pound 1921:vii.
84. Courthope 1895:460.
85. Courthope 1895:445.
86. Courthope 1895:466.
87. Gummere 1901:138-compare 1901:163.
88. Kittredge 1904:xi. My italics.
89. Kittredge 1904:xviii,xix.

90. Kittredge 1904:xx.
91. Kittredge 1904:xxvii.
92. Gummere 1907:14.
93. Henderson 1910:56.
94. Henderson 1910:66.
95. Henderson 1910:67.
96. Henderson 1910:70-1.
97. Henderson 1910:71.
98. Sidgwick 1914:9.
99. Sidgwick 1914:11.
100. Sidgwick 1914:15-compare 1914:21,23.
101. Ker 1909:191.
102. Ker 1909:191.
103. Gummere 1907:288.
104. Pound 1921:85.
105. Pound 1921:9.
106. Pound 1921:233.
107. Pound 1921:157.
108. Gerould 1932.
109. Gerould 1932:184.
110. Gerould 1932:184.
111. Gerould 1932:184-5.
112. Pound 1921:91-see also 1921:25.
113. Gerould 1932:186.
114. Courthope 1895:445.
115. Henderson 1910:64.
116. Henderson 1910:361-2.
117. Henderson 1912:123.
118. Henderson 1912:123.
119. Henderson 1910:14.
120. Henderson 1910:360-1-compare 1910:17-8.
121. Ker 1909:197-8.
122. Ker 1909:195.
123. Sidgwick 1914:20.
124. Sidgwick 1914:23-4.
125. Sidgwick 1914:35.
126. Quiller-Couch 1910:vii.
127. Sidgwick 1914:30.
128. Alexander Keith, cited in Wilgus 1959:104.
129. See above, pp.128-9.
130. Kittredge 1965:xxvi.
131. Gummere 1907:16.
132. Kittredge 1904:xi.
133. Kittredge 1904:xi.
134. Kittredge 1904:xxii.
135. Kittredge 1904:xxii.
136. Kittredge 1904:xxiii.
137. Kittredge 1904:xxiii.
138. Kittredge 1904:xxiii.
139. Kittredge 1904:xvii.
140. Gummere 1907:321.
141. Gummere 1907:13,170-see also 1907:135,140,141-2.
142. Gummere 1907:321. See below p.251, for Lloyd's use of the 'pebble' idea.
143. Pound 1921:232.
144. Pound 1921:234-5.
145. Pound 1921:104.
146. Pound 1921:104.
147. Pound 1921:91.
148. Pound 1921:91.
149. Pound 1924:449.
150. Pound 1921:90.
151. Pound 1921:118.
152. Pound 1921:119.
153. Pound 1921:119.
154. Pound 1924:451.
155. Pound 1929:627.
156. Pound 1921:232.
157. Pound 1921:89.
158. Pound 1921:89. For a later article on 'dialect', see Pound 1945.
159. Barry, quoted in Wilgus 1959:69.
160. Barry, quoted in Wilgus 1959:69-70.
161. Barry, quoted in Wilgus 1959:70.
162. Barry 1929:xvii.
163. Barry 1929:xxxii.
164. Barry 1929:xxi.
165. Barry 1929:xvii.
166. Barry 1929:xxi.
167. Barry 1927:143.
168. Barry 1929:146. Compare Gerould 1932:242-5.
169. Barry 1929:xvii.
170. Gerould 1932:186.
171. Gerould 1932:12.
172. Gerould 1932:165.
173. Lloyd 1967:134. Compare Seeger 1940.

Chapter 7

1. See Harker 1976, for an account of what happened in the north-east to broadside publishing.
2. For what happened in the north-east see Harker 1981.
3. Peter Bailey and Jacky Bratton are currently editing two books on the British music hall for this series.
4. For biographical information on Engel, see Grove 1954:944-5.
5. Engel 1866.
6. Engel 1879. All quotations from Engel derive from this edition.
7. Engel 1879:1.
8. Engel 1879:1-2.
9. Engel 1879:3.
10. Engel 1879:3.
11. Engel 1879:2.
12. Engel 1879:6-7.
13. Engel 1879:22.
14. Engel 1879:32.
15. Engel 1879:34.
16. Engel 1879:53.
17. Engel 1879:32-3
18. Engel 1879:99.
19. Engel 1879:99.

20. Engel 1879:99-100.
21. See Mackerness 1964 for an account of many of the following developments.
22. G. Bruce 1905 is a hagiography written by his son, and is used here with caution.
23. Lloyd 1965:vi.
24. There is no adequate biography of Lucy Broadwood. Gammon 1980 gives a useful sketch, which is used here. See also Ford 1929, and R. Vaughan Williams 1927 and 1948. Some of her letters were published in *JEFDSS*, 1964:9,233-68, edited by Dean-Smith. See also L. Broadwood 1889, for her updated republication of Dusart 1843.
25. Grove 1954:**3**,522-3.
26. Baring-Gould wrote two volumes of autobiography — Baring-Gould 1923 and 1925. W. Purcell 1957 and Dickinson 1970 wrote biographies. See also Addison 1947.
27. Grove 1954:**1**,457.
28. There is no adequate biography of Frank Kidson.
29. J. Bruce and Stokoe 1882:vii-viii.
30. See Harker 1971:xxvi-xxviii.
31. J. Bruce and Stokoe 1882:ix.
32. J. Bruce and Stokoe 1882:x. These articles are pasted up and bound together in one volume in Newcastle Central Reference Library.
33. Stokoe 1878-81:1.
34. Stokoe 1878-81:6.
35. Stokoe 1878-81:44.
36. Quoted in Harker 1971:xlix.
37. J. Bruce and Stokoe 1882:ix-x.
38. G. Bruce 1905:210.
39. Baring-Gould 1923:i.
40. Dickinson 1970:15.
41. Baring-Gould 1923:327.
42. Baring-Gould 1923:327.
43. Dickinson 1970:20.
44. Dickinson 1970:20.
45. Baring-Gould 1923:139.
46. Baring-Gould 1923:285.
47. Baring-Gould 1923:226,232,237.
48. Purcell 1957:94.
49. Dickinson 1970:40. See also Baring-Gould 1923:271.
50. Baring-Gould 1923:224.
51. Dickinson 1970:33.
52. Baring-Gould 1923:ix,90.
53. Dickinson 1970:176-85 gives a bibliography of some of his works.
54. Baring-Gould 1923:89.
55. Baring-Gould 1923:x.
56. Baring-Gould 1923:x.
57. Baring-Gould 1923:vii.
58. Baring-Gould 1923:x.
59. W. Purcell 1957:162.
60. Baring-Gould 1925:184. Dickinson 1970:123.
61. Baring-Gould 1925:184.
62. Baring-Gould 1925:6.
63. Baring-Gould 1925:102.
64. Baring-Gould 1925:184.
65. Dickinson 1970:125.
66. Baring-Gould 1895a:ix.
67. Baring-Gould 1895a:ix.
68. Baring-Gould 1895a:ix.
69. Dickinson 1970:126.
70. Baring-Gould 1925:211.
71. Baring-Gould 1925:185.
72. Baring-Gould 1925:185.
73. Baring-Gould 1925:186.
74. Baring-Gould 1895a:ix.
75. Baring-Gould 1895a:ix.
76. Baring-Gould 1925:212.
77. Baring-Gould 1895a:vii-viii.
78. Baring-Gould 1923:327.
79. Baring-Gould 1925:213.
80. Baring-Gould 1895a:v.
81. Baring-Gould 1895a:x.
82. Baring-Gould 1895a:xi.
83. Baring-Gould 1895a:xi.
84. Baring-Gould 1895a:xi.
85. Dickinson 1970:176-85.
86. Baring-Gould 1925:212-3. See also Dickinson 1970:140.
87. Dickinson 1970:136.
88. Barrett 1891:Preface.
89. Barrett 1891:Preface.
90. Graham 1927.
91. Kidson 1891:v. The remaining quotations in this and the next paragraph are all from this source.
92. Kidson 1891:xii.
93. Kidson 1891:xiii-xiv.
94. Kidson 1891:xvi.
95. Kidson 1891:71.
96. Kidson *Lecture* is the source of all quotations in this paragraph.
97. Kidson *Articles*:8.
98. Vaughan Williams 1927:137-8.
99. L. Broadwood and Fuller-Maitland 1893:iv.
100. L. Broadwood and Fuller-Maitland 1893:iv.
101. See Harker 1971:xxx.
102. For Allan, see Harker 1981b:27-30.
103. For Hepple and his texts, see Harker and Rutherford 1985.
104. Baring-Gould 1925:190.
105. Baring-Gould 1895a:viii. Compare Sharp 1905a:viii and Baring-Gould 1925:198.
106. Baring-Gould 1925:201.
107. Baring-Gould 1895a:vi.
108. Baring-Gould 1895a:vi.
109. Baring-Gould 1895a:viii.
110. Baring-Gould 1925:190.
111. Baring-Gould 1925:190.

112. Baring-Gould 1925:191.
113. Baring-Gould 1923:142. See also Baring-Gould 1895a:ix, Reeves 1960:6 and W. Purcell 1957:145-6. Hitchcock 1974 has texts from the manuscript collection.
114. Baring-Gould 1925:204.
115. Baring-Gould 1925:195.
116. Baring-Gould 1925:185.
117. W. Purcell 1957:150.
118. Baring-Gould 1925:185.
119. Baring-Gould 1895a:x; 1925:185.
120. Baring-Gould 1925:186.
121. Baring-Gould 1925:187.
122. Baring-Gould 1925:187.
123. Dickinson 1970:130-2 gives most of their names and occupations.
124. Baring-Gould 1925:190.
125. Baring-Gould 1925:199. See also Baring-Gould 1895a:viii.
126. W. Purcell 1957:153-4.
127. Baring-Gould 1925:200.
128. Baring-Gould 1895a:vii.
129. Baring-Gould 1895a:viii.
130. Baring-Gould 1895-8.
131. Broadwood and Fuller-Maitland 1893:v.
132. Barrett 1891:Preface.
133. *JEFDSS*, 1948:**V**, No.3,129.
134. *JEFDSS*, 1948:**V**, No.3,129.
135. *JEFDSS*, 1948:**V**, No.3,129.
136. Kidson *Lecture*:16-17.
137. *JEFDSS*, 1948:**V**, No.3,129.
138. *JEFDSS*, 1948:**V**, No.3,129.
139. Kidson 1891:xii.
140. Kidson 1891:31.
141. Gammon 1980:65ff. is the source of information in this paragraph. See L. Broadwood 1904-5 for her views on collecting from 'peasants'.
142. Parry 1899:2.
143. See Harker 1971:xlvi-lii. Lloyd 1965:x.
144. Baring-Gould 1925:184.
145. Baring-Gould 1925:189. See also Sharp 1905:XI.
146. Baring-Gould 1925:189.
147. Baring-Gould 1925:189.
148. Baring-Gould 1925:191-2.
149. Baring-Gould 1925:191.
150. Baring-Gould 1925:205.
151. W. Purcell 1957:155.
152. W. Purcell 1957:155.
153. Baring-Gould 1925:199, Purcell 1957:156.
154. Broadwood 1927:42-3.
155. Green 1970:vii.
156. Gammon 1980:68-72 is used as the chief source in this paragraph.
157. R. Vaughan Williams 1948:137.
158. Keel 1948:111. See also Fuller-Maitland 1927.
159. Keel 1948:111-2.
160. Keel 1948:111.
161. R. Vaughan Williams 1948:137.
162. Keel 1948:112.
163. Keel 1948:111.
164. Keel 1948:111-2.
165. Keel 1948:113.
166. Parry 1893.
167. Jacobs 1893:235-6.
168. Parry 1899 is the source of all quotations in the next two paragraphs.
169. Parry 1899:3.
170. Parry 1899.3.

Chapter 8

1. This chapter began life as Harker 1972 and was used as the basis of Harker 1976:462-91. I would like to thank the Editor of the *Folk Music Journal* for allowing me to use sections of that article here. An updated version of that article was produced at the request of the Editorial Collective of *History Workshop Journal*, though it failed to appear in anything like the form in which it was submitted. Even the acknowledgement to the original article in *Folk Music Journal* was edited out, without consultation, and no apology was printed when this omission was brought to their attention. I mention this simply to show how 'mediation', even today, is not always the fault of authors.
2. Fox-Strangeways is used as the source of all biographical information on Sharp in this chapter, except for those points which are otherwise attributed. The revised editions done by Sharp's former amanuensis — Karpeles 1955 and 1967 — would form the basis of an interesting essay on the practices of hagiographers. Beware, also, Karpeles 1948 and 1959.
3. Sharp Collection: letter from Lillian Purdom to Fox-Strangeways, 1.9.1931.
4. Sharp Collection: letter from H.W. Fulford to Fox-Strangeways, 24.9.1931.
5. Sharp Collection: letter from Sharp to Mrs Howard, 22.12.1891.
6. Sharp Collection: letter from Sharp to Mrs Howard, 9.3.1892.
7. Sharp Collection: letter from Sharp to Mrs Howard, 7.8.1892.
8. Sharp Collection: letter from Sharp to Mrs Howard, 14.8.1892.
9. Sharp Collection: letter from Sharp to unknown recipient, 26.6.1893.
10. For Marson, see Yeo 1968.
11. Sharp Collection: letter from Sharp to Mrs Howard, 22.8.1892.
12. See above, p.169.

13. Sharp 1902.
14. Sharp 1902:v-vi.
15. Sharp 1902:vi.
16. Sharp 1902:vi.
17. Sharp 1902:vi.
18. See above, pp.142-6.
19. Sharp 1902:vii.
20. Sharp 1902:vii.
21. Sharp 1902:viii.
22. Sharp 1902:viii.
23. Sharp 1902:viii.
24. Sharp 1907:vii. This edition of Sharp's theoretical work is the only reliable one, 'since the others were edited by Ms Karpeles. See above, note 2.
25. Fox-Strangeways 1933:33. For Mattie Kay, see Fox-Strangeways 1933:26. For Sharp's collecting methods, see Etherington 1959 and Sharp 1908.
26. See above, p.174.
27. Sharp Collection.
28. Sharp Collection: *Morning Post*, 27.11.1903.
29. Sharp Collection.
30. Sharp Collection.
31. Sharp Collection: *Somerset County Gazette*, 21.5.1904.
32. Sharp Collection: *Fabian News*, July 1904.
33. Sharp Collection: *Fabian News*, July 1904.
34. Sharp Collection: letter from Milford to Sharp, 13.7.1904.
35. Sharp Collection: *Morning Post*, 12.10.1904.
36. Sharp and Marson 1904-9:1,xi-xii.
37. Sharp and Marson 1904-9:1,ix-x. My italics.
38. Sharp and Marson 1904-9:1,xiii.
39. Sharp and Marson 1904-9:1,xiii.
40. Sharp and Marson 1904-9:1,xv.
41. Sharp and Marson 1904-9:1xiii-xiv.
42. Sharp and Marson 1904-9:1,xv.
43. Sharp and Marson 1904-9:1,57.
44. Sharp 1905b:2.
45. Sharp 1905b:3.
46. Sharp 1905b:2.
47. Sharp 1905b:3.
48. Sharp Collection: *Bristol Times*, 24.1.1905.
49. Sharp Collection: lecture at Hampstead, March 1905.
50. Board of Education 1905, quoted in Reeves 1958:5.
51. Board of Education 1905, quoted in Reeves 1958:5. My italics.
52. Sharp Collection: *Morning Post*, -.10.1905.
53. See R. Williams 1963:130,183.
54. See above, Chapter 4, for collectors of this period.

55. Sharp Collection: lecture notes, 14.12.1905.
56. Fox-Strangeways 1933:45.
57. Sharp Collection: *Musical Herald*, 1.12.1905.
58. Sharp Collection. For the Tonic Sol-Fa Association, see Mackerness 1964.
59. Sharp Collection: lecture note, 14.12.1905.
60. Kidson 1905.
61. Graham 1927:50.
62. Sharp and Marson 1904-9:2,xii.
63. Sharp and Marson 1904-9:2,64.
64. Sharp 1905a:V.
65. Sharp 1905a.V.
66. Baring-Gould 1923:202. See also Baring-Gould 1925:200,206 and Dickinson 1970:128.
67. Sharp Collection: *Morning Post*, 19.4.1906.
68. Sharp and Marson 1904-9:3,ix-x.
69. Sharp Collection: letter from Sharp to Gilmour, 8.4.1906.
70. Quoted in Fox-Strangeways 1933:59-60.
71. Sharp Collection: letter from Sharp to Etherington, 14.10.1906.
72. Sharp and Baring-Gould 1906.
73. Sharp 1907.
74. Sharp 1907:x.
75. Sharp 1907:89-90.
76. Sharp 1907:135-6.
77. Sharp 1907:137.
78. Sharp 1907:133.
79. Sharp 1907:129.
80. Sharp 1907:129.
81. See above, pp.27-8,32-3.
82. Sharp 1907:4.
83. Sharp 1907:3-4.
84. Sharp 1907:119.
85. Sharp 1907:viii.
86. Sharp 1907:105.
87. Sharp 1907:1.
88. Sharp 1907:3.
89. Sharp 1907:4. For Vaughan Williams' comments, see the Sharp Collection.
90. Sharp 1907:33.
91. Sharp 1907:100-101.
92. Sharp 1907:105.
93. Sharp 1907:119.
94. See above, pp.128-30.
95. Sharp 1907:10.
96. Sharp 1907:16.
97. Sharp 1907:87.
98. Sharp 1907:17. See also Harker 1972a:229ff.
99. Sharp 1907:17.
100. Sharp 1907:17.
101. Sharp 1907:23.
102. Sharp 1907:16. Compare Baring-Gould, above, pp.150,160.
103. Sharp 1907:29.

104. Sharp 1907:29.
105. Sharp 1907:29.
106. Sharp 1907:30.
107. Sharp 1907:30.
108. Sharp 1907:30.
109. Sharp and Marson 1904-9;1,Preface.
110. Sharp and Marson 1904-9:1,xiv.
111. Sharp and Marson 1904-9:1,xvi.
112. Sharp and Marson 1904-9:1,xiv.
113. Sharp and Marson 1904-9:1,xii.
114. Sharp 1907:viii-ix.
115. Sharp and Marson 1904-9:1,ix.
115. The analysis of Sharp's notebooks in Clare College Library, Cambridge, was carried out in 1972. My card index was donated to the Centre for English Cultural Tradition and Lore, University of Sheffield.
117. Sharp 1905b:1.
118. Sharp 1905b:2. For Baring-Gould, see above, p.151.
119. Sharp 1905b:3.
120. Sharp Collection. Vaughan Williams was commenting on the proofs of *Conclusions*.
121. Harker 1972a:225ff. gives a sketch of some of the more obvious material factors.
122. Gough 1967 gives an account of mining in the Mendip district.
123. Sharp 1907:ix.
124. Sharp 1905b:2.
125. Sharp 1905b:2.
126. Tongue 1968:74-84.
127. Tongue 1968:28-34.
128. Tongue 1968:68-73.
129. Marson 1914. See also Raymond 1910: 389.
130. Dyer 1833 and Bayly 1844.
131. Carew 1745.
132. Littlewood 1922.
133. Sharp 1907:110.
134. Sharp 1907:110.
135. Sharp 1907:101.
136. Sharp Collection: letter from Kidson to Sharp, 1906.
137. Sharp Collection. See also Sharp 1907:17.
138. Sharp Collection.
139. Sharp Collection:lecture notes, 14.12.1905.
140. Sharp 1905b:3.
141. Sharp 1905b:2.
142. Sharp and Marson 1904-9:1,xii.
143. Sharp Collection
144. Harker 1972:234.
145. Harker 1972:234.
146. Sharp 1907:18.
147. Sharp and Marson 1904-9:1,xiii.
148. See, for example, Lomax 1959.
149. Sharp 1907:106.
150. Sharp 1907:72.

151. Grainger 1908.
152. Sharp Collection:*Musical Herald* 1.12.1905.
153. Sharp 1905b:1.
154. Sharp and Marson 1904-9:2,xi.
155. Sharp and Marson 1904-9:1,xvi.
156. Sharp and Marson 1904-9:1,xvi.
157. Sharp and Marson 1904-9:1,60.
158. Sharp and Marson 1904-9:1,60.
159. Sharp and Marson 1904-9:2,xi.
160. Sharp and Marson 1904-9:1,65.
161. Sharp and Marson 1904-9:2,75. See below, p.223.
162. Sharp and Marson 1904-9:2,xi.
163. Sharp 1907:103.

Chapter 9

1. U. Vaughan Williams 1964:66. Foss 1950 has some additional information.
2. Gardiner 1909a:247-see also *The Edinburgh Academy Chronicle*, May 1910:112-3.
3. H. Hammond 1907:59. See also *The Edinburgh Academy Chronicle*, June 1910:128.
4. *JEFDSS*, Vol.IX, 1961, No.2:113. Bird 1976 is the most recent biography of Grainger.
5. Grove 1954:1, 1049-50.
6. Keel 1948:125.
7. Purslow 1967.
8. Purslow 1968.
9. U. Vaughan Williams 1964.
10. See below, p.209.
11. Dawney 1976. For his published songs, see also Butterworth 1913.
12. Fox-Strangeways 1933 is again the source for otherwise unreferenced information in this chapter.
13. Sharp Collection: letter from J. Spencer Curwen to Sharp, 21.11.1907.
14. Sharp Collection: letter from Sharp to Etherington, 24.2.1908.
15. Karpeles 1955:111.
16. Sharp diaries:12.5.1916. When I wrote Harker 1972a, 1976, 1980 and 1983, I relied on a 'pirated' version of Sharp's diaries, loaned to me by a colleague who had access to the originals. His typescript extracts, though not totally accurate, were so to a remarkable degree. The extracts quoted here are from the original diaries, and have been checked for me by Mike Yates and Malcolm Taylor, to who I am very grateful.
17. Sharp diaries:23.6.1917, 31.12.1917.
18. Sharp Collection: letter from Mrs Sidney Webb to Sharp, 7.5.1913.
19. Karpeles 1967:19.
20. Sharp diaries: 5.3.1918.

21. Sharp diaries: 1.1.1918.
22. Sharp diaries: 1.9.1918.
23. Sharp diaries: 8.12.1918-see also 31.8.1918.
24. Sharp Collection: letter from Sharp to his son Charles, 31.1.1918.
25. Sharp diaries: 13.11.1918.
26. Baring-Gould 1923:56.
27. Karpeles 1967:179.
28. See Newman 1912.
29. Sharp 1912b:543.
30. Sharp 1912b:545-6.
31. Fox-Strangeways 1933:91.
32. Sharp Collection: letter marked 'Batchelor', 24.10.1915.
33. Sharp diaries: 7.9.1916.
34. R. Vaughan Williams 1948:137.
35. R. Vaughan Williams 1948:138. But see Broadwood 1908:ix.
36. L. Broadwood 1908.
37. R. Vaughan Williams 1948:138.
38. Dean-Smith 1964:246.
39. Dean-Smith 1964:238.
40. Kidson 1929. See *JEFDSS*, 1948:V, No. 3, 129-30.
41. Sharp Collection: letter from Kidson to Sharp, 1906.
42. Kidson 1908.
43. Kidson and Neal 1915.
44. H. Hammond 1907:59. For other published songs, see Hammond 1908.
45. Gardiner *Articles* for the source of all quotations from Gardiner not otherwise cited. He also wrote an interesting piece on German bands — see Gardiner 1902.
46. Gardiner 1909a.
47. See above, p.164.
48. Kidson and Neal 1915:51.
49. H. Hammond 1907:59.
50. R. Thomson 1972.
51. Grainger 1980:147.
52. Grainger 1908:148.
53. Grainger 1908:149.
54. Grainger 1908:159 note.
55. Grainger 1908:150.
56. Grainger 1908:151.
57. Grainger 1908:151.
58. Grainger 1908:152.
59. Grainger 1908:154. See O'Shaughnessy 1968 for some of Grainger's collected songs.
60. Grainger 1908:164.
61. U. Vaughan Williams 1964.
62. Sharp Collection: letter from Vaughan Williams to Sharp, 1907, on *Conclusions* proofs.
63. R. Vaughan Williams 1912:10.
64. R. Vaughan Williams 1912:13-4.
65. R. Vaughan Williams 1912:15. See R. Vaughan Williams 1906 and 1908 for his collected songs.

Chapter 10

1. All biographical information on Williams, unless otherwise indicated, is derived from Clark 1969. Byett 1933 and Jones 1950 are not very useful. Unwin 1954 includes him amongst 'peasant' poets!.
2. A. Williams *Letter* 5.
3. Clark 1969:21. He generally voted Conservative, but never joined a party.
4. A. Williams 1915:289.
5. A. Williams 1915:32-3.
6. A. Williams 1915:227-see also 1915:47,71-2,166,168 and 216.
7. A. Williams 1915:5,38,52,73-4,182-3,186,218-9,304.
8. A. Williams 1915:306.
9. A. Williams 1915:122.
10. A. Williams 1915:64.
11. Clark 1969:59.
12. Clark 1969:58.
13. Clark 1969:117.
14. A. Williams *Letter* 59.
15. A. Williams *Letter* 4.
16. A. Williams *Letter* 87.
17. A. Williams *Letter* 89.
18. Jeffreys 1980. For Williams' views on the General Strike, see Clark 1969:176-7.
19. A. Williams *Letter* 4. For his financial struggles in the 1920s, see Clark 1969:169-91.
20. Clark 1969:93.
21. This analysis is based on the catalogue in Swindon Reference Library, done by Bathe, Clissold and Purslow, which is a little confusing.
22. A. Williams 1923:9.
23. A. Williams 1923:10.
24. A. Williams 1923:28.
25. See, for example, A. Williams 1912:88 and A. Williams 1922:197.
26. A. Williams 1922:130.
27. A. Williams 1923:21.
28. A. Williams 1922:285.
29. A. Williams 1923:39.
30. A. Williams 1922:285.
31. A. Williams 1923:10.
32. A. Williams 1922:294ff.
33. A. Williams 1923:22.
34. A. Williams 1923:22.
35. A. Williams 1923:20-21.
36. Purslow 1969:303.
37. A. Williams *Letter* 59.
38. A. Williams 1923:16.
39. A. Williams 1923:20.
40. A. Williams 1923:20.
41. A. Williams 1923:14.
42. A. Williams 1923:201.
43. A. Williams 1912:122.
44. A. Williams 1923:39,222.

45. A. Williams 1913:204.
46. A. Williams 1923:41.
47. A. Williams 1923:65.
48. A. Williams 1923:69.
49. A. Williams 1923:38.
50. A. Williams 1923:223.
51. A. Williams 1922:67.
52. A. Williams 1912:243.
53. A. Williams 1922:232.
54. A. Williams 1923:170.
55. A. Williams 1922:232.
56. A. Williams 1913:279. My italics
57. A. Williams 1922:36.
58. A. Williams 1913:90.
59. A. Williams 1923:52.
60. A. Williams 1923:11-2.
61. See A. Williams 1923:95 and 1922:213, where he proceeds by example.
62. A. Williams 1922:196.
63. A. Williams 1923:12.
64. A. Williams 1913,viii.
65. A. Williams 1923:12-3.
66. A. Williams 1923:19.
67. A. Williams 1923:20. See also A. Williams 1913:104-5.
68. A. Williams 1913:3.
69. A. Williams 1922:7.
70. A. Williams 1923:268.
71. A. Williams 1922:165.
72. A. Williams 1923:14.
73. A. Williams 1923:11.
74. A. Williams 1913:28.
75. A. Williams 1913:29.
76. A. Williams 1923:12.
77. Madden Collection: **M23**.
78. A. Williams 1923:224.
79. A. Williams 1923:182.
80. A. Williams 1913:105.
81. A. Williams 1913:105.
82. A. Williams 1913:104. My italics.
83. A. Williams 1913:279.
84. A. Williams 1923:249.
85. A. Williams 1923:292.
86. A. Williams 1923:14.
87. A. Williams 1923:24.
88. A. Williams 1913:94.
89. A. Williams 1923:22.
90. A. Williams 1923:21-2.
91. A. Williams 1923:23.
92. A. Williams 1923:23-4.
93. A. Williams 1923:23.
94. A. Williams 1923:24. For Baring-Gould and the police, see Baring-Gould 1925:203. For recent collecting in the same district, see Baldwin 1969.
95. Clark 1969:160.
96. A. Williams 1923:9.
97. Clissold 1969:297-8.
98. A. Williams 1923:11.
99. Clissold 1969:298.
100. Clark 1969:160.
101. Clark 1969:164.
102. Purslow 1969:301-3.
103. A. Williams 1923:24.
104. A. Williams 1923:10-1.

Chapter 11

1. This study began life as part of my thesis — Harker 1976:492-501. It was developed as part of an updated article on Sharp — see above, p.278, note 1 — but when that article was published none of the material on Lloyd was printed. An unedited version was given as a paper to the 1983 second international conference of the International Association for the Study of Popular Music, at Reggio Emilia, Italy.
2. By Georgina Boyes and Elisa Mantin.
3. All biographical material on Lloyd, except where otherwise noted, comes from Dave Arthur's obituary of him — Arthur 1983 — and from information kindly communicated by Dave in private letters. Apparently, Lloyd 'wasn't very forthcoming with information on many aspects of his early life; other than the very general romantic images that he seemed to enjoy propagating'. Any reader with information on Lloyd which might be useful to the biography which Dave Arthur is preparing should send it to him, care of *English Dance & Song*, EFDSS, Cecil Sharp House, 2 Regents Park Road, London NW1 7AY. Harker 1980 was *wrong* about Lloyd being born in Wales.
4. See, for example, Deutscher 1966.
5. A short critique of some of the disastrous consequences of Stalin's mistakes is in Callinicos 1983.
6. Lloyd 1967a:5-6.
7. Arthur 1983:438.
8. There is a sketch of MacColl and an analysis of some of his work in Harker 1980:150-5,180-5.
9. Arthur 1983:438. Most of the following three paragraphs is based on Harker 1980:150-5.
10. *JEFDSS*, 1956:**VIII**, No.1,49-50.
11. R. Vaughan Williams and Lloyd 1959. See also U. Vaughan Williams 1964:394, where the work is described in one sentence.
12. See Jefferys 1980.
13. Jefferys 1980.
14. Lloyd 1961.
15. Lloyd 1967a:5-6.
16. Lloyd 1978:11.
17. Howkins 1983:213-4.

18. The debate around this issue, by a former CP-member, is raised in R. Williams 1977. Eagleton 1976 is a short introduction to this and related problems inside marxism.
19. I owe this point to Mike Pickering.
20. *JEFDSS*, 1944:**IV**, No. 5, 207-8.
21. Morton 1938.
22. Lloyd 1944:12-3.
23. Lloyd 1944:13.
24. Lloyd 1944:45.
25. Lloyd 1952:106.
26. For a fuller account see Harker 1976, on which the following paragraph is based.
27. For Chicken, see also Welford 1895:**1**:546-9.
28. See Harker 1985 for a lengthy analysis of a song about a north-east pitman.
29. See Harker 1980:166-71.
30. Meredith 1983. See also Scott 1983. I am grateful to Malcolm Taylor of the Vaughan Williams Memorial Library for drawing these Australian articles to my attention.
31. A. Scott 1983.
32. R. Vaughan Williams and Lloyd 1959:7-11.
33. For how this formula developed, see below, pp.248-50.
34. Lloyd 1961:172.
35. Lloyd 1967a:5.
36. Lloyd 1967a:6.
37. Quoted in Lloyd 1967a:15.
38. Lloyd 1967a:16-17.
39. *FMJ*, 1968:1, No. 4, 270-273.
40. Lloyd 1967a:316.
41. Lloyd 1967a:330.
42. Lloyd 1967a:330.
43. The following paragraph is based on Harker 1980:159-77 and Harker 1976.
44. Harker 1983 attempts to survey the available literature on which to base the future study of English workers' songs and culture, and Harker 1976 was an early attempt to produce a historical account of an English region, the north-east, using songs as historical evidence.
45. Harker 1973.
46. Lloyd 1967a:409.
47. Lloyd 1967a:22-23.
48. Lloyd 1967a:31.
49. Lloyd 1967a:69.
50. Lloyd 1967a:69.
51. See Harker 1980:180-5.
52. Lloyd 1967a:179.
53. See E.P. Thompson 1968:9 10.
54. Lloyd 1967a:317-8.
55. See Harker 1981b.

Conclusion

1. Harker 1985 expands on this general analysis, and gives a provisional example of how to understand a particular song, historically.
2. Harker 1980:219-20.
3. Trotsky 1960:180, quoted above, p.99. Lombardi-Satriani 1974 has some interesting ideas about the relationship between 'folk-lore' and marxism. For other, similar works, see Harker 1983. For an analysis of Hungarian 'folk' research, see Marothy 1974:134ff. K. Thompson 1980 is an example of a British approach to 'folklore' from sociology.
4. Details of IASPM can be had from John Shepherd, Department of Music, Carleton University, Ottawa, Ontario K1S 5B6, Canada.

Bibliography

NB. Place of publication for books is London, except where otherwise indicated.

Aberdeen Cantus 1662, *Cantus, Songs and Fancies*, Aberdeen.

Addison, William 1947, *The English Parson*.

Allan, Thomas 1891, *Tyneside Songs*, Newcastle (reprinted 1972).

Andrews, William 1885, *Modern Yorkshire Poets*.

Arthur, Dave 1983, 'Albert Lancaster Lloyd', *Folk Music Journal*, 1983:4, 436-9.

Baldwin, John 1969, 'Songs in the Upper Thames Valley:1966-1969'. *Folk Music Journal*, 1969:1, No. 5,315-49.

Baring-Gould, Sabine 1895a, *A Garland of Country Songs*.

Baring-Gould, Sabine 1895b, 'A Historical Sketch of English National Song', (published in Baring-Gould 1895-8) (reprinted, N.D.).

Baring-Gould, Sabine 1895-8, *English Minstrelsie*.

Baring-Gould, Sabine, 1923, *Early Reminiscences*.

Baring-Gould, Sabine 1925, *Further Reminiscences*.

Baring-Gould, Sabine and H. Fleetwood Sheppard 1890, *Songs & Ballads of The West*.

Barke, James and S.G. Smith 1965, *The Merry Muses of Caledonia*.

Barrett, William 1891, *English Folk Songs* (reprinted 1973).

Barry, Phillips 1910, 'The Origin of Folk Melodies', *Journal of American Folklore*, 1910:**XXIII**, 440-5.

Barry, Phillips 1912, 'William Carter', *Journal of American Folklore*, 1912:**XXV**, 156-68.

Barry, Phillips 1913, 'An American Homiletic Ballad', *Modern Language Notes*, 1913:**XXVIII**, No.1, 1-5.

Barry, Phillips 1914, 'The Transmission of Folk-Song', *Journal of American Folklore*, 1914:67-76.

Barry, Phillips, Fannie Eckstorm and Mary Smith 1929, *British Ballads from Maine*, New Haven, USA.

Bayly, Thomas 1844, *Songs, Ballads, etc.*

Bell, John 1812, *Rhymes of Northern Bards*, Newcastle (reprinted 1971).

Bell, Robert 1856, *Early Ballads*.

Bell, Robert 1857, *Ancient Poems, Ballads and Songs*.

Bewick, Thomas 1975, *A Memoir of Thomas Bewick*.

Bird, John 1976, *Percy Grainger*.

Board of Education 1905, *Handbook of Suggestions for the Consideration of Teachers*.

Board of Education 1906, *Suggestions for the Consideration of Teachers*.

Boase, F. 1965, *Modern English Biography*.

Bradford, Gamaliel 1969, *As God Made Them: Portraits of Some Nineteenth-Century Americans*, New York (reprint of 1929 edition).

Brimley-Johnson, R. 1912, *A Book of British Ballads*.

Broadwood, Lucy 1889, *Sussex Songs*.

Broadwood, Lucy 1904-5, 'On the Collecting of English Folk-Song', *Proceedings* of the Royal Musical Association 1904-5: 89-109.

Broadwood, Lucy 1908, *English Traditional Songs and Carols*.

Broadwood, Lucy 1927, 'Frank Kidson', *Musical Times*, January 1927: 42-3.

Broadwood, Lucy and J.A. Fuller-Maitland 1893, *English County Songs* (reprinted 1915).

Bronson, Bertrand 1938, *Joseph Ritson: Scholar-at-Arms*, Berkeley, USA.

Bronson, Bertrand 1945, 'Mrs Brown and the Ballad', *California Folklore Quarterly*, 1945:**IV**, 129-40.

Bruce, Gainsford 1905, *The Life and Letters of John Collingwood Bruce*, Edinburgh.

Bruce, John and John Stokoe 1882, *The Northumbrian Minstrelsy*, Newcastle (reprinted, Pennsylvania, USA, 1965).

Buchan, David 1972, *The Ballad and the Folk*.

Buchan, Peter 1825, *Gleanings of Scotch and English and Irish Scarce Old Ballads*, Peterhead.

Buchan, Peter 1875, *Ancient Ballads and Songs of the North of Scotland*, Edinburgh (first edition, Edinburgh 1828).

Butterworth, George 1913, *Folk Songs from Sussex*.

Byett, Henry 1933, *Alfred Williams, Ploughboy, Hammerman, Poet and Author*, Swindon.

Bynum, David E. 1974, 'Child's Legacy Enlarged: Oral Literary Studies at Harvard Since 1856,' *Harvard Library Bulletin*, 1974:**22**, 237-67.

Callinicos, Alex 1983, *The Revolutionary Road to Socialism*.

Carew, Bampfylde 1745, *The Life and Adventure of Bampfylde Moore Carew*.

Chambers, Robert 1826, *The Popular Rhymes of Scotland*, Edinburgh.

Chambers, Robert 1829, *The Scottish Ballads*, Edinburgh.

Chambers, Robert 1835, *A Biographical Dictionary of Eminent Scotsmen*, Edinburgh.

Chambers, William 1884, *Memoir of Robert Chambers*, Edinburgh.

Chappell, William 1838-40, *A Collection of National English Airs*.

Chappell, William 1965, *The Ballad Literature and Popular Music of the Olden Time* (first edition, 1859).

Cherry, Steven 1981, *Our History — A Pocket History of the Labour Movement in Britain*, Norwich.

Child, Francis 1857-9, *English and Scottish Ballads*, Boston.

Child, Francis 1861, *English and Scottish Ballads*.

Child, Francis 1873, 'Old Ballads. Prof. Child's Appeal', *Notes and Queries*, 4th Series, Jan. 4, 1873:**XI**.

Child, Francis 1895, 'Ballad Poetry', *Johnson's Universal Cyclopaedia*, **1**.

Child, Francis 1965, *The English and Scottish Popular Ballads*, New York (first edition, Boston, 1882-98).

Clark, Leonard 1969, *Alfred Williams, His Life and Work*, Newton Abbot (first edition 1945).

Cliff, Tony 1975-8, *Lenin*.

Clissold, Ivor 1969, 'Alfred Williams, Song Collector', *Folk Music Journal* 1969:**1**, No. 5, 293-300.

Courthope, William 1895, *A History of English Poetry*.

Craig, David 1961, *Scottish Literature and the Scottish People*.

Cromek, Robert 1810, *Remains of Nithsdale and Galloway Songs*.

Crotch, William n.d., *Specimens of National Music*.

Crotch, William 1831, *The Substance of Several Courses of Lectures on Music Read at Oxford*.

Cunningham, Allan 1825, *The Songs of Scotland*.

276   *Fakesong*

Cunningham, John 1766, *Poems chiefly Pastoral*.

Davidson, Thomas 1884, 'Prof. Child's Ballad Book', *American Journal of Philology* 1884:5, 466-78.

Dawney, Michael 1976, 'George Butterworth's Folk Music Manuscripts', *Folk Music Journal*, 1976:3, No. 2, 99-113.

Day, Cyrus 1959, 'Introduction' to D'Urfey 1959.

Deacon, George 1983, *John Clare and the Folk Tradition*.

Dean-Smith, Margaret 1954, *A Guide to English Folksong Collections*, Liverpool.

Dean-Smith, Margaret 1957-8, 'The Work of Anne Geddies Gilchrist', *Proceedings* of the Royal Musical Association, 1957-8: 43-8.

Dean-Smith, Margaret 1964, 'Letters to Lucy Broadwood', *Journal* of the English Folk Dance and Song Society, 1964:**IX**, No. 5, 233-68.

Deutscher, Isaac 1966, *Stalin: a Political Biography* (first edition, 1949).

Dick, James 1903, *The Songs of Robert Burns*.

Dickinson, Bickford 1970, *Sabine Baring-Gould: Squarson, Writer and Folklorist, 1834-1924*, Newton Abbot.

Dixon, James 1845, *Scottish Traditional Versions of Ancient Ballads*.

Dixon, James 1846, *Ancient Poems, Ballads and Songs of the Peasantry of England* (reprinted 1973).

Dobie, Marryat 1940, 'The Development of Scott's Minstrelsy', *Transactions* of the Edinburgh Bibliographical Society 1940:**II**,Pt.1, 67-87.

Dorson, Richard 1968, *The British Folklorists: A History*.

D'Urfey, Thomas 1719-20, *Wit and Mirth; or, Pills to Purge Melancholy* (reprinted 1959).

Dusart, G. 1843, *Old English Songs, as Now Sung by the Peasantry of the Weald of Surrey and Sussex*.

Dyer, Robert 1833, *Nine Years of an Actor's Life*.

Eagleton, Terry 1976, *Marxism and Literary Criticism*.

Engel, Carl 1866, *An Introduction to the Study of National Music*.

Engel, Carl 1879, *The Literature of National Music*.

Etherington, Francis 1959, 'Cecil Sharp: Some Personal Reminiscences', *Journal* of the English Folk Dance and Song Society, 1959:**8**, No. 4, 194-6.

Evans, Thomas 1777, *Old Ballads*.

Farmer, Henry 1962a, 'Foreword', to G. Thomson 1962.

Farmer, Henry 1962b, 'Foreword' to Johnson 1962.

Fischer, Ernst 1963, *The Necessity of Art*.

FMJ: Folk Music Journal.

Ford, Walter 1929, 'Lucy Etheldred Broadwood', *Journal* of the Folk Song Society, 1929:**8**, Pt.3, 168-9.

Fordyce, William 1857, *The History and Antiquities of the County Palatine of Durham*, Newcastle.

Foss, Herbert 1950, *Ralph Vaughan Williams*.

Fox-Strangeways, A. 1933, *Cecil Sharp*.

Fuller-Maitland, J. 1927, 'The Beginning of the Folk-Song Society', *Journal* of the Folk Song Society, 1927:**8**, Pt.1, 46-7.

Furnivall, Frederick 1868, *Bishop Percy's Folio Manuscript. Loose and Humorous Songs*.

Gammon, Vic 1980, 'Folk Song Collecting in Sussex and Surrey, 1843-1914', *History Workshop Journal*, Autumn 1980:**10**, 61-89.

Gammon, Vic 1984, 'Popular Music in rural society; Sussex 1815-1914', unpublished PhD thesis, University of Sussex.

Gardiner, George 1902, 'The Home of the German Band', *Blackwood's Magazine*, Oct. 1902:**172**, 451-65.

Gardiner *Articles:Hampshire Chronicle*, *c.* 25.12.1907 and 20.2.1909: *Hants and Sussex News*, 5.5. 1909;*Hampshire Observer*, 16.10.1909.

Gardiner 1909a, 'Songs collected in Hampshire', *Journal* of the Folk Song Society 1909:**III**, No.13.

Gardiner 1909b, *Folk Songs from Hampshire*.

Gerould, Gordon 1923, 'The Making of Ballads', *Modern Philology*, 1923:**XXI**, 15-28.

Gerould, Gordon 1932, *The Ballad of Tradition*, Oxford (reprinted 1957).

Gilbert, Davies 1823, *Some Ancient Christmas Carols*.

Gilfillan, George 1858, 'Life of Thomas Percy', in Percy 1858.

Godman, Stanley 1957, 'John Broadwood: New Light on the Folk-Song Pioneer', *Monthly Musical Record*, May-June 1957: 105-8.

Godman, Stanley 1964, 'John Broadwood, the earliest English folksong collector', *West Sussex Gazette*, 30.1.1964.

Goldstein, Kenneth 1964, *A Guide for Field Workers in Folklore*, Pennsylvania, USA.

Gough, John 1967, The Mines of Mendip, Newton Abbot.

Graham, John 1927, 'The Late Mr. Frank Kidson', *Journal* of the English Folk Dance Society, 2nd series, 1927: No. 1, 48-51.

Grainger, Percy 1908, 'Collecting with the Phonograph', *Journal* of the Folk Song Society, 1908:**III**, No.12, 147-67.

Green, Anthony 1970, 'Foreword' to Kidson 1970.

Green, Anthony 1972, 'Foreword' to Harland and Wilkinson 1972.

Gregory, Mark 1983, 'The Lloyd Controversy', *Stringybark and Greenhide*, 1983:**4**, No.3, 13.

Grove 1954, *Grove's Dictionary of Music and Musicians*.

Gummere, Francis 1901, *The Beginnings of Poetry*, New York (reprinted 1970).

Gummere, Francis 1907, *The Popular Ballad*, Cambridge, Mass., USA (reprinted 1959).

Gummere, Francis, 1909, 'A Day with Professor Child', *Atlantic Monthly*, March 1909:**103**, 421–5.

Hales, John and Frederick Furnivall 1867–8, *Bishop Percy's Folio Manuscript*.

Halifax, Noel 1983, 'Music and Class', *Socialist Review*, September 1983.

Halliwell, James 1842, *The Nursery Rhymes of England*.

Halliwell, James 1851, *The Yorkshire Anthology* (reprinted 1973).

Hammond, Henry 1907, 'Songs Collected in Dorset', *Journal* of the Folk Song Society, 1907:**III**, No.7.

Hammond, Henry 1908, *Folk Songs from Dorset*.

Harker, Dave 1971, 'John Bell, the "Great Collector"', in John Bell 1971.

Harker, Dave 1972a, 'Cecil Sharp in Somerset: Some Conclusions', *Folk Music Journal*, 1972: 220-40.

Harker, Dave 1972b, 'Thomas Allan and "Tyneside Song"', in Allan 1972.

Harker, Dave 1973, *George Ridley*, Newcastle.

Harker, Dave 1976, 'Popular Song and Working-Class Consciousness in North-East England', unpublished PhD thesis, University of Cambridge.

Harker, Dave 1980, *One for the Money: Politics and Popular Song*.

Harker, Dave 1981a, 'Francis James Child and the "Ballad Consensus"', *Folk Music Journal* 1981: 146-64.

Harker, Dave 1981b, 'The Making of the Tyneside Concert Hall', *Popular Music* 1, 1981: 27-56, Cambridge.

Harker, Dave 1983, 'Song and History in England: a working bibliography of "folksong" and related sources', International Association for the Study of Popular Music, Goteborg, Sweden, Internal Publications, 1983.

Harker, Dave 1985, 'The Original Bob Cranky?', *Folk Music Journal*, 1985.

Harker, Dave and Frank Rutherford 1985, *The Bell/White Manuscript Song Collection*, Durham.

Harland, John 1865, *Ballads and Songs of Lancashire*.

Harland, John and T. Wilkinson 1870, 'An Essay on Songs and Ballads', *Transactions* of the Historical Society of Lancashire and Cheshire, New Series 1870:**11**, 87-118.

Harland, John and T. Wilkinson 1882, *Lancashire Folk-Lore* (reprinted 1972).

Harris, Nigel 1983, *Of Bread and Guns*, Harmondsworth.

Hart, Walter 1906, 'Professor Child and the Ballad', *Proceedings* of the Modern Languages Association, 1906:**XXI**, No. 4, (reprinted in Child 1965).

Hecht, Hans 1904, *Songs from David Herd's Manuscripts*, Edinburgh.

Henderson, Hamish and Francis Collinson 1965, 'New Child Variants from Oral Tradition', *Scottish Studies* 1965:**9**, 1-33.

Henderson, Thomas 1910, *Scottish Vernacular Literature*, Edinburgh (first edition, 1898).

Henderson, Thomas 1912, *The Ballad in Literature*, Cambridge.

Herd, David 1769, *The Ancient and Modern Scots Songs*, Edinburgh.

Herd, David 1776, *Ancient and Modern Scots Songs*, Edinburgh (reprinted 1973).

Hitchcock, Gordon 1974, *Folk Songs of the West Country Collected by Sabine Baring-Gould*, Newton Abbot.

Hogg, David 1875, *Life of Allan Cunningham*, Dumfries.

Hogg, James 1874, *The Jacobite Relics of Scotland*, Paisley (first edition 1819-21).

Howes, Frank 1943, 'A Centenary', *Journal* of the English Folk Dance and Song Society, 1943:**IV**, No. 4, 157-60.

Howes, Frank 1961, 'Percy Aldridge Grainger', *Journal* of the English Folk Dance and Song Society, 1961:**IX**, No. 2, 113-4.

Howkins, Alun 1983, 'A.L. Lloyd (1908-1982)', *History Workshop Journal*, Spring 1983: **15**, 213-4.

Hustvedt, Sigurd 1916, *Ballad Criticism in Scandinavia and Great Britain during the Eighteenth Century*, New York.

Hustvedt, Sigurd 1930, *Ballad Books and Ballad Men*, Cambridge, USA.

Jacobs, Joseph 1893, '*The Folk*', Folk-Lore, June 1893:**IV**, 233-8.

James, Thelma 1933, 'The English and Scottish Popular Ballads of Francis James Child', *Journal of American Folklore*, 1933:**XLVI**, 51-68.

Jamieson, Robert 1806, *Popular Ballads and Songs*, Edinburgh.

JEFDSS 1932-, *Journal* of the English Folk Dance and Song Society.

Jefferys, Steve 1980, 'The Communist Party and the Rank and File', *International Socialism*, 2nd Series, Winter 1980/1:**10**, 1-23.

Johnson, James 1962, *The Scots Musical Museum*, Pennsylvania, USA (first edition, 1787-1803; reprinted 1853).

Jones, Joseph 1950, *Williams of Swindon*, Swindon.

Karpeles, Maud 1948, 'Cecil Sharp', *Journal* of the English Folk Dance and Song Society, 1948:**V**, No. 3, 139-41.

Karpeles, Maud 1955, *Cecil Sharp*.

Karpeles, Maud 1959, 'Cecil Sharp: Collector and Restorer of English Folk Music', *Journal* of the English Folk Dance and Song Society 1959:**VIII**, No. 4, 179-81.

Karpeles, Maud 1967, *Cecil Sharp: His Life and Work*.

Keel, Frederick 1948, 'The Folk Song Society', *Journal* of the English Folk Dance and Song Society, 1948:**V**, No. 3, 111-26.

Ker, William 1909, 'On the History of the Ballads, 1100-1500', *Proceedings* of the British Academy, 1909:**IV**, 179-205.

Kidson *Articles* : 'Notes on Old Tunes', *Leeds Mercury* (?*c*.1890-1900), Mitchell Library, Glasgow.

Kidson, Frank 1891, *Traditional Tunes*, Oxford (reprinted 1970).

Kidson, Frank 1905, 'The Ballad Sheet and Garland', *Journal* of the Folk Song Society, 1905:**II**, No. 7, 70-8.

Kidson, Frank 1906, *Lecture*, 'Yorkshire Folk Song', notes for a lecture in Sheffield, 15.9.1906, Moir Collection, Mitchell Library, Glasgow.

Kidson, Frank 1908, Review of Sharp's *Conclusions*, *Musical Times*, 1.1.1908.

Kidson, Frank 1929, *English Peasant Songs*.

Kidson, Frank and Mary Neal 1915, *English Folksong and Dance*, Cambridge.

Kinloch, George 1827a, *The Ballad Book*, Edinburgh (reprinted in Stevenson 1868).

Kinloch, George 1827b, *Ancient Scottish Ballads*.

Kittredge, George 1904, *English and Scottish Popular Ballads*, Boston, USA.

Kittredge, George 1965, 'Francis James Child', in Child 1965.

Laing, David 1853, 'Advertisement' to Johnson 1853.

Lang, Andrew 1910, *Sir Walter Scott and the Border Minstrelsy*.

Legman, Gershon 1966, *The Horn Book*, New York (first edition, 1964).

Lewis, Mary 1976, '"The Joy of my Heart" : Robert Burns as Folklorist', *Scottish Studies*, 1976:**20**, 45-67.

Littlewood, Sidney 1922, *Somerset and the Drama*.

Lloyd, Albert 1944, *The Singing Englishman*.

Lloyd, Albert 1945, *Corn on the Cob*.

Lloyd, Albert 1952, *Coaldust Ballads*.

Lloyd, Albert 1961, 'The Folksong Revival', *Marxism Today*, June 1961: 170-3.

Lloyd, Albert 1965, 'Foreword' to Bruce and Stokoe 1965.

Lloyd, Albert 1967a, *Folk Song in England*.

Lloyd, Albert 1967b, 'Popular Music', *Encyclopaedia Britannica*.

Lloyd, Albert 1978, *Come all ye bold miners* (first edition, 1952).

Lockey, Elizabeth n.d., 'The Bell Family', unpublished BA Lib (PT) dissertation, Newcastle.

Lockhart, John 1902, *Life of Sir Walter Scott*.

Lomax, Alan 1959, 'Singing Style', *American Anthropologist*, 1959:**61**, 927-54.

Lombardi-Satriani, L. 1974, 'Folklore as Culture of Contestation', *Journal* of the Folklore Institute, June-August 1974:**XI**, Pts1/2, 99-121.

Lyle, Emily 1972, 'The Matching of Andrew Blaikie's Ballad Tunes with their Texts', *Scottish Studies*, 1972:**16**, 175-80.

Lyle, Emily 1975, *Andrew Crawfurd's Collection of Ballads and Songs*, Vol. **1**, Edinburgh.

Lyle, Thomas 1827, *Ancient Ballads and Songs*.

M'Conechy, James 1881, 'Memoir' in Motherwell 1881.

Mackenzie, Eneas 1827, *A Descriptive and Historical Account of the Town and County of Newcastle upon Tyne*, Newcastle.

Mackerness, Eric 1964, *A Social History of English Music*.

Madden Collection : Madden Collection of Broadsides, Cambridge University Library.

Maidment, James 1824, *A North Countrie Garland*, Edinburgh (reprinted in Stevenson 1868).

Maidment, James 1844, *A New Book of Old Ballads*, Edinburgh (reprinted in Stevenson 1868).

Mair, Carlene 1961, *The Chappell Story*.

Marothy, Janos 1974, *Music and the Bourgeois/Music and the Proletarian*, Budapest.

Marson, Charles 1914, *Village Silhouettes*.

Mason, Marianne 1877, *Nursery Rhymes and County Songs*.

Meredith, John 1983, 'A Depreciation of A.L. Lloyd', *Stringybark and Greenhide* (Australia) 1983:**4**, No. 3, 14.

Montgomerie, William 1956, 'Sir Walter Scott as Ballad editor', *Review of English Studies*, New Series, 1956:**7**, 158-63.

Montgomerie, William 1957, 'Some notes on the Herd Manuscripts', *Transactions* of the Edinburgh Bibliographical Society, 1957:**3**, 189-98.

Montgomerie, William 1958, 'William Motherwell and Robert A. Smith', *Review of English Studies*, New Series, 1958: **9**, 152-9.

Montgomerie, William 1963, 'William Macmath and the Scott Ballads', *Studies in Scottish Literature*, 1963:**II**.

Montgomerie, William 1966-70, 'A Bibliography of the Scottish Ballad Manuscripts, 1730-1825', *Studies in Scottish Literature*, 1966: Part 1, **IV**, 3-28; 1966-7: Part 2, **IV**, 79-88; 1966-7: Part 3, **IV**, 195-227; 1967-8: Part 4, **V**, 107-32; 1968-9: Part 5, **VI**, 91-104; 1969: Part 6, **VII**, 60-75; 1969-70: Part 7, **VII**, 238-54.

Morton, Arthur 1938, *A People's History of England*.

Motherwell, William 1827, *Minstrelsy Ancient and Modern*, Glasgow (reprinted 1968).

Motherwell, William 1881, *The Poetical Works of William Motherwell*, Glasgow.

Munro, Ailie 1976, 'The Abbotsford Collection of Border Ballads', *Scottish Studies*, 1976:**20**, 91-123.

Newman, Earnest 1912, 'The Folk-Song Fallacy', *English Review*, 1912:**V**, 255-68.

Norton, Charles n.d., 'Francis James Child', *Proceedings* of the American Academy of Arts and Science, **XXXII**, 334-5.

Norton, Charles 1897, 'Francis James Child', *Harvard Graduates' Magazine*, (USA) 1897:**VI**, 161-9.

O'Shaughnessy, P. 1968, *21 Lincolnshire Folk Songs*, Oxford.

Oswald, Harold 1936, *The Theatres Royal in Newcastle-upon-Tyne*, Newcastle.

Parry, C. Hubert 1893, *The Evolution of the Art of Music*.

Parry, C. Hubert 1899, 'Inaugural Address', *Journal* of the Folk Song Society, 1899:**1**, No.1, 1-3.

Percy, Thomas 1858, *Reliques of Ancient English Poetry* (first published 1765).

Phillips, Ambrose 1723-5, *A Collection of Old Ballads*.

Pickering, Michael 1982, *Village Song and Culture*.

Pickford, John 1867, 'Life of Bishop Percy', in Hales and Furnivall 1867.

Pinkerton, John 1781, *Scottish Tragic Ballads*.

Pinkerton, John 1783, *Select Scottish Ballads*.

Playford, John 1651, *The English Dancing Master*.

Playford, John 1661, *An Antidote against Melancholy*.

Plomer, Henry, *et al.* 1968, *A Dictionary of the Printers and Booksellers who were at work in England, Scotland and Ireland from 1726 to 1775*, Oxford (first published 1932).

Pound, Louise 1921, *Poetic Origins and the Ballad*, New York.

Pound, Louise 1924, 'The Term:"Communal"', *Proceedings* of the Modern Languages Association, 1924:**XXXIX**, 440-54.

Pound, Louise 1929, 'A Recent Theory of Ballad-Making', *Proceedings* of the Modern Languages Association, 1929:**XLIV**, 622-30.

Vaughan Williams, Ralph 1948, 'Lucy Broadwood 1858-1929', *Journal* of the English Folk Dance and Song Society, 1948:**V**, No.3, 136-8.
Vaughan Williams, Ralph and A.L. Lloyd 1959, *The Penguin Book of English Folk Songs.*
Vaughan Williams, Ursula 1964, *RVW.*
Walker, William 1915, *Peter Buchan and Other Papers*, Aberdeen.
Walker, William 1930, *Letters on Scottish Ballads*, Aberdeen (reprinted 1977).
Watson, James 1706-11, *A Choice Collection of Comic and Serious Scottish Poetry*, Edinburgh (reprinted 1977).
Welford, Richard 1895, *Men of Mark 'Twixt Tyne and Tweed*, Newcastle.
Whistle-Binkie 1878, Glasgow (first published 1853).
Whittell, Thomas 1815, *The Poetical Works of Thomas Whittell*, Newcastle.
Wilgus, Donald 1959, *Anglo-American Folksong Scholarship since 1898*, New Brunswick, New Jersey, USA.
Williams Collection : The Alfred Williams Collection of Folk Songs, Swindon Reference Library.
Williams Letters : '100 Letters from a Worker to Workers' MS, Swindon Reference Library.
Williams, Alfred 1912, *A Wiltshire Village.*
Williams, Alfred 1913, *Villages of the White Horse.*
Williams, Alfred 1915, *Life in a Railway Factory* (reprinted 1969).
Williams, Alfred 1922, *Round About the Upper Thames.*
Williams, Alfred 1923, *Folk Songs of the Upper Thames* (reprinted n.d.).
Williams, Raymond 1963, *Culture and Society*, Harmondsworth (first published 1958).
Williams, Raymond 1965, *The Long Revolution*, Harmondsworth (first published 1961).
Williams, Raymond 1971, 'Literature and Sociology: in memory of Lucien Goldmann, *New Left Review* 1971:**67**.
Williams, Raymond 1973, *The Country and the City.*
Williams, Raymond 1977, *Marxism and Literature*, Oxford.
Williams, Raymond 1983, *Keywords* (first published 1976).
Wright, Thomas 1839, *The Political Songs of England.*
Yeo, Stephen 1968, *For Christ and People* (edited by Maurice Reckett).

Index

Kidson, Ethel 205
Kidson, Frank 117, 147, 153–6, 157, 163–4,
    165, 167–8, 169, 176, 179, 180, 183,
    193, 198, 199, 205–6, 209, 229, 255
Kilbarchan 66
Kilmarnock 19, 67
Kincardine 198
King Family 218, 222
King, Francis 90–1
King, Tom 223
King, William 191, 195
Kingsbury Episcopi 190, 195
King's College (Aberdeen) 59
Kingston Barton, Dr James 173
Kingstone Lisle 221
Kinloch, George 39, 44, 53, 65, 67, 73, 75,
    104, 113, 115, 116, 117
'Kinmont Willie' 60, 70
Kipling, Rudyard 131
Kirk–Bean 61
Kirkhill 58
Kirkwhelpington 158
Kittredge, George 122–37
Knight, George 30
Knight, Job 93

L., W. 29
Labour Party xvii, 200, 202, 215, 233, 237,
    246, 256
Ladhope 63
'Lady Anne' 70
Lady of the Lake 46
Laidlaw, Mr 41
'The Laidley Worm' 31
Laidlaw, William 41, 58
Laing, David 43, 45, 62–3, 68, 75, 89, 104,
    115
Lamb, Lizzie 63
Lambe, Rev Robert 31, 113
Lament for the Death of a Bull Fighter 234
Lanark Grammar School 16
Lanarkshire 8, 30
Lancashire 28, 79, 82, 88, 92, 96, 164
Lancing College 199
Langport 190, 191
Larcombe, Henry 188, 193
'Lassie, lie near me' 71
Latton 225
Lausanne 80
Lawrence & Wishart 235, 238, 239
The Lay of the Last Minstrel 43
Leadenhall Press 156
Lechlade 216, 219
Lee, Kate xiv
Leeds 147, 155, 164
Leeds Festival 200
Lenin, V. I. xi, xiii, 232, 242, 254, 255
Lesly, Charles 63, 65, 68
Leviathan LP 246
Lew Trenchard 150, 160, 189
Lewis, Captain 191

Lewis, 'Monk' 40
Leyden, John 40, 59, 60
Leyden Public Library 89
Liberal Party 175, 212, 215
Liddesdale 58
Life in a Railway Factory 212–3
'Life Let us Cherish' 225
Lincolnshire 194, 198
Linton 91
Lisbon 29
Literature and Revolution 99
The Literature of National Music 142
Littlewood, Joan 235
Liverpool 175
Livingstone, Mr 58
Liszt, Franz 146
Lloyd, A. L. xii, xvii, 137, 231–53, 255, 256
Lloyd, Ernest 232
Lloyd, Mabel 235
Local Historians Table Book 93
Lochaber 63
Lochwinnoch 66, 67
Lock, Mrs 191
Lohr, Mr 152
Lolley, Charles 163
Lomax, Alan 235
Londesborough, Lord 87
London 3, 4, 6, 8, 9, 11, 12, 16, 17, 18, 21,
    23, 25, 28, 39, 40, 42, 43, 44, 45, 47,
    49, 50, 52, 53, 61, 65, 80, 81, 82, 83,
    85, 87, 88, 91, 142, 145, 146, 147, 153,
    155, 158, 162, 169, 172, 174, 179, 190,
    191, 192, 193, 194, 195, 199, 200, 223,
    235, 236, 239
London Magazine 43
London Polytechnic School of Morris Dancing
    200
Long Benton 62
Longstaffe, W. H. D. 93
Lorca, Garcia 234
'Lord Bateman' 193, 218
'Lord Lovell' 137
'Lord Randall' 124
Luckenbooths (Edinburgh) 9
Ludgrove School 175, 176, 200, 201
Ludlow 79
Ludlow Grammar School 79
Luxton, Roger 151
Lyle, Thomas 90
Lyme 93
Lyne 79, 80, 146
Lyttleton, Humphrey 235
Lytton, E. Bulwer 83

McCarthy, Senator 250
Macartney, Margaret 61
Macclesfield 39, 42
MacColl, Ewan 235, 236, 251, 252
MacDonnel, Fred 173
MacFarren, George 81, 82, 92
Mackenzie, Sir Alexander 169